The Germanna Record

Official Publication of the
Memorial Foundation of the Germanna Colonies in Virginia, Inc.
P.O. Box 279, Locust Grove, Virginia 22508–0279

NUMBER EIGHTEEN

The Brawdus Martin Fort Germanna Visitor Center

The Second Germanna Colony and Other Pioneers

By John Blankenbaker
2008

The Second Germanna Colony and Other Pioneers

Copyright 2008
The Memorial Foundation of the Germanna Colonies in Virginia, Incorporated
All Rights Reserved
No part of this publication may be reproduced mechanically or electronically for any purpose whatsoever including print, magnetic, optical media, or the internet, without the express written permission of the publisher.

ISBN 978-1-940945-02-6

Published by:
The Germanna Foundation
The Memorial Foundation of the Germanna Colonies in Virginia, Incorporated
P.O. Box 279, Locust Grove, Virginia 22508
GERMANNA.ORG

First Printing 2008

Second Printing 2019

Dedicated to my granddaughter

Isabel Sabina Blankenbaker
born May 14, 2003

Contents

Foreword ix

Part I

Introduction 1
General History 2
    Col. Alexander Spotswood's Explanations of His Land Acquisitions............................2
    The 40,000 Acre Tract, also called the Spotsylvania Tract...3
    Origins in Germany and the Trip to America 4
    The German Homes 5
    St. Mary in the Strand (London) Lutheran Church Records
        (Andreas Mielke and Sandra Yelton) 7
    The So-called Fifth Return Party 8
    Captain Tarbett or Captain Scott? 9
    Head Rights List of Alexander Spotswood 9
    First Homes on the Spotsylvania Tract 10
    The Colonial Government 11
    Law Suits by Alexander Spotswood Against the Germans 12
    The Creation of Spotsylvania County and Free Land 14
    Proofs of Importation of Selected Germans in Spotsylvania Court, 1724 to 1729......14
    Patents in the Robinson River Valley of Virginia 16
    Moving to the Robinson River Valley 30
    The Second Colony Members' Account 30
    The Results of the Fund Raising Trip 31
    Orange County Tithables in 1739 31
    The Constitution of the German Evangelical Lutheran Congregation.........................34
    Petition of the German Congregation of the County of Culpepper..............................41
    Origins of the Planckenbühler (Blankenbühler) Family 42
    The Utz-Volck Complex 44
    The Clore-Weaver-Crigler-Yager Complex 45
    Anna Barbara Schön, Anna Barbara Mayer, and Susanna Klaar..................................46
    The First Colony Petition Taken to London by Zollicoffer 46
Improvements in the General History..47
Improvements in the Family Histories...48
References 50
    General Secondary 50
    Family Histories as Books 54
Hebron Lutheran Church 56
Original Culpeper County..57

Part II

Family History Summaries (Alphabetical without regard to the time of arrival).....................59

Part III

Photographs from Germany and Austria...133

Index..163

Foreword

More than forty years ago, B. C. Holtzclaw wrote the Sixth Volume of *The Germanna Record*. He tried to have something about every family in the Second Germanna Colony of 1717 and the Other Germanna Pioneers. Considering that he had only a few relatives in this group, his tremendous efforts were made in a true spirit of generosity. He consulted the courthouse records, the church records, and the work of other researchers.

Much has been discovered since then, both from the records in the German-speaking lands of Europe and from the records in America. The origins of many people and previously unknown surnames have been found. While there will always be work to be done, the Memorial Foundation of the Germanna Colonies in Virginia felt that it was time to rewrite the record of the Second Colony. Thomas Faircloth asked me to do this and I agreed. One of the starting points was the *Germanna Record* series.

For twenty years, I have tried to study the Germanna families without regard to whether they were my ancestors or not. To publish the findings of other researchers and myself, I started a newsletter/journal entitled *Beyond Germanna*. A total of 917 pages were published and many people contributed to this. I have extensively used their work here but this volume cannot begin to replicate all of the material to be found there. I have been a keen student of the records kept by the German Lutheran Church in the Robinson River Valley. This last effort, the work done by the people who wrote for *Beyond Germanna*, and the research that has been done in Europe have been the principal sources of new information.

I would like to thank these many co-workers who contributed, perhaps without knowing it, to the present work. First, let me name some people whose efforts were especially dear to me.

Stephen Broyles. Though Steve did contribute some short notes, most of his work is of a hidden nature. He is the creator of DeedMapper™ software for plotting land. All of the plotting that I published was done with this software.

James E. Brown. James did courthouse research and sent me final results which could be published as they stood. Though we did not always agree, it was always a pleasure to work with him. I wish that he were still with us.

Nancy Moyers Dodge. Nancy was an inspiration. She is filled with ideas to think about. She solved problems which were intractable to me and encouraged me to keep trying. Together we tackled the baptismal records and the communion lists of the Evangelical Lutheran Church in the Robinson River Valley.

Cathi Clore Frost. I wish that I could be as productive as Cathi is. Her monumental work of the first four generations of the Michael Clore family will stand as a model for future researchers.

John Gott. John offered encouragement from the beginning. It was his contribution of the material from some loose papers in the Fauquier County Courthouse that gave me hope the *Beyond Germanna* endeavor would be successful.

Elke Hall. Elke translated, from the old handwritten script and from printed page, material for use. She was always such a willing worker that I hesitated to ask her. She provided insight into customs and practices and the meaning of words which only a native German could provide.

Andreas Mielke. Andreas is a professional historian who has found the study of German emigration to be a field for serious study. He has found more obscure documents than anyone and these often require a revision to the history as we had known it. Also, as a native German, he has assisted in the reading and translation of German documents.

Richard and Gisela Plankenbühler. Richard is my tenth half-cousin whose research enabled me to see the tie between the American Blankenbakers, the German Blankenbühlers, and the Austrian Planckenbühlers.

Alexander Spotswood. Though he made no direct contributions to *Beyond Germanna*, he was responsible for more material than any other source.

Margaret James Squires. She made her research in the German records on the Blankenbühler and Utz families available to me for publication. With this material, I started Beyond Germanna which became an outlet for many other researchers.

Klaus Wust. With his study of the Virginia Germans, Klaus led the way to better understanding our ancestors. He contributed studies of rare events and gave new interpretations to replace the erroneous work of early writers. I have reread his works more often than those of any other writer.

In the fifteen years that I published Beyond Germanna, many people contributed. Without classifying their work with any degree of significance, I would like to name these co-workers: Klaus Ahne, John P. Alcock, Jeff Aylor, Margaret Brown Altendahl, Col. James W. Barnett, Sally Baughn, Michael Beall, David Beatty, Ruth Blankenbaker, David B. Boles, Karen Bowman, Tommie Brittain, David M.W. Brown, Donald Brown, Carol Ann Burdine, Nancy Hudson Burge, Charles F. Byran, Jr., Ellie Caroland, Cheri Caspar, Franklin Cochran, Louise Keyser Cockey, Mary Collins, Ronald Cornwell, Jan Creek, Jenell Rector Cremeans, Cynthia Crigler, Wanda Cunningham, Benjamin Dake III, Emma-Jo Davis, Gene Dear, Tom Deeter, Lynnea Dickinson, Darryl Diemer, Eleanor Rodgers Edmonson, Barbara Elwell, Steve Frady, Frances L. Franklin, Carolyn Frazee, Hallie Price Garner, Edith Garrison, Jean Gayle, Doris Gibbons, Gary Carl Grassl, Dorothy Ambergey Griffith, Joan Hackett, Pat Holtzclaw Hartgrove, Marilyn Hartley, Rebecca Hilbert, Barbara Rector Hill, Earl J. Hitt, Louise and James Hodge, William H. Hoffman, Linda Hope, Karl R. Hume, John Humphrey, Olin Hupp, Ardys V. Hurt, Stephen Jacobson, Jefferey Jewell, Ellen John, Elizabeth Yates Johnson, Lucie Jenkins Johnson, Craig Kilby, Barbara Kollhoff, Charline Robinson Kvapil, Harvey Linebeck, Barbara Vines Little, Robert Lotspeich, Virginia Vance Lovett, Echo Mallery, Rev. Marietta Mansfield, Dr. Donald J. Martin, William Martin, Suzanne Matson, James F. McJohn, Mary F. Mickey, Clovis Miller, Linda Nelson, Marylee Newman, Robert Nicholson, Michael Oddenino, Mary Padget, Patricia Pataky, Jean Peters, Ernest Petrey, Jr., Heinz Prinz, Robert Rabe, Dr. Douglas Sanford, Anita Schmidt, Evelyn Rector Schmidt, Doris P. Schultz, Phyllis Tanner Scott, Robert Selig, Peggy Schock, Ina Ritchie Sipes, Ann Nunamaker Smith, Julius Spradling, Helen Spurlin, Nancy Stanberg, Ryan Stansifer, Jean Zorn Strand, Thora and William Sutherland, Brenda Thomas, John Tillery, John Toler, Nancy Upshaw, Jimmy Veal, Shirley Venrick, Robert Vernon, Theodore Walker, Susan Pottenger White, Brigitte Wiehle, Mary Wiley, John C. Wilhite, Jr., Jane Crouch Williams, William R. Yeager, Jr., Sandra Yelton, and Charles Zahn.

It was only natural when I started the present work that I would turn to Beyond Germanna for material that was published there. As all of the names above attest, this was the work of many people. I have not hesitated to reference material from it under the assumption that most people will consult it. It is readily available in a CD format from the Germanna Foundation or the author. Many major libraries have copies, many of them bound.

Some of the material in Beyond Germanna was copyrighted by me or the author. Without negating those copyrights in any way, we grant permission to the Memorial Foundation of Germanna Colonists in Virginia to use such material in this volume subject to their own copyright.

I have said on many occasions that I am not a genealogist but a historian who specializes in the Germanna Colonies and their rich heritage. I feel that the story of these people is inspiring.

John Blankenbaker
Chadds Ford, Pennsylvania
July 20, 2008

Part I

Introduction

A definition for membership in the Second Germanna Colony does not exist. One definition could define the Second Colony members as those who arrived in Virginia in 1717. Another definition could define the Second Colony members as those who left Germany in 1717. These two definitions are not the same for the year of departure is not necessarily the year of arrival. In fact, one family of "later arrivals" left Germany in 1709. The time of departure or arrival means little.

Rather than trying to distinguish the people by departure or arrival times, the emphasis will be on all of the eighteenth century German families of Virginia who lived in the Robinson River Valley (roughly today's Madison County), or near Mt. Pony (in today's Culpeper County), or in the Gourdvine area of today's Rappahannock County. The present work does not discuss the Germans who lived in modern Fauquier County or in the Little Fork of Culpeper County who are discussed in several publications of The Memorial Foundation of the Germanna Colonies in Virginia, Inc.

Two independent strands of action converged accidentally to create the Second Colony. Lt. Gov. Alexander Spotswood, with some partners, wished to obtain 40,000 acres of land (equal to a tract eight miles by eight miles) extending far to the west of Fort Germanna. The new, undeveloped land, being exposed to the Indians, without roads, and having no navigable rivers, was unattractive to settlers. However, any new land had to have people living on it or it would revert to the Crown. Based on his favorable experience with the Germans in the First Germanna Colony, Spotswood envisioned that a large number of Germans, say a boat load, could be the solution. The Germans could be placed on the land as a community and by their numbers serve as protection from the Indians. No fort would be built for them.

Whenever he had the opportunity to talk with the captains of ships, Spotswood let them know that he and his partners would pay the transportation costs of "many" Germans. One of these captains was Andrew Tarbett who had lost his ship to pirates in the Spring of 1717. He gave a full report on this in person to Gov. Spotswood that is on record in the Public Record Office in England as document PRO C.O.5/1342. On his return to England, Capt. Tarbett acquired command of the ship *Scott*.

In this same year, 1717, large numbers of Germans, perhaps a thousand or more, were passing through London on their way to Pennsylvania. Most of these people were in London in the Spring or early in the Summer but many, perhaps about three hundred or more souls, were in London late in the Summer. This group also sought passage to Pennsylvania but the ships equipped for carrying passengers had left. These Germans found Capt. Tarbett and he agreed to take about eighty of them to Pennsylvania (usually he transported freight to and from Virginia). Before they could leave, Capt. Tarbett was confined in Debtors' Prison. During the delay while he reached an agreement with his creditors, the Germans met with the German Lutheran pastors in London, especially at St. Mary in the Strand, a German Lutheran church. They took communion, had two babies baptized, and made plans for a future pastor in America. It was here that the people formed the congregation that is known today by the name of Hebron (though this name was not used until about 1850). The *Scott* was too small to take all of the people who wanted to go and many were left behind. Instead of taking his passengers to Pennsylvania, Capt. Tarbett hijacked them to Virginia where he knew there were people who would pay the transportation of the Germans. Of those left behind, some, after a delay of a couple of years, did find their way to Virginia. Others probably returned to Germany or found homes in England.

This quick overview shows the difficulty of defining the members of the Second Colony. Should the definition be those who left Germany in 1717 or should it be those who arrived in Virginia in 1717? What about the family who left in 1709 but did not arrive in Virginia until 1720? In discussing the individual families, evidence of departure and arrival times will be given. For some families, there are no explicit times and this would further confound the classification of the Germans. Here "Second Germanna Colonist" will just mean, an early arrival in Virginia.

One problem in preparing a work of this nature is the question of how surnames should be presented. It was decided to use the most common English spelling if it is known. Some alternative English spellings are given and if possible some of the spellings in German. Some of the names have no English spelling as in the case of the men who had only daughters, e.g., Michael Käfer who had no sons, only daughters. In these cases, the German spelling, which is known, is used.

This work is divided into three parts. In Part I, there is a review of some eighteenth century documents providing a general history of the colony as a whole. Interspersed among these documents are plots of the early land patents and grants. A summary of improvements in the general and family histories is given. A list of references concludes Part I. In Part II, the individual families, listed alphabetically, are discussed, generally to the second generation if possible. Part III has photographs with short commentaries.

General History

Col. Alexander Spotswood's Explanations of His Land Acquisitions

Alexander Spotswood was asked by the oversight board in London to explain his land acquisition and he wrote a letter, dated June 16, 1724, to the Council of Trade and Plantations. Extracts from this letter follow:

> . . .to avoid all censure of my concerning myself with ye administration, I soon after my return from Albany [found I was no longer Governor] wch. is above a year and a half ago, took up my residence here in the wild woods [at Germanna], 140 miles distant from Williamsburg, which is as far as I could go, being got to one of the ye extreme western settlements of all H.M. Dominions; and in this retirement, not enduring to spend my days in idleness, nor giving over ye thoughts of serving my Country, I assiduously apply'd myself to pursue the scheme, wch. I had laid while I was Governour, of raising in this part of the world all manner of Naval Stores: and I have now made such a progress therein, as I believe upon my arrival at home I shall be able to render your Lordshps an agreeable accot. of that undertak- ing . . .with respect to the lands in the new counties of Brunswick and Spotsylvania, the enclosed letter to the Auditor here gives a particular accounting of the lands which I have taken up.

From a letter written March 28, 1724, to Col. Nathl. Harrison, Deputy Auditor of H.M. Revenue, which was enclosed with the above letter:

> . . . The first tract that I became possessed of was that of 3229 acres called the Germanna tract from my seating thereon several families of German Protestants, to the number of 40 odd men, women and children, who came over in 1714, bringing with them a Minister and Schoolmaster in order to be provided for and setled upon land in these parts by Barron Graffenriede pursuant to an agreemt. he had made with them in Germany. But before their arrival the Baron being nonpluss'd in his affairs here, and forced to return to Switzerland, those poor people would have been sadly distress'd, and must have been sold for servants, had I not taken care of them, and paid down £150 sterling which remained for their pas- sage and ye Council Journals of 28th April, 1714 will shew that to my charity for these strangers I joyned my care for the security of the country against Indian incursions, by choosing to seat them on land 12 miles beyond the then usual course of our rangers, and making them serve for a barrier to the most naked part of our frontiers; and so far from my thoughts was it, to take up the land for my own use, that during the six years [? parts of 1714, 1715, 1715, 1717, 1718, 1719 ?] they remained on the land I never offered to plant one foot of ground thereon. My next tract of 3065 acres which being contiguous, I thought of fitting to take up, the better to accommodate those people when I found them grow fond of having their settlemts. enlarged, it having been concerted that I should convey to them by way of lease for lives, because as aliens their possessions would not descend to their children: but they being seduced

away by greater expectations elsewhere, left the land upon my hands: and so I was first engaged to purchase servants and slaves for seating plantations in this Colony. Soon afterwards I was drawn into another land concern. In Feb. 1717 [1718 by the modern calendar] Sr. Richard Blackmore writes to Mr. Secretary Cock to engage me to favour a design, which he, with several considerable men at home, had to set up an iron works in Virginia, and desires people might be imploy'd to find out the oar, and some thousands of acres taken up for that purpose. Accordingly I set my Germans [First Colony] to work to look for such oar, wch. search cost me upwards of three score pounds: But about two years afterwards I rec'd a letter from Sr. Richard telling me that he had at length considered that he was advanced in years, that his health was of late impaired, and that the undertaking was at too great a distance, and therefore he was determined to drop the project. Whereupon, rather than enter in a contention for my reimbursements, I chose to joyn in with several Gentlemen here, who were willing to carry on the project, and bear their proportion of the charges that I had already been at; and so the mine tract, consist- ing of 15,000 acres of land, was in 1719 [1720 by the modern calendar] taken up by nine or ten Adventures [Adventurers or partners]. About the same time [February 1718 on the modern calendar] I fell into another partnership of land . . . Mr. Robert Beverly having discovered some excellent land among ye little mountains and made a survey thereof before the Proclamation issued in 1710, concern- ing the granting of land, but not daring to seat lands so remote from all Christian inhabitants, and exposed to Indians, found it in vain to take out a patent for the same under the new terms of cultiva- tion, until an oppertunity hapned of freeing a considerable number of German families imported in 1717 [which by his calendar would extend to March 24, 1718 of our calendar], when he invited me to become a sharer in the land, and at the same time admitted in some other partners, to the end that we might all joyn our abilities to make a strong settlement with a body of people at once. Accordingly I came into the proposal, as judging it no ways unbecoming to me, in the station of Governour, to con- tribute towards the seating of H.M. lands, and paying down the passage-money for 70 odd Germans, we settled them upon our tract as freemen (not servants) in 20 odd tenements, all close joyning to one another for their better defence, providing them there with a stock of cattle and all other things neces- sary for their support, without receiving (even to this day) one penny or penny's worth of rent from them. The tract then consisted of about 13,000 acres, but afterwards understanding that many others of the Germans, who had been sold for servants in this Colony, designed when the time of their servitude was expired, to come and joyn their country-folks, we thought it needful to inlarge the tract; and I find- ing, by the care which the Lords Commissioners of Trade took to send over the methods for making hemp and tar, that the Ministry at home was for encouraging the Plantations to raise Naval Stores, judged it convenient to take in a large quantity of piney lands, which lay contiguous and fit for tar and masts, and so it was increased to a tract of 40,000 acres. And considering the number of free people we have seated upon it (with whom we agreed to allot them out of it sufficient lands for their lives, and who are now about 100 Germans) it will not appear such an exorbitant possession as some persons have been pleased to represent it. . . [*Calendar of State Papers, Colonial Series, America and West Indies, 1724–1725*, v.34, ed. Cecil Headlam, Public Record Office, 1936. See also, "Col. Alexander Spotswood's Land Acquisitions," Beyond Germanna, v.5, n.6, p.295 for a slightly longer and fuller account than given here.]

The 40,000 Acre Tract, also called the Spotsylvania Tract

To the east of Fort Germanna or toward the sea, there were no large tracts of land available. There was good land though toward the Blue Ridge Mountains (called the Great Mountains then). Spotswood and several other men interested in acquiring land took a trip from Germanna in 1716 over the Blue Ridge Mountains. The major purpose of this exploration was to find land for their private use. (Spotswood officially defined the purposes of the expedition in security terms as he hoped to be reimbursed for the expenses.) The major result of the trip was the broad definition of a 40,000 acre tract (shown on the next page). It started just to the west of Fort Germanna (G) and ran along the south side of and parallel to the Rapidan River out to the mouth of the Robinson River. This part on the south side of the Rapidan River was the 13,000 acre contribution of Robert Beverley which he was claiming but had not patented. Crossing the Rapidan, the tract followed the Robinson River to Crooked (Meander) Run, along this water course and then overland to Mountain Run to the west of the present day Culpeper Court House (CH), then farther north and east before turning south, and then running east back to the start. Modern calculations of the area of the tract show that it was closer to 64,000 acres or equivalent to ten miles by ten miles.

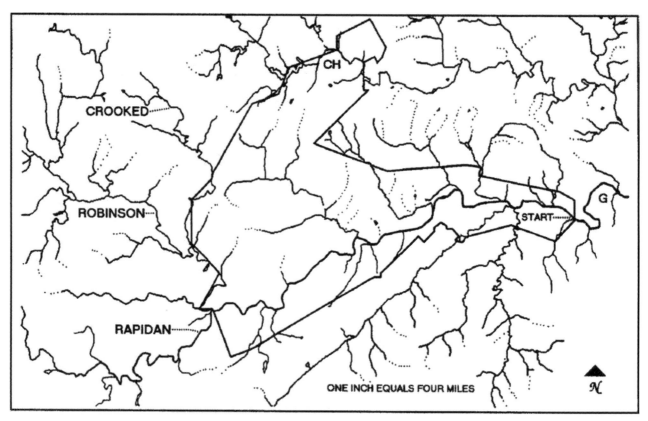

The Spotsylvania Tract. The straighter lines are the boundaries of the tract. The letter G shows the location of Fort Germanna and the Rapidan River loops around this. The CH shows the location of the modern courthouse for Culpeper County. The contribution of Robert Beverley was the land on the south side of the Rapidan River. Most of the land in the final tract lay to the north of the Rapidan River. Calculations today show that the tract contained about 64,000 acres, not 40,000 acres.

The land looked good and a general agreement was reached with several partners though it appears that Spotswood had more than a fifty percent interest and was the general manager of the partnership. The problem of finding settlers was the difficult part because this area was very isolated. He started working with the captains of ships and about six months later he took a report from Andrew Tarbett who had lost a ship to pirates. Spotswood explained his need for settlers and suggested that Germans might be the best answer. Tarbett could not promise any thing at the time as he had no ship and he probably had no idea of how he might find the Germans.

From the standpoint of Tarbett and the Virginia investors, it was lucky that in the year 1717 a large number of Germans decided to emigrate. Klaus Wust, largely based on the arrivals in America, estimated the number of Germans at one thousand and the evidence now suggests that he may have been low with respect to the number that left Germany that year. After the large number of Germans went to England in 1709, the English strongly discouraged German emigration and very few Germans passed through England up to 1717. As to why there were so many in this year, Wust thought war was a major factor. Most of these Germans came from southwest Germany, especially the areas which are known today as Baden, Württemberg, and the Palatinate. Also, Anabaptists may have come from Switzerland and the Alsace, especially Mennonites. Their co-religionists such as the Hans Herr party had left for Pennsylvania in 1709 and they were recruiting additional Anabaptists.

Origins in Germany and the Trip to America

Four of the Germanna families were from the German village of Gemmingen (six families left there in 1717). When the families left, the sexton in the church recorded their names in the register of deaths. (The individual families will be discussed in the family section later.) The sexton gave a bit of general history with the list of the people. This includes an alternative reason for leaving Germany though it does not explain why the departure was in 1717. The sexton wrote (in translation by Andreas Mielke and Elke Hall which was published in 𝔅𝔢𝔶𝔬𝔫𝔡 𝔊𝔢𝔯𝔪𝔞𝔫𝔫𝔞, v.15, n.6, p.907).

> On July 12th of this year [1717] the below listed persons including their children moved away from here at night with the intention to sail over to Pennsylvania in order to earn their piece of bread better than here through the hard work of cultivating the wilderness. Yet quite many people went away not only from here but also from other places, and all went there with the same intention.

July 12 was a very late time in the year to leave Germany. Two or even three months earlier would have been much better. By the time these people arrived in London, the ships for Pennsylvania had left. Finding a ship in August, the earliest time they could have been in London, was difficult. The ship *Scott* was probably the only choice and Capt. Tarbett could not have been in command for very long.

Gemmingen is in southwestern Germany. All of the emigrants from that region would have traveled down the Rhine River which flows to the north. Some might have started their trip on the Neckar River which flows into the Rhine River. The Rhine starts in Switzerland and passes by Strasbourg, Karlsruhe, Mainz, Wiesbaden, Koblenz, Bonn, Köln, Düsseldorf, and on to Rotterdam, see the map on the next page.

In 1717, the passengers divided the trip into three parts. First was the trip down the Rhine River to Rotterdam. Then passage on a ship to London would be obtained. There they would find another ship to America. In London, the Second Colony entered into agreement with Capt. Tarbett of the *Scott* to take them to Pennsylvania. After a few years, when the business of transporting Germans to American became larger and more consistent, the ships met the Germans at Rotterdam or Amsterdam. In 1717 though, the Germans had to use two ocean-going ships, one across the North Sea and the other across the Atlantic Ocean.

The German Homes

On the next page, the general localities of many of the emigrants in 1717 are located. Several of the Germanna immigrants left from homes and villages which have not yet been identified. However, researchers have found that emigrants often moved together, if not at same time, then at later times. A factor in this was the letters that the first immigrants wrote home. These were powerful sales tools. Thus, an examination of the names of residents of a village often show names that were later comers if not fellow immigrants.

Some of the names found in Oberöwisheim and Neuenbürg include: Blanckenbühler, Bender, Christler, Debelt/Debold/Debolt, Diehl, Fin(c)k, Fischer, Fleischmann, Gerhard, Hepp, Hirsch, Jäger, Käfer, Kappeler, Klar, Krieger, Lang, Lederer, Lepp/Lipp, Mack, Maier/Mayer/Meier/Moyer, Motz, Rauch, Rausch, Rücker, Sauter, Schad, Schaible/Schaiblin/Scheiblin, Schlüchter, Schneider, Schön, Sieber, Silber, Thoma/Thomas, Uhl, Vogt/Voigt, Weidmann, Weingard, Zimmermann (not all of these families were present in 1717).

Just a few miles away at Diefenbach, these names are found: Böhm, Fin(c)k, Fleischmann, Frei/Frey, Hipp, Hirsch, Hitt, Jäger, Kappler/Keppler, Kirchner, Klar, Krieger, Lang, Lapp, Maier, Mauch, Öhler, Sauder, Scheible, Schlatter, Schön, Schwindel, Sieber, Silber, Späth, Thoma/Thomae, Uhl, Vogt, Wieland, Ziegler.

Most of the earliest Second Colony people came from a small area of Germany. Gary Zimmerman and Johni Cerny, using the known villages of a few families searched other nearby villages and found many more Second Colony people. Though their search was extensive, they may not have exhausted the possibilities. If a family cannot be found in a specific village, it may pay to search in nearby villages for the ancestral home.

The next page is a map of Germany reproduced from the *Superatlas Deutschland 2001-2002* courtesy of Falk publishers. There are 232 pages of maps in this very detailed atlas.

When the atlas is opened, two pages are displayed. The rectangles here are the two pages though, like a book, each page is numbered. These pages are made at a scale where one inch is just about equal to three miles (they were created at two kilometers per centimeter or a scale of 200,000 to 1). Here one rectangle is about 44 miles east to west and 32 miles north to south.

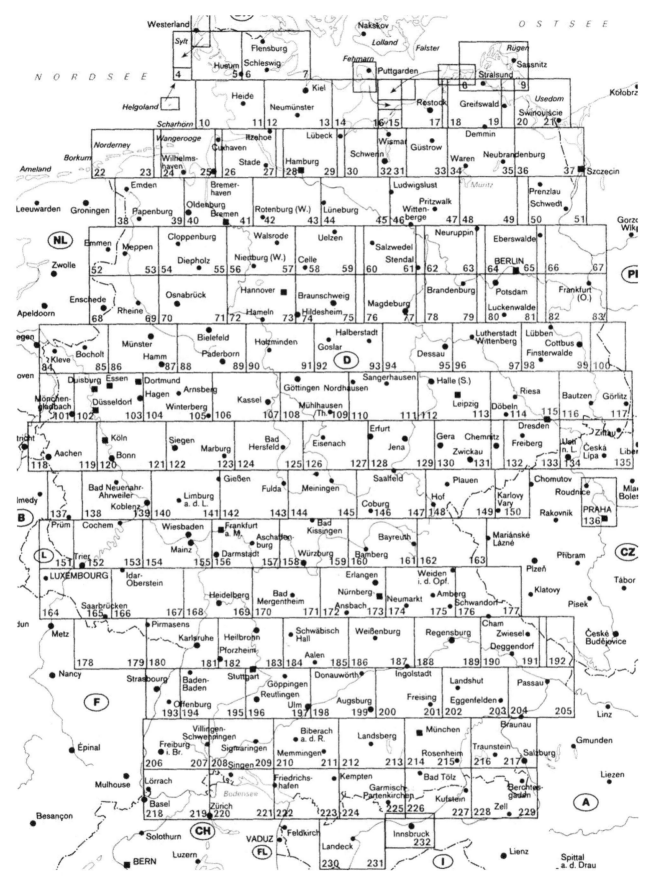

Germany in 2008. In 1717, there was no "Germany." There was the Holy Roman Empire which included hundreds of independent regions, some of them of a major size (e.g., Württemberg) and some of them were individual villages. For convenience today, we speak of Germany and its states.

About 80% of the earliest families came from the northern half of page number 182. This is an area of about 22 miles by 16 miles. The area includes parts of a cultural region called the Kraichgau and sometimes the Second Colony is identified as coming from the Kraichgau though it not a perfect match. Gemmingen and Schwaigern are in the Kraichgau, but several of the villages such as Neuenbürg, Sulzfeld, and Ötisheim were not a part of the Kraichgau. The northern half of page 182 lies today in the state of Germany named Baden-Württemberg. In 1717, the eastern area of page 182 was in Württemberg and the western area was mostly in Baden but there were lands belonging to the Bishops of Speyer, i.e., the Catholic Church, which in 1717 were not a part of Baden. Also, many of the villages were semi-independent with a knight as the head. These knights were loosely associated while trying to maintain their independence from Württemberg, Baden, and the Palatinate. This was especially true in the Kraichgau.

The Palatinate today lies to the west of this region across the Rhine River. The Yager family came from page 167 which lies in the Palatinate. The Utz-Volck complex came from page 169, Castler came from page 196, Crisler and Lotspeich came from page 168, Wayland from page 183, and Garr from page 185 (in Bavaria). These locations surround the dominant center of the majority.

Some of the Germanna families had not been long term residents of the villages from which they left for America. Cyriacus Fleshman had come from Klings on page 144, the Käfers were from Ansbach on page 172, and the Blankenbakers had come earlier from Austria. Some Germanna people have Swiss origins.

The land on page 182 is approximately bounded on the east by the Neckar River which flows through Heilbronn. The Neckar, after flowing north, turns to the west and flows by Heidelberg and shortly thereafter empties into the Rhine. To the west of page 182 is the Rhine River which flows through Karlsruhe.

The First Germanna Colony came from the vicinity of Siegen on page 122. This is about fifty miles east of Cologne (Köln). While all areas had an agricultural base, there were differences. The Second Colony came from a region where grapes were grown and wine was made. Several of the Second Colony people have been identified as vine tenders. In the Siegen area, there was ore extraction, metal working, and leather making.

The map shows several of the modern letter codes used to identify the countries. The letter D stands for Deutschland, CH for Switzerland, F for France, B for Belgium, NL for the Netherlands, I for Italy, A for Austria. The map shows some of the adjacent areas such as the city of Prague on page 136 and some of the areas of Switzerland and Austria. The German language is used in these areas.

St. Mary in the Strand (London) Lutheran Church Records
(Andreas Mielke and Sandra Yelton)

When the Second Colony people reached London they made contact with a German Lutheran church there. Having been without the service of a pastor for several weeks, they would have had a desire to attend services. They hoped they could make arrangements for a pastor to come to them after they were in America. Perhaps they wanted the blessing of the pastors for their journey; certainly, they had communion. Children were born to them in London and they were baptized.

On 31 AUG 1717, Matthias Schmidt and his wife Regina Catharina had a son Johann baptized. The baby had been born two days previously. One of the sponsors was Johann Georg Forckel.

On this same day, Maria Barbara Weiland and Matthias Schmidt were sponsors at the baptism of Maria Barbara Förckel, daughter of Johann Georg and Susanna Förckel.

On 9 SEP 1717, Johann Michel Koch and his wife Barbara had their daughter Maria Dorothea baptized. One sponsor was Henrich Schneider. The baby was born the previous day.

These events show that the group was still in London in September and perhaps later. See Beyond Germanna, v.15, n.6, p. 905 for more information. The original record is in the Public Record Office as RG4/4625 and a copy was obtained by Sandra Yelton. The Crown copyright is preserved.

The So-called Fifth Return Party

Henry Z Jones, Jr. found a document (T.1/208) in the Public Record Office in London which helps clarify why the definition of the Second Colony membership is difficult. Only an extract is given here and the full list is given in the book by Henry Z Jones, Jr. and Lewis Bunker Rohrbach, *Even More Palatine Families*, Vol. 3, Picton Press, 2002. Only a few names will be given here. The date of the list is 16 September 1717 and it is a petition by about fifty-two heads of families, representing two hundred people, who state:

> A Liste of Those Poor Palatines, Wirtembergers, Etc. Who Are Willing to Return into Germany, and Humbly Desiring His Majesty's Most Gracious Bounty, for Their Transportation into Holland, for Their Charges to Their Own Country, Taken the 16th September 1717.

One consecutive group of six names is: Johannes Scheff, Hans George Forchel, Christofle Uhl, Fredric Kapler, Hans George Long, Melchior Feiser.

We recognize that Uhl, Kapler, and Long are Germanna citizens who originated in Sulzfeld, Baden. The name Scheff certainly suggests the name Chelf who was found in the Germanna community later. Frederick Kapler stated in his proof of importation that he came in 1719. We immediately know that not everyone who left Germany in 1717 made it to Pennsylvania or Virginia in 1717. For some of them, there was a delay.

We do not know if this petition was approved; there is no evidence saying that it was. Probably some of the Germans found jobs in England until they could find transportation. Some of them would have gone to Pennsylvania while others had friends who went to Virginia. Notice that those who did eventually go to Virginia must have had letters back from Virginia saying they were in Virginia and not Pennsylvania. For example, Christopher Zimmerman from Sulzfeld did make it to Virginia in 1717 (against his will) and perhaps he sent word back that he was in Virginia.

Possibly, Uhl, Kapler, and Long did return to Sulzfeld where they received a letter from Zimmerman or others who did get to Virginia which told where they were. Or if Uhl, Kapler, and Long remained in England, possibly the communication was to the pastor of St. Mary in the Strand.

An important point is that some people were stranded in London in September 1717 and perhaps not all of them signed this petition.

It might be considered that the date of the petition indicates the *Scott* had left London but this would be an invalid conclusion. It might simply show that the petition signers had become discouraged whether there was even going to be a trip or whether they would be included if the *Scott* did leave. Capt. Tarbett was in Debtor's Prison and whether he would be released was unknown. In the face of the uncertainties, many people may have petitioned for aid to return to Germany.

Two other names in the list are of interest where four consecutive names are: Kilian Reiß, Hans George Heer, Hans Martin Volck, Christofle Gemelich.

The second of these names is believed to be a son of Hans Herr, an early Mennonite immigrant to Pennsylvania. The third of these names, Volck, is found among the members of the Second Germanna Colony and the early pioneers. The Heer family (an acceptable variant of Herr) lived on the Unterbiegelhof estate and many Volcks are found in the neighborhood of the Wagenbach estate. These two large farms are almost back to back. (If the identity of George Heer is correct, he would be the son of family tradition who did not go to Pennsylvania but settled in England.)

> Considering how long it too to cross the ocean, where ten weeks was typical though this could be much longer, it is not certain that they arrived by December 31 of 1717. If they had arrived up to the following March 24, they still would have said it was 1717 because the Old Style (OS) calendar was in use in the English-speaking world. Had it been in the period from January to March 24, we would say, using today's calendar, that it was in 1718.

Captain Tarbett or Captain Scott?

The claim that the captain of the ship which brought the Second Colony was Scott rested on a Spotsylvania County, Virginia Court record and duplicated in two other records of the same date in which occurs these three words, "...in Captain Scott..." Originally, the people who reported this bit of history added a question mark after Scott because of the strange nature of the remark. Soon people were omitting the question mark and just simply saying that Capt. Scott brought the Second Colony. Of course, the original courthouse record is to be questioned because one normally comes in a ship and not "in the captain." A search of the microfilms at the Virginia State Library of the Colonial records from England (which have been partially indexed) does not show a civil captain named Scott but it does show a ship named *Scott*. The captain of this was Andrew Tarbett. A search for information about this man shows that he had lost a ship to pirates and that he gave testimony to Alexander Spotswood about the loss in the Spring of 1717. It appears that on this occasion Spotswood made known his desire for a large number of Germans for whom he would pay the transportation costs. Just the previous Fall, the trip across the Blue Ridge Mountains had been made and the plans had been made to claim a large tract of land. An analysis of the case of Capt. Tarbett was made in Beyond Germanna, v.9, n.5.

Head Rights List of Alexander Spotswood

When Alexander Spotswood was issued a patent (11 APR 1732) for a 28,000 acre tract, he gave forty-eight names as head rights to help pay for the land [see *Virginia Patent Book 14*, p.378ff]. These are an important part of knowing who came in 1717. Since, in his history, Spotswood said there were seventy-odd Germans, the difference was must lie in the fact that his partners paid the transportation of the remaining Germans, perhaps about thirty of them. Spotwood's headrights include: [as read from the original patent],

Pale [Balthasar] Blankebuchner
Margaret Blankebuchner
Mathiaas Blankebuchner
Anna Maria Blankebuchner
Hans Jerich Blankebuchner
Wolf Michel Kefer
Hendrich Schlucter
Hans Jerich Chively [Scheible]
Maria Clora Chively
Anna Martha Chively
Anna Elizabetha Chively
Anna Maria Chively
Michel Cook
Mary Cook
Henry Snyder
Dorathy Snyder,
Hans Jerich Otes [Utz]
Parvara [Barbara] Otes
Ferdinandis Sylvania Otes [two people,
    Ferdinand Utz and Sabina Volck]
Anna Louisa Otes [her surname was Volck]
Joseph Wever [Weaver]
Susanna Wever
Hans Fredich Wever

Maria Sophia Wever
Wabburie [Walburga] Wever
Hans Michel Cloar [Clore]
Anna Maria Parva Cloar
Andrea Claus Cloar
Agnes Margaret Cloar
Hans Jerich Cloar
Hans Michael Smiedt [Smith]
Anna Creda Smiedt
Hans Michael Smiedt
Hans Jerich Wegman
Anna Maria Wegman
Maria Margaret Wegman
Maria Gotlieve Wegman
Hans Nicholas Blankebuchner
Applona Blankebuchner
Zacharias Blankenbuchner
Coz [Cyriacus] Jacob Floschman [Fleshman]
Anna Parva Floschman
John Peter Floschman
Maria Catharina Floschman
Hans Michel Milcher
Sophia Catharina Milcher
Maria Parvara Milcher

In the list, the order is father, mother, and children generally in the order of descending age, sometimes with a priority of sons over daughters.

First Homes on the Spotsylvania Tract

The histories of the Second Colony often state that the Germans lived south of the Rapidan River near the iron works or iron mine. This would be thirteen miles down the river from Germanna and nearer civilization. The statement is, on the face, doubtful because the Second Colony arrived in Virginia just as the First Colony started their search for iron ore. Furthermore, Alexander Spotswood is clear that the Second Colony worked on naval stores.

The Rev. Hugh Jones in his 1724 book, *The Present State of Virginia*, reprinted at Chapel Hill, North Carolina says, "Beyond this [Germanna] are seated the Colony of Germans or Palatines, with allowance of good quantities of rich land, at easy or no rates, who thrive very well, and live happily, and entertain generously." Since the Rev. Jones' experience in Virginia ended in 1722, the Germans he refers to are the Second Colony (as other statements of his make clear) who have not moved to their permanent homes.

The suggestion of Jones is that the Second Colony is beyond or to the west of Germanna and not east or closer to civilization. Looking at detailed maps of the area immediately to the west of Germanna, one is struck by two geographical features. These are Fleshman's Run which flows into the Rapidan and German Run which flows into Fleshman's Run. Cyriacus Fleshman was a member of the Second Colony so the names of these two small streams suggest where the Second Colony lived. (The official name of Fleshman's Run today is Field's Run though the people in the area still refer to it as Fleshman's Run. A reversal of the name back to Fleshman's Run is pending.)

At the Germanna Seminar in 1992, after hearing the suggestion that the Second Colony did live in this area, Mr. David M. W. Brown made this statement:

> In the late 1950s, my grandfather, E.P. Martin, and my uncle, James E. Martin, who is now one of the Trustees of the Germanna Foundation, owned and operated the lumber mill which still stands one and a half miles west of Germanna bridge on the south side of Route 3. Adjoining the mill property on its western property is a tract of pasture and woodland to which we always referred as the the Field's Place as it had been purchased by my grandfather from the Field family. This tract includes acreage on both sides of Field's Run, formerly known as Fleshman's Run.
>
> In those days, my grandfather kept a small herd of Angus cattle pastured on the Field's Place, and occasionally I would accompany him to check on it. On one such occasion, we went for a walk through the woods in a southward direction, paralleling Field's Run. Being very interested in the Civil War, I asked him if there were any campsites in the area, to which he replied that he thought not, but that there had been a settlement in the area many years earlier, and that it had probably disappeared long before the war.
>
> I never went back to the area to explore, for I did not regard the alleged settlement as likely to be of any great historical significance. Over the years I all but forgot the possibility, until I heard the theory at the Seminar regarding the home of the Second Germanna Colony. It was then that I recalled my grandfather's words and how they just may have held a hint as to the location of what is indeed a very significant historical site, the home of the 1717 Germanna Colony.

Spotswood leased land to Thomas Byrn and Martha his wife and it is recorded 17 DEC 1728 in *Spotsylvania Deed Book A*. Phrases in the lease include "fork of the Rappahannock," "New German Town," and "parcels number 18 and 19." All of these strongly confirm that the Second Colony was in the Great Fork of the Rappahannock on the north side of the Rapidan River. Still, this lease did not define exactly where parcels 18 and 19 were.

Joy Q. Stearns found information in the Orange County books which helped define the range better. One lease to John Bond on 14 July 1735 includes metes and bounds (*D.B. 1*, p.110–114). It starts at the lower corner of lot 18 of the German tenements on the Rapidan River. The drawing of the tract made by George Hume, the surveyor, shows two homes on it.

The conclusion now is that the Germans were spread out along the Rapidan River from Fleshman's Run almost to Potato Run. The homes were not as close as Spotswood's phrase, "closely joyned" might suggest.

The map below shows many of these features. The Germanna Tract was on both sides of the Rapidan River. The eastern part of the 40,000 acre Spotsylvania Tract is depicted. The part of this south of the Rapidan was Robert Beverley's claim and contribution. To this was added land north of the Rapidan. Fleshman's Run and German Run are shown. Bond's lease which refers to the German tenements is four to five miles west of the eastern point of the Spotsylvania Tract.

For more information see, 𝔅𝔢𝔶𝔬𝔫𝔡 𝔊𝔢𝔯𝔪𝔞𝔫𝔫𝔞, v.2, n.6; v.4, n.5; and v.10, n.3.

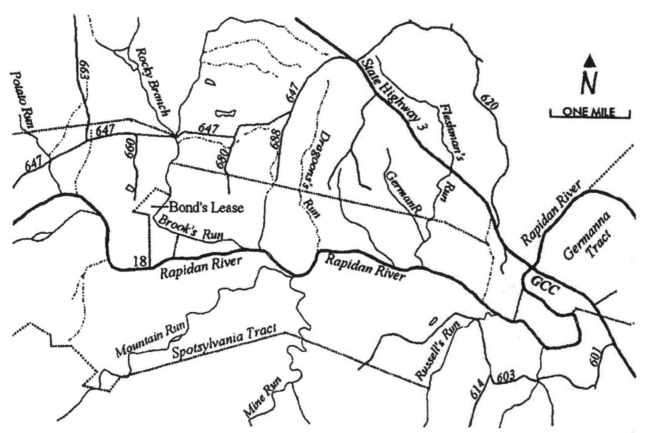

First Homes of the Second Colony. A portion of the Spotsylvania Tract is shown. The "Germanna Tract" legend is close to the site of Fort Germanna. The letters "GCC" show the location of Germanna Community College and the Visitor's Center of the Memorial Foundation of Germanna Colonists. Just to the west, Fleshman's Run and German Run can be located. The area of the homes of the Second Colony started in this general region and ran west out almost to Potato Run. Bond's lease was marked with two homes, one by the Rapidan and the other at the point where Brook's Run made a sharp turn to the north.

The Colonial Government

In 1717 Virginia, the Governor of the Royal Virginia colony was Lord Orkney in England. He took no active part in the routine affairs. This was delegated to the Lt. Governor who, from 1710 to 1722, was Alexander Spotswood. The Lt. Governor was usually called the Governor and, in effect, the Lt. Governor did act fully like the Governor.

In Virginia, besides the Governor, there was a Council of twelve men and a House of Burgesses. The Council acted as an upper legislative body and was also an adviser to the Governor. Appointments to the Council were made in England upon the recommendations of the Governor. Mostly these were large land owners (the "peers") and often they were related by marriage. The lower legislative body was the House of Burgesses which was composed of two men elected from each county plus two from William and Mary College. The House of Burgesses enacted legislation which was reviewed by the Council and perhaps sent back to the House for reconsideration. When an act was approved by the House and Council, the Governor signed it at a meeting of himself and Council. However, the legislation could not be regarded as law until it was reviewed in England where it might be rejected.

Law Suits by Alexander Spotswood Against the Germans

In a series of actions for which the motivation is not clearly understood, Spotswood sued many of the Germans. Nearly all of the Germans on his head right list were sued (we presume he had paid the transportation of these) and at least one who had had his transportation paid by a partner. Spotswood acquired his contract when he bought out his partners. Still, many of the Germans were not sued. The first of his suits was brought on September 6, 1723 against Jacob Crigler for £34 18s 4p. This was a tremendous sum for a man who had been working for almost six years for Spotswood, presumably without pay. On March 3, 1724(NS), by the consent of both parties, the case against Jacob Crigler was dismissed with the "defendant assuming to pay ye cost of the suit." The costs would have been but a small fraction of the amount originally sought which leaves us wondering what the basis of the suit had been and why did the plaintiff give in so abruptly.

Spotswood maintained that the Germans had failed to satisfy the terms of the agreement "made by them in consideration of money advanced upon their transportation." Despite their repeated efforts to have him produce the agreement, he steadfastly refused to do so.

George Utz and Cyriacus Fleshman, after their frustrations in obtaining legal help, petitioned the House of Burgesses for help:

1. In pursuance of the advise of the honorable Major Holloway have wee desired Colonell Spotswood to give us the Copy of the Covenant which wee at our arrival here made with him, but he will not give it. Wee have desired the Justices of the Spotsylvania Court to assist us and to be our witnesses that the Colonell will not deliver above mentioned covenant, but they refuse to have anything to do with it, therefore we humbly ask further advice.
2. Colonell Spotswood hath arested above 25 of us, wee not knowing wherefore we are arested, therefore humbly ask your honour's advice if it is proper to give in a petition to the Gentlemen of the house of burgess' to assist us and order one who might plead for us in forma pauperis.
3. Wee design to go to England and from thence to germany to bring in a Minister for us high germans who are here, do humbly ask if it proper to desire the governor to give us an attestation & passport to witness that we are inhabitants here, the Burgesses from Spotsylvania County know that we are by the rest of our Countrymen sent in that behalf.
Wee who are to go out our names are Michial Coock, Zerachus Flishman. [The two who actually went were John Motz and Cyriacus Flishman.] (The above petition was reprinted from the *Virginia Historical Magazine*.)

At a meeting on April 24, 1724, the Council sided with the Germans and decreed that the deputy attorney for the king should represent the petitioners in the Spotsylvania County Court:

On reading at the Board of Petition of Zacharias Flishman and George Ouds [Utz] on behalf of themselves and fourteen other high-Germans, now residing in Spotsylvania county near Germanna, complaining that Col. Spotswood hath unjustly sued them in the Court for the non-performance of a certain Agreement pretended to be made by them in consideration of money advanced them upon their transportation into this colony, although they have heretofore performed, and always ready to perform any Agreement thy made the said Col. Spotswood; but though they have often applied to him for a copy of the said Agreement they made with him, he hath refused to give them any such copy and therefore praying this board to commiserate their condition on being strangers and to make such order as they shall think proper to have the Agreement produced; the Governor with the advice of the Council is pleased to order as it is hereby ordered: That in regard to the petition, poor condition and ignorance of the laws of this Colony, the person acting as Deputy Attorney for the King in the said County of Spotsylvania do appear for the Petitioners in the said suits brought against them in that court, that so the Petitioners may have the benefit of a fair tryal.

From the date of the response, it appears that Spotswood had been discussing the matter with the Germans for some time before the lawsuit against Jacob Crigler. The Germans believed that more than twenty-five of them would be sued. Trials were held for thirteen Germans and six cases were dismissed before trial. From the first to the last trial, more than two years elapsed. At the trials, Spotswood was represented by a series of lawyers since he was in England. The results of the nineteen lawsuits were:

		Sued for			Awarded			Spotsylvania Co.
Date	Defendant	£	s	d	£	s	d	O. B. (1724–30)
3-24-1724(NS)	Jacob Crigler	34	18	4	dismissed*			p. 51**
7-08-1724	Andreas Bellenger				dismissed			
7-08-1724	Micheal Holt				dismissed			
7-08-1724	George Utz				dismissed			
9-01-1724	Michael Clore				dismissed			p. 8–9
10-6-1725	Phillip Paulitz	18	7	5	4	9	7	p. 20
10-5-1725	Conrad Amburge	32			2	13	1.5	p. 79
10-6-1725	Nicholas Jeager	35			7	3	2	p. 81–82
11-1-1726	Cyracus Fleshman				dismissed			p. 115
12-6-1726	Balthazer Blankenbucher	11	11	8	4	6	3	p. 130–131
12-6-1726	Hendrick Snyder	18	6	2	3	2	6	p. 131
12-6-1726	George Moyer	24	12	8	15	11	.5	p. 132
12-6-1726	Michael Cook	3	2	4		38	8	p. 133
12-8-1726	John Bryol	17	11	7	8	1	5	p. 133
12-8-1726	Michael Smith	14	3	1	4	14	4	p. 134
12-8-1726	Michael Kaifer	11	15	4	1	14	8	p. 135
12-8-1726	Mathias Blankenbucher	12	4	9	6	19	2	p. 135
12-8-1726	Nicholas Blankenbucher	9	2	.5	1	4	7	p. 135
12-8-1726	George Sheible	4	2	2	2	2	8	p. 136

* In the dismissals, the defendant agreed to pay the court costs.
** The action of dismissal for Jacob Crigler is in Spotsylvania Will Book A (1722–1749)

Since the action or decision that is recorded does not specify any of the details of the suits except the final conclusion, the reasons might have been some combination of the following:

The amount perhaps bears some relationship to the actual transportation expenses that Spotswood paid. This is a weak argument because George Sheible with five in his party was sued for only four pounds while the bachelor Michael Käfer was sued for eleven pounds.

Spotswood did supply cattle to the immigrants. In his leases, he supplied cattle on the basis that the lessee would return an equivalent number of cattle to Spotswood plus one-half of the increase. The other half of the increase could be kept by the lessee. There might be some merit in this but it is difficult to believe that all of the Germans would have been such poor husbandmen. Also, the cattle supplied to any individual would generally have fallen far short in value to the amount sought in the suits.

A popular argument is that Spotswood was attempting to keep the Germans for an additional time, perhaps as tenants. In this time period, his land claims were weak and he needed settlers on what he was claiming. Again, there is no rational explanation for the variation in the amount sought from the different Germans. In any case, the Germans left in 1725 which would be the normal expiration of their indenture. On November 1, 1726 they petitioned the court for a "German mountain road."

Yet another argument is that Spotswood was attempting to make money at the German's expense. This does not explain why the amounts sought varied so much and why the final result bore little correlation to the amount originally sought.

Possibly some of the Germans had personally paid something towards their transportation costs and the balance due to Capt. Tarbett was paid by Spotswood. But the eleven pounds for which the bachelor Michael Käfer was sued is about double the cost of one passenger fare.

The highest amount won by Spotswood was from George Moyer who had his transportation paid by Robert Beverley. The heir of Robert Beverley, who sold out to Spotswood, did testify at Moyer's trial. Apparently, he could present better evidence than Spotswood's lawyers could present.

The Creation of Spotsylvania County and Free Land

On November 18, 1720, the Burgesses took up legislation to create two new counties, Brunswick and Spotsylvania. Spotswood had apparently initiated the legislation for he had prepared the House by a presentation on the need for the better security of the frontier. Security against the French and the Indians was usually a persuasive argument in London. His argued that settlers in these new counties would enhance the security of the frontier.

The new county of Spotsylvania was to be bounded by the Rappahannock River on the north and was to extend westward over the mountains to the river on the other side. This would include the present counties of Spotsylvania, Orange, Culpeper, Madison, and Rappahannock plus land west of the Blue Ridge Mountains.

The most striking feature of the legislation was the liberal provisions for acquiring land in them. The act stipulated that settlers would be "free from publick levies" for ten years. Public levies were not defined but it was hoped that in England it would be interpreted as the quit rents (real estate taxes) and the head rights (the cost of acquiring the land). While men in Virginia were aware that the act had to be approved in England, many responded immediately by filing for land patents. Gov. Spotswood was among these though he used intermediates who would later sell him the land. The patents applications were not approved pending word from England on the legislation.

The legislation was ambiguous in other ways. It did not state what the status of land would be which had already been taken up. Would this be free from quit rents or not? There was no limitation on the quantity of land that an individual could take up.

Spotswood would be benefitted tremendously since he had or was to file for more than 80,000 acres of land in the new county.

In 1722, Spotswood could see his tenure as governor was drawing to a close. While he still could, he approved the pending patents and set up the government for the new Spotsylvania County. However, his patents (and all patents in the new counties) might be challenged. In fact, his patents were. It wasn't until late in the decade when he personally appealed to the King that the law was finally clarified and the conditions for his taking up the land were specified. In 1723, perhaps he wished to have settlers on his land until the patents were cleared. Still, this does not explain the basis on which the lawsuits against the Germans were made.

The Second Colony benefitted from the new legislation also. Though they were not acquiring such large quantities of land, what they did acquire was free for a period of years. They were still subject to the county and parish levies. By and large, it is for this reason that the Second Colony did not join the First Colony at Germantown. Willis M. Kemper and Harry L. Wright in their book, *Genealogy of the Kemper Family in the United States* (Chicago 1899), felt that there was an antagonism between the two Colonies because the Second Colony did not join the First Colony. The major difference he saw between the two Colonies was religion as the First Colony was German Reformed and the Second Colony was Lutheran. So Kemper ascribed their "antagonism" to this difference of religious faith. He completely overlooked that the Second Colony had the benefit of free land in Spotsylvania County. There is little reason to believe the two colonies were antagonistic. Several men of the Reformed faith moved to the Robinson River Valley, some very early.

Proofs of Importation of Selected Germans in Spotsylvania Court, 1724 to 1729

In 1705 the Virginia General Assembly enacted legislation designed to redefine the procedures pertaining to land acquisition, management, and land grants including the importation rights popularly called "head rights."

Each claimant had to be "free." Indentured servants were not eligible during their period of servitude, but upon fulfillment of the terms of their indenture they too were afforded the opportunity of land ownership. To establish eligibility, the free person had to petition the court and make proof of such importation upon oath, either in general or county court. A typical petition, such as that of Nicholas Yeager, dated May 2, 1727, reads as follows:

> On petition of Nicholas Yeager in order to prove his right to take up land according to his Majties Royale charter, made oath that he came into this Country about nine years since in Capt. Scott, and that he brought Mary his wife and two children named Adam and Mary with him, and that this is the first time of his proving the said Importations, Whereupon certificate is Ordered to be granted him of Rights to take up two hundred acres of Land. [Spotsylvania County, *Virginia Order Book (1724–1730)*, p. 142]

(This is one of three records in which the phrase, "in Capt. Scott," occurs. All three were made on the same day and it is obvious that the clerk simply copied the second two from the first entry.) Nicholas Yeager was now free to find two hundred acres of land and to have it surveyed (he had to pay the surveyor) whereupon he could be issued a patent (deed). There were terms and conditions to the patent as it required that some land be cleared and a house be built. Instead of using the head right to help pay for land, one could sell the head rights to others who could take up the land. Head rights were not especially significant to the Second Colony people because the legislation creating Spotsylvania County in 1720 stated that land in it would be free of the purchase price and quit rents (taxes) for ten years. Nevertheless, several members of the Second Colony and later comers did make their proofs of importations and these are valuable clues to the membership in the colony. Those that made application in Spotsylvania County are given below from the recording in the Order Book (others, not given here, are recorded in Orange County):

Petition Date (OS)	Petitioner	Arrived	Accompanied By	Acres	O.B. 1722–4	Granted Certificate
04–07–'24	Frederick Cobler	1719	Barbara, his wife	100	p.69	No entry
02–01–'25	John Motz	1717	Maria Pelona, his wife	100	p.89	03–22–'25
02–01–'25	Hans Herren Burgud	1717	Anna Purve, his wife and son Stephen	150	p.89	03–22–'25
04–05–'26	Christopher Zimmerman	1717	Elizabeth, his wife and sons John and Andrew	200	p.107	04–11–'26
05–05–'26	Henry Snyder	1717	Dorothy, his wife	100	p.107	04–11–'26
04–05–'26	Matthew Smith	1717	Katherina, his wife	100	p.108	04–12–'26
04–05–'26	Michell Cook	1717	Mary, his wife	100	p.108	04–12–'26
04–05–'26	Andrew Kerker	1717	Margeritta, his wife and daughter Barbara	150	p.108	04–12–'26
04–05–'26	William Carpenter	1721	Elizabeth, his wife	100	p.108	04–12–'26
04–05–'26	Christopher Parlur	1717	Pauera, his wife	100	p.108	04–12–'26
05–02–'27	Jacob Bryoll	1717		50	p.142	No entry
05–02–'27	John Bryoll	1717	Ursley, his wife and Conrad and Elizabeth	200	p.142	No entry
05–02–'27	Nicholas Yeager	1717	Mary, his wife, and children Adam & Mary	200	p.142	No entry
05–02–'27	Phillip Paulitz	1717	Rose, his wife and Margaret and Katherin	200	p.142	No entry
11–08–'27	Robert Turner	1720	Mary, his wife and Christopher, Christiana, Katherine, Mary & Parva	350	p.214	11–20–'27
10–07–'29	George Lang	1717	Rebecca, his wife	100	p.352	10–16–'29
11–04–'29	Thomas Wayland	no date	Mary, his wife, and Jacob and Katherine	200	p.356	12–08–'29

Patents in the Robinson River Valley of Virginia

Early Robinson River Valley Patents, Part I

When the crown sold land, it gave a deed called a patent. If a man wished to purchase land from the crown, he had to find land which no one else owned or was claiming. Then he staked out the land that he wanted to claim. A common method was to mark trees along the lines, perhaps by removing some bark and cutting his initials. Typically the person establishing a claim would not be a surveyor and the estimate of the amount to buy could be in error. The general tendency was to mark more land than was expected to be purchased. A surveyor would be called in to measure a specified quantity, say 400 acres. The surveyor would file his survey with the Colony of Virginia and the person purchasing the land would pay his fees, either in cash or by head rights. He would be issued a deed, called a patent. Two copies of the patent were made, one for the purchaser and one for the files of the colony. Those for the colony have been preserved and are accessible today from the Virginia State Library. This is the source information about the patents. There are published book indices to the patents and grants, see the referenced books.

The surveyors tended to be generous and their survey often included more acreage than the stated amount (much the same effect would be achieved if the surveyor used chains, the unit of lineal measurement, that were longer than the correct value). Even if the surveyor were generous, the final tract, as surveyed, might not fill out the original piece of land as initially marked. Thus, the original patents would not fill all of the space. Eventually, on a resurvey, the tract might grow in size as the extra land was added in. When patents are plotted, the tendency is to fill up all of the space with the patents and to leave no gaps between them. However, gaps were not uncommon. In the plots to be shown here, one will recognize cases where the claim was larger than the patent states.

In 1940 D. R. Carpenter, a surveyor and Germanna descendant, drew a map of the first patents in what became Madison County, Virginia. When one attempts to recreate his map from the metes and bounds (the measures) in the patents, the patents do not fit together as neatly as Mr. Carpenter drew them. To achieve his results he had to use input from other sources. Some of the de facto boundaries are preserved in aerial photographs and in the layouts of the roads which came later and often followed boundary lines where reasonable. Some of the best anchor points come from features, such as waterways, that are still recognizable today.

The 1940 Carpenter map has been redrawn in an attempt to improve the clarity even though not all of the information in the Carpenter map was retained. That information is available here in other plots. Modern names were used and thus Tower becomes Thomas and Schnidow becomes Snyder. The false identification of Castler with Crisler was corrected.

The location of the Motz and Harnsberger patent, which should be a rectangle, does not fit well within the Carpenter map. The Carpenter map is not a complete set of the early patents. There were more to the north, the south, and the east of these though probably not many to the west in the first years.

On the plot here, the old route 29 is shown angling from the center at the bottom to the center on the left but the modern bypass route is not shown. Another major road is the Blue Ridge Turnpike which meets route 29 at the western end of the George Long patent. The larger roads are shown as two "parallel" lines. The Robinson River flows down from the upper right corner toward the left bottom corner. Other water courses, namely, Island Run, Dark Run, Little Dark Run, Deep Run, and Pass Run are also shown. The Robinson River and Island Run (also known as White Oak Run) have been darkened. Note that North is at the right side of the map.

The land on the north side of the map here is the north side of the Robinson River while the land to the south is the south side of the Robinson River. The question will naturally arise, for those people who had land on both sides of the river, on which side they lived. This is answered in the 1739 Orange County tithe list which had separate lists for the north and south sides of the Robinson River. For another orientation view of the Robinson River, see the map of the original Culpeper County on page 57.

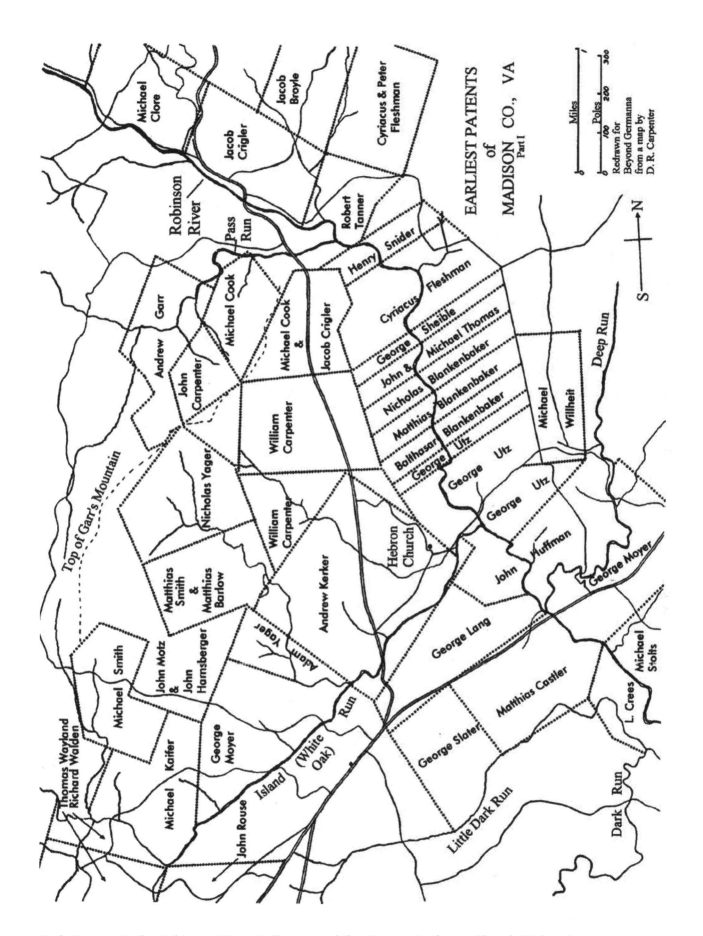

Early Patents in the Robinson River Valley around the German Lutheran Church (Hebron).

Robinson River Valley Patents, Part II

Plotting patents is frustrating and humbling. The answer is often to guess.

D. R. Carpenter, who drew the first map of the patents in Madison County, did a good job but he still had some errors. For example, it is impossible to fit the Motz and Harnsberger patent into his larger picture without a serious conflict. It also seems that he had the John Carpenter, Michael Cook, and Andrew Garr patents in the wrong locations. He was attempting to leave no unpatented land at the top of Garr's Mountain. D. R. Carpenter plot- ted the Henry Snider patent much larger than the patent metes and bounds state but what he plotted may have been the de facto lands.

To correct some of the errors but in particular to extend the area of plotting to the north of the previous set of patents, the map on the next page was created. Shaded areas on the map are conflicts for which no attempt at resolution was made. In other cases, adjustments were made to the metes and bounds before plotting. The patent dates are not the best clues as to when the land was settled. Many of the Germans were living on the land when the patent was issued.

The entry in the table below under "VPB" is the volume and page number in the *Virginia Patent Book*.

Modern Name	Part	Acres	Year	VPB	Notes
Ralph Banks	II	400	1734	15:297	
William Banks #1	II	590	1728	13:264	
William Banks #2	II	400	1728	13:264	
Balthasar Blankenbaker #1	II	360	1728	14:40	Paul Plunkepee
Balthasar Blankenbaker #2 (B.B.)	II	160	1733	15:19	Paulas Blancumbaker
Matthias Blankenbaker	II	320	1728	14:39	Matthew Plunkapee
Jacob Broyles	II	400	1728	13:389	
John Carpenter	II	150	1733	15:55	
Michael Clore	II	400	1726	12:447	Michall Clore
Michael Clore & John Clore	II	698	1728	13:391	Michael Clawse & John Clawse
Michael Cook	II	224	1732	14:430	
Michael Cook & Jacob Crigler	II	400	1726	12:480	Michael Cook & Jacob Krugler
Jacob Crigler	II	400	1730	13:536	
Henry Downs	II	1000	1727	13:96	repatented by Benj. Walker in '33
Cyriacus Fleshman	II	390	1726	12:474	Cyriacus Fleishman
Cyriacus & Peter Fleshman	II	400	1728	13:477	Sericus & Peter Fleshman
Andrew Garr	II	250	1734	15:352	Andrew Care
John Huffman					John Huffman had several patents
John Malden	II	1000	1728	13:343	
Richard Malden	II	813	1728	13:459	
Thomas Phillips	II	1000	1727	13:168	
Benjamin Rush	II	387	1726	12:349	
William Rush	II	400	1726	12:350	
Henry Snider	II	78	1726	12:475	Henry Schnieder
Edward Southall	I	500	1727	13:163	
Robert Tanner #1	II	216	1728	14:96	
Robert Tanner #2	II	200	1735	16:156	
Thomas Taylor	II	378	1728	14:100	repatented by Robert Brooke in '36
John Thomas #1	II	400	1728	14:97	
John Thomas #2	II	400	1734	15:470	
William Vinegunt	II	500	1728	14:32	
Christopher Yowell #1	II	400	1728	14:103	Christopher Atwell
Christopher Yowell #2	II	124	1733	15:120	Christopher Awel
John Zimmerman	II	400	1734	15:466	John Zimberman

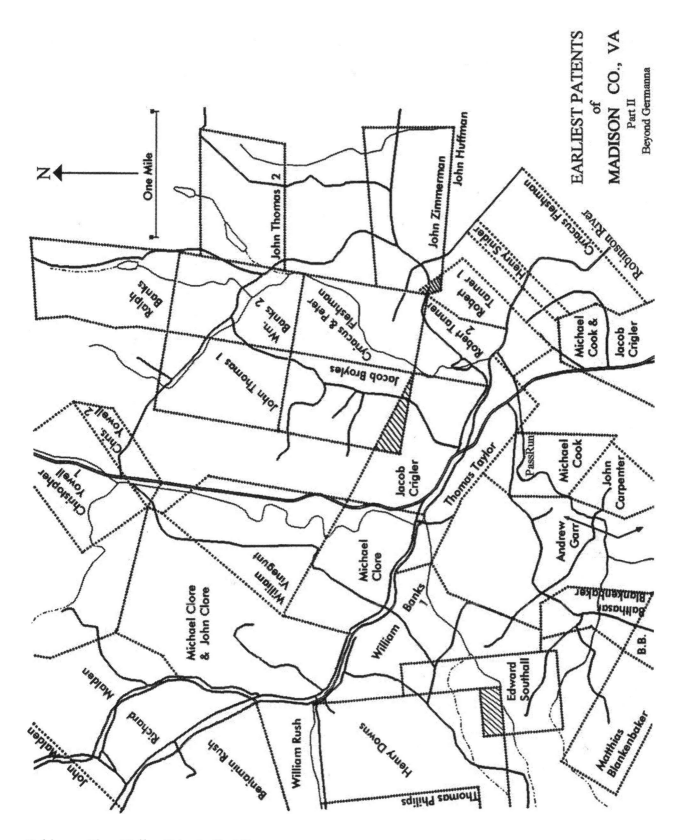

Robinson River Valley Patents, Part II

Robinson River Patents, Part III

The patents on the opposite page generally lie to the south of the modern town of Madison. There are several English people in this region.

Route 29 is shown with the modern bypass of the main street of the older part of Madison.

The specification of the Thomas Wayland patent overlapped the John Broyles patent almost perfectly. It took a lawsuit to straighten this out (Steven Broyles helped clarify this case.) Because Broyles had the earlier patent, he was upheld and Wayland was left with only the land that was outside the Broyles patent.

In the plotting here, the Motz and Harnsberger patent is assuming a more reasonable position. The Rouse patent was for 610 acres and the plot here is to that acreage though it required some small adjustments to the metes and bounds. In doing so, it made the William Eddings 2 patent touch a waterway as it is supposed to do. The description of the Eddings 3 patent does not jibe well with other facts. The plots for the Andrew Kerker, George Moyer, and the Eddings 3 patent all include substantially more acreage that is stated in the patent. All three are a con- nected set of tracts. However, the expansion in the plotting helped to create the space for the Motz and Harnsberger patent.

In some of these plots, lakes are shown which were not there when the patents were issued. They have been made since then.

The earliest patents of 1726 were to the Germans. Andrew Kerker was delayed two years but it was probably due to the larger size of his patent.

Modern Name	Part	Acres	Year	VPB	Note
Elizabeth Batteley	III	500	1733	15:8	widow of Robert Taliaferro
John Broyles	III	400	1726	12:476	John Prial
John Bruce	III	400	1735	15:526	
Robert Cave & David Philips	III	400	1735	15:498	
Edward & John Daughtary	III	400	1735	15:501	
John Eddings	III	525	1728	14:111	
William Eddings #1	III	400	1731	14:246	
William Eddings #2	III	400	1731	14:246	
William Eddings #3	III	1725	1734	15:355	
Michael Holt #1	III	400	1726	12:477	
Michael Holt #2	III	245	1728	14:100	
Michael Käfer	III	400	1726	12:479	Michael Kaffer
Andrew Kerker	III	850	1728	13:389	Andrew Kirker, @ 1219 acres
James King	III	300	1728	13:337	
George Long	III	300	1731	14:359	George Lang
Richard Malden	III	100	1728	13:343	
John Motz & John Harnsberger	III	400	1726	12:475	
George Moyer	III	400	1726	12:478	George Meyer, @ 582 acres
William Rice	III	400	1736	17:120	
John Rouse	III	610	1728	14:110	
John Rucker	III	977	1727	13:162	
George Slaughter (Schlatter?)	III	300	1734	15:144	
Matthias Smith & Matthias Barlow	III	400	1726	12:480	Smith & Beller, @ 372 acres
Michael Smith	III	400	1726	12:478	
Mary & Elizabeth Taliaferro	III	1482	1733	15:8	
Thomas Wayland	III	504	1728	13:433	Thomas Weyland, @ 120 acres
Adam Yager	III	100	1737	17:327	Adam Yayer

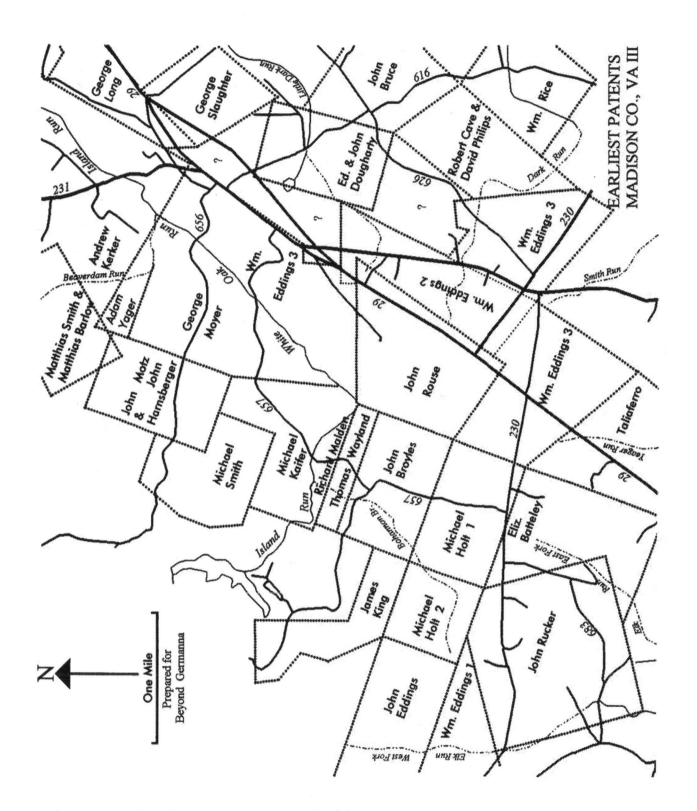

Early Patents in the Robinson River to the South of the Core Patents.

Robinson River Patents, Part IV

The plots on the opposite page are from four to eight miles from the German Lutheran Church (now called Hebron) in a northeasterly direction, far enough to carry over the modern county line between Madison and Culpeper. At the time the patents were issued, neither Madison or Culpeper County was in existence. The land was in Spotsylvania County starting in 1720, in Orange County in 1734, in Culpeper County in 1749, and finally in Madison County in 1792.

The placements here are reasonable but decidedly inexact. Some of the de factor patents were larger in practice than recorded in the patent. In particular, see the Vogt and Clements patents.

The John Kains patent has its southeast corner on Conical Run which is not shown on the map here. Scaling its location from other maps, the placement, especially in the east-west direction, should be correct. When this is done, then Route 604 seems to lie along the west side of the patent. The Butler and Gunnel patent should lie on the west side of the Kains patent but with the negative aspect that it is too long to fit in neatly.

The Jacob Manspiel and Edward Ballenger patents are tied to Deep Run. The Manspiel patent is said to have a corner "near to the corner of Ballenger." The Christian Clements and the John Paul Vogt patents have western lines that match John Kains. However, the Clements patent's southern-most corner should be east of Deep Run. One wonders if the patent was in effect bounded by Routes 640 and 609. Clements and Vogt should share a line and the Vogt patent would seem to stretch from Route 607 to the Kains patent.

The Bloodworth patent requires modifications to fit in but the lines now parallel to Route 607 are shown as specified. The Ambergey and Coleman patents seem to be bounded by the roads on the south side. The patent of Bloodworth and Ambergey shares one line with Coleman but the information to complete the plot is not available.

The feeling is that, if the areas of the patents were expanded, a reasonable fit might be obtained. More of the surrounding patents would help to define these better.

The dates for Bloodworth (700 acres) and for George Martin are new style years. The actual date in the patent will appear to be the previous year.

Name	Part	Acres	Date	VPB	Notes
Conrad Amburger	IV	400	1733	15:51	
Edward Ballenger	IV	400	1733	15:59	499 acres plotted
Joseph Bloodworth	IV	700	1735	15:424	1194 acres, inc. earlier patent
J. Bloodworth & C. Amburger	IV	400	1736	17:140	
John Butler & Nicholas Gunnel	IV	400	1734	15:361	453 acres plotted
Christian Clements	IV	600	1734	15:384	633 acres, Christian Clemond
Robert Coleman, Sr.	IV	400	1734	15:209	433 acres plotted
John Kains	IV	400	1736	17:57	397 acres plotted
Jacob Manspiel	IV	400	1734	15:351	434 acres plotted
George Martin	IV	400	1734	15:186	411 acres, John Paul Vought
John Paul Vogt	IV	640	1735	16:510	618 acres plotted

> Generally, German children were given two names. The first was their saint's name and the second was their personal name, also called their "calling" name. A few people might use both names. Anna Elisabetha might be called Anna or Anna Elisabetha besides being called just Elisabetha.

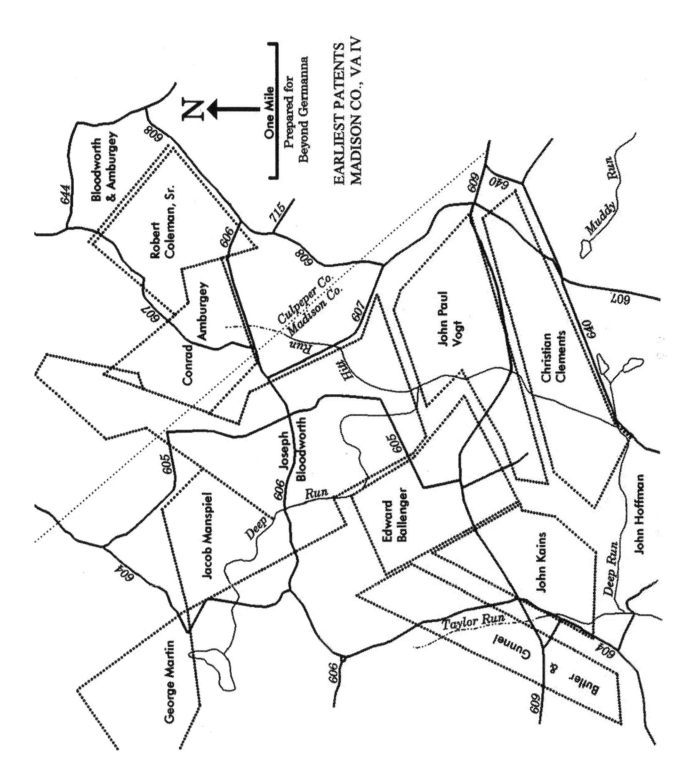

Early Patents in the Robinson River Valley Northeast of the Central Patents.

Patents in the Robinson River Valley, Part V

Some of the patents on the facing page duplicate earlier presentations. The same scale essentially is used but some of the patents are plotted to a different size. For instance, the Kerker patent is shown smaller here. In preparing these plots, use was made of water ways, reference to adjoining patents, the roads, and modern tax maps which show the present property boundaries. These boundaries have changed radically through the years but occasionally a clue is found. Here, the Castler patent on its southeast side coincides with a modern boundary for a significant distance. Considering the near match to a road on the southwest side, the Castler patent is a high confidence patent.

The Lorenz Crees patent is a low confidence one. It references Dark Run though it lies on Little Dark Run. Even with adjustments, it plots out to more acreage than claimed. The patent of Wilhide (Willheit) and Walk refers to branches of Deep Run which seems also to be a mistake. Therefore the confidence rating of this patent is also low. The eastern-most point of this patent should touch the Beverley line but nothing gives a north-south location.

It seems very questionable that a huge gap, defined by parallel lines should exist between the Baumgardner and Weaver patents on one hand and the Willheit-Walk patent on the other. One suspects that the de facto patents probably had a line in common here. And in fact, when the Baumgardner sons repatented (as a grant), the tract was found to contain more than 900 acres. Again, this shows that the defacto lands were often quite different from the patent description.

The Stoltz and Maulden patents should touch. The Beverley and Maulden patents are high confidence even though the Maulden acreage is vastly different in size from the stated area in the patent. The book *Cavaliers and Pioneers* refers, in the description of the Maulden patent, to John Michael Holt which is a mistake for John Michael Stolts.

Name	Part	Acres	Date	VPB	Notes
Frederick Baumgardner	V	400	489	17:122	Pamgarner
William Beverley	V	3300	1728	13:317	3572 acres plotted
Balthasar Blankenbaker	V	157	1726	12:483	Blankenbucher
Matthias Blankenbaker	V	156	1726	12:481	Blankenbucher
Nicholas Blankenbaker	V	156	1726	12:475	Blankenbucher
Matthias Castler	V	406	1728	13:474	
Lorenz Crees	V	200	1732	14:528	Laus Crest
Cyriacus Fleshman	V	390	1726	12:474	Fleishman
John Huffman	V	1800	1736	17:56	Incorporates earlier patents
Andrew Kerker	V	850	1728	13:389	Plotted as 827 acres
George Long	V	300	1731	14:359	Lang, plotted as 347 acres
Richard Maulden	V	800	1735	15:459	As 1327 acres, touches the German Road
George Moyer	V	498	1728	14:107	Plotted as 434 acres
George Sheible	V	78	1726	12:481	
George Slater	V	300	1734	15:144	Slaughter
Michael Stolz	V	291	1732	14:438	John Michael Stolts
John & Michael Thomas	V	156	1726	12:476	Tomer
George Utz #1	V	78	1726	12:479	
George Utz #2	V	312	1726	12:479	
George Utz #3	V	196	1728	13:390	George Woods
Peter Weaver	V	400	1736	17:125	
Michael Willheit	V	289	1728	14:113	Wilhide
Tobias Willheit & Martin Walk	V	400	1736	17:127	Wilhide

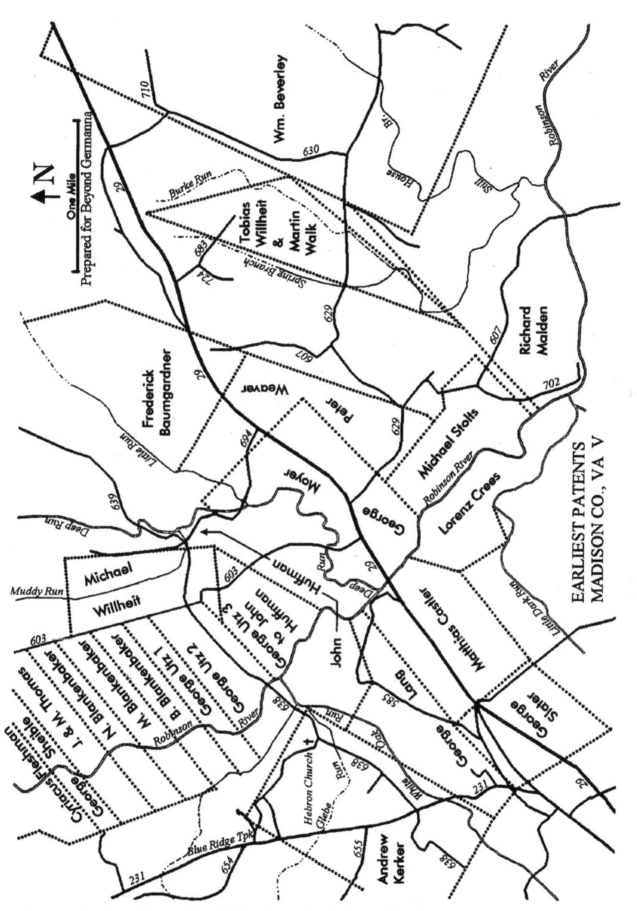

Early Patents in the Robinson River Valley East of the Lutheran Church.

The John Hoffman Grant of 1753

In the previous plots of the original land division in the Robinson River Valley, the land of John Hoffman/Huffman was not emphasized because the information for his patents is of a poor quality. The specifications of the metes and bounds were poor and the quality of the recorded images was also poor.

Hoffman had a series of patents and grants for contiguous land wherein many of these incorporated earlier land acquisitions. The descriptions for these land parcels were not consistent with each other nor were they consistent with the neighbors.

The text of the 1753 grant was slightly better because of the redundancy which is intrinsic to the statements. That is, phrases such as "up the courses of the run to a maple" can often be read, even if half of the letters are missing. But to show how bad the problem is, Gertrude E. Gray, who abstracted the Northern Neck Land Grants, which includes the Hoffman grant, read the name of a run in the Hoffman patent as Dry Run for the correct reading of Deep Run. Knowing that Deep Run was a prominent run in this area, it can be understood as Deep Run.

The elements or parcels of the final grant were:

1. The Huffman patent date 27 SEP 1729 of 800 acres (*VPB 13*: 388) adjacent to Michael Wilhide,
2. The Huftman patent of 400 acres on both sides of the Robinson River, adjacent to Andrew Kirker, White Oak Run, mouth of Deep Run, his own land, Micall Wilhide, and George Wood (Utz). This patent was dated 31 AUG 1731 (*VPB 14*: 252),
3. The George Utz (his wife's stepfather) patent of 196 acres dated 28 SEP 1728 (*VPB 13*: 390) which Hoffman purchased from Utz,
4. The Huffman 27 JAN 1734/5 patent of 400 acres (*VPB 16*: 414) in the Island Line (N45°W), on Deep Run, adjacent to George Shively (Sheible) and himself,
5. All four of the previous tracts plus four acres of surplus land were incorporated in one patent of 5 JUN 1736 for 1800 acres (*VPB 17*:56),
6. All of the previous plus 1,425 acres of surplus land were included in a grant for 3,221 acres dated 29 SEP 1748. As a grant this was from Lord Fairfax (*Northern Neck Grant Book G*, p. 126),
7. Finally, all of the previous plus 304 acres of surplus land were incorporated in a grant dated 2 APR 1753 (*Northern Neck Grant Book H*, p. 268).

Though this seems like a lot of information, more is required. Some of this comes from the neighbors who had grants which redefined their boundaries. Using the definitions of the neighbors and what can be deduced about the lands of John Hoffman, the plot on the next page is obtained.

In John Hoffman's grant of 1748, he found 1,425 acres of "waste land." He was not alone in laying claim to land which he had not patented. The original Baumgardner patent had been for 400 acres but the Baumgardner sons found unclaimed land ("surplus") on their east side. This brought their grant up to 993 acres which more than doubled the size of the patent. Peter Weaver had an original patent of 400 acres. Later he bought 189 of George Moyer's 28 SEP 1728 patent. Then Weaver found 706 acres of surplus land on his east side and he obtained a grant of 1295 acres on 28 MAY 1763 to include everything. By the time the grants for Baumgardner and Weaver had been issued, the angle of the line between them had been redefined. The final set of grants and patents for Baumgardner, Weaver, and Willheit & Walk probably filled all of the space over to Beverley and Malden.

There was a small conflict between the original Moyer patent and the claims of Hoffman on the west side of Hoffman's Branch which was assigned in favor of Hoffman. A conflict between Kerker and Hoffman at the northeast corner of Kerker was assigned to Kerker. John Carpenter obtained a grant (*Northern Neck Grant Book K*, p. 155) which included the original patent of Andrew Kerker which he inherited plus 395 acres of surplus land. George Utz consolidated his earlier two patents into one along with 82 acres of surplus land. What is plotted is his 1 JUN 1764 grant of 472 acres (*Northern Neck Grant Book M*, p. 279).

In the corner between W. Carpenter, the original Kerker patent, and Utz, there was an unclaimed parcel of 33 acres for which Matthias Rouse obtained a grant (marked "R" on the map here). This grant refers to the "old German chapel" which stood nearby. Close to this is the present day Hebron church which is marked with a †.

The Hoffman grant is most uncertain in its northwest corner. To obtain the present plots, the location of the Broyle patent, the northern Fleshman patent, and the eastern boundary of the Crigler patent were moved and the Burdyne grant was inserted. This incorporated the earlier Tanner patent and added some surplus land. The plot of John Snider (*Northern Neck Grant Book G*, p. 41) was helpful in defining the north-south line of Hoffman in this region. The resulting plot for Hoffman contains close to the stated amount.

In the Northern Neck, when an individual found a desirable tract of "waste and ungranted" land, he applied to the proprietor's office. A warrant was issued by the office to a surveyor to measure and mark the tract. When the survey was completed, a plat with the land location, description and adjoining property owners was submitted to the office. If there were no infringements on the property of another, a grant was issued to the applicant.

At the warrant stage, the warrant could be transferred from one individual to another. Often these transfers were within the family and the endorsement yields genealogical data (in the discussion of the Garr family there are some very good examples of this). For easy access to these documents, see the several volumes by Peggy Shomo Joyner in the reference list.

After 1743, the land between the Rappahannock and the Rapidan Rivers (the Great Fork) was decided to be a part of the Northern Neck. Many of the people took out grants for their land to replace the patents. The old patents were still valid but any new claims were in the form of grants, not patents. Thus, in the case of John Hoffman, his last deeds were grants, not patents.

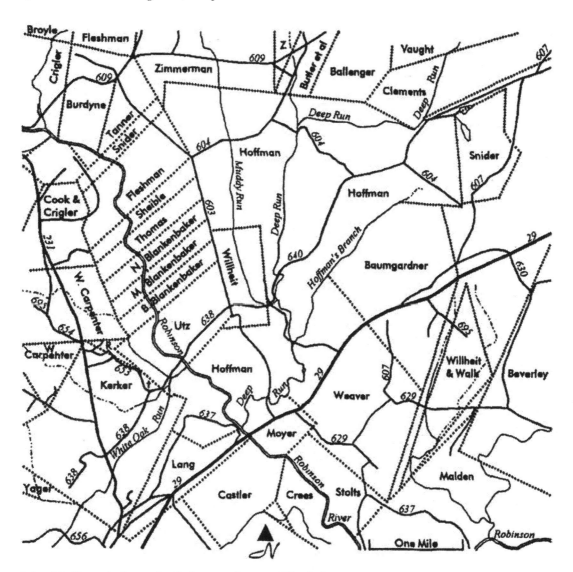

John Hoffman's Grant in Culpeper County, Virginia

Robinson River Valley Patents and Grants, Part VI

The final presentation shows all of the previous plots on one sheet. Because there are more than one hundred separate plots, the detail has to be abbreviated. Individual plots are identified by numbers and a summary of information pertaining to that plot is given below. Use was made of grants and patents. All dates are by the new style calendar. The scale is 1.52 miles per inch with north at the top. Two features are identified by letters: **R** for the 33 acre Rouse tract between 68, 78, and 79 and **H** for the location of the German Lutheran Church which was on property originally patented by Andrew Kerker, number 78. Some of the tracts overlap, i.e., they conflict. Gaps exist for which the original property owners have not been found. The abbreviation "inc." means *including* or *includes*.

1. John England, 1728, 1000a, **2.** William Duff, 1728, 358a, **3.** John Shotwell, 1763, 542a, inc. 408a in Stonehouse of 28 SEP 1728, **4.** Rachel Evans, 1728, 1000a, **5.** James Maxwell, 1750, 634a, inc. 507 in Stonehouse of 28 SEP 1730, **6.** John Malden, 1728, 1000a, **7.** Richard Malden, 1728, 813a, **8.** Nicholas Copeland, 1734, 350a, plot is incorrect, location is uncertain, **9.** Christopher Yowell, 1728, 400a, uncertain location, **10.** Christopher Yowell, 1733, 124a, uncertain location, **11.** Ralph Banks, 1734, 400a, uncertain location, **12.** Samuel Hennings, 1756, 400a, **13.** George Martin, 1734, 400a, **14.** John Towles, 1748, 300a, **15.** John Kilby, 1748, 400a, **16.** Joseph Bloodworth, 700a, inc 400a of Bloodworth of 1733, plot has many uncertainties, **17.** Anthony Strother, 1735, 50a, **18.** Benjamin Rush, 1726, 387a, **19.** Michael and John Clore, 1728, 698a, **20.** William Vinegunt, 1728, 500a, **21.** Michael Clore, 1726, 400a, **22.** John Thomas, 1728, 400a, **23.** William Banks, 1728, 400a, **24.** Jacob Broyles, 1728, 400a, **25.** Cyriacus and Peter Fleshman, 1728, 400a, **26.** John Thomas, 1735, 400a, **27.** Robert Hutchinson, 1761, 254a, **28.** John McKenzie, 1748, 400a, **29.** Jacob Manspile, 1734, 400a, **30.** Conrad Amberger, 1733, 400a, **31.** Robert Coleman, 1734, 400a, **32.** Joseph Bloodworth and Conrad Amberger, 1736, 400a, very incomplete plot, line in common with Coleman #31, **33.** Thomas Kennerley, 1748, 499a, **34.** Francis Thornton, 1748, 785a, **35.** John Zimmerman, 1748, 556a, overlaps #36, **36.** John Zimmerman, 1748, 400a, overlaps #35, **37.** John Zimmerman, 1756, 805a, inc. 400a of Zimmerman of 1734, **38.** John Butler & Nicholas Gunnell, 1734, 400a, **39.** Edward Ballenger, 1733, 400a, **40.** John Kains, 1736, 400a, **41.** John Paul Vaught, 1736, 640a, **42.** Christian Clemans, 1734, 600a, **43.** Thomas Phillips, 1727, 1000a, **44.** William Rush, 1726, 400a, **45.** Benjamin Walker, 1733, 1000a, was Downs of 1727, **46.** Not used, **47.** William Banks, 1728, 590a, **48.** Edward Southall, 1727, 500a, conflict with #45, **49.** Jacob Crigler, 1730, 400a, **50.** Robert Brooke, 1736, 378a, repatent of Thomas Taylor, 1728 378a, **51.** Richard Burdyne, 1749, 266a, inc. 216a of 1728 Tanner, **52.** Robert Tanner, 1735, 200a, **53.** Henry Aylor, 1753, 34a, description in error, location generally correct, **54.** Henry Snider, 1726, 78a, **55.** Matthew Blankenbaker, 1728, 320a, **56.** Balthasar Blankenbaker, 1728, 360a, **57.** Balthasar Blankenbaker, 1733, 160a, location not proven, **58.** Andrew Garr, 1734, 250a, description uncertain, location generally correct, **59.** Michael Cook, 1732, 224a, **60.** John Carpenter, 1733, 150a, **61.** Michael Cook & Jacob Crigler, 1726, 400a, **62.** Cyriacus Fleshman, 1726, 390a, **63.** George Sheible, 1726, 78a, **64.** John Hoffman (see previous pages), **65.** John Snider, 1748, 368a, **66.** Nicholas Blankenbaker, 1728, 400a, **67.** Nicholas Yager, 1726, 400a, **68.** Nicholas Blankenbaker, 1733, 400a, **69.** William Carpenter, 1726, 400a, **70.** John & Michael Thomas, 1726, 156a, **71.** Nicholas Blankenbaker, 1726, 156a, **72.** Matthew Blankenbaker, 1726, 156a, **73.** Balthasar Blankenbaker, 1726, 157a, **74.** Michael Willheit, 1728, 289a, **75.** Baumgardner brothers, 1766, 993a, inc. 400a of 1736 Baumgardner, **76.** Matthew Smith & Matthew Barlow, 1726, 400a, **77.** William Carpenter, 1728, 193a, **78.** John Carpenter, 1760, 1245a, inc. 850a from Kerker of 1728, **79.** George Utz, 1764, 472a, inc. two patents of 1726 minus sale to Hoffman, **80.** George Moyer, 1728, 498a before selling 189a to Weaver #81, **81.** Peter Weaver, 1763, 1295a, inc. 400a 1736 Weaver, purchase of 189a from Moyer's #80, **82.** Tobias Willheit & Martin Walk, 1736, 400a, **83.** William Beverley, 1728, 3300a, **84.** Michael Smith, 1726, 400a, **85.** John Motz & John Harnsberger, 1726, 400a, **86.** Adam Yager, 1737, 100a, **87.** George Moyer, 1726, 400a, **88.** George Long, 1731, 300a, **89.** Matthew Castler, 1728, 406a, **90.** George Slaughter (Schlater), 1734, 300a, **91.** John Michael Stoltz, 1732, 291a, **91.5.** Lawrence Crees, 1732, 200a, **92.** Dr. William Lynn, 1749, 378a, **93.** Richard Malden, 1735, 800a, **94.** Richard Malden, 1735, 800a, **95.** James King, 1728, 300a, **96.** Michael Käfer, 1726, 400a, **96.5.** Richard Malden, 1728 100a, **97.** Thomas Wayland, 1728, 504a but lost 384 in disputed lands, **98.** John Broyles, 1726, 400a, **99.** William Eddings, 1734, 1725a, 325a from Rouse 1728, 400a from Eddings 1731, balance new land, **100.** John Rouse, 1728, 610a but not showing the 325a sold to Eddings, **101.** Edward & John Dougharty, 1735, 400a, **102.** not used, **103.** John Bruce, 1735, 400a, **104.** John Eddings, 1728, 525a, **105.** William Eddings, 1731, 400a, **106.** Michael Holt, 1728, 245a, **107.** John Rucker, 1727, 977a, **108.** Michael Holt, 1726, 400a, **109.** Elizabeth Batteley, 1733, 500a, **110.** Mary & Elizabeth Taliaferro, 1733, 1482a, **111.** Robert Cave & David Philips, 1735, 400a, **112.** William Rose, 1736, 400a.

Early Patents and Grants in the Area of the Robinson River

Moving to the Robinson River Valley

In 1725, the majority of the Germans moved to the Robinson River Valley where they had made land claims. This was about 25 miles from their first homes but the Germans said they had to move this far because the nearer land had been taken up by "greater people" even though no one was living on the land. In the Robinson River Valley, they almost immediately built a chapel and held services led by lay people. A few of the Germans chose to stay near Mt. Pony, apparently because they were coopers and they felt the need to be closer to the market for barrels and casks.

The letters to London asking for a pastor to be sent to them were not being answered. They sent Cyriacus Fleshman and John Motz to London to plead in person for a pastor. They were unsuccessful.

In 1732 a school teacher, Johann Caspar Stöver, Sr. from North Carolina, was in the Robinson River community. The residents appreciated that he was educated and they said he could be their pastor if he could be ordained. Stöver and George Sheible went to Pennsylvania where they found Johann Christian Schultz, a Lutheran pastor, who ordained Stöver, Sr. and also his son Stöver, Jr. Also, the son was married, again by Schultz. In Virginia, the congregation raised money to buy a glebe on which they built a house for Stöver. The financial history of the congregation from the appearance of Stöver to his departure to Europe for fund raising is known, see James Brown et al, "The Hebron Church Account," in 𝔅𝔢𝔶𝔬𝔫𝔡 𝔊𝔢𝔯𝔪𝔞𝔫𝔫𝔞, v.6, n.4 for an annotated discussion of the financial record and, by implication, some social customs.

The congregation was hard pressed to raise money to pay Stöver a respectable salary. They cited the fact that they had to support the Anglican church, the official church of Virginia. The decision was made to send Pastor Stöver, Michael Smith, and Michael Holt to Europe to raise money.

The Second Colony Members' Account

When Johann Caspar Stöver, Sr., Michael Smith, and Michael Holt were in London in 1734 on the fundraising trip, they wrote a history for the benefit of the London pastors. To paraphrase their comments:

> Seventeen years ago, a small group of Protestant Lutheran people from Württemberg, Qualtzbach [unidentified] and the Electorate Palatinate arrived in London and had themselves transported to Virginia on their expenses. Before their departure, they consulted with the Rev. Protestant Lutheran German preachers then present regarding the future care of their souls. To this they added the most obedient request that a pastor and a contribution be sent to them. The Rev. Clergy showed themselves to be inclined. The people were given communion and enjoined to remain faithful to the Protestant Lutheran truth.
>
> After the arrival of these people in Virginia and as soon as it was possible after they completed the hard Servitude on then Gov. Spotswood's land, they began with divine services by reading the divine word, singing and praying, and asking untiringly with tears and sighs for a pastor. They wrote letters to the Rev. Preachers but received no response.
>
> Eight years ago the Congregation raised the money to send two deputies named Cyriax Fleischmann and Johann Mutz [Motz] to London. In all hope, the Congregation took up their permanent lands so that they could live together and benefit from divine services. They moved 40 English miles [25 would be closer] into the wilderness to the foot of the high mountains on the River Rappahannock because all land in between had been taken up by greater people even though the lands were uninhabited [the Robinson River flows into the Rapidan which flows into the Rappahannock so that their settlement on the Robinson River could be said to be on the River Rappahannock].
>
> Here, at this new place, they immediately built a meeting house in the midst among them, as well as they could, and again continued their services as mentioned on Sundays and Holidays and Apostle days and also ordered that each first Friday of every month to be a day of repentance and prayer.

The original letter, *"Brief von Johann Caspar Stoever an die Geistlichen der deutschen lutherischen Gemeinden in London,"* is in the Francke-Nachlass der Staatsbibliothek zu Berlin-Preussischer Kulturbesitz as Microfilm No. 18, 363–365. Andreas Mielke, working with Petra Stallboerger, Dipl. Bibl., became aware of this letter. The translation, as published in 𝔅𝔢𝔶𝔬𝔫𝔡 𝔊𝔢𝔯𝔪𝔞𝔫𝔫𝔞, v.15, n.1, is copyrighted (2002) by Andreas Mielke.

The Results of the Fund-Raising Trip

The trip was lengthy. Michael Holt returned after a couple of years apparently because he and Rev. Stöver did not agree on policy. During the trip, Stöver hired an assistant pastor, George Samuel Klug, and sent him on to Virginia. Klug stayed for a while in London, perhaps to learn the English language and he seems to have arrived in Virginia in 1738. The departure of Stöver and Smith was delayed while Stöver spent several months in theological study (in this area his background was weak). The pair started home in 1738 and Stöver died while they were at sea, late in 1738 or early in 1739. He left a will which was first filed at Philadelphia.

Financially, the trip was a success. The money was sufficient to build a church and to buy a large farm and slaves to tend it.

Orange County Tithables in 1739

The law in eighteenth century Virginia colony required that a survey be made of all the tithables which included the white males 16 and above and all blacks 16 and above but only the heads of households are listed. A levy on each tithable was made to support the Anglican church. Lists of the tithables were made by visiting every home and farm. The collector wrote the information as he went from one home to another. We have a picture of the route he took when we know where people lived. For the Germans, the plots of their patents enable us to trace the path of the person making the survey. Few of these tithe lists have been preserved but there are lists for parts of Orange County in 1739 that cover the Robinson River Valley. This is an especially interesting year because the Lutherans built their new church in 1740 so the list is an excellent approximation of who was living in the community when the church was built. A detailed analysis of the names shows some problems in the conventional histories which makes these lists of tithables even more interesting.

Some adjustments to the list are required to account for families such as the Criglers. The father, Jacob Crigler, had died in 1734 leaving a wife and children. His wife, Susanna, married Nicholas Yager and the two Crigler sons became a part of his household. Had they been 16 or older they would have been tithes chargeable to Nicholas Yager and their names would not show up on the lists.

One list was made by James Pickett and it covers the area south of the Robinson River down to the Rapidan River. The easterly portion of this has many English names in it. Probably starting at the junction of the Robinson and Rapidan Rivers, the collector worked his way west through 49 English names until he came to Michael Holt who was on the extreme southern side of the German settlement. He went through 23 more English names. The German names then start with some English names interspersed, usually in a block. The second list was made by John Mickell and it includes the homes north of the Robinson River.

In the list below, the first column is a line number, the second is the name in the original list, the third column is the number of tithes, the fourth column is the name as it is commonly spelled with comments after it. The microfilms with this information are in the State Library in Richmond. They have been read and printed by Peggy Shomo Joyner in *Northern Neck Warrants & Surveys, Orange & Augusta Counties*, v.1, 1985, and in other publications. A microfilm of them is available from the Latter Day Saints, number 1869674, but it is not recommended because of the poor images.

> In 1717, there were two calendars in use in the Christian world. In the English speaking world, they were still using the Old Style (OS or Julian) calendar where the year started on March 25. In the German speaking world, they were using the New Style (NS or Gregorian) calendar where the year started on January 1. Besides the difference between the starting dates for the year, the old style calendar was eleven days behind the new style. On 2 SEP 1752 adherents of the Julian calendar shifted to the Gregorian calendar and the next day became 14 SEP 1752.

James Pickett's Precinct (South of the Robinson River) 1739

    49 English names (not given here)
1. Michael Holt — 3 Michael Holt

    23 English names (not given here)
2. Lau: Crees — 2 Lawrence Crees
3. Cortney Browel — 1 Conrad Broyles, see lines 21 & 43
4. George Lung — 1 George Long/Lang
5. John Hoffman — 1 John Hoffman
6. Jon Carpenter — 2 John Carpenter
7. Mathias Castler — 1 Matthias Castler
8. Michael Cook — 1 Michael Cook
9. Henry Snider — 1 Henry Snider/Snyder
10. Robt Tenner — 1 Robert Tanner
11. Geo: Tenner — 1 George Tanner
12. Lodowick Fisher — 1 Lewis Fisher, see line 38
13. Geo: Teter — 1 George Teter

    4 English names (not given here)
14. Adam Carr — 3 Adam Gaar/Garr
15. Wm Carpenter — 4 William Carpenter
16. Nichs Yager — 5 Nicholas Yager

    8 English names (not given here)
17. Daywall Cristler — 1 Theobald Crisler, see line 24
18. Adam Yager — 1 Adam Yager
19. Mathew Smith — 2 Matthew Smith
20. Henry Crowder — 1 ??? (?Krauter or Sauter?)
21. Christley Browel — 1 ??? Broyles, see lines 3 & 43
22. John Hansborgow — 1 John Harnsberger
23. Michael Smith — 3 Michael Smith
24. Daywat Cristler — 1 Theobald Crisler, see line 17
25. Michael Keiffer — 1 Michael Käfer
26. Geo: Moyers — 2 George Moyers
27. John Rowse — 2 John Rouse
28. Thos Wayland — 1 Thomas Wayland
29. Mark Finks — 2 Mark Finks

    13 English names (not given here).

John Mickell's Precinct (North of the Robinson River) 1739

    16 English names (not given here)
30. Tobias Wilhite — 1 Tobias Willheit
31. John Stolts — 1 John Stoltz
32. Frederick Bumgarner — 1 Frederick Baumgardner
33. Christopher Moyers — 1 Christopher Moyers
34. Peter Weaver — 1 Peter Weaver
35. Mitchell Wilhite — 1 Michael Willheit
36. George Woods — 3. George Utz
37. Pals Plunkabeaner — 1 Balthasar Blankenbaker
38. Ludwick Fisher — 1 Lewis Fisher, see line 12
39. Mathias Plankabeaner — 2 Mathias Blankenbaker
40. Nicholas Plancabeaner — 2 Nicholas Blankenbaker
41. George Shively — 1 George Sheible
42. Conrat Pater — 1 Conrad (the original document can be read as Slater)
43. Jacob Broil — 1 Jacob Broyles, see lines 3 & 21
44. Zacharias Flefhman — 2 Cyriacus Fleshman
45. Peter Fleshman — 2 Peter Fleshman

46.	Richard Burdine	2 Richard Burdyne (married a German)
47.	John Wilhide	1 John Willheit
48.	Michael Claur	— Michael Clore (unknown why there are no tithables)
	8 English names including Michael O'Neall	
49.	David Ouell	1 David Yowell
50.	John Kynes	3 John Kynes
51.	Christopher Ouell	2 Christopher Yowell
	Thomas Fargarson	
52.	John Thomas	1 John Thomas
53.	Henry Sluter	1 Henry Slucter
54.	John Zimmerman	1 John Zimmerman
	5 names including Joseph Bloodworth	
55.	John Full	2 John Paul Vogt
56.	Christian Clemon	1 Christian Clemons
57.	Jacob Manfpoil	1 Jacob Manspiel

Isaac Hadok's Precinct for 1737 (includes Mount Pony area)

58.	Frederick Cobbler	1 Frederieck Kabler
59.	Christopher Zimmerman	1 Christopher Zimmerman

There are some problems in these lists, at least by the conventional histories.

Lewis Fisher (Ludwig Fischer) is an expected name; the problem is that the name occurs twice in the 1739 tithables, once in line 12 and once in 38.

There seem to be two Theobald Crislers, lines 17 and 24 which were taken by the same collector.

There are too many Broyles as heads of families, see lines 3, 21, 43. One resolution is that one of these was born in Virginia but perhaps died before he had left a major mark in the community.

John Thomas is in the lists but his brother Michael is not. By our usual counting, Michael was born before 1723 so he should be in the list (perhaps he had not set up housekeeping on his own).

Henry Crowder, line 20, is an unknown. If the collector was hard of hearing, perhaps the name was Sauter which is a name known in the Germanna community. Henry Crowder is close to Michael Smith in the list whose wife's maiden name was Sauder.

Conrad Pater (?Slater or Slucter?) is another unknown.

George Tanner, who would seem to be a relative of Robert Tanner, is an unknown.

The Criglers, the Barlows, and the Aylors are missing though they are in the community. Apparently, there were no males who were old enough and who had set up a household on their own.

The Constitution of the German Evangelical Lutheran Congregation

[When Rev. Jacob Franck came in 1775 as the minister at the German Lutheran church, he led an effort to write a constitution defining the responsibilities of the congregation, elders, and the minister. This was written before the Declaration of Independence was written and certainly before the constitution of the United States was written. The document was in German and Elke Hall made the translation for publishing in Beyond Germanna in v.9, n.1. The value of the document, besides the general interest, is that it has the names of the male members of the congregation. There were the initial signers, then as men were confirmed or moved into the community they signed. So the presence of a name does not mean that person was present in 1776.]

Church Order

We, the undersigned, the current, properly called, teacher as well as the trustees, elders, chairmen and communing members of the German Evangelical Lutheran Community in Culpepper County in Virginia, unite in the following church order.

Chapter 1
Regarding the Doctrine

1.
The current, properly called, teacher and his properly called successors – at the usual time on Sundays and holidays, at funerals and other solemn functions – shall announce God's Word according to the proclamation by the Apostles and prophets and according to the unchanged original creed, publicly, aloud, clearly, thoroughly, and originally; and they are to strive honestly, according to Christ, their Master's command, to abundantly sow God's Word like a living seed, and to direct the community to their eternal bliss, in genuine penance, living faith and through the power of God's salvation.

2.
The proper teacher shall, at the right time, dispense the Holy Sacraments as trusted keeper of God's mysteries to those who truly desire them and who are, at least outwardly, able and worthy to receive them, but he also must be ready and conscientious enough to refuse the Holy Communion and the ability to be baptismal witnesses to those who, obviously, or according to credible report, are found to have committed gross sins and transgressions against the moral laws of our Lord, until they show improvement.

3.
He shall not refuse, if he is able to, to visit the sick of the community as soon as he has been told, and if he had been requested to do so, to teach them about God's Word, to inquire, to take in, to edify, to comfort and to give them the Last Supper, with all their ability and dignity and to prepare them for a blessed departure.

4.
He shall recommend a program for our young people to be taught to them in the church as well as in the school house. He shall have the supervision over the community, school and school teacher as well as over everything belonging to the community. He shall set up a wholesome school order and hold examinations; he shall diligently visit the school; he shall encourage the young people to follow God's Word and our catechism taken from it, and also the remaining teaching books as well as the Providence, to instruct them to follow Christ and also raise them as useful community members.

5.
He shall also be empowered to preside over the annual church meetings and other regular meetings of the church administration; to take part and assure that everything proceeds orderly and in a Christian manner in church administrative meetings, during the election of the trustees, elders and chairmen; and to work for the benefit of the community.

6.
He shall be obligated to keep a journal of his remaining work for the community, in addition to the baptismal and communion book, and to assemble from it an annual report and to send it to the Ministry, so that those fathers, who hold the well-being of the community in their heart, will be able to see if he carries out his work for the community faithfully and sincerely or not.

7.
He shall not refuse to take part in the General Church Meetings or to go to meetings of respectable preachers – members of the German North American Lutheran Ministry – if he is able to and if his health and other circumstances permit him to take on such a distant journey.

8.

He shall carry out his duties himself, as they have been assigned to him, within the church and school, as best he can and according to the strength and health given to him by God, as a trusty keeper of the House of God, and no other preacher or student preacher, who has not yet been examined according to our Evangelical Church Order, will be called or shall replace him as long as he is found to be healthy and able by the above mentioned Ministry. In case he should become ill for some period and he is not able to carry out his duties, or due to some other valid cause, and the community has been duly informed of that fact, then we will ask for help through bonds from the church coffers belonging to the previously mentioned ministry who will offer aid as their regular obligations permit. We are not against giving our proper teacher the freedom to call for regularly called and united preachers and have them preach for him as long as he is present, for the enrichment of the community, as the united preachers and communities, through the love of Christ and according to Christ's regulations, are obligated to each other. *Matthew 7, v. 12.*

However, an itinerant or vagabond preacher, who does not belong to the above mentioned ministry, shall not be permitted to step foot on our pulpit because such people are not only thieves who steal the community's money, they are also God's blasphemers and the downfall of preachers, and they are violators of our Christian Church because, through their behavior, they go against their beliefs, and through their sinful life they cause nothing but irritation and trouble within the community.

9.

If our preacher, who is serving the community, should go against God, either through his teachings or morals, or against the church order of the community, causing any trouble or problems, then any costs occurring due to this shall be handled as follows:

1. The elders or two thirds of them shall present the problems, as stated or confirmed by two or three credible witnesses, in reference to his teaching or his life, in a kind manner and they shall warmly admonish him to improve.
2. If this does not happen, then the church administrators, in presence of the officials from the united community, shall invite him to a friendly place and shall repeat the admonishment in their presence.
3. If this does not result in the desired solution, then the matter shall be brought to an extra ordinary convention or via the annual preacher's convention to the North American German Lutheran Ministry, who shall handle the matter through two or three credible witnesses, two of the elders and one from the community, or one of the elders and one from the community; they shall check on the matter in detail, and if the preacher is found guilty and damaging to the community, then he shall be relieved immediately from his position and benefits, and shall be suspended and asked to leave.

10.

The members belonging to the ministry shall have the right, after the preacher has been suspended and relieved, to look for another preacher for the community, so that the damage can be undone, and the labor of the Lord can be continued, the sacraments can be dispensed, and old and young alike can be served again according to paragraph 1 and 2 of this order. However, if a preacher, against whom nothing improper or damaging can be proven according to this order, wants to leave himself, or wants to leave the community because of slight problems, he must first obtain the approval of the church administrators and two-thirds of the community, in addition to the consent of the ministry.

11.

The election of a preacher shall happen as follows, namely:

1. The preacher selected by the ministry shall come as a guest lecturer and give a sample sermon, so that the community can hear if he teaches loudly, clearly, understandably, edifyingly, and according to the teachings of the Apostles or not.
2. The next day, the elders and the chairmen, in addition to the complete community, will assembly and think over the matter impartially, in front of God, and will decide if the intended preacher will do for the community or not.

And so that the election of the new preacher will occur without any displeasure, all communing members will cast their vote in the school building, as it is usually done for any other election, if the intended preacher will do for the community or not. If two thirds of the church administrators and two thirds of the communicating members of the community agree, then he may be called up, and asked if he wants to take on the community and if he wants to be initiated as the teacher.

However, if no teacher can be obtained from the American ministry, then the community reserves the right, with consent of the before mentioned ministry, to write to the blessed consortium ministry in Europe and to ask them for a preacher, under the condition that he is well educated and properly knowledgeable in Evangelical teaching and that his life and morals are according to the teaching.

12.

The teacher for our community, who truly carries out his duties according to his ability and the grace of God according to Christ and his demand, shall be properly supported by the community so that he can carry out his difficult duties and does not have to fend for his daily bread.

1. We promise to place the preacher, for his support and benefit, on the plantation, which has been inhabited since the establishment of the German community here by a preacher, and which contains 180 acres; but our present teacher has given 40 acres for the support of our school teacher, the other 140 acres will remain for the support and benefit of the preacher as long as he serves the community according to the church order.
2. He also is to receive annually a payment of money as is agreed upon by the elders of the community and has been agreed upon when he was called up; part of which will come from the income of the estates which belong to the church, and part from the community.

This support, as previously mentioned, will benefit our rightfully called up preacher, who was either placed by the before mentioned higher administration or by the committee ministry, as long as he serves the community faithfully and sincerely, until he dies or moves away with the consent of the ministry and the community.

13.

The public church services, the administration of the Holy Sacraments as well as the remaining church functions shall be held by the teacher according to our usual agenda and custom until the united ministry and the community deem it necessary or beneficial to add or remove something.

14.

No church service shall be missed by our teacher, without our previous knowledge, unless it is due to a sudden illness or most important business; however, if the preacher misses a Sunday or holiday sermon due to his own fault, or because he is carrying out his own business, then he shall pay for this, and 20 shillings will be deducted from his salary.

Chapter 2
Regarding the External Administration of the Community

Our community, which has been growing from year to year, has been served by trusted members, trustees, elders and chairmen since its beginning, now already for 48 years, they have with great effort built up and lovingly carried the community and their problems so that it could flourish, but sometimes a lack of order could be felt by the community. For that reason, we have, according to local customs, and due to necessity, brought forth the Christian Church Order and accounting procedure, with the approval of the community.

And we have greatly pondered the appointment of the officials for this external administration, which consists of trustees, elders and chairmen, and we have, with the approval and to the satisfaction of the community members, decided the following:

1.

The community, with this New Order, shall have the continuing freedom to elect and confirm the necessary community officials and servants in Christian order, through the majority of votes.

2.

The community and church administration shall consist of capable trustees, as well as elders and chairmen, all properly elected and confirmed by the community.

3.

And even though our community has been served since its beginning – with God's blessed support – by trustees, elders and chairmen with unexpected diligence, but since we are now introducing this new order, the following regulations are set forth, with the approval of the community, namely:

1. The following persons shall remain rightful trustees, elders, chairmen and remain as such a) until they can be rightfully convinced that they are no longer able to carry out their duties, b) or until they step down by themselves, or–if they have sufficient cause–until they want to be released, with consent of the members of the church administration, and the community, c) or until they move away from this region, namely, Adam Gaar, Adam Weyland, Andreas Zimmermann, Johannes Weber, Nicolaus Grickler, Johannes Jager, Christoph Blanckenbücher, and Adam Breil.

Above persons will hold the trusteeship, position of elders and chairmen according to local custom, over all and everything – without exception – which has been entrusted to them as trustees, elders and chairmen by their community, and which has been recorded in a deed and declaration under their guardianship; namely what belongs to the community to date, such as land, Negroes, but also money, bonds and bills, and what will be added in the future, until they either become unfit to serve in their positions, until they die or move away.

4.

If some of the above trustees, elders and chairmen relinquish their position in a manner as stated above, then the community is to have the freedom to choose others to take their place, in a manner as stated below.

5.

The election of the trustees, elders and chairmen shall be held as follows, on Three Kings Day, namely:

1. The remaining elders shall, let's say on the previous day, review the names of the community members who have signed this order, and according to their best know-how and conscience, without prejudice, without looking at the person – if one needs to be replaced, they are to select two names – if two or three or more must be selected, they should select 4 or 6 Christian honorable men, who have a good reputation, write down their names legibly and present them to the community on the day of election.
2. On the day of election, the community members present have the freedom and the right to select one or more elders from the 2, 4 or 6 presented names, by majority vote. The selected then remain in this position until they become unfit to serve, until they die or move away.
3. After the election is over, the preacher, as president, shall protocol the elders or chairmen, who were elected by the majority, in the church order book, and on the following Sunday he shall present them to the community, remind them publicly of their duty, and take a verbal promise of their loyal service.

[Note in Margin
On Three Kings Day 1806, this paragraph, in this article in the chapter Church Order, has been repealed by the church administration after it was previously repealed by the community.]

However, if one or more of the elders, who were elected by the majority of the members of the community, want to refuse to take on this difficult duty without just cause, then they shall not get off without giving a donation to the church coffer; it shall not be less than 20 shillings. In case two or more have the same number of votes, then the church administration shall decide. The church administration consists of trustees, who also serve as elders and chairmen for the community.

6.

If any important matters arise in the community, regarding the preacher, the school teacher, the parish or school house properties, Negroes, money or anything else that belongs to the community at that time, then it shall not be decided by the preacher alone, nor by one or the other of the elders, but the complete church administration shall confer about it well and long, decide on the matter by at least a two thirds majority, and then present it to the community and have it approved by at least two thirds of the members. Especially in matters where the members shall contribute funds, the complete church administration should be publicly invited by the preacher and no member or members shall stay away without just cause, and no decision should be made which has not been approved by at least two thirds of the above mentioned community members, and they should sign the protocol book with their own hand to avoid any possible conflicts and the community will be blessed, illustriously and flourishingly.

7.

The duties of the trustees, elders and chairmen serving the community are as follows, namely:

1. They shall, through God's mercy and support, not only run their own houses in a Christian manner, but also be an example to the community through their Christian life and behavior.
2. In addition to the teacher, they shall assure that the Evangelical teaching and Christian order is retained and continued within the community.
3. They shall assure that any income from estates, Negroes, outstanding loans and bonds, etc. is collected, used and retained to the advantage of the community.
4. They shall assure that the teacher is supported by the community as Christ demanded.
5. They shall properly handle the income and expense accounts for the community, and they shall present them to the church administration annually, and on the next day, on Three Kings Day, they shall read them aloud to the community, point for point, and then write them down into the church record books for retention.
6. They shall take part in public and special church services, distribute the sacraments, help especially during children's services, and make sure that discipline and good order are maintained among the young people; so that everything is handled properly and orderly according to the teachings of the Apostles.
7. If any disorder, disagreement or problem arises within the community, and they become aware of it, they shall try, as much as they are able to,

to settle the matter, or to present it to the church administrators, so that it may be settled in time, to prevent any damage.

8.

And because the church officials and servants in this country, even though they hold important positions before God, are nevertheless subjected to many unfavorable comments and suspicion by people lacking sound judgment, if they direct these people according to God's Word, no complaint shall be accepted against the teacher, elders and chairmen, unless it is supported by two or three credible witnesses, according to *1 Timothy 5, 19*.

However, if truly mistakes or transgressions according to *Galatians* 5, 19, *Chapter 6, 1* were made by one or the other, God forbid, then the complete church administration shall appoint an unbiased committee, they shall check out the matter and shall handle the charges in a trusty manner, according to Christ's teachings, without regard of the person.

Chapter 3.
Regarding the Community Members

1.

Anyone who wants to be an active member of our German Evangelical Lutheran Church in Culpepper, has a right to vote, take part and enjoy any of the privileges, as well as serve in some capacity, must at least – according to Christ's order – as can be seen outwardly:
1. be baptized,
2. enjoy the Holy Communion according to the blessing of the Lord and Christ,
3. not live in the revealing effects of the flesh according to *Galatians 5, chapter 19, 20, 21.*
4. live according to Christian ways, and not carry out any illegitimate deeds,
5. give willingly to the church, school and care of the preacher, for love and ability, as long as it is necessary, may it be little or much, even if it would be only a cold drink of water,
6. follow the Christian order and let himself be reprimanded in brotherly love if he went astray,
7. and – in addition to God and the dear authority – he shall act towards his trusty teacher, elders and chairmen in such a way, that they will carry out their duties with pleasure and not with a sigh.

2.

Anyone who fails on any of the above points or on one or the other part in particular, willfully or intentionally, and who does not better himself with God's Grace and benevolence, nor wants to take part in the Christian order, he can and shall be no member of our Evangelical Lutheran Church; shall take no part and enjoy none of the privileges, much less have a vote and carry out a function within the community.

3.

Even though the estates belonging to the church are considered to be gifts from well-meaning hearts and well-wishers of Christ's kingdom from Europe and other places, they nevertheless had to be collected through great effort and danger; assembled from the first beginnings and up to now maintained by regular community members; otherwise they would long ago have been depleted and returned to its previous nothing.

Because it would not be right, according to God's worldly laws, even against the nature of things themselves, that anybody, wherever he might come from, can take part of these privileges, who have been sent by people before us and which regular members have supported up to now through their contribution, we have—to be fair—set down the following basic points necessary for the acceptance of a new community member:

1. A person or persons, who came from another part of America, or who moved here from Europe, and never have been members of the community themselves, nor their parents, shall and may report to the preacher and the elders—if they want to be members of the community—and show testimony to their good behavior or show through good morals that they are worthy of calling themselves or becoming members of this Christian community.
2. After the preacher or the elders have checked out the character of such a person or persons, and at least two thirds of the community have agreed to accept the new member, then the new member shall pay a fee which shall be placed into the church coffer for the use of the community.
3. These persons shall sign this church order, and shall conduct themselves accordingly.

4.

In case one or another of the communicating members – may God's grace prevent this – should commit gross errors or commits any sins of the flesh or fraud and falls in the hands of Satan, and if such is proven to be so by truthful and credible witnesses, then
1. they shall be reprimanded by the preacher himself and asked to repent and strive for truthful reconciliation, and if that does not help,
2. they shall again be reprimanded by the preacher in front of the elders and the chairmen and if that does not help,

3. they shall be expelled from the community by the church administration and shall not take part in any of the privileges or have a voice until they return through God's grace, wisdom and sincerity and if they apologize through the preacher in front of the community, without having to give their name; in such a case they shall be taken on again as community members, if they demonstrate through their moral behavior that a real change and improvement has taken place.

The above church order shall be upheld by all, without any changes, completely and in every part, especially by our Evangelical Lutheran community church and anybody connected to it, and shall remain and be valid until the complete church administration and community or at least two thirds of both, namely the administration and the communing members, find it necessary to make a correction, to add or to eliminate something. We attest to this with our signature.

Written in Culpepper County, Virginia,
the 27th of May in the Year of our Lord 1776
Jacob Frank, preacher

Adam Gaar
~~Adam Weyland~~

Johannes Jäger
Andreas Carpenter
Johannes Weber
Niclos Griegler
~~Christoph Blankenbücher~~
Adam Jäger Sen.
Conrad Delp   dead
J....
Georg Koch
Martin Roush

Johann Schmidt
Johannes Carpenter Sen.
Georg Utz Sen.
Mathuis Weber
Henrich Öhler, Sen.
Georg Chnstler
Jacob Blankenbicher
Johannes Carpenter Jun.
Henrich Lipp
Georg Schlater
Philip Jelf
Georg Utz Jun.
Michael Fleischmann
Michael Utz Jun.
Johannes Gaar
Zacharias Blankenbücher
Michael Schmidt

Mathuis Rausch
Adam Koch
~~R... Rausch~~
Michael Jäger
Zacharias Breil Sen.
Nicolaus Schmidt Sen.
Philip Schneider
Eberhard Reiner
Friednch ~~Gerber~~ Tanner
Markus Fincks
Johannes ~~Gerber~~ Tanner
~~Johannes Weyland, Jun.~~
Wilhelm Carpenter Sen.
Michael Utz Sen. dead
Johannes Fincks
Conrad Gensle
Andreas Gaar
Peter Klor
Michael Delp

Christoph Gerber
Mathuis Hauss
Georg Reiser
Peter Weber
Adam Christler
Henrich Öhler Jun.
Adam Utz
Michael Schneider
Peter Breil
Johannes Blankenbücher
Johannes Zimmermann
Johannes Freh dead
Martin Hirsch Sen. dead
Michael Carpenter Sen.
Johannes Schmidt
Michael Carpenter
Daniel Böhme
Georg Wilheit
Valentin Bungard
~~Nicolaus Lederer~~
Nicolaus Schmidt Jun.
Michael Koch
Ludwig Nunnemacher
Henrich Christler
Bejamin Gaar
Christoph Gnckler
Christoph Zimmermann
Johannes Jäger Jun.
Aron Grickler
Johannes Hirsch
Peter Benenger
Ruben Grickler
Henrich Wayland
Samuel Carpenter Sen.
Wilhelm Carpenter Jun.
Andreas Hirsch
Carl Vrede

Johannes Blankenbücher Jun.
Georg Utz - Jünger

Ephraim Utz
Abraham ~~Gerber~~ Tanner
Joseph Carpenter
Cornelius Carpenter
Ludwig Grickler
Ludwig Blanckenbücher
Ephraim Rausch
Josua Jäger
Jacob Rausch
Michael Hauss
Salomon Carpenter
Ephraim Fleischmann
Zacharias Fleischmann
Daniel Koch
Martin Hirsch Jun.
Peter Koch
Jacob Lipp
Jacob Bungard
Georg Rausch
Ludwig Wayland
Joseph Schneider
Ephraim Freh
Andreas Carpenter Jüngere
Michael Schmidt Jun.
Josua Zimmermann
Johannes Bungard
Ludwig Utz
Lorentz Gaar
Johannes Koch
Abraham Grickler
Mathuis Hauss Jun.
Zacharias Breil Jun.
Samuel Schmidt
Nicolaus Jäger
Daniel Utz
Benjamin Jäger
Thomas Blankenbücher
Abraham Grigler
Ludwig Koch
Daniel Reiser
Jacob Blankenbücher
Jonas Blankenbücher
Ephraim Koch
Michael Schmidt Sen.
Ludwig Rausch

Samuel Blankenbücher
Thomas Blankenbücher
Andreas Carpenter Jun.
Jacob Holsklau-
~~Mathuis Haus~~
Jacob ~~Holsklau~~ Hauss,
Friederich Zimmermann
Henrich Holsklau
Abraham Christler
Jacob Crigler
Ephraim Tanner
Michael Tanner
Ambrosius Koch
Aron Breil
Johann Jesse
Aron Koch
Simeon Gaar
Elijah Fleischmann
Joel Carpenter
Jacob Tanner
Johannes Rausch
Solomon Koch
Simeon Carpenter
Absalom Aylor
Moses Weber
Friedrich Julius Schad
Georg Philip Schad
Benjamin Aylor
Josua Crigler
Simeon Tanner
Lewis Crigler Jun.
Elijah Rousch
Abraham Carpenter
Aaron Hauss

Aaron Blankenbücher
Lewis Utz
Moses Tanner
Aaron Tanner
Joel Crigler
Nicolaus Rausch
Joel Utz
Daniel Utz Jun.
Jeremias Carpenter
William Tanner
Nicolaus Crigler
Josua Hauss

[The internal evidence of the above list is that these names were generally not signatures made by the person. Crossed out names probably represent death. In a few cases, the word "dead" is entered. After the initial names were made, members coming later added their names to the list. In the later part of the list, more modern spellings are used.]

Petition of the German Congregation of the County of Culpepper

To the Honorable, the President and Delegates of the Convention of the
Commonwealth of Virginia
The Petition of the German Congregation
of the County of Culpepper Showeth

That our Fathers who lived under an Arbitrary Prince in Germany, and_____by the Honorable William Penn Esq. Proprietor of the Province of Pennsilvania to settle his Province, which with the faith they had in the Provincial Charter, given and granted from the British Crown, and that the Germans there, enjoyed freedom in the exercise of Religion as well as other ways, and that they supported their own Church and Poor. Our Fathers ventured their Lives and Fortunes to come into a Land of Liberty (i e) from a European Egypt, to an American Canaan, to enjoy those Sweets of Freedom which God created for all Men. They journeyed from Germany to London, & there agreed with a Captain, to land them and their Families in Pennsylvania; but he proved false, and landed them against their will and agreement in Virginia, and sold them for Servants.

On their Arrival, the loss of their Estates, and the Snare the Captain had draged them in, was not equal with the loss they were at, in not understanding the English Tongue, which rendered it impossible to join in the Worship of God; till they were Free, and the Lord directed a Door for them, where they could exercise themselves in the Christian Religion as they were taught by their Parents in Europe.

Soon after they were gathered to the Place where we now live, they concluded to erect a Church and School House. But 1st, they being just free were too poor; 2nd, the laws of the Country was against them, & 3rd, the Arbitrary Power of Bishops_____Prayer to God, that he would be Merciful to them, they petitioned the Governor & House of Burgesses, acquainted them with their Distress, and asked redress of all Grievance, which was so far granted they had a license to collect Money, build a Church, call a Minister, worship God in a congregation, & practice the Christian Religion as they were taught by their Parents in Europe.

[The petition goes on to ask the privilege of having their own independent church without having to support the state church.]

[The full petition is to be found as Appendix C of *History of the Hebron Lutheran Church, Madison County, Virginia, from 1717 to 1907* by Rev. William P. Huddle *With Epilogue 1908 to 1989* by Margaret Grim Davis, Hebron Lutheran Church, Madison, Virginia, 1990.]

[The names of the male members of the church are given.]

1. Adam Gaar
Adam Wayland 2
3. Johannes Jaeger
4. Andreas Carpenter
5. Johannes Weber
6. Nicholaus Grickler
7. Christoph Blankenbuecher
8. Conrad Delp
9. George Koch
10. Vallendin Bangert
11. Matheis Hauss
12. Michael Fleischmann
13. Michael Utz
14. Johannes Gaar
15. Zacharias Blanc..buchler
16. Bernhard Fischer

17. Rudolph Urbach
18. Michael Schmitt
19. Matheus Rausch
20. Adam Koch
21. Nicolaus Breul
22. Adam Mayer
23. Samuel Rausch
24. Michael Yaeger
25. Zachariah Broyle
26. Michael Leather
27. Nicholas Smith
28. Phillip Snyder
29. Abirhart Riner
30. Frederick Tanner
31. John Winegard
32. Marck Fink

33. Jacob Broyle
34. John Wayland, Junr.
35. Jacop Broils
36. Adam Barler
37. Willhelm Carpenter
38. Michael Utz, Junior
39. Adam Pander
40. John Fink

1. Mardin Rausch
2. Henrich Christler
3. Adam ? –der?
4. Paulus Leatherer
5. John Smith
6. Johannes Zimmerman
7. Niclaus Jaeger

1. Christian Reiner
2. Georg Utz, Junr.
3. Jacob Handrexson
4. Matheus Weber
5. Heinrich Ehler
6. Georg Christler
7. Daniel Dosser
8. Stephen Fisher
9. Jacob Blankenbuecher

1. Nicholaus Wilheit
2. Johannes Carpenter
3. John Fleischmann
4. Friedrich Lipp
5. John Broyl
6. Robert Fleischmann
7. Georg Flathes [Slater?]
8. Philip Jelf
9. Georg Utz

1. Conrad Kenszle
2. Michael Gaar
3. Andreas Gaar
4. Peter Clar
5. Michal Utz
6. Daniel Delp

7. Christopher Gerber
8. Michael Swindle
9. Ziriakus Breil
10. Johannes ????
11. Georg ?Rieser?
12. Peter Weber
13. Adam Grickler
14. Heinrich Oeler
15. Adam Utz
16. Michael Clore
17. Michael Schneider
18. John Clore, Junr.
19. Adam Clore
20. Peter Breil
21. Rudolph Crecelius
22. Johannes Freh
23. Martin Hirsh
24. Michael Zimmerman
25. Georg Lehman
26. John Clore
27. Christoph Barlow
28. Johannes Schmid
29. Michael Carpenter
30. Daniel Peemon
31. John Swindle
32. Christoph Mayer

33. George Wilheit
34. Nicolas Lederer
35. Nicholas Smith, Junr.
36. Michael Cook
37. Ludwig Nunenmacher
38. Mich'l Blankenbecker
39. Benjamin Gaar

1. Christoph Crigler
2. Adam Broil
3. Christoph Zimmermann
4. Zacharias Smith
5. Christoph Maier, Junr.
6. John Yeager, Junr.
7. Johannes Zimmermann
8. Adam Yaeger, Senr.
9. John Carpenter, Senr.
10. Joseph Rausch
11. Benjamin Gaar
12. Jurt Tanner
13. Joseph Holtzclaw
14. John Wilhoit
15. John Backer
16. John Dear, Senr.
17. Henry Miller

Origins of the Planckenbühler (Blankenbühler) Family

Four families who came to America can trace one line of their ancestry to Gresten, Austria. The detailing of their descent from 1600 to their departure from Germany is not easy but fortunately it has been accomplished thanks to very dedicated work of researchers. Because so many Germanna families can trace a line through these families, it is desirable to recap the information here. This was a turbulent period involving the Reformation, the counter-Reformation, and the Thirty Years' War and all of these factors had some influence on the decisions of people. In this early phase, religion was an important question.

In Gresten, Austria, about fifty miles west of Vienna, the Catholic church became Lutheran about 1550 in the sense that the building was now used by the Lutherans who were the majority of the citizens. It returned to the Catholic faith about 1630 during the Thirty Years' War by order of the Kaiser. The Lutheran church records have disappeared and only civil records, still in private hands, serve as a record of events in these years. The Catholic records commence about 1630. These and the estate records are the sources of information. The civil records have never been filmed for public distribution but Pastor Georg Kuhr of Mittelfranken in Bavaria worked with these records for many years. He photographed them in the archives of Schloss Stiebar in Gresten and typed up the data. Richard and Gisela Plankenbühler of Nürnberg worked with Pastor Kuhr and obtained information which answered many questions. Pastor Kuhr once remarked that it was a hardship to work with the family in Austria because of the many spellings that were used (a characterization that continues today). He decided to standardize the spelling as Planckenbühler to avoid confusion by the many spellings.

The estate records are an important source of information that tells how assets were to be divided after the death of a person. Even without any certain knowledge of Austrian seventeenth century estate law, the main points are easy to understand. On the death of a mother with the father surviving and with the father keeping a farm, he had to pay to the children their share of the mother's estate. Sons and daughters were not treated equally but they were all entitled to a share. When the father died, the farm would go to one of the sons, probably the oldest son. This son had to pay the other children their share of the father's estate.

On 24 September 1620, Martha Planckenbühler died. She and her husband Kilian (also given as Colman and other variations) were the parents of seven children, namely, Jacob, Hannß (I), Paul (I), Thomas, Michael, Maria, and Barbara. Barbara died before her mother did. The first child to receive a payment was Jacob. A record of 1644 identifies Jacob with the farm Plözenperg (Pletzenberg today) which is very close to the farm Plankenpichel (Plankenbichl today) where Kilian lived.

Kilian Planckenbühler married again. The second wife was also Martha and again her maiden name is unknown. Before 1640, they were the parents of ten children, Blasius, Matthias, Hannß (II), Paul (II), Adam, Magdalena, Christoph, Elisabetha, Sophia, and Potentiana. Kilian died in 1646 and Martha in 1647. Blasius assumed the possession of the Plankenpichel farm and paid, over the course of time, his brothers and sisters their shares of the estate. It is mentioned in the estate records that Blasius' brother Mathias is "im Rom. Reich bay Langenbruckh in das Bistumb Speyer gehörig verheyrath." This remark may be read as "[he is] married in the [Holy] Roman Empire at or near Langenbrücken which belongs to the Speyer diocese." This is the record that clearly identifies Matthias Blankenbühler, the ancestor of the 1717 Blankenbakers, as belonging to the Austrian family Planckenbühler at Gresten. (The record may be cited as from the Schlossarchiv Stiebar b. Gresten, in the general reference works *Herrschaftbücher Hausegg*, specifically in the *Bäuerliches Waisenbuch I [1603–1636]* and *II*. The specific quotation pertaining to Matthias appears to be best given by the date 26 October 1660 and *Waisenbuch II*.

Langenbrücken is found five miles west and slightly north of Neuenbürg. It has been merged with Bad Schönborn. Matthias soon moved to Neuenbürg, a very small village located less that two miles north of the town of Oberöwisheim. The village had only a Catholic church but Oberöwisheim had a Lutheran church and the events of the Blankenbühler family are recorded in the church that served both communities. Matthias and his wife Margretha were baptismal sponsors in 1667. This is the first record of him at Neuenbürg. The only known child of Matthias is Hans Thomas Blankenbühler who married Anna Barbara Schön 2 November 1680 at Neuenbürg (she had just turned sixteen). Anna Barbara's father was Quirin Schön and her mother was Maria Barbara.

Four children of Anna Barbara Schön and Johann Thomas Blankenbühler were born and baptized in the Lutheran church in Oberöwisheim:

Hans Niclas Blanckenbühler,	b. 02 JAN 1682
Hans Balthasar Blanckenbühler	b. 29 APR 1683
Hans Matthias Blanckenbühler	b. 29 DEC 1684
Anna Maria Blanckenbühler	b. 05 MAY 1687

Anna Barbara Schön Blanckenbühler married secondly, on 03 NOV 1691 Johann Jacob Schlucter. There is a gap in the church records, probably war related, so the death of her first husband is not recorded. Johann Jacob Schlucter was born 1652/53 and he died 13 FEB 1698 in Neuenbürg. Not long before his death, a son had been born, the only child of this union known:

Henerich Schlucter	b. 07 MAY 1697

After the death of Johann Jacob Schlucter, Anna Barbara Schön Blanckenbühler Schlucter married, as her third husband, Cyriacus Fleischmann on 05 MAY 1701 in Neuenbürg. Three children were born to Anna Barbara and Cyriacus in Neuenbürg:

Maria Catharina Fleischmann	b. 08 MAR 1702 (died yonng?)
Maria Catharina Fleischmann	b. 26 JAN 1704
Hans Peter Fleischmann	b. 10 APR 1708

(At the birth of Hans Peter, Anna Barbara had seven living children with a span of 26 years in their ages.)

Anna Maria Blanckenbühler was the first child to marry. On 18 NOV 1711 in Neuenbürg, as the age of 24, she married Johann Thomas, son of Albrecht Thomas. They had three children in Neuenbürg:

Hans Wendel Thomas	b. 17 APR 1712
Ursula Thomas	b. 08 MAY 1714, d. the same day
Anna Magdalena Thomas	b. 24 NOV 1715

Johann Nicholas Blanckenbühler married Apollonia Käfer in Neuenbürg on 6 MAY 1714. Two children were born in Neuenbürg:

Maria Barbara Blanckenbühler	b. 22 DEC 1714, d. next day
Zacharias Blanckenbühler	b. 21 OCT 1715

The day after Johann Nicholas Blanckenbühler's wedding, Johann Mattheus Blanckenbühler, tailor, married Anna Maria Mercklin on 7 MAY 1714 in Oberderdingen, Württemberg. A birth of a child is recorded in this same town:

Hannes Jerg Blanckenbühler	b. FEB 1715 [the day is impossible to read]

No marriage was found in Germany for Hans Balthasar Blanckenbühler who was recorded with a wife, but no children, on Spotswood's importation list. All of the above people who departed Neuenbürg lived through the voyage to Virginia.

The family of George Sheible left Neuenbürg at the same time. He was probably related to the complex of people above for these reasons: first, from the Plankenbichl farm outside Gresten, Austria, one can see an adjacent farm, Scheiblau; second, George Sheible was living in Neuenbürg; third, in Virginia, George Sheible had his land in the midst of the people from Neuenbürg. So in three widely different locations, the family seems to be very close to the Blankenbakers. Probably he was related.

For further information see: Margaret James Squires, "Anna Barbara Schön," *Beyond Germanna*, v.1, n.3, p21; John Blankenbaker, Richard & Gisela Plankenbühler, "The Origins of the Blankenbaker Family in America," *Beyond Germanna*, v.13, n.5, p.761; Karl Diefenbacher & Klaus Rösser, *Ortssippenbuch Oberöwisheim-Neuenbürg*, 1995; Johni Cerny and Gary Zimmerman, *Before Germanna*, v.3, "The Ancestry of Blankenbaker, Fleshman, and Slucter Families."

The Utz-Volck Complex

Margaret James Squires found the origins of George Utz and the Volck family of the Wagenbach estate farm and the associated church at Hüffenhardt, Baden. Hans (or Johann) Michael Volck of Wagenbach married, about 1685, Anna Maria_____. (The sound of the name Volck suggests also the spelling Folg.) They were the parents of seven children before Anna Maria died. Johann Michael Volck married Anna Barbara Majer(s) (or Maier or Mayer) on 27 JAN 1709. To this couple, three children were born:

Maria Sabina Charlotta Barbara,	b. 19 MAR 1710
Louisa Elisabetha,	b. 23 MAR 1711
Maria Rosina	b. 22 AUG 1712

Johann Michael Volck died 7 APR 1714 at the age of 51 years. The widow, Anna Barbara (Majer) Volck married Johann Georg Utz on 10 JUL 1714. Two children were born in Germany (others were born in Virginia):

Ferdinand,	b. 03 APR 1715
Johannes,	b. 25 JUL 1716

The daughter Maria Sabina became the second wife of John Hoffman, the 1714 colonist who moved to the Robinson River Valley. Some people believe, with good reason, that Elisabeth became the wife of Peter Weaver. Ferdinand survived the trip to Virginia but died as a young person in Virginia. Johannes Utz and Maria Rosina Volck did not survive the trip to Virginia. In Virginia, three more children of George and Barbara Utz were born:

> Michael who married Susanna Crigler,
>
> Mary Margaret who married John Blankenbaker,
>
> George who married Mary Kaifer.

Thus, Anna Barbara Maier Volck Utz was the mother of eight children.

In the baptisms of the children of John and Mary Hoffman, one of the sponsors was listed by John Hoffman as "The Mother of My Wife," without telling us her name which was Mrs. George (Barbara) Utz. For a complete listing of the baptisms of the John Hoffman's children and the sponsors, see "John Hoffman: Records from his Bible, 1663–1813," *Beyond Germanna*, v.11, n.2.

More information about these families is to be found in *Before Germanna*, v. 4, "The Ancestry of the Weaver, Utz and Folg Families." See also Margaret James Squires, "The Mother of My Wife," *Beyond Germanna*, v.1, n.1.

The Clore-Weaver-Crigler-Yager Complex

The Lutheran Church records of Gemmingen record the marriage of Phillip Joseph Weber and Susanna Klaar on 26 Jan 1706. She was the sister of Michael Klaar (Clore). At the time of their marriage, Susanna was about fourteen years of age. Six children of this union are to be found in the Gemmingen baptismal records:

> Hans Martin, christened 26 APR 1707 and died 4 MAY 1707,
>
> Johann Georg, christened 23 MAR 1708 and died 23 MAY 1708,
>
> Hans Georg, christened 7 MAY 1709 and died 9 MAY 1709,
>
> Hans Dieterich, christened 8 NOV 1710,
>
> Maria Sophia, christened 26 OCT 1713,
>
> Johann Georg, christened 17 DEC 1715 and died 15 APR 1717.

For a more complete reading of these baptisms, see John Blankenbaker, "Gemmingen Baptisms of the children of Joseph Weber and his wife Susanna Klaar," *Beyond Germanna*, v.15, n.6. In the Gemmingen Lutheran Church Death Register, the people leaving Gemmingen on 12 JUL 1717 included:

> Joseph Weber (30 years of age) and his wife Susanna (25)
>
> Hannes Deiterich (7) who was studying the catechism,
>
> Sophia (under 4), an infant.

For a complete transcription of this departure list, see Andreas Mielke and Elke Hall, "Emigrants in the Gemmingen 'Departure List' of July 1717," *Beyond Germanna*, v.15, n.6.

Alexander Spotswood's head right list has these names for the Weber [Weaver] family:

> Joseph Wever,
>
> Susanna Wever,
>
> Hans Fredich Wever,
>
> Maria Sophia Wever, and
>
> Wabburie [Walburga] Wever.

This is the last record of Joseph Weaver and he appears to have died within a few years of their arrival in Virginia. Hans Dieterich became Peter Wever in Virginia. It appears that Peter married Elisabeth Volck. Maria Sophia married Peter Fleshman, son of Cyriacus Fleshman and his wife Anna Barbara. Walburga, known as Burga, married John Willheit, son of Michael Willheit and Anna Maria Hengsteller.

After the death of Joseph Weaver, his widow Susanna married Jacob Crigler and they had four children (sequence not certain):

> Nicholas who married Margaret Käfer,
> Christopher who married Catherine Finks,
> Susanna who married Michael Utz,
> Elizabeth who married Michael Yager.

The birth of these four children may be taken as occurring in the decade of the 1720s or possibly into the 1730s. Jacob Crigler died, probably in 1734. By the time of the 1739 tithe list, Susanna was married to the 1717 immigrant Nicholas Yager but there were no children.

Anna Barbara Schön, Anna Barbara Mayer, and Susanna Klaar

In the immediately preceding three sections, one person stands out in each story. In each, this is the matriarch. The stories of these three ladies is filled with history and inspires our profound respect. There is hardly a Germanna Second Colony descendant who is not descended from at least one of these three. Susanna was a mother eleven times though not all of her children lived to adulthood. Anna Barbara Schön was a mother eight times (one died as an infant) and there was a spread of 26 years between her oldest and youngest. Anna Barbara Mayer was also a mother eight times but we only know of five who lived to be adults. Counting her great-grandchildren is mind boggling for one daughter had twelve children and each of them had several offspring.

Two of the three had three husbands and the other one had two. Two of them married as very young persons, Anna Barbara Schön just past her sixteenth birthday and Susanna Klaar when she was about fourteen By the standard of their times, they lived to an old age.

Anna Barbara Schön was 53 years old when she came to America. This is in an age when most people of that time would be thinking about retiring, not starting on a life threatening adventure.

By the time of the second or third generation after these women, their genes have spread through many families. The descendants of Peter Weaver are all cousins of the Clores. All people of the Fleshman name descend from Sophia Weaver and in turn a Clore. All of the Germanna Thomases and Fishers descend from Anna Barbara Schön as well as "three-quarters" of the Garrs. All of the Aylor surname have Anna Barbara Schön as an ancestor. Of course the Blankenbakers and the Fleshmans have a common ancestor in her.

The First Colony Petition Taken to London by Zollicoffer

Several points in the history of the Germanna Colonies have been taken from the petition submitted to the Society for the Propagation of the Gospel on 2 OCT 1719. The assumption is made, even though the internal evidence does not support the idea, that this document, was written by the Germans from both colonies in Virginia. It was carried to London by Jacob Zollikoffer. This document, in English, was not the one written by the Germans in Virginia. Zollicoffer, to increase the appeal to the English, submitted a considerably different thing and it must be regarded as a work of fiction with several errors. The document written by the Germans is (in a translation from the German by Andreas Mielke):

> To all pious Christian Readers of this in Europe, we wish God's Mercy and Blessing through Christ Jesus our Lord. Since in none other is salvation; and also since man is given no other name under the sky in which he can be blessed than in the name of JEsus Christ, Acts 4; It is therefore an unspeakable goodness of God, and to man a joyful message; that he gave man not only his son for our salvation but also

that he has this gospel be preached to the entire world, Matt. 24, as initially in the Orient, so also now in recent times here in the Occident, in America; as we see various people come together from Europe and elsewhere almost daily: Because we note with them a big difference in their divine service, we have concluded to establish also here in the land Virginia Christian churches and schools for us Germans, so that our children and offspring shall not get into heathendom, enthusiasms, or other sects and errors, and thus would lose the blessedness so dearly gained by Christ: But rather maintain the true Evangelical-Reformed divine service after our death, and publicly preach in the German language according to the guide line of the divine word, administer the holy sacraments according to Christ's order, teach the youth in schools (especially the catechism known in the Heidelberg lands), maintain the teacher; all to the honor of God and the blessing of the people. Therefore we, the undersigned, sent to Europe to you our fellow brothers in Christ him who shows this, the honorable Mister Jacob Christoff Zollickoffer, born out of the city St. Gall, of Switzerland, to pleadingly request a merciful contribution to above mentioned Christian endeavor in the hope that every Christian Reader of this shall contribute according to his ability and expect for it the blessing of God which we wish to all of you to enjoy constantly in this transitory and afterwards in the eternal life

(L. S.)

Henrich Häger/ Servant of God with the Germans in Virginia 1719.

Johann Jost Merdten.

Hans Jacob Richter/ Elders. In the name of the congregation.

Clearly, the original document was the work of the First Colony in which the Second Colony had no participation. There is no count of the number of families by the people who would know best, the Germans themselves. These counts of the number of families are sometimes used as the basis of the claim that there was a Third Colony. It is true that some of the people did come later but it would not be appropriate to call them a colony.

Improvements in the General History

Third Colony
The statement that there was a third colony is erroneous (see the previous section). People did continue to come after 1717 but there was no organized group. The concept that there was a Third Colony arose from the statement that Zollicoffer made to the Society for the Propagation of the Gospel. Purportedly, this was a joint statement of the First Colony and the Second Colony but in fact only the First Colony made the appeal. Zollicoffer ignored their statement and submitted one of his own. He was not well informed about the details.

South of the Rapidan
The Second Colony was not placed south of the Rapidan; on the contrary they were north of the Rapidan.

Worked in the Mines
The Second Colony did not work in the mines; they worked on naval stores.

Spotswood Sold the Germans Land in the Robinson River Valley
The land on which the Second Colony took patents belonged to the Crown. Spotswood did not sell them the land nor did he sign the patents. He was retired from the government in 1722 and had no official capacity after that time in the Virginia government.

Spotswood Sued the Germans to Force Them to Work Another Year
The claim of the lawsuits against the Germans seems to have been strictly monetary. We do not entirely understand the basis of the suits, but Spotswood sought money, not more time. The time that the Germans worked for Spotswood was seven years, part of 1718, 1719, 1720, 1721, 1722, 1723, and 1724. They left him, probably early in 1725. (They arrived too late to do any work in 1717.) The evidence says they worked seven years for him, not eight or nine.

George Samuel Klug was hired by John Caspar Stoever and not by Michael Holt.

Capt. Scott
The ship that brought the Second Colony was the *Scott* and its captain was Andrew Tarbett.

"The Knights of the Golden Horseshoe"
This phrase originates in a work of fiction in the nineteenth century, more than a hundred years after the 1716 expedition across the Blue Ridge Mountains. It is even doubtful that the "golden horseshoes" ever existed.

Antagonism Between the First and Second Colonies
Willis Kemper was the originator of the idea that the Second Colony and the First Colony were antagonistic towards each other. He blamed it on their religious differences and overlooked the free land in Spotsylvania County at the time the Second Colony was to move to their permanent homes. In fact, many Reformed people, the religion of the First Colony people, did chose to live in the Robinson River Valley.

Improvements in the Family Histories

Henry Aylor and Margaret Käfer
Michael Käfer's will mentioned a daughter Margaret Coller. (Spelling in this document is very bad.) There was no Coller in the community. Analysis of other documents by Nancy Moyers Dodge and others have shown that Henry Aylor married Margaret Thomas. See "Found– Margaret Aylor," in 𝕭𝖊𝖞𝖔𝖓𝖉 𝕲𝖊𝖗𝖒𝖆𝖓𝖓𝖆, v.10, n.4.

Daniel Beemon's (Böhme) wife was Nancy Chelf, the daughter of Philip Chelf by a marriage previous to his marriage to Barbara (Yager) Clore. At the baptisms of two of the children of Daniel and Nancy, Philip Chelf (Schelpf) is a sponsor. His choice would be most unusual unless he were the father of Nancy.

Anthony Berry and Elizabeth Thomas
This couple almost certainly were a husband and wife. See "The Wife of Anthony Berry," in 𝕭𝖊𝖞𝖔𝖓𝖉 𝕲𝖊𝖗𝖒𝖆𝖓𝖓𝖆, v.6, n.3.

Matthias Blankenbaker
The 1717 immigrant, Matthias Blankenbaker, married Anna Maria Mercklin in Germany. He did not marry Mary Yager. See Margaret James Squire, "Anna Barbara Schoen." 𝕭𝖊𝖞𝖔𝖓𝖉 𝕲𝖊𝖗𝖒𝖆𝖓𝖓𝖆, v.1, n.3.

Balthasar Blankenbaker did not marry Margaret Utz. His wife's surname remains unknown.

Els or Alcy Blankenbaker
Els_____was the wife of Zacharias Blankenbaker, the son of the 1717 immigrant John Nicholas Blankenbaker. Prior to her marriage to Zacharias, she had been married and was the mother of two daughters. Some speculation or family history says her first husband was a Finks. By age analysis, the man would be a brother of Mark Finks, Sr. One daughter was Elizabeth who married Peter Broyles and the other daughter, Mary Magdalena, married Henry Wayman. See "Elizabeth, Wife of Peter Broyles," in 𝕭𝖊𝖞𝖔𝖓𝖉 𝕲𝖊𝖗𝖒𝖆𝖓𝖓𝖆, v.15, n.3.

Jacob Blankenbaker, son of John Nicholas Blankenbaker
Jacob was married only twice. The statement that he married an Utz woman is mistaken.

Jacob Blankenbaker and Elizabeth Reiner
John Blankenbaker and Elizabeth Weaver
Aaron Blankenbaker and Elizabeth Utz
Jacob Blankenbaker, #12 in the *Germanna Record* 13, married Elizabeth Reiner. The eventual fate of this family is unknown. Elizabeth Weaver, #25 in *Germanna Record* 13, married John Blankenbaker, #25 in *Germanna Record* 13. Elizabeth Utz, #45 in *Germanna Record* 10 married Aaron Blankenbaker, #68 in *Germanna Record* 13. All of these cases were discussed in two articles "Husbands and Wives," in 𝕭𝖊𝖞𝖔𝖓𝖉 𝕲𝖊𝖗𝖒𝖆𝖓𝖓𝖆, v.11, n.3 on p.626 and 628.

Julius Blankenbaker
The individual given in *Germanna Record* 13 as Julia F. (#68b) was a male, Julius. For a copy of the Bible record in which he is listed correctly, see 𝕭𝖊𝖞𝖔𝖓𝖉 𝕲𝖊𝖗𝖒𝖆𝖓𝖓𝖆, v.7, n.5. Also, the individual listed as Ellen F. in *Germanna Record* 13 was Frances Helen in the Bible record.

Peter Broyles
He married Elizabeth, the step-daughter of Zacharias Blankenbaker. Perhaps her surname was Finks; one book, *Some Martin, Jeffries, and Wayman Families and Connections of Virginia, Maryland, Kentucky, and Indiana*, suggests that this was the case.

Jacob Crigler Family
Good evidence says that Jacob Crigler and his wife Susanna Clore Weaver had four children, Nicholas, Christopher, Susanna, and Elizabeth. Susanna became the wife of Michael Utz, the son of the immigrant George Utz. Elizabeth became the wife of Michael Yager, the son of the young immigrant, Adam Yager. There was no Margaret Crigler. For a more a detail analysis, see the articles "Susanna, the Wife of Michael Utz" and "Elizabeth, the Wife of Michael Yager," both of which are in 𝕭𝖊𝖞𝖔𝖓𝖉 𝕲𝖊𝖗𝖒𝖆𝖓𝖓𝖆, v.15, n.3.

Fleshman Family
The young immigrant, Peter Fleshman, married Maria Sophia Weaver, the daughter of Joseph Weaver and Susanna Clore. The analysis which leads to this conclusion shows the power of association in pointing to unknown people. It was published as an article, "The Wife of Peter Fleshman," in 𝕭𝖊𝖞𝖔𝖓𝖉 𝕲𝖊𝖗𝖒𝖆𝖓𝖓𝖆, v.13, n.5.

Peter Fleshman, Jr., the son of the above Peter Fleshman was married twice and his first wife was Winifred Smith, the daughter of Isaac Smith, Sr. and Margaret Rucker. See the note by Darryl J. Diemer, "Mistaken Identify (Wife of Peter Fleshman, Jr.)," in 𝕭𝖊𝖞𝖔𝖓𝖉 𝕲𝖊𝖗𝖒𝖆𝖓𝖓𝖆, v.4, n.2. The thought that Barbara Tanner married Peter Fleshman is now considered false.

John Frey
By the baptism records at the Lutheran church, John Frey married Rebecca Swindle, not Rebecca Yowell. There is no evidence that a Rebecca Yowell ever existed while the associations at the church point to John Frey's wife being Rebecca Swindle.

Matthias House
Not everyone agrees, but the church baptismal records indicate that Matthias House wives, Mary Margaret and Margaret, were different people. The second wife was Margaret Zimmerman and she was the mother of Moses and Sara and probably Aaron. See "The Matthias House Family in the Hebron Church Records," 𝕭𝖊𝖞𝖔𝖓𝖉 𝕲𝖊𝖗𝖒𝖆𝖓𝖓𝖆, v.15, n.2. An analysis of ages shows that it is extremely improbable that Margaret Zimmerman married Jacob Lipp.

Conrad Kuenzle
He married Rachel Barlow. An analysis of this was in 𝕭𝖊𝖞𝖔𝖓𝖉 𝕲𝖊𝖗𝖒𝖆𝖓𝖓𝖆, v.12, n.3.

Jacob Lipp
While Jacob Lipp did marry a Margaret, it is very unlikely that she was Margaret Zimmerman. From the church records, it would appear that Margaret Zimmerman was about ten years older than Jacob.

John Railsback and Elizabeth Thomas
The church records and the land records of John Thomas show that Elizabeth Thomas married John Railsback.

Ephraim Rouse married first Mary Huffman who was the daughter of Jacob Huffman and the granddaughter of John and Mary Sabina (Volck) Huffman. See 𝕭𝖊𝖞𝖔𝖓𝖉 𝕲𝖊𝖗𝖒𝖆𝖓𝖓𝖆, v.1, n.3.

Abraham Tanner, the son of Christopher Tanner, Sr., married Elizabeth Huffman, the daughter of Jacob Huffman and the granddaughter of John and Mary Sabina Huffman. See 𝕭𝖊𝖞𝖔𝖓𝖉 𝕲𝖊𝖗𝖒𝖆𝖓𝖓𝖆, v.1, n.3.

John Swindle and Hannah Weaver
Hannah, the daughter of Peter and Elisabeth Weaver, was unmarried when her father died and she was named as Hannah Weaver in his will. There are a number of baptisms at the German Lutheran church which clearly point to John Swindle as being the husband of Hannah Weaver. See "The Timothy Swindle Family" in Beyond Germanna, v.7, n.4.

Dorothea Tanner married Reginald Burdyne.
Catherine Tanner married Richard Burdyne.
Several articles on the Burdyne family are in Beyond Germanna. See Nancy Stanbery, "The Richard Burdyne Family," (v.7, n.5), Frances L. Franklin, "John Burdyne," (v.7, n.6), and Carol Ann Burdine, "The Burdyne/Burdine Family," (v.11, n.4; v.11, n.5; and also v.11, n.6 for a correction on page 657).

John Thomas, Jr. had four daughters and one son, Michael. John Thomas moved to North Carolina with Michael. DNA testing has proven that descendants of this Michael are descended from John Thomas, Sr.

Family of George Utz and Mary Käfer
The church records show two additional children in this family in addition to the ones usually given. There was a Michael and an Elizabeth who married George Willheit.

Michael Willheit
The early Germanna settler, Johann Michael Willheit, married Anna Maria Hengsteller as his second wife. She was the mother of all of his children. Michael's wife was not Mary Blankenbaker.

Nicholas Willheit and Mary Margaret Fisher
These two were husband and wife (Nicholas Fisher did not marry Elizabeth Fisher). See Ellen John, "Mary Margaret Fisher," Beyond Germanna, v.14, n.3.

John Willheit and Walburga Weaver
John Willheit, the son of the early immigrant Johann Michael Willheit, married Walburga Weaver, the daughter of Joseph Weaver and Susanna Clore. An analysis was made in "Burga," in Beyond Germanna, v.6, n.3.

References

General Secondary

Germanna Records
This is a series of about eighteen books of a historical or a genealogical nature. Some are being rewritten and new ones are being added. The publisher is The Memorial Foundation of Germanna Colonies in Virginia, Inc. For a current list, one may contact the Foundation at Post Office Box 279, Locust Grove, Virginia 22508 or one may access the Foundation on the Internet (www.germanna.org).

Beyond Germanna
In 1989, John Blankenbaker started publishing a newsletter/journal at the rate of six issues per year. Eventually, the publication became more of a research journal and less of a newsletter. The material pertained to the ancestry of the Germans, their trip to America, their life and families here, and the movement away from Germanna. It covered both the First and Second Colonies and other Germans up to 1800. After fifteen years and 917 pages of information, publication ceased. Many major libraries have bound copies of Beyond Germanna. Print copies are still available from John Blankenbaker but the recommended source media today is a compact disk (CD) in the Portable Document Format (pdf) which can be produced at a much lower cost. This is available from him or the Germanna Foundation. Readers would do well to note there are two distinctly different references here with similar names, Beyond Germanna and *Before Germanna*. The different type font used for the name Beyond Germanna is used to emphasize the difference between the two.

Before Germanna
Johni Cerny and Gary Zimmerman spent man-years in searching through the church records in southern Germany, Austria, and Switzerland for information pertaining to the ancestors of the Second Colony Germans and the later people. They found a great wealth of information which was published in a series of small volumes, starting in 1990, by American Lending Library, Bountiful, Utah. Unfortunately, the volumes are difficult to obtain now. The research was very time consuming and the sale of the copyrighted volumes provided the return on the effort and expense in researching the material. While the volumes are referenced in the work here and some information is given from them, the majority of the details of the research are not given unless another researcher has read the church records and is willing to have his information freely published.

"Hebron" Baptismal Register
The German Evangelical Lutheran Church of Culpeper County has a record of baptisms from 1750 to about 1813. The record is not entirely what one might assume and a detailed study of its history is necessary to understand it. The period from 1750 to 1776 was rewritten and in the process some errors were made and some families, who had moved away, were omitted. The great value of the Register is that the sponsors are given and these were not a random choice of people but were nearly always relatives of the same age as the parents. John Blankenbaker, with assistance from Nancy Moyers Dodge and Andreas Mielke, transcribed the original German records and added the relationship of the sponsors to the parents to the basic data. The result was privately printed by John Blankenbaker and is available from him or from the Germanna Foundation. For more about the interpretation of the original data, see "The Baptismal Register of the Evangelical Lutheran Church of Culpeper County." in Beyond Germanna, v.11, n.6.

"Hebron" Communion Lists
From 1775 to 1813, the names of people who partook of communion at the Evangelical Lutheran Church were recorded. The original records in German script are in the possession of the church and have been microfilmed. These were transcribed by John Blankenbaker, Andreas Mielke, and Nancy Moyers Dodge. Because of the pattern that the Lutherans used in the process of serving communion, these lists of names are a good approximation of the seating order. It has been found from known cases that one was most likely to sit with one's relatives, either by blood or by marriage. These associations extended down to the cousins and second cousins. A study of these people has been useful in deciding the names of some of the unknown women of the early church. The lists have been privately printed by John Blankenbaker and are available from him and from the Germanna Foundation.

Ortssippenbücher
These are a series of books (in German), each covering one village in Germany, which have very complete family histories. Unfortunately, only a few villages have them but more are being issued. For a complete list, search on the Internet with the keyword Ortssippenbuch. For an example of how they may be used, see "Ortssippenbücher," Beyond Germanna, v.14, n.5. The following are known to exist:

Oberöwisheim-Neuenbürg Ortssippenbuch. This has information on the Fleshman, Blankenbaker, Thomas, Schlucter, and Scheible families.

Sulzfeld Ortssippenbuch has information on the Zimmerman, Kabler, Yowell, and Long families.

The Culpeper Classes
In 1781 as the Revolutionary War campaigns were heating up in Virginia, the Commonwealth of Virginia decreed that the counties in Virginia were to raise quotas of troops. In old Culpeper County, consisting of today's Culpeper, Madison, and Rappahannock Counties, the assignment was 106 men. The militia in Culpeper County was divided into 106 classes with thirteen or fourteen men in each class. One name was drawn at random from each class and this person was to either serve or to find a substitute. One of the interesting aspects of this was that each class was centered on a small region so the men in one class were near neighbors. The original sheets at the Virginia State Library were transcribed and published in a booklet, *The Culpeper Classes*, which was privately published by John Blankenbaker. The book is available from him or from the Germanna Foundation.

The 1787 Census of Virginia, Culpeper County
In the absence of a census for Virginia in this time period, Netti Schreiner-Yantis and Florene Love put together a substitute based on the personal property tax lists for the year 1787. While basically it names only the heads of households, it does provide a wealth of economic data. In addition, the lists are in order of the route that the collector took while composing the lists which means that neighbors are listed together. An alphabetical index is provided. The publisher was Genealogical Books in Print at Springfield, Virginia in 1987.

Cavaliers and Pioneers
There are several volumes in this series which are abstracts of the land patents issued by the crown. The books are arranged chronologically. The earliest ones, up to 1732, were compiled by Nell Marion Nugent and published by the Virginia State Library. The balance were issued by the Virginia Genealogical Society. (The complete patents are available at the Virginia State Library and can be accessed via the Internet.) These very well indexed books are essential to locating the patents of which there are tens of thousands. The volumes of highest interest to researchers of the Germans in the Robinson River Valley are:

Volume III (1695–1732). This covers the initial settlement of the RRV.

Volume IV (1732–1742). This is the period of rapid expansion in the RRV.

Volume V (1741–1749). The activity in the RRV is tapering off.

Virginia Northern Neck Land Grants
While *Cavaliers and Pioneers* are abstracts of the first deeds issued by the crown (called patents), the grants are abstracts of the deeds issued by the Northern Neck proprietors. Many of the Second Colony landowners had both patents and grants as the area between the Rappahannock and Rapidan Rivers (The Great Fork) that was declared in 1743 to be a part of the Northern Neck. All of the grants are filed at the Virginia State Library and can be accessed via the Internet. Two volumes are of most interest to researchers in the Robinson River Valley:

(1694–1742). This covers Grant Books 2 through 5 and A through E.

(1742–1775). This covers Grant Books F through P. During the time covered by this book, the land in the Robinson River Valley was declared to be in the Northern Neck.

Images of the Patents and Grants
The web site http://www.lva.lib.va.us/ may be followed through as indicated below:

- What we have
- Land records
- Virginia land office patents and grants/Northern Neck grants and surveys
- Chronological (it is helpful to know the book and page number as can be found in the books above). This leads to images of the patents and grants which may be downloaded.

Northern Neck Warrants & Surveys
Peggy S. Joyner compiled, in several volumes, the Warrants and Surveys which were the first step in obtaining a grant in the Northern Neck. Because the warrants were often transferred between individuals, especially relatives, they are a source of genealogical information. Two of the volumes, number 1 and number 3, are of special interest because they include the Robinson River Valley area (all include the words *Northern Neck Warrants & Surveys* as the first words in the title):

Volume 1, Orange & Augusta Counties with Tithables, Delinquents, Petitioners, 1730–1754.

It is this volume that contains a list of tithables in 1739 in Orange County who lived in the area of modern Madison County.

Volume 3, Dunmore, Shenandoah, Culpeper, Prince William, Fauquier & Stafford Counties, 1710–1780.

In the discussion of the families, these works will be referred to as Joyner, v.1 or Joyner, v.3. A reference to the 1739 Orange County tithables is an alternative reference to Volume 1 of these books.

Margaret G. Davis, *Madison County, Virginia, A Revised History*. The Madison County Board of Supervisors issued this revision in 1977 to Claude Lindsay Yowell's *A History of Madison County, Virginia* which had been printed in 1927.

J. Vogt, T. W. Kethley, Jr. compilers, *Madison County Marriages, 1792–1850*, Iberian Publishing Co., Atlanta, 1983.

W. A. Crozier, ed., *Virginia County Records, Spotsylvania 1721–1800*, Genealogical Publishing Co. Baltimore, 1971.

W. W. Scott, *A History of Orange County*, Virginia, Regional Publishing Co. Baltimore, 1974.

R. T. Green, compiler, *Genealogical and Historical Notes on Culpeper County*, Virginia, Regional Publishing Co., Baltimore 1971. This is available from the Germanna Foundation.

Margaret G. Davis, *History of the Hebron Lutheran Church, Madison County, Virginia*. The original volume by Rev. William Peter Huddle was issued in 1907 and Margaret G. Davis added an *Epilogue* and the revised book was issued by Hebron Lutheran Church in 1990. It is available from the church or from the Germanna Foundation.

A History of the Lutheran Churches in Boone County, Kentucky, Rev. H. Lentz, privately printed, 1902. Many Germanna families are mentioned in this book.

The Lutheran Church in Virginia, 1717–1962, William Edward Eisenberg, Trustees of the Virginia Synod, Roanoke, Virginia, 1967.

Pastors and People: German Lutheran and Reformed Churches in the Pennsylvania Field, 1717–1793, Charles H. Glatfelter, The Pennsylvania German Society, Breinigsville, Pennsylvania, 1980.

Arthur Leslie Keith, "The German Colony of 1717," *William and Mary College Quarterly*, First Series, Vol. 26, pp. 79–95, 178–195, 234–249. This early work is the foundation of many later genealogies but it does contain some significant errors.

E. P. Alexander, ed., *The Journal of John Fontaine*, The Colonial Williamsburg Foundation, Williamsburg, 1972.

Klaus Wust, *The Virginia Germans*, The University Press of Virginia, Charlottesville, 1969.

W. A. Knittle, *Early Eighteenth Century Palatine Emigration*, Genealogical Publishing Co., Baltimore, 1970.

H. Schuricht, *History of the German Element in Virginia*, Genealogical Publishing Co., Baltimore 1977. Reprinted from original works of 1898 and 1900. Not recommended because of errors.

J. W. Wayland, *The German Element of the Shenandoah Valley of Virginia*, C. J. Carrier Co., Harrisonburg, Virginia, 1989 (reprinted from 1907 original).

S. Kercheval, A History of the Valley of Virginia, C. J. Carrier Co., Harrisonburg, Virginia, 1994 (reprinted from editions back to 1833).

P. S. Feller, *Forgotten Companions*, Historic Publications of Fredericksburg, Fredericksburg, Virginia 1982.

A. S. Fogleman, *Hopeful Journeys, 1717–1775*, University of Pennsylvania Press, Philadelphia, 1996.

A. G. Roeber, *Palatines, Liberty, and Property*, Johns Hopkins University Press, Baltimore, 1998.

Family Histories as Books

Amburgey Ancestry in America by Dorothy Amburgey Griffith. This was issued as a looseleaf notebook with updates as new information became available. For locating copies, check the Internet at the web site www.amburgeyfamily.org.

The Aylor Family by Sarah Aylor Lewis. Issued as a part of *Germanna Record* 12 by the Memorial Foundation of Germanna Colonists in Virginia, Inc.

Berry-Berrey Family, the Family of Elijah Berry by Lynn Berry Hamilton. Privately published by Mrs. C. H. Hamilton, Jr., 1980.

The Blankenbaker Family by Claude L. Yowell. Issued as a part of *Germanna Record* 13 by the Memorial Foundation of Germanna Colonists in Virginia, Inc.

Ancestors and Descendants of Felix and Mary Crisler Blankenbaker compiled by Patricia Blankenbeker Wally, privately published, 1985.

Blankenbeckler Family of Southwest Virginia and Related Families by William P. Blankenbeckler, 1941.

The Carpenter Family by B. C. Holtzclaw. Issued as a part of *Germanna Record* 11 by the Memorial Foundation of Germanna Colonies in Virginia, Inc.

Carpenter Ancestors and Cousins by Winton Burell Cain. Published by McDowell Publications, Utica, Kentucky, 1999.

The First Four Generations of the Michael Clore Family by Cathi Clore Frost. Issued as *Germanna Record* 16 by the Memorial Foundation of the Germanna Colonies in Virginia, Inc.

A History & Genealogy of John Fray of Culpeper County, Virginia by Florence Virginia Fray Lewis, 1958.

Genealogy of the Descendants of John Gar or More Particularly of His Son Andreas Gaar by John Wesley Garr and John Calhoun Garr, privately printed, 1894. This widely reprinted and used book is commonly called the *Garr Genealogy*.

Johannes Hoffman, A Compilation of the Ancestors and Descendants of the 1714 Immigrant to Germanna by Melvin L. Miller, 1996. Primarily tracing descendants of Daniel (grandson of 1714 John) Hoffman and his wife Margaret Catherine Bunger.

The Genealogy of the Holtzclaw Family 1540–1935, B. C. Holtzclaw, 1935, reprinted by The Memorial Foundation of the Germanna Colonies, Inc., 1990 as their *Germanna Record* 14. The two youngest sons of Jacob Holtzclaw lived in the Robinson River Valley.

(Revision of) The House Family by Gary Lee House, privately printed, 2004. *The House Family* was originally published by Susie House Cooper in 1972 but the print run was exhausted.

John Rouse of Virginia and His Descendants 1717–1980 by Nancy E. Rouse, 1982.

Our Families: Shuck, Fleshman, Sydenstricker, Smith, Lewis, Kincaid, Keister et al of West Virginia by Larry G. Shuck, Gateway Press, Baltimore, Maryland, 1995.

The Descendants of Richard Smith of Northumberland County, Virginia by Darryl J. Diemer. Privately published, 1995.

The Snyder Family by Claude L. Yowell. Issued as a part of *Germanna Record* 12 by the Memorial Foundation of the Germanna Colonies in Virginia, Inc. The author treats the families of John Snyder and Philip Snyder and considers that they are brothers which is probably not true. However, the work is valuable.

Stöver - Stoever - Staver - Stiver, by Vernon Stiver, 1992.

Swindall-Austin Families of Virginia and North Carolina 1622–1995 compiled by W. H. and T. M. Sutherland, published by Hetty Jean Swindall Sutherland 1995.

The Swindle Family - Three Centuries in America, B. Dale Swindle.

The Tanner Family by B. C. Holtzclaw. Issued as a part of *Germanna Record* 12 by the Memorial Foundation of Germanna Colonists in Virginia, Inc.

The Utz Family of Germanna by Claude L. Yowell. Issued as a part of *Germanna Record* 10 by the Memorial Foundation of Germanna Colonies in Virginia, Inc.

Descendants of Christley Vaught, Grandson of the Immigrant John Paul Vaught by Helen Spurlin and Mickey Martin, published by The Vaught Association of the United States, first edition, 1989.

The Wayland Family by B. C. Holtzclaw. Issued as a part of *Germanna Record* 11 by the Memorial Foundation of Germanna Colonies in Virginia, Inc.

Descendants of Peter Weaver, The Immigrant by B. C. Holtzclaw. Issued as a part of *Germanna Record* 13 by the Memorial Foundation of the Germanna Colonists in Virginia, Inc.

The 300 Year History and Genealogy of One Weaver Family by Edward A. Weaver, Jr., privately printed, probably in 1997.

The First Four Generations of the Wilhoit-Wilhite Family in America by John Connie Wilhite, Jr. Issued as a part of *Germanna Record* 13 by the Memorial Foundation of the Germanna Colonies in Virginia, Inc.

The Yager Family of Germanna by Claude L. Yowell, issued within *Germanna Record* 10 by the Memorial Foundation of Germanna Colonies in Virginia, Inc.

Following John, Documenting the Identity and Path of John Yager by Elizabeth Yates Johnson, Gateway Press, Baltimore, Maryland, 2004.

Yowell and Related Families by Ann Yowell Cook, privately printed, 1994.

Hebron Lutheran Church

Hebron Lutheran Church stands peacefully on a small hill overlooking the fertile meadows along the Robinson River east of the Blue Ridge Mountains in Madison County, Virginia. In 1725 about a hundred German immigrants moved to farms surrounding the site of this church. Their first house of worship was a log building which they built soon after moving here (to the left of this building). They were without a minister until the spring of 1733 when Johann Caspar Stöver, Sr. became their minister. A fund-raising trip in Europe yielded enough money to build this church in 1740, buy a farm, and secure slaves to work on the farm.

The original building of 1740 was rectangular and forms the transept of the modern building. Late in the eighteenth century a nave was added which converted the church into a cruciform plan. In 1802, an organ made by David Tannenberg in Lititz, Pennsylvania, was installed and is still used in the worship services today.

The eighteenth-century ministers were: Johann Caspar Stöver. Sr. from 1732 to 1738; Georg Samuel Klug from 1739 to 1764; Johannes Schwarbach from 1766 to 1774; Catechist Heinrich Moeller from 1774–1775; Jacob Franck from 1775 to 1778; J. Michael Schmidt, a native son, from 1782 to 1785; Christian Streit (supply pastor) from 1786 to 1788; William Carpenter, a native son, from 1789 to 1813.

Family historians appreciate the birth, baptism, and communion records. The Baptismal Book has birth and baptism records from 1750 through the first decade of the 1800 though unfortunately not all of the births in this period are recorded. From late 1775 and continuing for more than 35 years, there are lists of the people who took communion here. These documents, mostly in German, are kept in a bank vault for safety.

This is the oldest building in use as a Lutheran house of worship in America. It even predates the Lutheran church at Trappe, Pennsylvania, built under the leadership of Melchior Muhlenberg. Hebron Church is the work of dedicated lay people who kept the congregation together for sixteen years until Stöver became their minister and then for five years more while he was absent in Europe.

Adjacent to the church is a modern social hall and educational building. The complex stands outside the town of Madison, Virginia. Visitors are always welcomed.

Original Culpeper County

The original Culpeper County included the land between the Rappahannock River and the Rapidan River (which was the South Fork of the Rappahannock) up to the crest of the Blue Ridge Mountains. All of this area was referred to as the Great Fork. By the time that Culpeper County was formed, it was considered to lie in the Northern Neck which was the land between the Rappahannock and the Potomac Rivers. Madison County was split off from the southwest corner of Culpeper in 1792 and Rappahannock County was split off from the northwest corner in 1833.

The Robinson River watershed does not match the boundaries of Madison County perfectly, especially in the south where there were many English settlers. The Germans were almost entirely confined to the Robinson River Valley. There were some exceptions at the Madison and Rappahannock boundary where a few Germans lived in the area that became Rappahannock County.

Fort Germanna was in the bend of the Rapidan that is just below the words "Great Fork" above. Fairfax was the old name of the town of Culpeper. Some First Colony members and their friends and relatives had land in the Little Fork. From where the Rappahannock and Rapidan split to the northern most point of the original Culpeper County is about 44 miles. From where the Second Colony was living (the area above the word "Rapidan") to where they built their log church in the Robinson River Valley is about 22 miles though the route they took may have been longer.

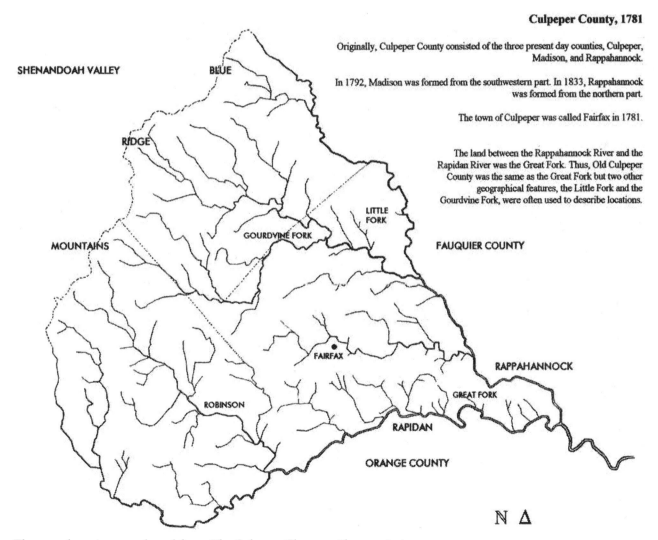

The map here is reproduced from *The Culpeper Classes* with permission.

Culpeper County was formed from Orange County in 1748. Orange was formed from Spotsylvania County in 1734. Spotsylvania was formed in 1721/2 from Essex and other counties. Arguably, the Second Germanna Colony people were the first people to live in what became Culpeper County. A few of the early Second Colony people lived in Essex, Spotsylvania, Orange, Culpeper, and Madison. Zachariah Blankenbaker, for example, was born in Germany and died in Madison County.

Part II

Family History Summaries

(Alphabetical without regard to the time of arrival)

Altap. Elizabeth Altap communed at the German Lutheran Church 29 AUG 1784.

Amberger (Ambergey very often in America). Hans <u>Conrad</u> Amberger was born 2 FEB 1683 in Bönnigheim, Württemberg. He became a vine dresser and married Anna Catharina (Schulnig) Rohleder on 13 NOV 1714 at Bönnigheim. She was a widow with a daughter, Maria Magdalena, born 1708. Two children born to Conrad and Magdalena did not survive. For more German history, see "The Ancestry of the Snyder, Amburger, Kerker and Kapler Families," *Before Germanna*, v. 8. Anna Catharina and her daughter did not reach Virginia since Conrad's proof of importation, 15 May 1736, does not mention that he was accompanied by anyone (Brockman, *Orange County Families*, v.1, p.50). Conrad was sued by Spotswood in 1724 for £32 but the jury awarded Spotswood only 2£ 13s 1½d. Peter Weaver used Conrad's head right in taking a grant of land 20 JUL 1736.

Conrad married Barbara_____, perhaps about the time of the lawsuit. Under the name Connorat Ambyon, he was granted 445 acres 28 SEP 1728 (*Virginia Patent Book 13*, p. 327) which was located southeast of Mount Pony on Potato Run in present day Culpeper County. This land may be identified as being south of Stevensburg along the east side of road 661 and north of road 723. There was another grant of 400 acres 20 JUN 1733 (*Virginia Patent Book 15*, p. 51) on branches of Deep Run and Buttock Run to Conrade Amburger. This land was in the Robinson River community though it was about eight miles northeast of the German Lutheran Church and straddles the line dividing today's Culpeper and Madison Counties. Another 400 acre grant (*Virginia Patent Book 17*, p.140) in the same general vicinity was taken jointly by Joseph Bloodworth and Conrade Amberger on 20 AUG 1736. He sold the first grant of 445 acres near Mt. Pony to Christopher Zimmerman 22 SEP 1737 (*Orange D.B. 2*, p.100) and 200 acres to Joseph Cotton 22 NOV 1738 (*Orange D.B. 3*, p.34).

Conrad Amberger died in Orange County in 1742. His widow Barbara was appointed administratrix 23 JUL 1742 with Christopher Zimmerman as security (*Orange W.B. 1*, p.229). The valuation of his estate showed personal property of just over £34. One other record of Barbara Amberger occurs at this same time. She was ordered by the Orange County Court to teach Anne Stuart the fine arts of reading, writing, and spinning. Presumably this was in English, suggesting that was her native language.

Conrad had at least one son, John Amburger, whose mother was probably Barbara. In a grant for John Towles, John Ambargo was a chain carrier in 1747 which suggests he was born before 1730. In a grant for Thomas Kennerly in 1747 on branches of Deep and Devils Runs, adjacent to Joseph Bloodworth, Samuel Coleman, Conrade Amburger (deceased by then), and John Paul Vaught, the chain carriers were John Amburger and John Towles. In still another 1747 grant to John Kilvy (Kilby) on branches of Deep Run, the chain carriers were Thomas Kennerly and John Ambargo. The repeated appearance of the names of John Towles and Thomas Kennerly suggests there may have been a relationship between these families. In 1759 John was a witness to James Gillison's will. After that he appears frequently in the land records. The Culpeper Rental of 1764 shows John Amburger with 400 acres (apparently 200 acres of the 1733 grant to Conrad and 200 acres being half of the joint grant to Conrad Amburger and Joseph Bloodworth in 1736). John Amburger married Anne_____in 1750. They probably had three children, Anne, born about 1751; William, born about 1756; and John, Jr., born 1758 (see Revoltuionary War Pension application R174). Francis Lucas and his wife Elizabeth transferred 82 acres to the Ambergers 20 OCT 1763 (*Culpeper D.B. D*, p.301). In 1765 John and Anne gave 100 acres to their daughter, Anne, and son-in-law, John Hawkins. Not long after this, the mother Anne apparently died and John married Margaret_____. John and Margaret sold the 82 acres 20 JUL 1769 to Thomas Johnston (*Culpeper D.B. E*, p.709) which had been owned by Francis Lucas and his wife Elizabeth. In 1774 John and Margaret sold 300 acres from Conrad Amberger's patent. In JAN 1772 John Amburger and Margaret his wife deeded 50 acres to William Watts (*Culpeper D.B. F*, p.494), and, on 3 DEC 1774 they deeded 300 acres adjoining Bloodworth and Hawkins to Zacharias Wall (*Culpeper D.B. G*, p.469). On 20 FEB 1775 John Hawkins and Ann his wife deeded to John Broyle 100 acres, part of a tract which had been given to Hawkins by John Amburger (*Culpeper D.B. G*, p.463).

About 1775, John Ambergey, Sr., John Ambergey, Jr., Tim Holdway (Holloway?) and John Hawkins moved to Surry County, North Carolina. With a change in boundaries, the county became Wilkes County. John, Sr. and John, Jr. both procured land. In the census of 1787, both Johns are listed. John, Sr. may have had by his second wife a daughter, Margaret who as a "Peggy Amburga" joined the Roaring River Baptist Church in 1789. John Ambergey, Jr. married Elizabeth Hamons (3 JUL 1787) and twelve children are known for them.

More information about the Amburgeys is to be found in Dorothy Amburgey Griffith's book, *Amburgey Ancestry in America*, and her assistance here is acknowledged. She wrote an article, "Conrad Amberger" which appeared in v.6, n.6, of Beyond Germanna. The Ambergey collection of documents has been microfilmed by the Kentucky Historical Society and is available in Frankfort, Kentucky.

Some German researchers find that the name is spelled Anberger in the early records.

Aylor (Öhler in German). Hans Jacob Öhler was born at Botenheim, Württemberg 3 MAY 1688. He married Anna Magdalena, the only child of Hans Heinrich Schneider (Henry Snider) and Anna Dorothea Schilling of Botenheim who were 1717 immigrants to Virginia. Jacob and Anna Magdalena did not come to Virginia at that time. Two children of Jacob and Anna Magdalena Öhler, Georg Heinrich, born 3 OCT 1718, and Elisabetha Catharina, born 6 MAR 1720, are found in the Botenheim records. More information from Germany is given in "The Ancestry of the Aylor, Castler, Manspiel, and Reiner Families," *Before Germanna*, v. 7. Other workers, in particular Alfred Benz, have found more ancestors in the *Ehningen Ortssippenbuch*.

Hans Reichert, the maternal grandfather of Anna Dorothea Schilling, was born about 12 NOV 1629 in Ehningen in Württemberg (Ehningen is about 28 miles south of Botenheim). He married on 25 NOV 1651 Anna Magdalena Böringer in Botenheim where the new family settled. Hans Reichert died 25 JUL 1687 at Botenheim. The father of the previous Hans Reichert was another Hans Reichert who was born about 28 NOV 1609 in Ehningen. His wife was Agnes for whom no additional information is available. The father of the last Hans Reichert, Ulrich Reichert, was born 8 JAN 1577 in Ehningen. He married 20 AUG 1600 Magdalena Holl who was born in Schwieberdingen in Württemberg. This village lies between Botenheim and Ehningen. The parents of Ulrich Reichert were another Ulrich Reichert and his wife Barbara. Their marriage was before 1567. Magdalena Holl's mother was Lore Holl and the absence of any information on the father may indicate he was not publically known. These findings were presented by Dr. Donald J. Martin et al in "Extensions to the Aylor-Snyder Ancestry in Germany," Beyond Germanna, v. 15, n.4.

In Virginia, records of the family are scarce and indirect. There is no land grant to or naturalization of John Jacob Aylor nor is there a naturalization of the son, Henry, who was born in Germany. Henry Snider's will in 1742 mentions that his daughter is a widow with a son, Henry Aylor, and with a daughter, Elizabeth, who was already married to Christopher Tanner. Anna Magdalena Aylor, after 1742, became the second wife of John Harnsberger, the 1717 colonist, and is mentioned in his will in 1760, along with her two children, Henry Aylor and Elizabeth Tanner. The son, Henry Aylor, married Margaret Thomas, the daughter of John Thomas, Sr. Henry died in Madison County in the early 1800s leaving six children:

> Henry who married Barbara Carpenter,
> Jacob who married Frances Murray,
> Abraham who married Mary Shearer,
> Susannah wife of James Murray,
> Delilah wife of Muscoe Newman, and
> Magdalena wife of Adam Delph.

Henry Aylor, the father, was a witness (1760) to the will of John Michael Smith (Jr.). The men had married sisters. He was named as co-executor in Philip Hoop's (Hupp) will (1761). Henry Aylor's wife, Margaret, was a first cousin of another Margaret Thomas who was a daughter-in-law of Philip Hupp. Henry Aylor was an appraiser of the estates of Peter Clore, Henry Huffman, and George Utz, in 1763, 1766, and 1767, respectively. Henry Eiler had a 34 acre grant for which Christopher Tanner and Michael Thomas were chain carriers (Joyner, v.1, p.4). Christopher Tanner was a brother-in-law of Henry and Michael Thomas was the uncle of Henry's wife (or perhaps other possibilities). Though the survey was made in 1748, the grant was not issued until 1753 (*Northern Neck Land Grants H*, p.410).

Baccon. Maria Baccon communed at the Lutheran Church on Easter 1777. She sat with Mary Utz and Elizabeth Böhme.

Bach (Back). Hermann Bach left Freudenberg in Nassau-Siegen in 1738 and traveled to America on the ill-fated ship *Oliver* which had a great loss of life (two out of three passengers). For the story of this voyage, see Klaus Wust, "The Year of the Destroying Angels – 1738," Beyond Germanna, v. 10, n.1 and following issues. In Germany, Hermann Bach had married Anna Margaret Hausmann but due to the great loss of life on the voyage it cannot be said with certainty that she was his wife in Virginia. He did have two sons in Virginia, Henry and John, who married daughters of John Huffman. For more information, see *Germanna Record* 3 and 5.

Bädl. Margaretha Bädl (Bädi?) communed at the Lutheran Church on 23 NOV 1788. She is listed between Jemima Holtzclaw and Susanna Holtzclaw.

Ballenger (the origin and the spelling of this name are unknown). Andrew Ballenger was sued by Spotswood but the suit was dismissed 8 JUL 1724 because neither party appeared at court. His inclusion in the law suits is the basis of his claim to be a member of the Second Colony. He does not appear in the records after 1724. He may have been a bachelor immigrant in 1717 and died without issue. On the other hand, it is possible that he was the father of Edward Ballenger, who was granted 400 acres of land (*Virginia Patent Book 15*, p.59) in 1733 adjacent to Joseph Bloodworth on Deep Run in the Robinson River Valley. Edward was married to his wife Mary in 1736, indicating that he was probably born at least as early as 1715. On 4 MAY 1736 Edward Ballenger of Spotsylvania County deeded to Joseph Bloodworth of Orange County 400 acres of land in Orange and Edward's wife Mary gave up her dower 18 MAY 1736 (*Orange D.B. 1*, p.249). In return, on 17 MAY 1736, Joseph Bloodworth deeded to Edward Ballenger 200 acres in Orange County adjoining Christopher Zimmerman in the Mt. Pony area (*D.B. 1*, p. 253). In 1764, Frederick Zimmerman had a grant on the east side of Mt. Pony which adjoined Edward Ballenger, Sr. and Nicholas Kabler. Edward Ballenger continued to live in Orange (later Culpeper) County all his life and died there in 1780. His will, dated 9 DEC 1779 and probated 20 MAR 1780 (*Culpeper W.B. B*, p. 360), mentions his son Edward; son-in-law Stokely Towles and daughter Margery Tolls; grandson Gabriel Wilhoit; daughter Agatha Kilbee; daughter Susannah; and makes residuary legatees "my children," Francis, John, Edward, Mary, Margery, and Agatha. A James Ballenger was deeded 405 acres of land by John Threlkeld and Nancy his wife on 17 MAR 1777 (*Culpeper D. B. H*, p.403). He is not mentioned in Edward's will, but may have been a son who predeceased his father. Edward Ballenger's grandson, Gabriel Wilhoit, was the son of Michael Wilhoit, who was a son of Tobias Wilhoit, the eldest son of Michael Willheit, the early Germanna settler. Families whose names occur in connection with the Ballengers often are or have an association with known Germanna families.

From the Culpeper Will Books, Edward Ballenger was an appraiser of John Blanton (1750). Margaret Connor in her will leaves an equal part of her clothing to Sarah Balynger, 1745. Francis Balleger and Sarah Balleger were witnesses to the will of Elias Powell (1756). Francis Ballenger was an appraiser (Frederick Zimmerman was another appraiser) of the estate of Elias Powell.

Barlow (uncertain spelling in Germany). Christopher Barlow came to Virginia in 1717 with his wife Pauera (Barbara) according to his proof of importation which does not mention any children. He was not sued by Col. Spotswood nor did he have a land grant in his own name. On 5 MAY 1730 Christopher Parlow and Cyracus

Fleshman were freed from levies (*Spotsylvania O.B. 1724–30*, p.388). Perhaps this does not indicate that Barlow was an elderly man, since Barlow seems to have had several sons, all born after his arrival in this country. He was perhaps excused from taxes because of some physical disability.

Matthias Beller was granted 400 acres of land 24 JUN 1726 jointly with Matthias Smith, the 1717 colonist (*Virginia Patent Book 12*, p. 480) which might indicate kinship between the two men. (Perhaps Matthias Beller was not of age and Matthias Smith joined in the patent as a "guardian.") At present Matthias is regarded as Christopher's eldest son. On 19 OCT 1747 Matthew Smith deeded to Jacob Barlow 200 acres, half of the patent to Matthias Smith and Matthias Beller of 24 JUN 1726 (*Culpeper D.B. A*, p.51). This strongly suggests that both Christopher Barlow and his presumed eldest son, Matthias, were both dead by 1747 (Matthias without issue), and that Jacob Barlow, the eldest surviving son, was heir of the land. Jacob must have been born at least as early as 1726. In the 1739 Orange County tithables, no Barlow is listed. Matthias Smith is included with two tithes.

There is no mention of Christopher Barlow, the immigrant, after 1730, but he appears to have had at least four sons, Christopher, Adam, Jacob, Matthias, and there may have been another son, John, see below. On 18 JAN 1753 Jacob Barlow and Mary his wife deeded to Christopher Barlow 100 acres, half of the land deeded him by Matthew Smith (*Culpeper D. B. A*, p.477).

Adam Barlow, probably the youngest son, was married to Mary, daughter of Michael Smith, Jr. and Anna Magdalena Thomas as early as 1759 as shown by the German Lutheran Church records. Michael Smith made a deed of gift on 15 APR 1762 of 100 acres of land to his son-in-law, Adam Barlow (*Culpeper D.B. D*, p.3). Adam and his brother Christopher were foot soldiers in the Culpeper militia in 1756 during the French and Indian War. Adam Barlow died in 1786. A tentative list of children for Adam and Mary is:

Joshua who married Rhoda Thomas of English descent,

Rachel who married Conrad Kuenzle,

Jemima who married Dietrich Hoffman,

Leah,

Anne who married Moses Harbinson,

Ambrose who married Ann Smith,

Adam,

Enoch, and

perhaps Michael.

Christopher Barlow, the presumed son of the immigrant, died and a copy of his will is filed in Madison County, Virginia in 1810 (*W.B. 2*, p.249) and in Boone County, Kentucky (*W.B. B*, p.82). (Apparently Christopher wrote his will in Madison County, Virginia and later moved to Kentucky where there is a record of an estate sale for him. The witnesses to the will lived in Madison County, so the will was proven there and a copy was transferred to Kentucky.) This will names children:

Joseph,

Ephraim,

Michael,

Aaron Barlow who married Catherine Beemon 28 APR 1801. Three of their children are in the Baptismal Register under the name Perler,

Daniel,

Mary who married John Millbanks, and

Margaret who married John Delph, son of George Conrad Delph.

Christopher Barlow's wife was Catherine, a daughter of Peter Fleshman and a granddaughter of Cyriacus Fleshman. This is shown in 1773 when Adam Cook, Christopher Barlow, and Christopher (Christian) Reiner agreed to take the estate of the deceased Peter Fleshman at the valuation of George Hume, Adam Wayland, and John Zimmerman and to make bond in case any one of them forfeited the agreement (*Culpeper D.B. G*, p.222).

This agreement was signed not only by the three men mentioned, but also by John and Peter Fleshman, sons of the deceased. Ellie Caroland wrote a note on the family of John Millbanks and Mary Barlow, "Mary Barlow Millbank," Beyond Germanna, v.3, n.1.

Jacob Barlow, the eldest surviving son of the immigrant Christopher, last appears in the records of Culpeper County in a deed in 1779, at which time he and his wife Mary (maiden name unknown) were living in Rockingham County, Virginia. (*Culpeper D.B. I*, p.277). The children of Jacob and Mary appear to be:

Lewis who married Mary Graves,

Christopher, Jr. who married Barbara Mayer,

John,

William Henry who married Jane Marshal,

Cornelius,

perhaps Elizabeth who married a Taylor, and

perhaps Samuel who married Elizabeth_____.

In Rowan County, North Carolina, John Gerhard/Garrett left a will dated 5 AUG 1757 which mentions several Germanna people including daughter Mary Myers (widow of George Blankenbaker and wife of Michael Myers) and the daughter Cathrin the wife of Martin Wollox (Walk). One of the witnesses to the will was John Parlor and the suggestion is that John Parlor may be another member of the Barlow family. If he were a Barlow, he might be a fifth son. See also the Klug history and the petition for a land grant which included John Barler as one of the petitioners.

The lack of good evidence at many points in the family history of the Barlows shows that more research is needed.

[There is an ongoing DNA study to help in separating the several Barlow families who have different national origins. This has been a material help to identify descendants of the Germanna Barlows. These results are available on the Internet, search on "Barlow."]

Battern (also Batten and Batton). John Battern, who probably was not a German, married Ann (Rhoda Ann?) Cook in Culpeper County on 11 May 1791 so that his descendants qualify as Germanna colonists. Anna Battern appears in the German Lutheran Church communion list for the 12th Sunday after Trinity in 1791. The evidence implies strongly that Ann was of German descent, the daughter of Adam Cook and Barbara Fleshman, who was born about 1774. She died in Madison County 29 Dec 1851. John Battern is given a birth date of 23 NOV 1765 in Culpeper County. His father was probably George Battern and his mother was Elizabeth_____. John died 17 June 1819 in Madison County. They had twelve children who married into the following Germanna families: Lipp, House, Wilhoit (twice), Tanner, Huffman, Wayman, Finks, Broyles, and Clore. Other families are recognizable Robinson River Valley names. For more information, see Linda Nelson et al, "The Battern Family of Madison County, Virginia," Beyond Germanna, v.14, n.5, p.830.

Baumgardner (many descendants are known as Bumgarner). Johann <u>Frederick</u> Baumgardner was baptized 5 JUN 1706 in Schwaigern, Württemberg as the son of Hans Jacob Baumgartner and Catherine Willheit. Catherine was the sister of Johann Michael Willheit, an early Virginia immigrant. (Frederick had a younger brother, Gottfried, who settled in Pennsylvania.) Frederick arrived in Philadelphia on 19 SEP 1732 on the *Johnson*. He soon went to the Robinson River area where he (as Frederick Pamgarner) received a patent for 400 acres on 20 JUL 1736 in the Great Fork of the Rappahannock River on a branch of Deep Run (*Virginia Patent Book 17*, p.122). Frederick married Catherine whose maiden name is unknown. On 27 JAN 1743 he was naturalized along with his neighbor Peter Fleshman whose son Robert later married Frederick Baumgardner's daughter Dorothy.

The will of Frederick Bumgarner, dated 8 SEP 1745, in Orange County devised 100 acres each to his four sons and to his daughter Dorothy the value of her share. Besides the five children named in the will, there was a sixth child, Eve, who was born posthumously in 1746. Administration was granted Catherine 27 FEB 1745(OS).

Catherine then married John Deer (Hirsch) who died in 1781. Eve and Dorothy were treated equally in the will of John Deer and neither was called a child. The Baumgardner sons obtained a grant (6 AUG 1766) on their father's (erroneously stated to be Adam's) 400 acre tract patented 20 JUL 1736 finding, in the process, that it contained 993 acres (*Northern Neck Land Grants N*, p.94). The six children of Frederick and Catherine are:

> Adam married about 1766/68 Elizabeth Clore,
>
> George never married and his estate went to his siblings. He moved to Washington County, Pennsylvania about 1769,
>
> Frederick married Sarah Swindell and left a will in Madison County dated 1817 which names heirs,
>
> Joel never married and he left his land in his will of 3 OCT 1773 to his mother "Catron Deer" and at her death to his brother Frederick,
>
> Dorothy married about 1755/58 Robert Fleshman, the son of Peter Fleshman and grandson of Cyriacus Fleischmann and Anna Barbara Schön. Robert and Dorothy moved to Greenbrier County, Virginia (now West Virginia) in 1790.
>
> Adam Bumgardner married about 1766/68 Elizabeth Clore. Adam's estate was appraised 19 APR 1770 in Culpeper County. In the division of his estate 15 NOV 1779 it is noted that John Baker (Becker) married the widow of Adam and a guardian was appointed for "the boy." Elizabeth and John Baker were married in 1770 and the German Lutheran Church Register implies Jesse (born 6 JUN 1769) is the son of Johannes and Elizabeth Becker but several records determine that Jesse was the son of Adam Baumgardner. Elizabeth and John Becker had several children of their own as given by the church records.
>
> George Bumgarner presumably never married as his estate went to this siblings as heirs. He moved to Washington County, Pennsylvania about 1769.
>
> Eve (born posthumously) married Mordecai Boughan and left ten children. (This interesting story was developed by Sally T. Baugh as "Eve Baumgardner Boughan" in 𝔅𝔢𝔶𝔬𝔫𝔡 𝔊𝔢𝔯𝔪𝔞𝔫𝔫𝔞, v.3, n.4, p.161.)

Information about the Baumgarder family is to be found in these locations: "Johann Frederick Baumgartner" by Ardys V. Hurt in 𝔅𝔢𝔶𝔬𝔫𝔡 𝔊𝔢𝔯𝔪𝔞𝔫𝔫𝔞, v.1, n.5 with credit to Mary F. Mickey; Larry Shuck, *Our Families*; in "The Ancestry of the Christler, Baumgartner, Deer, Dieter, and Lotspeich Families," *Before Germanna*, v.11 by Zimmerman and Cerny; and *Germanna Record* 6 by B.C. Holtzclaw.

Becker (perhaps Bacher, Beker, or Becker). Johannes Becker and his wife Elizabeth had four children baptized at the German Lutheran Church from 1769 to 1776. The first of these, Jesse, was not John Becker's son but was his wife's son by Adam Baumgardner, her first husband. This conclusion is supported by documentation in the Baumgardner family. For the baptism of Jesse, Frederick Baumgardner, the uncle of Jesse, was included. That Elizabeth was a Clore is supported by the inclusion of Clores as sponsors at each of the baptisms.

A Samuel Becker was in the Orange 1739 tithe list next to Nicholas Christopher.

Beemon (Boehme or Böhme is perhaps the German spelling of the name). Daniel Beemon was probably born about 1750–55 as his first child was born in 1777. A Harman "Bahmer," who witnessed a deed from Matthew Smith to Jacob Barler in 1747 in Culpeper County (*Culpeper D.B. A*, p.51) was perhaps his father. Elizabeth Boehme, who was a communicant at the German Lutheran Church in 1775 and was a sponsor for Daniel's son John in 1779, was probably his mother. In the civil records the name is usually spelled Beemon or sometimes Beemy. Daniel Boehme signed the German Lutheran Church covenant 27 MAY 1779 but used the name Daniel Beemon when he signed the petition of the church members 22 OCT 1776 to be freed from levies to the state church.

His wife was named Nancy, and judging by the sponsors of their children, it would appear that she was a daughter of Philip Chelf. Daniel Beemon last appears in the records of Madison County, Virginia in 1808. The family moved to Boone County, Kentucky. On 2 JUL 1810, John Beemon and Peggy his wife of Boone County deeded

46 acres to Samuel Carpenter. Nine children of Daniel Beemon (Boehme) are shown in the Robinson River Lutheran Church records as follows:

- Susannah was born 28 SEP 1777 and she married (as Susannah Beemy) Daniel Barlow on 2 FEB 1797. In the marriage bond, Daniel Beemon was called her father. Daniel Barlow was the son of Christopher Barlow,
- John Beemon was born 31 DEC 1779 and he married Margaret Zimmerman (born 1 AUG 1782), the daughter of Christopher Zimmerman and his wife, Mary Tanner. This family moved to Boone County, Kentucky,
- Joshua Beemon was born 14 FEB 1781,
- Catharine Beemon was born 4 FEB 1783 and married Aaron Barlow in Madison County, Virginia on 28 APR 1801. Aaron was the son of Christopher Barlow. Daniel Beemon was on the bond. In the Lutheran Baptismal Register, the surname is given as Perler,
- Nancy Beemon, born 28 JUL 1785,
- Rosina Beemon, born 27 DEC 1787,
- Daniel Beemon, born 22 OCT 1790,
- Mary Beemon, born 13 DEC 1795,
- Anna Beemon, born 18 JAN 1799.

The information on the Beemon family comes principally from the German Lutheran Church records. B.C. Holtzclaw left a short typescript on the family which was used in the preparation of this section. An analysis of the family, in two articles, starts in Beyond Germanna, v.4, n.5, p.221. The elder Daniel had sisters in the community, perhaps as many as four, Catherine, Elizabeth, Margaret and Eva. There are opportunities for further research on the family.

Bender. Johann <u>Adam</u> Bender married Demilia Broyles. Their son, Heseckiel, born 16 JUN 1776, was baptized 28 JUL 1776. Sponsors were Andrew Carpenter and his wife Barbara, Moses Broyles, and Elizabeth Broyles. Adam Bender was a communicant 25 DEC 1775. On Easter Sunday (7 APR) in 1776, Adam Bender was a communicant while Demilia was confirmed. On Pentecost in 1776, Adam Bender was a communicant and at Christmas in 1776, Adam Bender and wife were communicants. Adam Pander signed the petition in the fall of 1776 made by the church members to be freed of the support of the state church. He is not found though as a signer of the church constitution of May 1776.

The father of Adam Bender was Johann Jorg (John George) Bender who was killed during the French and Indian War at what is now called "Indian Fort Stock Farm," in Shenandoah County, Virginia that is still owned by his descendants. The settlement was called Ft. Painter and Paintersville. Johann Jorg's wife, son, and five daughters were captured by Indians and held captive for two years. The wife, son, and two daughters were then released. The captivity is documented in the Revolutionary War pension application of Adam Painter in which he notes he served five tours of duty. The pension application states he lived in Culpeper County and that he left there about 1782 and moved to what is now Washington County, Tennessee. The tax records of 1783 for Washington County, North Carolina, (now Greene County, Tennessee) show Adam and his son Ezekiel. "Old Adam," as he was sometimes called, served in the War of 1812 for 14 months with his son Ezekiel.

There were other children besides Ezekiel who lived and died in Greene County, Tennessee. One, Aaron, moved to Missouri. Ezekiel moved to Georgia and then Alabama where he died.

More information on the Bender/Painter family is from *A History of the Valley of Virginia* by Samuel Kercheval.

Benneger. See Pinnegar.

Berry. John Berry (about 1700 to 1779) married Jemima_____. They lived in the Robinson River Valley and were in contact with many Germans as their descendants married several Germanna people. Of their children (an incomplete account here),

John Berry, Jr. married Susanna Smith, the daughter of John Michael Smith, Jr. and Anna Magdalena Thomas. An article on a son of John, Jr. by Lynnea Dickinson, "Research on the Jesse Berry and Anna Miller Family," appeared in Beyond Germanna, v.13, n.3).

Anthony married Elisabeth Thomas, the daughter of Michael Thomas (see "The Wife of Anthony Berry," Beyond Germanna, v.6, n.3).

Elijah married Anna Hurt, the daughter of James and Sarah Hurt of Culpeper County. (The previous Michael Thomas married as his second wife, Eve Susanna Margaret Hurt/Hart. It appears there were connections between the Berry family and the Thomas family.)

Jeriah married Adam Yager, Jr. who was born 9 MAY 1738. Adam, Jr. was the son of the young 1717 immigrant Adam Yager.

Acrey or Acra, the son of John Berry, Sr., married Mary Hurt/Hart and his children married people from the Yager, Finks, and Thomas families.

Grandchildren of John Berry, Sr. married Broyles. For more information on the Berry family see, Lynn Berry Hamilton, *Berry–Berrey Family*, privately published, 1980.

Beyerback. Henry Frederick Beyerback was deeded land by Peter Weaver in 1742 and 1744 and died early in 1746. In his will he mentions his wife, Hannah, and his daughter, Catherine Jones. He nominated Richard Burdyne as an executor but Burdyne refused to serve. His origins in Germany have been found and the rich history is documented in "The Ancestry of the Yager, Stolts, Crees, and Beyerbach Families," *Before Germanna*, v.10. As Heinrich Friedrich Beyerbach, town watchman and vine-dresser, he married Anna Maria and had one child christened at Öhringen, Württemberg. This was their daughter, Anna Catharina, born 29 SEP 1716, who married_____Jones in Virginia.

Blankenbaker, Balthasar (many spellings in Europe such as Blanckenbühler). The origins of Balthasar Blankenbaker from Neuenbürg, Baden have been elaborated by many researchers, see Part I and the section on the Blankenbühlers. No marriage in Germany was found for Balthasar but he was married to Margaret when he came to Virginia but without any children, see the Spotswood importation list. Balthasar was accompanied by his two brothers (Nicholas and Matthias) and their families, perhaps his sister (Anna Maria) and her Thomas family, his mother (Anna Barbara Schön) and step-father (Cyriacus Fleshman) and three half-siblings (Henry Schluchter, Catherine Fleshman and Peter Fleshman). He was sued by Col. Spotswood in 1724. From 1726 to 1733, he received three grants of land in the Robinson River valley with the rest of the 1717 group. These were for 157 acres (*Virginia Patent Book 12*, p.483), for 360 acres (*Virginia Patent Book 14*, p.40) and for 160 acres (*Virginia Patent Book 15*, p.19) under the names Balthasar Blankenbucher, Paul Plunkepee, Paltas Blancumbaker, respectively. The first of the patents was on both sides of the Robinson River in the midst of grants to the people from Neuenbürg. The last two grants were on the back side of Garr's Mountain on branches of Pass Run. On 17 DEC 1759 he made a deed of gift to Adam Wayland, "his wife Elizabeth being my daughter." His will, dated 7 JAN 1762 and probated in Culpeper County 1 APR 1774, mentions only his wife, Anna Margaret, and his two daughters, Anna Barbara, wife of Lewis Fisher, and Elizabeth, wife of Adam Wayland. Balthasar Blankenbaker thus left no male heirs, and all his descendants are through the Fishers and Waylands.

There is a mystery about Balthasar's wife who might be related to the wife of George Utz and to the wife of John Hoffman or to the Maiers (Moyer). John Hoffman's second wife was Maria Sabina Volck whose mother Barbara was the wife of George Utz. Barbara Utz was born Anna Barbara Majer (Maier, Mayer) and married Johann Michael Volck (see the section on the Utz-Volck complex in Part I). Balthasar Blankenbaker was a witness at the baptism of all twelve of the children of John and Mary Sabina Hoffman including one who was named for him. Considering also that Balthasar lived on land adjacent to George Utz who was adjacent to John Hoffman who was adjacent to George Moyer and considering the similarity of the names Majer, Maier and Moyer, (where "j" is a vowel which substitutes for "i" and "y"), perhaps Anne Margaret Blankenbaker was a part of this complex. Since no marriage was found for Balthasar in Germany and Bathasar and Margaret had no children when they arrived in Virginia, perhaps Balthasar and Anne Margaret met and were married on the trip.

Blankenbaker, Matthias (many spellings in Europe such as Blankenbühler but Blankenbaker, Blankenbeker, and Pickler are the frequent variations for his descendants in America). At his marriage in Oberderdingen, Württemberg to Anna Maria Mercklin on 7 May 1714 he was said to be a tailor. One child, Hans Jerg (George) was born at Oberderdingen in FEB 1715 (day unknown). Matthias (or Matthew) with his wife, Mary, and young son, George, appears on Spotswood's importation list. The family was accompanied by many relatives including the Fleshmans, (probably) the Thomases, Henry Schluchter and Matthias' two brothers. He was sued by Col. Spotswood in 1724 and was granted land with the other colonists on the Robinson River. He had only two patents, one for 156 acres (*Virginia Patent Book 12*, p.481 as Matthias Blankenbucher, 24 June 1726) and another for 320 acres *(Virginia Patent Book 14*, p.39 as Matthew Plunkepee, 28 SEP 1728). The first straddled the Robinson River and the second was on the west side of Garr's Mountain adjacent to other land of his brothers. Matthew Blanckenbücher, 52 years of age, applied to Orange County Court on 21 May 1746 to be free of the county levy. He stated he had been been unable to work for three years (Orange County loose papers). On 14 OCT 1746, Mathas Plancit Pecker was discharged from paying the parish levy by the vestry of St. Mark's Parish. As can be seen, the name was subject to many variations in spelling. Matthias' will, probated in 1763, but written in 1746 (NS) mentions his wife Mary, sons Christopher and John, and a grandson, John Blankenbaker, Jr., who was the son of Matthias' deceased son, George. It appears that the death of the son George was a shock and Matthias decided that he should write his will while he could. However, he lived seventeen more years.

> The son, Christopher, married Christina Finks, the daughter of Mark Finks. They had children born 1754–78 as documented in the German Lutheran Church records.
>
> The son, John, married Mary Margaret Utz, daughter of the 1717 immigrant George Utz.
>
> The son, George, left one heir, his son John. This John moved with his mother, Mary (Gerhardt or Garrett), and stepfather, Michael Mires (Moyers) to Rowan County, North Carolina. John married Jane Davis and they had four sons (Jesse, Davis, Joseph and John) who adopted the name Pickler. There were also two daughters, Mary and Nancy.

Blankenbaker, Nicholas (many spellings in Europe such as Blanckenbühler but Blankenbeker, Blankenbaker, Blankenbeckler, Blankenbecler, Blank, and Beckler are variations in America). John Nicholas came to Virginia in 1717 with his wife Apollonia Käfer and his son Zacharias and appears on Spotswood's importation list. He, too, was sued by Spotswood in 1724. He received three land grants, one on 24 JUN 1726 for 156 acres (as Nicholas Blankenbucher, *Virginia Patent Book 12*, p.475), another on 28 SEP 1728 for 400 acres (as Nicholas Plunkepee, *Virginia Patent Book 14*, p.36) and another on 20 JUN 1733 for 300 acres (as Nicholas Blancumbaker, *Virginia Patent Book 15*, p.20). He died in Orange County in 1743, signing his full name to his will as John Nicholas Blankenbeckler. The will mentions his wife Apollonia, sons Zacharias, Jacob, and Michael, and daughters Ursula, wife of John Zimmerman (son of the immigrant Christopher Zimmerman), Dorothea, wife of Lawrence Garr, and Elizabeth Blankenbecker (who later married John Fleshman).

> The son Zacharias was naturalized 27 JAN 1742(OS) at the Orange Court. He and his wife Els (Alcy, Elizabeth) had children born 1750–1767 (German Lutheran Church records). Alcy was a widow with two daughters and her first husband may have been a Finks, perhaps a brother to the immigrant Mark Finks. At present there is no proof as to her maiden name or her first husband's name. Zacharias was appointed constable in the place of Richard Burdyne in 1746 but he seemed reluctant to accept the post. After one year's service as constable, he was replaced. Zacharias was also appointed to survey and count the tobacco plants. This Zacharias had a son, Zacharias, Jr. who moved to southwest Virginia and many of his descendants spell the name as Blankenbeckler or Blankenbecler. An account of this family is given in William P. Blankenbeckler's *Blankenbeckler Family of Southwest Virginia*. The senior Zacharias also had a son, Jacob, who married Elizabeth Reiner, not Elizabeth Weaver, as has been reported in the *Germanna Records*. The eventual fate of this Jacob is unknown but he did have children by his wife Elizabeth Reiner.
>
> The son Jacob of Nicholas married first his first cousin once removed, Mary Barbara, daughter of John Thomas, Jr., an early immigrant. Second, Jacob married Hannah Weaver, another first cousin once removed. The statement that Jacob married Barbara Utz is false (due to an erroneous reading of George Utz' will). Jacob and all of his children moved to Jefferson and Shelby Counties, Kentucky. Many later individuals from this family moved to Indiana and farther west.

Michael Blankenbaker married Elizabeth Barbara Garr, daughter of Andrew Garr. All seven of the children were girls. This family is found in the *Garr Genealogy*.

Germanna Record 13 contains a fuller account of the Blankenbakers by C.L. Yowell, but the account contains some errors. Some Blankenbaker material is contained in Virginia Fray Lewis' *Fray Genealogy*.

Bloodworth. This name could be English or it could derive from a German name (Blutwert). Joseph Bloodworth was involved in land transactions with the Germans, especially with Conrad Amberger where they had a joint patent.

Bohannon. Margaret Bohannon was a sponsor for two children of Christopher Zimmerman and his wife Mary Tanner.

Braun. David Braun communed at the German Lutheran Church on 22 MAY 1785.

Broyles (Briles is a variation in America). Johannes Breuel or Breyhel, the eldest son of Conrad and Margaretha (Schelling) Breyel, was christened 1 MAY 1679 in Dusslingen, Württemberg. Conrad Breyel died 8 OCT 1703 in Dusslingen, five days after falling out of a crab apple tree and breaking his back. Shortly thereafter, Johannes moved to Ötisheim about forty miles away where he was a weaver. There he married Ursula Ruop, daughter of Hans Jacob Ruop, gravedigger, on 6 NOV 1703. Six children of Johannes and Ursula are recorded in the church records at Ötisheim. Hans Jacob and Conrad, twins, were christened 26 MAR 1705. This Conrad died young. The next son, Mattheus, was christened 24 NOV 1706 and died before his second birthday. Another Conrad was christened 2 JAN 1709. Jerg Martin, was christened 1 AUG 1711 but there is no further record of him. Maria Elisabetha was christened 5 JUL 1716. This data is furnished by a descendant, Stephen H. Broyles, who researched the church records (see *Beyond Germanna*, v.3, n.4). More on the family is given in "The Ancestry of the Broyles, Paulitz, Moyer, and Motz Families," *Before Germanna*, v.6."

John Broyles came to Virginia on the ship *Scott* stating in his proof of importation that he brought his wife, Ursula, and children, Conrad and Elizabeth. The eldest son, Jacob, proved his own importation in 1727. John Broyles was sued by Spotswood. As John Prial, he took a grant 24 JUN 1726 on a branch of Island Run for 400 acres (*Virginia Patent Book 12*, p.476). The son, Jacob, took a grant of 400 acres on 28 SEP 1728 adjacent to Jacob Crigler (*Virginia Patent Book 13*, p.389). There were several miles between these grants with the father in the south and the son in the north of the Robinson River community.

John Broyles, the 1717 immigrant, died in 1734. His will, written 7 MAR 1731(OS) and probated 5 FEB 1733(OS) (*Spotsylvania W.B. A*, p.209), mentions his wife and "my children, male and female." The will was proven by Urseley Broyle and Paultus [Balthasar or Paul] Blankenbaker.

The son Jacob Broyles was naturalized 27 JAN 1742(OS) in the Orange Court. He married Mary Catherine Fleshman, the daughter of Cyriacus Fleischmann. They were the parents of twelve children: Adam, Catherine, Nicholas, Cyrus, Elizabeth, Jacob, Peter, Michael, John, Zacharias, Matthias, and Mary. Except for Mary for whom nothing is known, the children lived to adulthood and married.

The son Conrad Briles (he originated this spelling of the surname) married Margaret_____ about 1735 and this family moved to North Carolina in 1754. Nine children are assigned to them: Mary, Michael, Frederick, Rachel, Adam, Rebecca, Elizabeth, George, and Susanna though Rebecca and Elizabeth are not proven children.

The daughter Elizabeth has no known marriage.

The daughter, Catherine, born in Virginia about 1719, married Adam Wilhite, the son of Johann Michael Willheit and his wife Anna Maria Hengsteler. They were the parents of five children: John, Michael, Elizabeth, George, and Mary.

The report that there was a John Broyles who testified on 7 APR 1724 that he came to Virginia in DEC 1719 (citing *Spotsylvania W.B. A*, p.68) was a misreading of the court record and there was no John Broyles (the name in the record is John Bell).

In the 1739 Orange County tithables, there is a Christley Broyles, who is distinct from Conrad and Jacob who are listed also. This Christley is presumably a son who was born in Virginia and died as a young man.

In 1744, Jacob and Conrad Broil conveyed to Adam Wilhite 200 acres of land patented 24 JUN 1726 by John Broil and bequeathed to them. This was their inheritance and would indicate that their mother had died. Also, since John Broil owned 400 acres at his death, this would indicate that there were four children when this sale was made.

A. L. Keith left a typescript, *The Broyles Family*, in the Chicago Newberry Library which is available on microfilm through the Latter Day Saints Family History Centers.

Bunger (perhaps Bungard in Germany). Valentin or Felta Bunger made his first appearance in the Robinson River Valley just before the Revolutionary War. He bought 100 acres on a branch of Deep Run from Michael Wilhite and his wife on 1 AUG 1775 (*Culpeper D.B. H*, p.111). He signed the church constitution at the German Lutheran Church and the petition asking to be freed from levies to support the established church. Both of these events were in 1776. He was involved in several land transactions and appears in the 1803 personal tax list for the last time. The will of Felta Bunger was executed in Greenbrier County, Virginia (now West Virginia) on 11 MAR 1806.

His wife was named Elizabeth. The Bunger and House families seem to have some connection to judge by the many interactions at church. The lists of baptisms and confirmations at the German Lutheran Church indicate that Valentin and Elizabeth Bungard had seven children:

- John, born 1762/3, confirmed in 1782 age 20. He married Eva House about 1786/7. Four children are given in the baptismal register at church from 1788 to 1794. John last appears in the tithables in 1803.
- Magdalena born about 1763/4, confirmed in 1782 age 18. She married about 1783 Rev. Daniel Huffman, son of John Huffman and grandson of John Huffman, the 1714 colonist.
- Anna Margaret, born 1766/7, confirmed in 1782 age 15. She married 19 JAN 1790 Daniel Huffman, son of George Huffman and grandson of John Huffman, the 1714 colonist.
- Jacob, born 1768/9, confirmed in 1785 age 16. He married 1788/9 Margaret House and had moved to Rockingham County by 1799. It appears that they had thirteen children.
- Philip was confirmed in 1789 and he was probably born about 1770/1. He married 9 JAN 1798 Mary Garriott, the daughter of Thomas Garriott. The family moved to Kentucky where they bought a farm in Hardin County.
- Henry was confirmed in 1794 and he was probably born about 1772/3. He married Barbara Garriott, the sister of Mary. They moved to Meade County in Kentucky.
- Catherine Bunger was confirmed with her brother Henry and she was probably born about 1774/5. She married Samuel Mossbarger 16 OCT 1806 in Greenbrier County Virginia (now West Virginia).

For more information see Ina Ritchie Sipes, *Bunger Ancestors and Descendants and Allied Families*. There is also a short note in Beyond Germanna, v.5, n.4 with information contributed by B. C. Holtzclaw and Mrs. Sipes.

Carpenter, John (Zimmermann in Germany). John Carpenter, the brother of William, must have been born about 1700 and perhaps he came to Virginia in 1721 with William. John Carpenter was granted 150 acres 20 JUN 1733 (*Virginia Patent Book 15*, p. 55). He married by 1721 or 1722 Anna Barbara, only daughter of Andrew Kerker the 1717 colonist, for in 1739 he is shown with two tithables in his family, indicating a son born prior to 1723. He was administrator of the estate of his father-in-law, Andrew Kerker, 27 JUL 1738 (*Orange W.B. 1*, pp.50–51). On 24 JAN 1742(OS) he was admitted to citizenship as "John Zimmermann alias Carpenter," along with a number of other Germans of the Lutheran Church community (*Orange O.B. 3*, p.313). On 20 MAR 1750 John Carpenter deeded to Lawrence Garr the 150 acres that he had patented in 1733 (*Culpeper D.B. A*, p.256) and on 1 JUN 1760 was granted 1,245 acres of land adjoining John Huffman (Joyner, v.3, p.46). To quote the abstract from Joyner: "1,245 acres on White Oak Run in a patent granted 28 SEP 1728 to Andrew Kirker, deceased, (now said Carpenter's) adjoining John Huffman, George Long, Dr. William Lynn, John Mutts [Motz] now Nelson's, Adam Yeager, Jacob Barlow, Matthias Rouse, William Carpenter, deceased, George Utz' line at a place where the old German Chapel stood." John Carpenter was thus the owner of 1645 acres, which in 1762 he and his wife, Barbara, deeded to their four sons:

> John Carpenter, Jr., born about 1723, married Dorothy, daughter of the 1717 immigrant, Michael Cook (see Cook). He made deeds of gift of land to his sons John and Michael (*Culpeper D.B. H*, pp. 441 and 442). John Carpenter died in 1804 in Madison County, leaving a will which mentions six children, John, Michael, Samuel, Mary Cook, Margaret Carpenter, and Susannah Jesse.
>
> Andrew Carpenter married about 1752 Barbara, the widow of George Clore who died in 1751. Barbara was the daughter of Peter Weaver who came as a young boy in 1717 with his parents (see Weaver). Andrew Carpenter died in Madison County in 1795, leaving a will which mentions his sons Andrew, Joseph, Cornelius and Simeon, and daughters Barbara Aylor, Ann Crigler, and Nancy Carpenter.
>
> William married Mary Willheit, daughter of Adam Willheit and granddaughter of Michael Willheit, the Germanna pioneer. The births of six children of William Carpenter (called Zimmermann in the record) and his wife, Maria, namely, Barbara, Samuel, William, Elizabeth, Mary, and Anna, are recorded in the Lutheran Church books from 1757 to 1771. He died in Madison County in 1808, leaving a will which mentions the above children. [Adam Willheit's will in 1763 calls his daughter Mary, not Mary Carpenter, but Mary Willheit, which would normally indicate that she was unmarried in 1763.]
>
> Michael married Mary Christler, daughter of Theobald Christler, a later comer to the Robinson River community (see Christler). Michael Carpenter (called Zimmermann in the church records) and his wife Mary had seven children, whose births are recorded at the Lutheran Church from 1761 to 1781: Solomon, Dinah, Rebecca, Andrew, Aaron, Moses and Ephraim. Michael Carpenter's will, written in 1805 and probated at the time of his death in 1808 in Madison County, mentions all these children except Rebecca (who probably died young), and adds another child, Peggy Carpenter, who was probably born after 1781.

John Carpenter, Sr. died as quite an old man in 1782. His will, dated 20 JUN 1782 and probated 16 SEP 1782, mentions only the wife, Ann Barbara, and "my four children," (*Culpeper W.B. B*, p.524).

What has been recounted above is the standard history of the early Carpenter family. There are problems which are given next. At the baptism of a slave child on 9 JUN 1778, the mother of the child, then deceased, is said to have belonged to "Old John Carpenter's Estate." This would seem to refer to the John Carpenter who was the immigrant. This statement is confirmed by another statement, "Barbara Carpenter, Sen. Carp. Widow" in the list of communicants the Sunday after Easter in 1778. The implication of these two statements is that there was another John Carpenter, perhaps the father of John and William. The two statements which have been quoted come from the German Lutheran Church Baptismal Register as are the statements in the next paragraph.

Another problem occurs in that there is another Michael Carpenter who is unaccounted for in the history. On Easter Sunday in 1776, the communicants included "Michael Carpenter and w. Margaretha." Four names away in the list, there is a "Michael Carpenter and w. Maria". Also in the slave baptism just referred to, one of the sponsors was "Marg. Carpenter Mich. Wife." Thus the existence of a Michael Carpenter who is married to Margaret is twice verified, but the standard history, for example *Germanna Record 11*, makes no mention of this individual.

Carpenter, William (Zimmermann in Germany). William Carpenter on 5 APR 1726 stated that he came into this country in 1721 with his wife, Elizabeth, *Spotsylvania O.B. 1724–30*, p.108. As William "Cimberman," he was granted 400 acres in the Robinson River neighborhood 24 JUN 1726 (*Virginia Patent Book 12*, p. 477) among the patents of those who arrived in 1717. As William Carpenter, he received another grant of 193 acres 28 SEP 1728 (*Virginia Patent Book 13*, p. 389). He deeded this last grant of 193 acres on 4 DEC 1733 to Michael Smith and

Michael Cook, wardens and trustees of the German church, to serve as a glebe for the pastor (Crozier, *Spotsylvania County Records*, p. 128). William Carpenter was a member of the first Grand Jury convened in Orange County in 1735. He was awarded 140 pounds of tobacco for an old wolf's head in 1736.

Both William Carpenter and his brother John were usually called Carpenter rather than Zimmermann in the records. Occasionally the Carpenters were called Zimmerman in the German Lutheran Church records, but it is moderately easy to distinguish this family from that of Christopher Zimmermann, the 1717 colonist who was not a related family. William Carpenter died in Orange County, Virginia in 1745 as the result of a kick by a horse, and his will, dated 4 OCT 1745, mentions his wife, Elizabeth, who is to have a life interest in the property. After her death the farm was to go to Catherine Proctor who was his mistress. For a longer version of this story, see "William Carpenter's Will" in Beyond Germanna, v. 12, n.4. He mentions John, William, and Andrew Carpenter who were his nephews, but strangely he does not mention his nephew Michael. From the will it appears that William Carpenter had no children and later deeds show that his brother John inherited his land after the will of William Carpenter was declared invalid.

Castler (Gessler in German). Matthias was married in Berg bei Stuttgart, Württemberg on 17 FEB 1711 to Susanna Christina Schnell. In this marriage record, the occupation of Matthias was given as a weaver. More information is given in "The Ancestry of the Aylor, Castler, Manspiel, and Reiner Families," *Before Germanna*, v.7. When the family came to Virginia is not known, but it would appear they came shortly after 1717. Matthias Castler was granted 406 acres near the Robinson River 28 SEP 1728 (*Virginia Patent Book 13*, p. 474). In 1739 he deeded 100 acres of this land for £4 to George Long (*Orange D.B. 3*, p. 325). The very low sale price suggests there may have been a family connection between Castler and Long. Castler sold another 100 acres to "Courtly" [Conrad] Broyle, son of the 1717 immigrant, John Broyle (*Orange D.B. 3*, 349). In 1739 Matthias Castler had two tithables in his family. This second tithable may have been his son-in-law, Conrad Delph (see Delph), though it could have been a son, born prior to 1723. But if it were a son, he died young. Matthias Castler was a witness to the will of George Utz on 28 JUN 1753. The Culpeper County Rental of 1764 shows "Mathias Carler" with 206 acres. He was survived by two daughters, Anna Magdalena, wife of Conrad Delph, and Susannah, wife of Rev. Samuel Klug, the second pastor of the Evangelical Lutheran Church. Matthias Castler last appears in the Culpeper records on 17 FEB 1775 when he deeded to his son-in-law, Conrad Delph, his 206 acres, "reserving 50 or 60 acres to be acknowledged by Delph to my grandson, Ephraim Klug" (*Culpeper D. B. G*, p.472). In accordance with these instructions, Conrad Delph and Ann his wife deeded 52 acres to Ephraim Klug on 13 APR 1775 (*Culpeper D.B. G*, p.533). Adam, Michael and Samuel Delph who witnessed these deeds were grandsons of Matthias Castler. For the descendants of Matthias Castler see Delph and Klug.

Caul or **Call**. See Kahl.

Chelf (the German spelling is unknown but Chelf, Zelf, Schelf, and Jelf are variations found in Culpeper County). Philip Chelf is known in Culpeper County as the second husband of Barbara Yager Clore. The occasion for this was the baptism of a child of Michael Yager and his wife Elizabeth Crigler in 1768. Michael Yager was the brother of Barbara Yager Clore Chelf. Peter Clore died in 1763 so the marriage of Philip Chelf and Barbara Yager Clore was in the 1763 – 1768 period. From the sponsorships at the baptisms in the German Lutheran Church, especially in the Beemon family, it appears that Philip probably had children already, i.e., he was a widower, when he married Barbara Yager. The girl Nancy who married Daniel Beemon certainly appears from the sponsorships at baptisms of her children to be his daughter.

In 1717, a petition by Germans in London asking for funds to return to Germany was signed by Johannes Scheff who was the head of a party of two, probably himself and a wife (Henry Z Jones and Lewis Bunker Rohrbach, *Even More Palatine Families*, vol. 3, Picton Press, Picton, Maine 2002). An interesting aspect of this is that the second, third, and fourth names after his were of people who eventually settled in the Robinson River Valley. These three families were all from Sulzfeld. Associations in lists of this type often are indicative of relationships or friendships.

In 1737, Hans Schnepff signed a road petition pertaining to a road over the Blue Ridge Mountains. Philip Chelf did live in the Shenandoah Valley where he was a chain carrier for Isaac Hite in 1762 (as Philip Chilf). In a 1762 Culpeper County deed, it is stated that Philip Chelf was a resident of Frederick County.

Philip Chelf left a will (*Madison County W.B. 4*, p.118f) written 6 OCT 1821in which he mentions that he had a deceased son Isaac, a son Elias, and a deceased daughter Catherine who married_____Crisler. No other children or a wife are mentioned. It is not certain who the mother was of these three. Adam Yager, the father of Barbara Yager Clore Chelf, does not include any Chelf children in his will while positively stating, "my other grand-children the heirs of Peter Clore begotten by my daughter Barbara." In other ways Adam Yager seems to be recognizing every grandchild but there is no mention of children of Philip and Barbara Chelf. The children, Isaac, Elias, and Catharine do not appear in the German Lutheran baptismal record which suggests they may have been born before the marriage of Philip and Barbara.

> Isaac, reportedly born 25 DEC 1765, died in 1796 in Wolford County, Kentucky. He married Anna Crigler in 1786. They had four children and the family tended to spell the name Jelf.
> Elias died in 1836 in Marion County, Kentucky. He married Catharine Weaver. They had nine children.
> Catherine married Lewis Crisler, the son of Leonard Crisler and Margaret Clore.

(Two of the mentions of Barbara Chelf in the German Lutheran Baptismal Register are mistakes made when the Register was rewritten.)

Christopher. Nicholas Christopher may not have been a German at all. He and his two sons, John and William, did not move to the Robinson River section with the majority of the 1717 colony, but lived in the Mt. Pony area. However, he appears in the Spotsylvania County records very early and in 1734 he is shown in the tithables of Orange County with two tithables in his family as "_laus Christopher," which may indicate the German name, Nikolaus. An early appearance of Nicholas Christopher was on 2 APR 1723 when he sued John Hix in Spotsylvania County (*Spotsylvania W.B. A*, p.26). On 2 FEB 1725(OS), "John Christopher, infant, by Nicholas Christopher, his next friend," sued Edward Southwell (same, p. 94). This record indicates that John was a son of Nicholas. On 20 JUL 1736 Nicholas Christopher was granted 400 acres on the Rapidan River (*Virginia Patent Book 17*, p.130), and on 8 MAY 1741 John and Francis Taliaferro of Caroline County leased to Nicholas Christopher 150 acres, "during the natural lives of Nicholas Christopher, John Christopher, and William Christopher" (*Orange D.B. 4*, p.421). This deed shows that John and William were both sons of Nicholas. Nicholas had an earlier grant jointly with William Phillips 17 AUG 1727, as shown by a deed from him on 24 MAY 1744 to William Beale for 572 acres, part of the land having been granted to him and Phillips in 1727, and the rest to him alone in 1736 (*Orange W.B. 9*, p. 80). Of the sons, John Christopher was head of a family in 1734 in Orange County, and witnessed deeds of Edward Ballenger, who may have been a son of Andrew Ballenger, the 1717 colonist, in 1736 (*Orange D.B. 1*, pp.249 and 253). John Christopher and Ann his wife gave a mortgage to Edward Spencer and Alexander Waugh 22 OCT 1747, and John last appears a few years later, when he deeded 150 acres to Cochran, Murdock and County (*Orange D.B. 10*, p.532, and *12*, p.175). William Christopher was also head of a family in 1734, and on 25 AUG 1741 the executors of Alexander Spotswood leased to William Christopher 150 acres "during the lifetime of William Christopher and Morton Christopher his son" (*Orange D.B. 6*, p.111). William deeded this lease to Thomas Jones 28 JUL 1743 (*D. B. 7*, p. 356). Morton Christopher, son of William, married about 1765/6 Elizabeth Wayland, daughter of Adam Wayland and granddaughter of Thomas Wayland, the early Germanna pioneer (see Wayland), and the births of their nine children, born 1767–1795, are shown in Keith.

Clements. The origin of Christian Clements and the German spelling of his name are unknown. Christian Clemon purchased 550 acres in the Shenandoah Valley of Jacob Stover 17 SEP 1735 for £28 (*Orange D.B. 1*, p.151f). He sold this land in 1737 for £60 to Ludwig Stone (*Orange D.B. 2*, p.256). He patented 600 acres of land on Deep Run 21 NOV 1734 adjacent to John Huffman (*Virginia Patent Book 15*, p.384) under the name Clemond. He married Catherine Margaret Vogt, daughter of his neighbor, John Paul Vogt. He sold 600 acres to Michael Smith, Jr. for £70 (*Orange D.B.7*, p.6).The Clements and the Vogts probably moved shortly after this to the Shenandoah Valley. Christian Clements' will was dated 13 FEB 1780 and proved 18 MAR 1783 in Augusta County, Virginia. He named his wife Catherine, eldest son Gaspar, son John, daughter Catherine married to George Trout, grandson David Trout and mentions but does not name his daughters married to Henry Liner and Philip Burger

(Barger, Barrier). Catherine (Vogt) Clements' will was dated 12 JUN 1783 and proved in 1793. The five children of Christian and Catherine (Vogt) Clements are:

Gaspar, born about 1746,

Mary Catherine who married George Trout,

John who married Elizabeth_____,

Eve who married Philip Barger and

Elizabeth who married Henry Lyner/Liner.

The grandson of Philip and Eve Barger, Wesley Kenerly Helm (1822–1871) left an extant notebook in which he wrote, "Philip Barger, Sr. was born September 1st 1747, maried February 4th 1765, Died August 28th 1803 aged 62. Eve Clemens was born May 1st 1747, maried to Philip Barger February 4th 1765, deceased October 7th 1791 aged 44. Philip and Eve Barger had 8 children, Casper, Jacob, John, Philip, Jr., Christa, Eve, Catharine, and Adam." This information was supplied by Larry P. Cornwell, a descendant of W.K. Helm.

Clore (Klaar, Klar, Clar in Germany and sometimes Glore in America). Hans Michael Klaar was the head of one of the families whose departure in 1717 was recorded by the sexton at Gemmingen. Another family in this group was Joseph and Susanna Weber, she being the sister of Michael Clore. The Michael Clore family is on Spotswood's importation list with three children. Michael Clore was sued by Spotswood in 1724 but, on the first of September that year, Michael appeared in court and "assumed to pay the cost of the Clerk's & Sheriff's fees, on which the plaintiff consented that the said suit be dismissed." Michael Clore was granted 400 acres on the north side of the Robinson River at the northern end of the German community on 24 JUN 1726 (*Virginia Patent Book 12*, p. 477). He and his son, John Clore, were granted 698 acres jointly 28 SEP 1728 (*Virginia Patent Book 13*, p.391) under the name Clawse. This land was west and north of the first patent. On 20 MAY 1735 a division of the 1728 patent was made between Michael Clore and his son John Clore (*Orange D.B.1*, p.32). Michael Clore sold 100 acres to Martin Wallick for 25£ 20 MAY 1735 (*Orange D.B.1*, p24ff). On this same day, Michael Clore sold 100 acres to Michael O'Neal for £25 (*Orange D.B.1*, p.28ff). Later O'Neal sold this land back to Michael Clore for £20 (*Orange D.B. 7*, p.220).

Michael Clore and his wife Barbara made a deed of gift to their son, George Clore, 15 NOV 1750 (*Culpeper D.B. A*, p.229). Michael's second wife, Ann Elizabeth, was married to him by 14 JUL 1760 when Peter Clore gave a bond to his father, Michael Clore, and his "mother-in-law," Ann Elizabeth Clore, to support them (*Culpeper D.B. C*, p.628). Michael Clore died in 1763. His will, dated 10 MAY 1762 and probated 17 MAR 1763 (*Culpeper W.B. A*, p.315), mentions his wife Elizabeth, sons John and Peter, daughter Agnes Margaret, the wife of Michael O'Neal, and daughter Margaret, wife of Paul Leatherer, and "grandchildren by my daughter Catherine, formerly the wife of Martin Walke", and the children of George Clore, deceased. The widow, Elizabeth Clore, died in 1766 (*Culpeper W. B. A*, p.110). From the *Gemmingen Parish Registers* and Virginia records the children of Michael and Barbara were:

Maria Barbara, baptized 4 OCT 1707, died 30 AUG 1712,

Hans Michael, baptized 26 NOV 1709, died 22 JUN 1713,

<u>Agnes</u> Margaretha, baptized 25 FEB 1712. She appears in the departure list and in Spotswood's head right list. She married Michael O'Neale. On 9 APR 1763 the O'Neales deeded to John Clore land that had been sold them by Michael Clore (*Culpeper D.B. D*, p.218), but O'Neale was dead by 19 OCT 1767, when his widow, Margaret, and his son, William O'Neale, deeded land to James Crane (*Culpeper D.B. E*, p.472). Nothing further is known of the O'Neals.

Andreas, baptized 17 DEC 1713, appears on the departure list and on Spotswood's head right list but that is the last record for him.

Johann <u>Georg</u>, baptized 20 APR 1716, appears on the departure list and on Spotswood's head right list. He died before his father in 1751, leaving a will and several children. His wife was his first cousin once removed, Barbara Weaver, daughter of Peter Weaver. After George's death she married second Andrew Carpenter, son of John Carpenter and grandson of Andrew Kerker, the 1717 immigrant.

John Clore married first Dorothy, daughter of Michael Käfer and Anna Maria (Blankenbaker) Thomas and married second Katherine_____. He died in 1785, leaving a will and nine children.

Catherine married Martin Walk (Wallick), a later comer to the Robinson River Valley. Michael Clore deeded land to Martin Walke 20 MAY 1735 (*Orange D.B. 1*, p.24) which probably indicates that the Walkes were already married.

Peter Clore, the third son, died in 1763, about the same time as his father, leaving several children named in his will. His wife was Barbara Yager, daughter of Adam Yager and granddaughter of Nicholas Yager, the 1717 immigrant. After Peter's death she married Philip Chelf.

Margaret Clore, married Paul Leatherer (Lederer), a later immigrant to the Robinson River community, so that all the Leatherers are descended from Michael Clore.

More German history is in "The Ancestry of the Clore, Kaifer, and Thomas Families," *Before Germanna, v. 2*. Keith (pp. 178–182) gives an account of Michael Clore. Claude L. Yowell has a history of the first four generations of the Clores in *Germanna Record 10*. The best reference source is *Germanna Record 16* by Cathi Clore Frost entitled *The First Four Generations of the Michael Clore Family*.

Cofer. A family of this name lived in the southern part of the Robinson River Valley in the mid-eighteenth century. The name is especially interesting because it might be derived from the German name Käfer. At the present, little is known about the Cofer family. George, Jacob, and Thomas Cofer were heads of families in the 1787 Culpeper Personal Property Tax lists. George and Joel Cofer were in the 1781 Culpeper Classes. There is no mention of Cofers in the German Lutheran Church records.

Cook (Koch in German). Michael Cook came in 1717 with his wife Mary from Schwaigern, Würtemberg, a town whence several Germanna settlers came. In some records, the wife's name appears as Mary while in others it is Barbara. It was Mary in Spotswood's importation list and in Michael Cook's head right application. The church records in Schwaigern show a marriage to Barbara Reiner not long before their departure. In London, they were the parents of Maria Dorothea born on 8 September 1717 but this child did not live. The mother is called Barbara in this record. Between this time and the time of Spotswood's head right list taken on arrival there would hardly be time for a second wife. For more German history, see "The Ancestry of the Christler, Baumgartner, Deer, Dieter, and Lotspeich Families," *Before Germanna*, v.11. Later, members of the Reiner family came to Virginia and they interacted closely with the Michael Cook family suggesting that Mary may have been a Reiner, perhaps Maria Barbara. (Using the first name sometimes and using the second name at other times or using both names is not unusual in the German community, especially for the women.)

Michael Cook was sued by Col. Spotswood in 1724. Jointly with Jacob Krugler (Crigler), he patented 400 acres near the Robinson River 24 JUN 1726 (*Virginia Patent Book 12*, p.480). Michael Cook had another patent for 224 acres on 11 APR 1732 adjacent to his own land (*Virginia Patent Book 14*, p.430). Michael gave Christopher Crigler, Jacob Crigler's oldest son and heir, a deed for 200 acres of the 400 acre grant on 24 JAN 1743(OS) as Jacob Crigler had died. Michael Cook was a leader in the community including an appointment as constable 3 MAR 1729 and service as a warden and reader in the German Lutheran Church in 1733 and 1740.

Michael left no will. The records do show that there were at least four children of Michael and Mary Cook and these were probably all of the children. They are:

Margaret married Philip Snyder,

Dorothy married John Carpenter, Jr, the son of John Carpenter and Barbara Kerker,

Adam married Barbara Fleshman, the daughter of Peter Fleshman and Sophia Weaver,

George married first Mary Sarah Reiner, the daughter of John Dieter Reiner and Mary Margaret Schleicher, and married second Anna Maria Hoffman, the daughter of Henry Hoffman and Elizabeth Catherine Schuster.

On 1 AUG 1751 Michael Cook made a deed of gift of 100 acres to each of his sons-in-law, Philip Snider and John Carpenter, Jr., (*Culpeper D.B. A*, p.316). Philip Snider was a later comer to the Robinson River Valley. The daughters, Margaret Snyder and Dorothy Carpenter, must have been the elder children of Michael and Mary Cook, for Michael Cook was charged with only one tithable in Orange County in 1739, see Part I, showing that both his sons were born after 1723. On 21 JUL 1757 Michael Cook made deeds of gift of 112 acres apiece to his sons, Adam and George Cook (*Culpeper D.B. B*, pp.536 and 538).

The Lutheran church records show that George Cook by his first wife, Maria Sarah Reiner, had a number of children, born 1751–68, and by his second wife, Anna Maria Hoffman of the Reformed faith, he had sons and daughters born 1772–1782. The estate of George Cook was ordered inventoried 25 NOV 1802 (*Madison W.B. 1*, p.24). Deeds in Madison County in 1805 by his thirteen surviving children provide valuable genealogical information, not only for this family but for allied families. In addition, the church records are a source of information. By his first wife, Mary Sarah Reiner, George Cook was the father of

    Mary <u>Barbara</u> married John Blankenbaker, son of Zacharias, Sr.,

    Margaret married Christopher Tanner,

    Magdalena married John Huffman,

    Elizabeth no marriage,

    Dorothy unmarried in 1805,

    Dina died young, and

    Lewis married Mary Yager.

By his second wife, Anne Mary Hoffman, George Cook was the father of

    Ambrose married Susanna Fleshman,

    Aaron married Leanna Garr,

    Sarah married Andrew Huffman,

    George married Jemima Wilhoit,

    Rosanna,

    Cornelius married Mary Wilkerson,

    Moses married Elizabeth Grayson,

    Unknown son who married Jemima Garr. The basis of this statement is the deed in 1805 which was signed by Jemima Cook with three Garrs as witnesses for her and her alone.

Adam Cook, the son of the immigrant Michael, married Barbara, daughter of Peter Fleshman and granddaughter of the 1717 immigrant Cyriacus Fleshman, for on 13 DEC 1773, Adam Cook, Christopher Barler, Christopher Ryner, John and Peter Fleshman signed an agreement regarding the valuation of the estate of Peter Fleshman, deceased. (*Culpeper D.B. D*, p.222). Adam Cook was probably the father of

    Frederick married Eva (Böhme?),

    Peter married Mary Carpenter,

    John married Mary Fleshman,

    Michael married Catherine Wilhoit,

    Adam, Jr. married Elizabeth_____,

    Daniel married Rosanna Wilhoit,

    Ann married John Battan,

    Mary,

    Barbara,

    Susan, and

    possibly Margaret.

There are references to Ephraim Cook (m. Jemima Fleshman), Ann Cook (m. Absalom Utz) and Elizabeth (m. Samuel Snyder) who are not clearly identified. The Lutheran Church records are rich in information on the Cook families though not all of the children above are represented sufficiently well to determine all of the relationships.

Cooper. Joseph Cooper had land in the vicinity of Mt. Pony. The estate of Barbara Cooper was administered 1734 by Jacob Prosie with Jacob Miller and John Vought as securities. Christopher Zimmerman, William Kelly, Charles Morgan, and Frederick Cobler were appointed to appraise her estate. The many known Germans involved in the estate suggest that the Joseph and Barbara Cooper may have been Germans. The presence of John Vought is unusual as he lived many miles away from Mt. Pony and apparently was newly arrived in Virginia. The other Germans lived in the neighborhood of Mt. Pony.

Crecelius. The earliest known ancestor of Otto Rudolph Crecelius is Dietrich "Theodore" Krekel (ca. 1540 - ca. 1628). He was the last Catholic instructor at the Institute of St. Serverus at Gemunden in the Duchy of Nassau before the Institute became Evangelical Lutheran during the Reformation period. Later, many members of the family were Lutheran pastors. The sons of Dietrich adopted the spelling Crecelius. The line of descent is Christian, Peter, Johannes, Johann Cristophal, and Johann to Otto Rudolph. Rudolph married, at Reichelsheim on 13 JAN 1750, Anna Margarethe Zubrod who died 29 JAN 1758. He married second Anna Ursula Gerlach, born 1740. She died in Philadelphia in 1765. They had two surviving children, one of whom was Elizabeth.

In 1765 Rudolph Crecelius and his wife, Anna Ursula Gerlach were the parents of Anna Magdalena who was baptized 30 MAR 1765 at St. Michael's and Zion Lutheran Church in Philadelphia. At this same church, Rudolph married Maria Elisabetha Diederle on 4 FEB 1766. About one year later, Maria Barbara Crecelius was christened on 24 MAR 1767 at the Evangelical Lutheran Church in Frederick, Maryland. This same year he was a witness of communion of Germans who wished to be naturalized. He was a schoolmaster at Frederick and perhaps in Monocacy in Maryland. Catharina Barbara Crecelius was born 22 MAR 1769. Rudolph Isaac Creselius was born 31 MAR 1772. By tradition, Dorothea (Dolly) Crecelius was born about this same time.

On 28 JUL 1776, Rudolph Crecelius was a sponsor for Margaret Diehl at the German Lutheran Church in Culpeper County. In 1777, on Rogate Sunday, (Maria) Elisabetha Crecelius was confirmed at the Culpeper German Lutheran Church. Later that year, Johannes, born 14 OCT 1777 to Rudolph and Maria Elis. Crecelius, was baptized on 30 NOV 1777 where the sponsors were Johannes Jager and his wife Maria. On another occasion, Rudolph Cecilius was a sponsor, as was Catharina Hirsch (Deer), for the child Marg. (born 12 MAR 1775) who was baptized 28 JUL 1776 with parents Daniel Diehl and his wife Elisabetha.

The next records are in Rockingham County, Virginia, where Rudolph Crecelius was granted land in 1782. On 15 JAN 1783, Jacob A. Crecelius was born. Rudolph was listed in the Rockingham tax lists this year. Later in the decade, Rudolph Crecilus bought land in Washington County, North Carolina (later Tennessee). His will was probated in November of 1787. Charles M. Bennett in *Washington County, Tennessee, Tombstones Transcriptions*, v.II, states that Rudolph Cretselious and Elizabeth Cretselious, the wife of Rudolph, are buried in the Old Dutch Meeting House cemetery. Other members of the family are here also. See Beyond Germanna, v.6, n.1, p.308; also v.11, n.2; and v.15, n.1 for more information.

The *Bulletin* of the Watauga Association of Genealogy in volume 7, numbers 1 & 2, has a transcript of the Crets(z)elious-Walters Bible which has the family of Samuel who was probably the son of John, who was born in 1777. This John operated a general store a few miles southwest of Johnson City, TN. Other names in the Old Dutch Meeting House records which might be of interest to Germanna researchers include Harnsbarger and Good.

Crees (Greys in German). Laurentius Greyss, Police Accountant, married Maria Euphrosina, daughter of Georg Sigmund Schott, local administrator at Göppingen (from the Evangelical Reformed church in Berg bei Stuttgart). Henriabout Louise was born to them at Unterturkheim, Württemberg 3 NOV 1716. He was still listed in the parish register in 1720. More information is given in "The Ancestry of the Yager, Stolts, Crees, and Beyerbach Families," *Before Germanna*, v.10. He may have made his first appearance in the Virginia records in the patent dated 16 JUN 1727 to Lancelot Crest for 200 acres of land in Hanover County (*Virginia Patent Book 13*, p.103). Laus Crest patented 200 acres of land 28 SEP 1732 on the south side of the Robinson River (*Virginia Patent Book 14*, p.528). The land was further described as "corner to Matthias Castler, on Dark Run." He was naturalized as Lawrence Grays 27 JAN 1743(OS) (Orange O.B. 3, p.313. He deeded the 200 acres to his daughter, Rebecca, and her husband Timothy Swindell in 1758 and 1762.

There was probably a son, Peter, who might have been old enough to have left heirs. The evidence is in a grant to Debold (Theobald) Christler in the Shenandoah Valley where one of the chain carriers is Peter Cree along with Lawrence Garr (Joyner, v.2).

Crible. George Frederick Crible landed at Philadelphia in 1743. In 1759, a grant to Joseph King was adjacent to the Dutch Quarter, George Frederick Cribble, Richard Young, and Robert King. There is no known grant for Crible and perhaps he was living on land for which he intended to have a grant. For King's survey, John Grissam and Michael Klug were chain carriers. Crible died intestate in Culpeper County in 1764. Appraisers of the modest estate were Joseph King, John Grisom, and Thomas Lillard.

Crigler (the surname and origin in Germany are unknown). Jacob Crigler was probably a bachelor when he came in 1717. He did not appear on the head right list but his claim to Second Colony status rests on being the first of the colonists to be sued by Alexander Spotswood. Why his patent (as Jacob Kruger) of 400 acres on 24 JUN 1726 was with Michael Cook is unknown (*Virginia Patent Book 12*, p.480) though this, plus the choice of sponsors on two occasions at the church, is evidence of some connection. Jacob Crigler was granted an additional 400 acres adjoining Michael Clore on 28 SEP 1730 (*Virginia Patent Book 13*, p.536). He married the widow Susannah (Clore) Weaver not long after coming to Virginia. Her husband, Joseph, has no records in Virginia after his importation by Gov. Spotswood. Jacob died as a comparatively young man in 1734, and on 3 APR 1734 his widow Susannah Creagler was appointed his administratrix, with Michael Clore, her brother, and George Utz as her securities (Crozier, *Records of Spotslyvania County*, p.56). Jacob and Susannah Crigler had four children:

Christopher who married Catherine Finks,
Nicholas Crigler who married Margaret Käfer,
Susanna who married Michael Utz, and
Elizabeth who married Michael Yager.
(There was no evidence for a daughter named Margaret.)

On 24 JAN 1743(OS) Michael Cook deeded to Christopher Crigler half of the patent of 400 acres that had been granted to Michael Cook and Jacob Crigler in 1726 (*Orange D.B. 3*, p.321) which indicates Christopher was the eldest son and heir of Jacob, and born prior to 1723 (if he were of age when this deed was made). On 21 JUL 1757 Christopher Crigler and Caty his wife deeded to Nicholas Crigler the 200 acres which was part of the patent to Michael Cook and Jacob Crigler in 1726. On the same date Nicholas Crigler and Margaret his wife deeded to Christopher Crigler 157 acres, part of the larger tract granted to Jacob Crigler. On 18 OCT 1759 Nicholas Crigler and Margaret his wife deeded to Henry Aylor the 200 acres which was part of the 1726 patent to Cook and Crigler (*Culpeper D.B. C*, p.234).

Christopher Crigler, son of Jacob, married Catherine, daughter of Mark Finks, a later immigrant to the Robinson River section. The Lutheran Church records show that Christopher Crigler and his wife had eleven children: Mary, Reuben, Jacob, Elizabeth, Susannah, Lewis, John, Christopher, Anna, James and William, born 1751–1778. The last record of Christopher Crigler and Catherine his wife was on 18 SEP 1782, when they made deeds (*Culpeper D.B. L*, pp.163 and 167).

Nicholas Crigler married Margaret, a daughter of Michael Käfer and the widow Anna Maria (Blankenbaker) Thomas. The baptismal records show seven children of Nicholas Crigler and Margaret his wife: Elizabeth, Aaron, Margaret, Nicholas, Susannah, Anna, and Abraham, born 1750–1771. Nicholas Crigler died in 1813, leaving a will (*Madison W.B. 3*, p.1).

Jacob Crigler's widow, Susannah, married Nicholas Yager, the 1717 immigrant, for on 6 APR 1764 Susannah Yager, widow of Nicholas, deeded slaves to Christopher and Nicholas Creeglar. This is the last appearance of Susannah in the records.

The family of Michael Jäger and his wife Elizabeth Crigler are given in the Lutheran baptismal record and shows the children to be John, Samuel, Barbara, Susanna, Eva, Elizabeth, Jemima, Michael, Hanna and Rachel. The family of Susanna Crigler and Michael Utz is not in the baptismal register which probably means that they had some children born before 1750.

The analysis which led to the decision that Elizabeth and Susanna were daughters of Jacob Crigler is in Beyond Germanna, v.15, n.3 in two articles, "Susanna, the Wife of Michael Utz," and "Elizabeth, the Wife of Michael Yager."

Mr. Arthur D. Crigler published a Crigler genealogy which has serious errors in the early generations.

Crisler (usually Crisler in America but never Chrysler). The Christler family left Lambsheim in the Palatinate in 1719 and emigrated to Pennsylvania when Johann Theobald Christler was ten years old. His mother's maiden name was Bender which was one of the families that emigrated with the Christlers. For more German history, see "The Ancestry of the Christler, Baumgartner, Deer, Dieter, and Lotspeich Families," *Before Germanna*, v.11. Theobald Christler was deeded 418 acres for £20 in Orange County in 1736 by John Trotter (*Orange D.B. 1*, p.262ff). There are other references to land transactions in the Garr section here. Deval Christler was paid 140 pounds of tobacco by the Orange County Court for one wolf's head in 1742. He was naturalized in 1743, and died in Culpeper County in 1776. Deobald Christler was a witness to the will of Lawrence Garr in 1753 (his brother-in-law) and of Michael Käfer in 1762. Deobald's wife was Rosina Garr, born in 1713 in Germany, the daughter of the immigrant Andrew Garr. The *Garr Genealogy* gives an account of their eleven children who all married into Germanna families:

> Henry Christler married Elizabeth Weaver, daughter of Peter Weaver and Elizabeth Volck,
>
> John George Christler married Anna Magdalena Smith, daughter of Michael Smith, Jr. and Anna Magdalena Thomas,
>
> Adam Christler married Elizabeth Crigler, daughter of Nicholas Crigler and Margaret Käfer,
>
> Leonard Christler married Margaret Clore, daughter of John Clore and Dorothy Käfer,
>
> David Christler married Elizabeth Wayland, daughter of John Wayland and Catherine Broyles,
>
> Michael Christler born 1752 married Mary Ann (Thomas) DeBolt, daughter of Michael Thomas,
>
> Dorothy Christler married Nicholas Broyles, son of Jacob Broyles and Mary Catherine Fleshman,
>
> Catherine Christler married Aaron Crigler, son of Nicholas Crigler and Margaret Käfer,
>
> Mary Crisler married Michael Carpenter, son of John Carpenter and Anna Barbara Kerker,
>
> Elizabeth Crisler married Michael Wilhoit, son of Adam Wilhoit and Catherine Broyles,
>
> Margaret Crisler married Adam Clore, son of Peter Clore and Barbara Yager.

A Dan'l (Daniel? or Deobald?) Crisler and Steven Hansbarger were chain carriers for Henry Souther (Joyner, v.3, p.79).

There is a possible reason, not proven but suggestive, as to why the Christlers moved to Virginia from Pennsylvania. The wife of Johann Caspar Stöver, Jr. may have been a first cousin of Theobald Christler. By this connection, Theobald Christler learned that there was a Lutheran minister and community in Virginia. This was at a time when there were few Lutheran pastors in America. For more on this possible connection, see "A Possible Connection Between Theobald Christler and Johanna Caspar Stöver, Jr.," Beyond Germanna, v.14, n.6.

Daher. See Ohlscheitt.

Dearet. One baptismal report shows this name but it is believed to be a mistake for Dear. John Dear (given as Dearet) and his wife Maria were sponsors for Jacob, son of Ambrose Garriott and his wife Elizabeth Blankenbaker. Maria was a cousin of the mother, Elizabeth Blankenbaker Garriott.

Deer or **Dear, John** (in German, Hirsch, but the close English equivalent of Deer is often used in America). Johannes Hirsch was born 2 NOV 1718 in Täbingen, Württemberg. More information appears in "The Ancestry of the Christler, Baumgartner, Deer, Dieter, and Lotspeich Families," *Before Germanna*, v.11. He was a brother to Martin Deer, see the following. John Deer married about 1746/7 Catherine_____, the widow of Frederick Baumgardner who died early in 1746 leaving four sons and a daughter plus a posthumous daughter Eva. Both Baumgardner daughters are mentioned in John Deer's will. On 5 MAY 1760, John Deer and Catherine his wife deeded to Harmon Spilman 100 acres bought of John Sutton (*Culpeper County D.B. C*, p.346) and he was the owner of 200 acres in the Culpeper Rent Roll of 1764. John and Catherine deeded 125 acres to John Brown 16 JUN 1777 (*D.B. H*, p.466) and 275 acres to Peter Pinegar 12 AUG 1778 (*D.B. O*, p.408). John Deer's will, dated 26 MAR 1781 and probated 18 JUN 1781 in Culpeper County (*W.B. B*, p.422), leaves bequests to his wife Catherine, unmarried daughters Mary and Elizabeth, son Moses; after the legacies are paid, the estate is to be divided among John Deer, Moses Deer, Catherine Rider, Susannah Brown, Mary Deer, and Elizabeth Deer; three pounds sterling are left to Dorothy "Fleshn" and the same amount to Eve "Bohon."

> John Deer married Mary Blankenbaker and they had ten children, Reuben, Lewis, Ephraim, Simeon (his descendants spell the name as Dear), Elizabeth, Jeremiah, Sarah, Abner, Jonas, and Mildred,
> Catherine married_____Rider,
> Susanna married_____Brown,
> Moses married Unknown with seven children: Lucy, Elizabeth, Mary, Larkin, Moses, Thomas, and Jemima,
> Mary,
> Elizabeth.

Deer, Martin (in German, Hirsch, but the close English equivalent of Deer is often used in America). Martin Hirsch, brother of John, was born 16 AUG 1715 in Täbingen, Württemberg. More information appears in "The Ancestry of the Christler, Baumgartner, Deer, Dieter, and Lotspeich Families," *Before Germanna*, v.11. Martin first appears in the Virginia records in 1751 when he was deeded 300 acres of land by George Long (*Culpeper D.B. A*, p.304). The deed should be consulted for an implication that Martin was a son-in-law of George Long. His wife seems to have been named Veronica but the name Frances or Franky is a common nickname for this. Martin and his wife Frances sold 150 acres of this land to Michael Russell in 1756 (*Culpeper D.B. B*, pp.428–431).

Martin Hirsch and wife Veronica were communicants in 1775 and 1777. Martin Hirsch (not listed as a Sr. on a day when there was a Jr.) had a wife An. Maria in 1782 at church. His children are determined only by inference. His brother John left a will which names John's children. Other mentions in this time period would seem to be Martin's children. A tentative set is:

> Andrew , born 1751, d. 1798, married Susannah, perhaps Racer,
> Martin, born 1755, d.1853, married Susannah_____,
> Veronica? married Michael Blankenbaker? and perhaps she died young,
> Frances married Peter Racer,
> Barbara married Ephraim Rouse.

On 22 MAR 1794 Martin Deer, "very aged and infirm and having the misfortune of my wife to elope from me," deeded his goods and chattels to his son, Andrew Deer, on condition of Andrew taking him into his house to live; should there remain any part of my estate undisposed of for my support, it is to be divided among my daughters" whose names are not given (*Madison D.B. 1*, p. 86). On this same date he made a deed of half of his land to his son Martin Deer, Jr. (same reference and page) and the other half to his son Andrew. A Barbara Deer, "daughter of Anna Deer," married Ephraim Rouse in Madison County in 1795 (bond given 16 MAR 1795). A Barb Hirsch was confirmed at the German Lutheran Church at the age of 17 in 1785 so born 1767/8.

Delph (Delp, Telph, or Telp could be the German spelling but the origins are unknown). Conrad Delph was born about 1720–25 and died in Culpeper County in 1791. He was excused from levies in Culpeper personal taxes around 1786 which commonly indicates an age of about 60 years. He was perhaps born in Germany and came with his parents. A Mary Delp, who might have been his mother, was ordered to be paid as a witness in Orange County in 1745 in a suit of George Moyer, Jr. and Sarah his wife against Conrad Broyle (*Orange O.B. 4*, p.279, also pp.74 and 149). Conrad Delph married about 1744–45 Anna Magdalena Castler, daughter of Matthias Castler, Germanna pioneer. Deeds show that she was sometimes called Ann and sometimes Magdalena and in the personal taxes she is shown as Nancy Delph in 1791 and 1792 just after her husband's death. Probably she did not die until 1807/8 for on 12 FEB 1808, her son, Adam Delph deeded away land she had given him in 1802 (*Madison D.B. 3*, p.143 and p.159). In 1782 Conrad and Anna Magdalena made a deed of gift of 62 acres to their son Henry (*Culpeper D.B. L*, p.217). Conrad's will, dated 26 OCT 1790 and probated 17 OCT 1791, leaves his property to his son Adam and appoints Adam Delph and Michael Snyder as executors (*Culpeper W.B. D*, p.19).

The records of the German Lutheran Church show there were eleven children of Conrad and Magdalena, eight sons and three daughters.

- Adam Delph (probably the oldest and born about 1745/46) was married by 1771 to Magdalena Aylor, daughter of Henry Aylor, Sr. and Ann Margaret Thomas.
- Michael Delph was probably the second son born about 1746/47 and he married Margaret Snyder, daughter of Philip Snyder and Margaret Cook. (Adam and Michael Delph witnessed the deed of their grandfather, Matthias Castler, to their father Conrad Delph on 17 FEB 1775 (*Culpeper D.B. G*, p.472).
- Daniel Delph, a soldier in the Revolution, is shown to be a son of Conrad Delph by his sponsorship of various grandchildren of Conrad in the church records.
- Susannah Delph (born about 1748/50) married John Carpenter, son of John and Dorothy (Cook) Carpenter.
- David Delph (born about 1750/52) appears only once in the records in 1772 when he was a sponsor of Anna Magdalena, daughter of John and Susannah (Delph) Carpenter.
- Mary Delph (born about 1752/53) was married by 1772 to Michael Snyder, son of Philip Snyder and his wife Margaret Cook.
- George Conrad Delph (born about 1754/56) married Elizabeth Snyder, daughter of Philip Snyder and his wife Margaret Cook. George Conrad appears in the records as George Conrad or George or Conrad.
- Samuel Delph (born about 1754/56 or possibly earlier) is only known by his signature as a witness to a deed by his parents to Ephraim Klug (*Culpeper D.B. G*, p.533).
- Rebecca Delph (born about 1757/59) married in 1776 Michael Carpenter, the son of John and Dorothy (Cook) Carpenter.
- Henry Delph (born about 1759/61) was a member of the Culpeper militia in 1781. He married Ann Powell but in 1786 has a wife Nancy. He disappears after 1790 and probably moved away.
- Matthias Delph (born about 1762/63) is only mentioned twice in the records. He was a sponsor at church once and is in the Culpeper Classes of the militia. Otherwise he never appears in the records of Culpeper or Madison County.

A longer discussion of the Delph family starts in *Beyond Germanna*, v.6, n.1 and extends through four issues based in part on a typescript left by B.C. Holtzclaw with contributions by Delph descendants.

Diehl (the spelling and origins in Germany are unknown but Deal or Deale is popular in America). Daniel Diehl and his wife Elizabeth brought their daughter, Marg, born 12 MAR 1775, to the German Lutheran Church for baptism on 28 JUL 1776. Sponsors for the child were Rudolph Crecilius and Catharina Hirsch. The Alexander Deale in Culpeper Class 15 was probably English. Daniel Deel was in Class 55. Peter Diel was in class 56. A Rosanna Deale, born about 1771, married Jonas Hoffman, the son of Michael Hoffman and perhaps Mary Fleshman. Johann Diel and his wife Christina were communicants in 1791, in 1801, and in 1808 at the German Lutheran Church. Elias Deal married Catherine Hoffman, born about 1780, the daughter of Nicholas Hoffman. In the *1787 Census of Virginia, Culpeper County*, there are two Deals, Daniel and John. From their position in the lists, they lived near the border of northern Madison County and southern Rappahannock County. Neighbors who lived close by include Thomas Garriott and Frederick Bumgarner.

Dicken. Several members of the Dicken family interact with the Germanna people. Most of these people were children of Christopher Dicken and Sarah Pulliam. Christopher Dicken wrote his will in Culpeper County, Virginia, on 21 AUG 1778 and it was recorded a month later on 21 SEP 1778 (*W. B. B*, pp. 273–5). He named eight children but stated there were fifteen children. From the will and other sources, the children were Susannah, Richard, Benjamin, William, Elizabeth, John, Ephraim, Joseph, Daniel, Charles, Isaac, Christopher, Sarah, Winifred, and Lot. Thirteen of these children are to be found in the Kentucky records.

Benjamin Dikons and his wife Rosina Garr (daughter of John Adam Garr and Elizabeth Käfer) had Rhode baptized 22 JUN 1777 at the Lutheran Church with Adam Fisher, Elizabeth Garr Fisher, and Eva Yager as sponsors. Rosina was a communicant at Christmas service in 1776. Elizabeth Dicken married John Burdyne, son of Richard and Catherine (Tanner) Burdyne. Christopher (Sr.) was a witness to the will of Anne Mary Gabbard (1762) and an appraiser of her estate (1762). Susannah Dicken married Joseph Render II (they moved to Georgia).

Several pages of information on the Dicken family will be found in *Kentucky Pioneer Genealogy and Records*, v.9, 1988, published by the Society of Kentucky Pioneers.

Doser / Dosser / Dozer. Daniel Doser and his wife were sponsors for the child Anna Barbara Urbach on 22 SEP 1776 at the Lutheran Church. Friedrich Dosser was confirmed in 1777 and Henrick Dosser was confirmed in 1782 at age 14. Leonard Dozier received cash of the estate of Philemon Kavanaugh (1752) as did Christopher Zimmerman. The family appears to have moved to Greenbrier County, now West Virginia, and some information is available in *Our Families* by Larry Shuck.

Eberhart. Elizabeth and Anna Maria Eberhart were communicants at Hebron Church in 1775.

Fähr. Caspar Fähr and his wife Catharina had Adam (born 1777) baptized on 2 NOV 1777 with Adam Wayland and his wife Mary (Finks) as sponsors. Adam was an elder in the church and probably his inclusion is a reflection of that position and not any relationship to the parents.

Finder. Michael Finder died intestate in Culpeper County in 1760. The appraisers of the estate were James Barbour, Jr., Adam Gaar and Adam Wayland.

Finks (the origin and journey to America are uncertain). Mark Finks was unquestionably Germanic but differs in some respects from the other Germanic families in the Robinson River community. Though he is said to have come to Virginia in the early 1730s, by 1734 he was a member of the first grand jury impaneled in Orange County which also included William Carpenter and George Woods (Utz) who had been there more than ten years. This suggests a familiarity with the English language by Mark Finks which is unusual in a person thought to have arrived just about this time. Though there is a proof of importation for Mark Finks, he was never naturalized. This, taken with the apparent knowledge of English, suggests that he may have been born on English soil. Two of his later descendants describe his origins as "high in the mountains" and "Switzerland." It is a possibility that the family left their original home many years before and lived for a while in lands under the dominion of England, perhaps in England, Ireland or Pennsylvania. Mark Finks was in court several times, often as a defendant in assault and battery cases. Michael Holt and Elizabeth his wife brought suit 21 SEP 1736 against Finks (*Orange County O.B. 1*, p.114).

While Mark Finks was living, the family had almost no presence at the German Lutheran Church. One daughter of Mark Finks, Catherine who married Christopher Crigler did not attend the baptism of her first ten children. This apparent opposition to infant baptism suggests that the family may have been Anabaptist which would be consistent with an origin in Switzerland. Another daughter, Elizabeth, who married Matthias Weaver, acts at church as though she were a Carpenter, not a Finks. It is believed that this situation arose at the birth of Elizabeth when her mother died. Probably John Carpenter and his wife Anna Barbara raised Elizabeth. Thus, she acquired the culture of the Carpenters. Mark Finks remarried and his second wife was Elizabeth. After Mark Finks died, the children are to be found at the Lutheran Church. Elizabeth, the wife of Mark Finks, is found once in the list of communicants after he died.

In 1739, the family of Mark Finks has two tithables. None of the children of Mark Finks would have been old enough to be a tithable and he was not a slave holder. Possibly this second tithe was a brother who married Alcy _____ and left two children before he died. Alcy then married Zacharias Blankenbaker by 1750. The tradition that Alcy_____married a Finks first is supported in the book *Some Martin, Jefferies, and Wayman Families and Connections of Virginia, Maryland, Kentucky and Indiana* which states that one of the wives of Henry Wayman was Mary Magdalena Finks. Baptisms at the church show that Mary Magdalena was a member of the family of Zacharias and Alcy (_____) Blankenbaker.

Mark Finks died in 1764 leaving a will which mentions his wife Elizabeth and children. The first three here are thought to be daughters of his first wife while the other children are by his second wife:

    Catherine who married prior to 1751 Christopher Crigler, son of the 1717 immigrant Jacob Crigler,

    Christina who married Christopher Blankenbaker, son of the 1717 immigrant Matthias Blankenbaker,

    Elizabeth married Matthias Weaver, son of the 1717 immigrant Peter Weaver,

    Mark, Jr. married Eve Fisher, daughter of Lewis and Anna Barbara (Blankenbaker) Fisher,

    John married Anna_____,

    Mary married Adam Wayland,

    Andrew married Sarah_____,

    Hannah married Henry Wayland, son of John Wayland and Catherine Broyles, and

    James.

Fisher (undoubtedly Fischer in German but his point of origin is unknown). In the 1739 Orange County tithables (see Part I), Ludwig or Lewis Fisher appears twice. In James Pickett's precinct, south of the Robinson River, he appears as Lodowick Fisher. In John Mickell's precinct, north of the Robinson River, he appears as Ludwick Ffisher. Whether these are two individuals or a mistake in the compilation is unknown. The possibility that they are two distinct individuals is increased by information from Germany. When Christoph Zimmermann and his first wife, Dorothea, had their son Johannes baptized in Sulzfeld, Baden on 12 APR 1711, one of the godparents was Anna Barbara Fischer. On 16 JUN 1715, when the parents Christoph Zimmermann and his second wife, Anna Elisabeth, had their child Johann Martin baptized, one of the witnesses was Ludwig Fischer (information from Margaret James Squires). Because of the tendency to migrate as friends and relatives and because Christopher Zimmerman did emigrate, the mention of Ludwig and Anna Barbara Fischer in Germany suggests they may be related to the Lewis and Anna Barbara Fisher known in Virginia. Confusion could certainly develop because the Fishers from Germany have the same personal names as the Fishers who are known in Virginia. A Lewis Fisher died in Culpeper County in 1773 and there is a reference to the estate of Lewis Fisher in Orange County in 1742 *(Orange County O.B. 3, 1741–43, p.190)*. On the surface, this suggests two Lewis Fishers but James E. Brown analyzed the reference in "Were There Two Ludwig Fishers in the Early Robinson River Settlement?" in 𝔅𝔢𝔶𝔬𝔫𝔡 𝔊𝔢𝔯𝔪𝔞𝔫𝔫𝔞, v.6, n.1 and he concluded it does not support the two Lewis Fishers theory. The question is unresolved and the information which follows pertains to the Lewis Fisher who died in 1773. There are many references to Lewis Fisher in the Orange County Court both as a defendant and as a plaintiff. For example, William Russell on behalf of himself and the King brought a suit of debt against Lewis Fisher in 1737. William Pierse brought a suit of assault and battery against Lewis Fisher in 1737. Harry, a Negro boy, belonging to Ludwick Fisher was judged to be ten Years of age by the Orange County Court in 1739.

Lewis Fisher married Anna Barbara Blankenbaker, the daughter of Balthasar Blankenbaker whose will confirms the marriage. The will of Lewis Fisher does not define his family completely. *The Garr Genealogy* gives one set of children and *Fisher Families of the Southern States* gives another set. When analyzed against the German Lutheran Church records, it is clear that both of these are incorrect. The correct set is believed to be:

Stephen who married Mary Magdalena Garr,
Adam who married Elisabeth Garr,
Barnett who married Eve Wilhoit,
Eve Fisher who married Mark Finks, Jr. and
Mary Margaret who married Nicholas Wilhoit.

The Garr's claim that daughters married a Watts and a Kalfus has confused granddaughters with daughters. The church records show that the wife of Nicholas Wilhoit was Mary Margaret, not Elizabeth. She alternated between using Mary and Margaret but never used Elizabeth.

The will of Lewis Fisher mentions an estate in Germany in which all of the children are to share if it is recovered. The estate was never defined and imaginations ran wild with the potential of it. There is no evidence that it was anything more than a typical citizen might have. The stories that Ludwig Fisher was a Baron and owned extensive properties in Germany including a castle on the Rhine River are not to be believed. See James E. Brown, "The German Estate of Lewis Fisher of Culpeper County, Virginia," in 𝔅𝔢𝔶𝔬𝔫𝔡 𝔊𝔢𝔯𝔪𝔞𝔫𝔫𝔞, v.9, n.3, p.501.

It is true that there are mentions of other Fishers in the Germanna community who are not descendants of Lewis Fisher. For example, Michael Klug married Elizabeth Fisher. This may be evidence that Lewis Fisher had a brother who had descendants.

Fite. Theobold Fite and his wife Barbara sold land to John Zimmerman, Jr. in 1759. In the Culpeper Rental of 1764, he is shown as "Tebald White." His given name would indicate that he was a German.

Fleit. Robert Fleit was a sponsor for a child of Dietrich Hofman and Jemima Barlow. Perhaps, Fleit is a misspelling of the name Floyd.

Fleshman (Fleischmann in German). Cyriacus Fleshman came in 1717 with his extended family namely, his wife, Anna Barbara (Schön) Blankenbaker Schluchter Fleshman; his son, Peter; his daughter, Mary Catherine; his stepson, Henry Schlucter; plus his four Blankenbaker step-children, Anna Maria, Nicholas, Matthias, Balthasar. Each of the latter four had their own families. All of these people had their origins at Neuenbürg just north of Bruchsal.

Cyriacus Fleshman was a leader in the Second Colony. He and George Utz filed a petition with the House of Burgesses asking for assistance to assure fair trials for the Germans being sued by Spotswood. He was sued by Spotswood in 1724 but the suit was dismissed in November 1726. Cyriacus Fleischman patented 390 acres across the Robinson River 24 JUN 1726 (*Virginia Patent Book 12*, p.474).

Shortly after the time that he moved to this land, he was one of two people whom the Lutherans sent to London (John Motz was the other) to secure a pastor but they were not successful in finding one. On this trip the two men cared for a "strange animal" which Lt. Gov. Drysdale was presenting to the King. An account of this visit to London was given by Andreas Mielke in "No Man-Eaters in Virginia," in 𝔅𝔢𝔶𝔬𝔫𝔡 𝔊𝔢𝔯𝔪𝔞𝔫𝔫𝔞, v.14, n.5. They did have an audience with the King and were rewarded by the King and Princess Caroline. He was one of the collectors of pledges for the church when John Caspar Stöver became the minister of the congregation.

He and his son, Peter, were jointly granted 400 acres in the same area 28 SEP 1728 (*Virginia Patent Book 13*, p.477). The father sold 156 acres of the original patent to Jacob Broyles and Mary Catharine his wife for £20 (*Orange D.B. 1*, p.74f).

Cyriacus was born in Klings where many Fleischmanns still live today. By occupation he was a stone mason and may have worked on Spotswood's "Enchanted Castle." Judging by the age of Anna Barbara, he was born about 1665 and was freed from county levies 5 MAY 1730 (*Spotsylvania O.B. 1724–30*, p.388). On 28 JUL 1737 he deeded 200 acres to Sarah Sluchter for £20 (*Orange D.B. 2*, p.84). Sarah, her maiden name unknown, was the wife of his stepson, Henry. The deed to Sarah would seem to indicate Henry was not a capable manager. Cyriacus last appears in the records of Orange County 1 JUL 1748, when he deeded 120 acres to Henry Huffman (*D.B. 11*, p.76). On this late deed, his wife is given as Margaret so she must have been a later wife. The 1748 Orange County Tithe List has the comment after the name of "Zachary" Fleshman of "gone to Germany." It is uncertain whether he died in Germany or Virginia.

> The daughter Mary Catherine married Jacob Broyle.
>
> The son Peter Fleshman, Sr. was naturalized 27 JAN 1742(OS) (Orange O.B. 3, p.313). He married Mary Sophia Weaver as is shown by strong implications in the church records (see Beyond Germanna, v.13, n.5 for an analysis of this situation). Peter and Sophia had six children:
>
>> John Fleshman married Elizabeth Blankenbaker, the daughter of Nicholas and Apollonia. Evidence for this marriage appears in a deed of 18 NOV 1762 when John Fleshman and Elizabeth his wife sold Michael Wilhoite 300 acres of land which had been a part of a patent to Nicholas Blankenbaker 20 JUN 1733 (*Culpeper D.B. D*, p.149). The 300 acres had been left to Elizabeth in her father's will.
>>
>> Robert married Dorothy Baumgardner,
>>
>> Peter, Jr, married first Winifred Smith, the daughter of Isaac Smith, Sr. and Margaret Rucker (see Darryl J. Diemer, "Mistaken Identity (wife of Peter Fleshman, Jr.)" in Beyond Germanna, v.4, n.2). Peter, Jr. married second Hannah_____.
>>
>> Elizabeth married Christian Reiner,
>>
>> Catherine married Christopher Barlow, and
>>
>> Barbara married Adam Cook.

The son of Cyriacus, Peter Fleshman, made a deed of gift of 200 acres, on 16 NOV 1753, to his son, John Fleshman, part of the 1728 patent to Peter and Cyriacus Fleshman (*Culpeper D.B. B*, p.32). John seems to have been of age at this time, so born at least as early as 1732. Peter Fleshman also made deeds of gift of land to his sons, Robert and Peter Fleshman 31 DEC 1763 (*Culpeper D.B. D*, pp.335 and 337). He died in 1773 and on 13 DEC 1773 Adam Cook, Christopher Barler (Barlow), Christopher Reiner, John Fleshman and Peter Fleshman made an agreement regarding the evaluation of his estate (*Culpeper D.B. D*, p.222). For some reason the son Robert did not sign this agreement.

The Lutheran Church records show a fair number of Fleshmans. Keith (pp. 183–185) devotes two pages to the Fleshmans. The most complete history is in L.G. Shuck, *Our Families*, Gateway Press, Baltimore, 1995. Material on the Fleshman family appears in Beyond Germanna in several articles.

Flohr. George Daniel Flohr was a British auxiliary in the Revolutionary War. After his return to Germany and his discharge, he lived there for a while before he returned to America, studied for the ministry, and became the pastor of a congregation in Wytheville, Virginia. When he returned to America in 1795, he lived first in Madison County where he studied theology under the Reverend William Carpenter (1762–1833) at the German Lutheran Church. He supported himself by teaching school. Flohr was licensed to preach and perform religious services by the Evangelical Lutheran Ministerium of Pennsylvania and Adjacent States in Lancaster, Pennsylvania. He accepted a call to serve among the German settlers in the New River Valley of southwestern Virginia around Wytheville (known as Evansham at the time). He served both Lutheran and Reformed Germans. He never married. On 30 APR 1826, four months before his 70th birthday, he died, and was mourned by the congregations that he had served for a quarter of a century. It is believed that he never told the members of his congregations that he had had an earlier life as a soldier. Samples of his handwriting from each period show that he was the same person. A fuller account of his life was told by Robert Selig in "Georg Daniel Flohr," Beyond Germanna, v.10, n.6. and in v.11, n.1.

Frady (Wrede). Carl Simon Wrede was a British auxiliary who remained in America after the Revolutionary War. He was listed as deserted in 1781. In the German records, he was in the Regiment von Rhetz, Lieb Company, 5 ft 6 in tall [English measurements], born at Braunschweig, 17[?] years old, Protestant, single, 5 years service, deserted 6 FEB 1781.

He was a Brunswicker captured as a part of Burgoyne's army at Saratoga. He had left Germany in 1776. Burgoyne's disaster on 17 OCT left Carl Wrede a prisoner of war. First, he was kept in Massachusetts and in January of 1779 the POWs were sent to Albemarle County, Virginia. He remained here until he deserted. Very soon after he left the POWs, Carl Wrede appears in Culpeper County where the name is given as Charles Frady, Carl Vorete, Carl Wrede, and Carl Vrede. A common saying was "German settlers [were] ready to aid the newcomers, the sick, the wounded, the stragglers, the deserters."

Twice he is mentioned in the Lutheran Church records. With a wife Barbara he is in the communicant lists at the church in 1782. At an uncertain date in the 1780s, he and his wife Sara apparently brought a child for baptismal but no child is listed and no sponsors are given. Since the name Sarah is used so much by his descendants, perhaps Sarah was the mother of his children. In the 1830 census, he appears with a wife Elizabeth.

Charles Frady left Virginia and became a landowner in several North Carolina counties. His family is thought to consist of twelve children:

Polly, born about 1782 in Virginia,

Henry (1784) in Virginia,

John (1786),

Ephraim (1790),

William, born 9 FEB 1793 in Virginia,

Sarah, born 18 MAR 1796 in North Carolina,

Charles, born 22 JAN 1797 in North Carolina,

Lewis, born about 1798 in North Carolina,

George W., born about 1801 in North Carolina,

Thomas H., born about 1804 in North Carolina,

Minnie or Winnie, born about 1805 in North Carolina,

Unknown son, born about 1812 in North Carolina.

A major researcher in the family is Louise F. Hodge who contributed three articles to Beyond Germanna: "The Search for Charles Frady," v.10, n.4; "Carl Simon Wrede, Brunswicker," v.11, n.5; "Charles Frady (Carl Simon Wrede)," v.11, n.3. In the last two of these articles, James D. Hodge is also given as an author.

Franck. Rev. Jacob Franck became pastor, on a trial basis, of the Culpeper Lutheran Church late in 1775. During the three years that he was pastor, the church was reactivated and attendance and the number of baptisms increased dramatically. Though he was popular with the congregation, he left the ministry and returned to Philadelphia as a silversmith. He and his wife Barbara had a son, Jacob, born 17 SEP 1776, baptized in the church. During his pastorate, a Constitution was written as was a petition to the Commonwealth of Virginia. These are valuable for the names of the male members. Rev. Franck also started the rolls of the people who took communion.

Fray. John Fray bought 90 acres in Culpeper County in 1764 from Adam Bumgarner (*D.B. D*, p.350). In 1782, he bought 60 acres of Henry Huffman and his wife Annie. At some point he purchased 112 acres from Valentine Hart. Though John Fray's wife, Rebecca, has been said to be a Yowell, the baptism sponsorships at the German Lutheran Church strongly indicate that she was Rebecca Swindel. John Fray died in 1791 with a will (Culpeper W.B. C, p.417) that mentions his wife, Rebecca, his sons Ephraim, Moses, and Aaron, his daughters, Mary, Elizabeth Ann, and Margaret.

> Ephraim was born 1762 and he married first, 2 NOV 1786, Mary Hoffman with nine children: John, Elizabeth, Mary, Margaret, Moses, Sarah, Rosanna, Nancy, and Ephraim. This information is from Ephraim's German Literature Book. Second, Ephraim married Nancy Snider on 11 FEB 1811 with five children: Ephraim Dutton, Hester Ann, Tabitha, Joseph Michael, and Martha.

Aaron married Lucy Snider 18 NOV 1806.

Moses married first Mary Hoffman and second Susannah Sellers.

Elizabeth married Elisha Hoffmans 15 JUN 1800. He was a widower with children but this marriage had no children.

Margaret married first Frederick Hoffman 29 SEP 1798 and second Joshua Fleshman 27 SEP 1813.

Florence Virginia Fray Lewis' *A History & Genealogy of John Fray of Culpeper County, Virginia* has more information down to the twentieth century though her writings have some erroneous statements.

Gabbard, Gybert. Anna Mary Gabbard wrote her will in Culpeper County on 17 DEC 1761 with witnesses John Clore, Christopher Dickens, and Michael Thomas. The estate went to her grandson, Henry Jones. A Michael Gabbert was a chain carrier for George Rindhart in 1761 in Frederick County.

Whether she was related to the following is unknown. The *Pennsylvania Merchant* in 1731 brought Frederick Gybert, Catrina Gybert, Elizabeth Gybert, Julian Reiner, Barnet Reiner, Sabina Gybert and Matthias Gybert from Schwaigern, Württemberg. The mother Catrina was the step-daughter of John Michael Willheit, early Germanna pioneer. Catrina had been married twice and Frederick was her second husband.

Garr (Gaar is a more common spelling in Germany). The origin of the family of Andreas Gaar and his wife Eva Seidelmann was Illenschwang in Bavaria. Thanks to the Theodore Walker family, extensive research on the family has been done in Germany which has found forty-five ancestors of Andreas and Eva. They came to Philadelphia 25 SEP 1732 on the ship *Judith* with five children:

John <u>Adam</u>, who was born 24 NOV 1711, married Elizabeth Käfer, daughter of Michael Käfer. He was a very active leader in the church. He was paid 140 pounds of tobacco for two wolves' heads in 1736.

Rosina, who was born 11 AUG 1713, married Theobald Crisler,

Lawrence, who was born 29 NOV 1716, married Dorothy Blankenbaker, daughter of John Nicholas Blankenbaker,

<u>Elizabeth</u> Barbara, who was born 11 FEB 1730, married Michael Blankenbaker, son of John Nicholas Blankenbaker, and

Mary Barbara, who was born 15 JUL 1728. She is said to have died in Philadelphia but there is evidence she reached adulthood in Virginia.

As Andrew Care, Andreas patented 250 acres on the back side of Garr's Mountain on branches of Pass Run (*Virginia Patent Book 15*, p. 352.) paying for this with five head rights (Andrew, Eve, Adam, Rosanna, and Lawrence). Some details of the standard Garr history are called into question by facts recorded in some land grants. In Peggy S. Joyner's *Virginia Northern Neck Warrants and Surveys*, v.3, there is this item:

Debold Christler, assignee of Christian Tival, assignee of Andrew Garr 2 OCT 1751 - 6 JUN 1752; south side of South Fork of Shannandoah River adjacent Zachory and Micall Blancumbaker. Chain carriers: Lawr. Garr, Peter Cree.

Above was a warrant to And. Garr and given to his son-in-law Christian Tival. Surveyed for C. Tival of Culpeper County.

Another warrant and survey shows the name Tivall in 1750. In Augusta County (v.1 of Joyner):

Lawrence Garr of Culpeper, 4 JAN 1749/50 - 3 FEB 1750, on South Fork Shannondoah. Chain carriers: Tivall and Zacharias Blancumbaker.

Another warrant and survey in Culpeper County also shows (Joyner, v.3):

Deobald Cristler, assignee of Christian Tivall; 12 MAY 1752 - 17 MAR 1752(OS); 62 a. on branches of Robinson R.; adj. His own land, Michael Smith, Andrew Gar. Chain carriers: Lawrence Gar & Henry Tivall.

A partial explanation of these statements might be that Andrew Garr had three daughters in Virginia where one of them was Mary Barbara who married Christian Tivall. The Tivall family moved away and Christian assigned his rights, which he had acquired from Andrew Garr, to his wife's brother-in-law (and another son-in-law of Andrew Garr).

Andrew, Adam, and Lawrence were all naturalized 27 JAN 1742(OS) in the Orange Court (*O.B. 3*, p.313).

The *Genealogy of the Descendants of John Gar* was published in 1894 after a fifty year long research project by John Wesley Garr and his son John Calhoun. This Gaar/Gar/Garr book of genealogy has been reprinted several times. A few errors are known for the book, for example, see the Lewis Fisher section here, but on the whole it has been a reliable guide for family research. A very detailed report on the forty-five ancestors of Andrew and Eva Gaar in Germany was given in 𝔅𝔢𝔶𝔬𝔫𝔡 𝔊𝔢𝔯𝔪𝔞𝔫𝔫𝔞, v.14, n.1.

Garriott. The origins of this family, including its nationality, are debated. In the Culpeper County, Virginia 1787 tax list there are Ambrose, John, Moses, Reuben and Thomas Garriott. That the family should be discussed here is quickly shown by the number of marriages with the Germanna families. Ambrose Garriott married before 1770 Elizabeth Blankenbaker, daughter of Jacob and granddaughter of John Nicholas Blankenbaker, a 1717 colonist. Philip Bunger married Mary Garriott, daughter of Thomas who gave his consent. Henry Bunger married Barbara Garriott with the consent of her father, Thomas, in 1798. Another daughter of Thomas Garriott, Levina, married Joseph Good (Goode, Gut) in 1803 with the minister of the German Lutheran Church officiating. Lewis Rouse, born 1756/7 in Culpeper County, Virginia married Elizabeth Garriott. Elizabeth Shirley, daughter of James Shirley and Judith Garriott, married William Wilhoite who was born about 1741. Another daughter of the Shirley couple, Nancy Ann, married James Yowell. Judith is said to be the daughter of Moses Garriott.

The spelling of the name is varied. In many records, the form Garrett occurs alongside Garriott though in later years the form Garriott is more universal. In the Orange County, Virginia Court Orders in the period 1734–1741 there are these mentions which might be the family: Thomas Garret, Edward Garrett, John Garrot, and Thomas Garrott. Both the first and last names suggest that this might include ancestors of the family members in the previous paragraph. Thomas Garrott, shoemaker, purchased 246 acres in the Robinson River Valley in 1737/8 (*Orange D.B. 2*, p.268). However, Thomas Garrett did not pick up the deed until 18 MAY 1744.

Land of John Garrot is mentioned in Prince George County in a patent of John Gibbs (*Virginia Patent Book 15*, p. 143). Probably this same land is mentioned in Thomas Webster's patent (*Virginia Patent Book 15*, p.217). Both of these events are in 1734. Prior to these mentions, John Garrett was a head right in 1714 and Tom Garret was a head right in 1714. John Garratt of Henrico County patented 400 acres in Prince George County 28 SEP 1730 (*Virginia Patent Book 13*, p.534).

In the Culpeper County tax list of 1783, there is listed a Garriott Vandyke which may be a clue to family associations. There is a Peter Vandyke in the 1787 Culpeper County tax list. In the 1781 Culpeper Classes there are Peter Vandyke and Garriott Vandyke.

One family historian suggests that the originator of the family in Virginia was John S. Garriott who married Catherine_____. One known son was Jonathan who married Sarah_____ and they had Ambrose, James, and Moses. Ambrose and his wife Elizabeth Blankenbaker had Phoebe, Elijah, Elizabeth, Barbara, Jacob (his birth is in the German Lutheran church register), Mary, Loving, William, Rhoda, Daniel, Simeon, John, and Lucinda. Moses was the father of Judith. However, this account is not complete as a comparison to the records above shows.

Gerhard. Nancy Dodge found a record for the Gerhard family in an earlier work of Barbara Vines Little who had abstracted information from the Orange County, Virginia Order Books. Nancy recognized the name under an alternative spelling. The significant portion of this 22 May 1740 record reads, "John Carehaut a German . . . imported himself, Mary, Elizabeth, Daniel and Catherine Carehaut immediately from Great Britain into this Colony at his own Charges . . ." Since no wife is specifically mentioned, John Gerhard was probably a widower who came with four children. Since he paid his own transportation, he could have arrived just before this date.

The children were older as Mary Gerhard married George Blankenbaker very soon after this date. Later records in North Carolina for the Gerhard family show an Elizabeth who had been previously unidentified but who may be a sister of the three previously known children, Mary, Daniel and Catherine. Apparently the Gerhards did not stay in Virginia for very long but moved to North Carolina.

A Barbara Garhert was a sponsor in 1787 when Henry Crisler and his wife Elizabeth baptized Rosina but there is no reason to believe she is associated with this family.

Graves. Nancy Graves was a sponsor about 1764 for a child of Michael Yager and wife Elizabeth Crigler.

Gut or **Good.** Daniel Gut and his wife Elizabeth had Ludwig baptized 24 NOV 1791. Sponsors for the four day old baby were Jacob Lip and his wife Margaret. Joseph Good married Levina Garriott in 1803. John Tanner married Susanna Good in 1791 in Culepeper County. Jonas Good married Sarah Tanner 9 NOV 1802 in Madison County. Their daughter Harriet, born about 1812/1814, married John Roberts. Jonas, born about 1770, was the son of Casper Good and Catharina Rothgeb. Caspar Good was the son of Hans Caspar Good/Gut (the latter may have been born in Switzerland). Hans Caspar Good married Anna Neff/Naf/Naef.

Hance. The head rights of several members of the Hance family (Susanna, Peter, Margaret, Catharine, and Adam), whose first names suggest a German origin, were used by Jacob Manspeil when he patented land. Adam Hance wrote his will 7 SEP 1746 and it was probated in Orange County 25 JUN 1747. His wife Catherine was appointed the executrix. The witnesses were John Walker, Patrick McNeil, and Isabell Walker. There was at least one child, Susanna.

Harnsberger (also Hansberger in America). Hans Heerensperger was born 1 April 1688 as is recorded in the Evangelical Reformed Church Parish book of Bussnang, Thurgau, Switzerland. He came in 1717 with his wife, Anna Purva (Barbara), and his son, Stephen. On his proof of importation, the name is recorded as Hans Herren Burgud showing the great difficulty in properly understanding the name. On 24 JUN 1726 he was granted 400 acres jointly with John Motz near the Robinson River (*Virginia Patent Book 12*, p. 475). Though the two men were perhaps related, there is no evidence of this. John Harnsberger names only one child, Stephen, in his will. After his wife, Anna Barbara, died, John Harnsberger married Anna Magdalena Aylor, the daughter of the 1717 immigrant, Henry Snyder. This was after 30 NOV 1742 when her father, Henry Snyder, wrote his will and described her as a widow. The will of John Harrensparger, dated 15 JAN 1759 and probated in Culpeper County on 20 MAR 1760, mentions his wife Anna Magdalene, leaves his land to his grandchildren, John, Barbara, Elizabeth, and Margaret Harrensparger who are children of his son Stephen by the latter's first wife, Agnes, and leaves a small bequest to the son Stephen, and mentions "my wife's children," Henry Aylor and Elizabeth Tanner (*Culpeper W. B. A*, p.56).

Stephen Harnsberger married first about 1741 Agnes Hoffman, the daughter of the 1714 immigrant John Hoffman by his first wife, Anna Catherine Häger. Agnes died about 1750. The son, Stephen Harnsberger, moved to Augusta, later Rockingham County, Virginia, and married, at about the same time, Ursula Scheitle. Their children include Adam, Henry, Stephen, Conrad and Robert. John Harnsberger, son of Stephen by his first wife, Agnes, was also living in Augusta County in 1779, when, he deeded away the land his grandfather had given him in Culpeper County. The Rockingham County marriages show many Harnsbergers from 1800 on. By 21 JUN 1770 Stephen's three daughters by his first marriage were all married, Barbara to Daniel Mauk, Margaret to Henry Huffman, and Elizabeth to Jacob Lingel for on this date the three couples deeded away the 100 acres that Hans Harnsberger had left them jointly (*Culpeper D.B. F*, p.96). Nothing further is known at present concerning the Mauks and the Lingels; but Margaret Harnsberger married Henry Huffman, son of Henry Huffman (1708–1765), brother of John Huffman, the 1714 Germanna immigrant (see *Germanna Record Three*). A four part article by Wanda Cunningham on the Harnsberger family appeared in Beyond Germanna starting with the January 1995 issue (v.7, n.1). An analysis of the wife of Stephen Harnsberger was made by Wanda Cunningham in "Who Was Agnes Harnsberger," in Beyond Germanna, v.12, n.4. Keith omits the Harnsbergers.

Hart (sometimes Hurt). Michael Thomas married, as his second wife, Eve Susanna Margaret Hart. Michael was the younger son of the 1717 immigrants, John and Anna Maria (Blankenbaker) Thomas, Sr.

Moses Hart was confirmed at the Lutheran Church in 1782 at the age of 17. Several Harts attended the Lutheran church, for example, Elizabeth Hart, Valentin Hart and his wife Anna Maria. The name, Valentin, itself suggests a Germanic origin for the family. See the Berry family for other connections within the Robinson River Valley.

Hendricks. Jacob Hendricks attended the German Lutheran Church at least four times in the period 1775 to 1785.

Holt (Hold in Germany). Michael Holt came as a 20 year old bachelor in 1717 from Stetten am Heuchelberg, Württemberg. He came with his mother, Anna Maria and her new husband John Spade, see "The Ancestry of the Scheible, Peck, Milker, Smith, and Holt Families," *Before Germanna*, v.5. The earliest known ancestor of Michael Hold was Jonas Hold (1601– 9 APR 1663) who was the mayor of Stetten. With his wife Anna they were the parents of eight children. The oldest of these was Martin who married on 7 NOV 1665 Barbara Waydelich. They had five children. After Barbara's death, Martin married Anna Maria Brückmann on 3 MAY 1687. Anna Maria was the daughter of Hans Jerg Brückmann and Anna Barbara Nägelin. Martin and Anna Maria had three children including Hans Michael born 30 DEC 1696. The research which yielded this information was paid for by Jimmy L. Veal who hired a German researcher (Rut Rosler) to reexamine the records that had been found by Gary Zimmerman and Johni Cerny and reported in "The Ancestry of the Sheible, Peck, Milker, Smith, and Holt Families," *Before Germanna*, v.5. The German researcher reported the spelling of Brückmann and Nägelin as Brickmann/Brickhmann and as Hägelin.

Michael Holt was sued by Col. Spotswood in 1724, and on 24 JUN 1726 was granted 400 acres in the Robinson River neighborhood (*Virginia Patent Book 12*, p. 477). He and his wife, Elizabeth, sued Frederick Cobbler (Kabler) early Germanna pioneer, 7 SEP 1725 (*Spotsylvania O.B. 1724–30*, p.72). Another grant of 245 acres was made to him 28 SEP 1728 (*Virginia Patent Book 14*, p. 100). He purchased 250 acres from William Eddings for £40 in 1740 in which the two witnesses were Christopher Yowell and Mark Finks (*Orange D.B. 3*, 164).

Michael Holt's wife, Elizabeth, was a daughter of George Sheible, the 1717 immigrant. Michael was a prominent member of the German Evangelical Lutheran Church community, being sent to Europe in 1734 with Michael Smith and the pastor, Rev. John Caspar Stöver, to solicit funds for the church. Holt returned before Smith and Stöver did. Michael Holt and his wife Elizabeth brought suit against Mark Finks for assault and battery on 21 SEP 1736. (This cannot be taken as positive evidence that Michael Holt had returned by then since the wives included their husbands in lawsuits even if the husband was not present, see Stöver.)

Michael Holt gave a bond for the execution of the will of John Rucker 28 JAN 1742(OS). Michael Holt was a witness to the will of Peter Rucker and he and George Holt gave a bond in the matter. On 23 NOV 1750, he was a witness to the will of George Clore. Michael Holt and his sons, George, Nicholas, Christopher, Michael, Peter and Jacob, all moved to Orange County, North Carolina some time after 1755. He was granted land 20 AUG 1759 in Orange County. (Some of this land is still owned by his descendants.) His will, naming his wife Elizabeth, is dated 31 OCT 1765 which was recorded two years later in North Carolina (*Orange W. B. A*, p.76). The children, all sons of Michael and Elizabeth, who were born in Virginia, are:

- George Holt married Mary Magdalena who was the young widow of John Caspar Stöver. George was probably born soon after his parents came to Virginia.
- Nicholas Holt married Eva Wilhoit about 1740 in Orange County, Virginia. She was the daughter of Johann Michael Willheit and Anna Maria Hengsteler. Eva died 16 APR 1807 in Orange County, North Carolina. Nicholas was probably born within a few years of his parent's marriage.
- Michael Holt, Jr. was born 6 MAY 1723 in Spotsylvania County, Virginia and died 20 JUL 1799 in Alamace County, North Carolina. He married first in Virginia Margaret (Peggy) O'Neil. Secondly he married Jean C. Lockhart. There were children by each wife.
- Peter Holt was born 1725. He married Rachel_____.

John Holt was born about 1726 and died in June of 1802 in Chatham District, Orange County, North Carolina. He married Mary Bobo.

Jacob Holt was born about 1729. Though he was married, her name is unknown.

Christopher Holt was born 1733. He married Elizabeth_____.

More information about the first three generations is in Robert Nicholson et al, "Michael Holt and Elizabeth Scheible," 𝔅𝔢𝔶𝔬𝔫𝔡 𝔊𝔢𝔯𝔪𝔞𝔫𝔫𝔞, v. 14, n.3.

Holtzclaw. Jacob and Joseph Holtzclaw were the youngest sons of the 1714 colonist, Jacob Holtzclaw, and they lived in the Robinson River community. They both married daughters of John Thomas, Jr. who had come as a very young boy with his father, John Thomas, Sr. and mother, Anna Maria Blankenbaker. (The Holtzclaws' eldest brother, John, had married a widow whose first husband was_____Thomas. Whether there was a connection between this Thomas and John Thomas is unknown but the later marriage of Jacob and Joseph to Thomas girls does raise questions.) Jacob married Susannah and they moved to Kentucky very early in its history. Jacob gave testimony at one point that he had raised a crop of corn there in 1775.

Joesph Holtzclaw married Mary Thomas but no descendants from this union are known. She died and he married Elizabeth Zimmerman, daughter of John and granddaughter of Christopher Zimmerman and Nicholas Blankenbaker, 1717 colonists. For more information, see B.C. Holtzclaw's works, *The Genealogy of the Holtzclaw Family* (reprinted as *Germanna Record* 14) and *Ancestry and Descendants of the Nassau-Siegen Immigrants to Virginia 1714–1750* (printed as *Germanna Record* 5).

House. The origins of Matthias House (Haus?) just prior to purchase of land in 1771 in Culpeper County are thought to be in Augusta County, Virginia. The German Lutheran Church in the Robinson River Valley records are filled with information about the family after they arrived in the Robinson River Valley. They show that Matthias' wife was Margaret or Maria Margaret which are the same person according to Susie House Cooper who was a major researcher and publisher of a history of this family.

The author here believes that Margaret and Maria Margaret are two different women. At the baptism of Salome in 1776 and of Catherine Elizabeth in 1778, both daughters of Matthias, the wife is Mary Margaret and sponsors are Valentin Bungert and wife, Elisabeth. At the baptism of Moses in 1787 and of Sara in 1789, children of Matthias, the wife is Margaret and the sponsors are (for Moses) Joseph Holtzclaw and his wife Elizabeth Zimmerman and (for Sara) Christopher Zimmerman and his wife Anne Mary Tanner. (Note that Elizabeth Zimmerman and Christopher Zimmerman are sister and brother and that they did have a sister, Margaret.) Matthias House married Margaret Mitchell (widow of Mark Mitchell) in Madison County in 1814. The association between the House and Bunger families is strong but the degree of relationship is unknown.

From the Lutheran Church records, Adam was confirmed in 1782 at the age of 18 though he was actually born 3 JAN 1763. Michael was confirmed in 1782 at 18. Matthias was confirmed in 1785 at 19. Elisabeth was confirmed 1783/4 at 17 but she is not included in the list of children of Matthias House by many researchers. Eva was confirmed 1785 at 17, Margaret was confirmed in 1785 at 16, Jacob was confirmed in 1792, Salome (born 1776) was confirmed 1794, Catherine Elizabeth (born 1778) was confirmed 1794, George was confirmed 1798, John was confirmed in 1800, Susanna was confirmed in 1800. Aaron signed the Lutheran Church covenant in 1776. Moses was born in 1787 and Sara was born in 1789.

Adam married Catherine_____and she died 10 MAY 1839. He married Hannah Seraphim in 1841 and he died in 1852 in Washington County, Missouri.

Michael married Susanna Zimmerman in 1789 though the marriage record gives her name as Nancy. They moved to Preble County, Ohio. Eleven children of Michael and Susanna are in the German Lutheran Church records.

Matthias, Jr. married Susanna Floyd in 1792 and they moved to Tennessee.

Eva married John Bungert (Bunger) with four children at the Lutheran church.

Margaret married Jacob Bungert with five children baptized at the church.

Mary Magdalena married John Floyd in 1789.

Jacob married Susanna Tanner in 1797 and they moved to Kentucky first, then Ohio.

Salome married Jacob Holtzclaw the son of Joseph Holtzclaw and Elisabeth Zimmerman in 1796 with three children noted in the Lutheran records. They moved to Boone County, Kentucky.

Catherine (Katy) married George Rookstool and moved to Preble County, Ohio.

John married Mildred Tanner in 1803. They moved to Boone County, Kentucky and then to Shelby County, Indiana. There were later marriages for John.

Moses is said to have married Margaret Garr, the daughter of John and Margaret (Wilhoit) Garr.

An analysis of the House family as revealed by the German Lutheran Church records is made in "Matthias House Family in the Hebron Church Records." 𝔅𝔢𝔶𝔬𝔫𝔡 𝔊𝔢𝔯𝔪𝔞𝔫𝔫𝔞, v.15, n.2. Another article in the same issue of 𝔅𝔢𝔶𝔬𝔫𝔡 𝔊𝔢𝔯𝔪𝔞𝔫𝔫𝔞, "Did Matthias House Marry Margretha Jäckler?" examines the question of the first wife and the history of Matthias House.

Huffman, Henry (Hofmann). Henry Huffman, a younger brother of John, below, was christened Johann Henrich Hofmann, at Roedgen on 11 MAR 1708. He trained as a carpenter and married Elisabeth Catherina Schuster. Three daughters are recorded in the church at Rödgen: Maria Elisabetha, baptized 29 JUL 1736, Anna Catharina, baptized 18 MAY 1738, and Elisabetha baptized on 14 JUN 1739.

This family moved to the Robinson River community in 1743. His will, dated 14 AUG 1765 (*Culpeper W.B. A*), was written in German and witnessed by Henry Ralsback (from the same village in Germany) and Peter Weaver (his son-in-law). Translation of the will from German to English was made by Samuel Klug.

Though the Hofmanns were of the Reformed faith in Germany, several descendants of Henry Huffman are found in the German Lutheran Church in the Robinson River community. Using these records and other sources, the children of Henry and Catherine Huffman can be taken as:

Mary Elizabeth, born in 1736 in Eisern and married Peter Weaver, Jr. in Virginia,

Anna Catherine, born in 1738 in Eisern and no marriage by the age of 30,

Elizabeth, born in 1739 in Eisern with no record in Virginia,

The birth sequence of the following, all born in Virginia, is uncertain:

Lewis, no marriage,

Anne Mary, married George Cook as his second wife,

Henry, married Margaret Harnsberger,

Ambrose, married Mary Railsback,

Teter, married Jemima Barlow,

Agnes, married Robert Fleit (Floyd?).

There is no evidence for Daniel as a son. For additional reading see the *Germanna Records* 1 and 5. See also "The Family of Johannes Henrich Hofmann and Elisabetha Catherina Schuster," in 𝔅𝔢𝔶𝔬𝔫𝔡 𝔊𝔢𝔯𝔪𝔞𝔫𝔫𝔞, v15, n.5, p.895; "The Henry Huffman Bottle" by David Beatty et al in 𝔅𝔢𝔶𝔬𝔫𝔡 𝔊𝔢𝔯𝔪𝔞𝔫𝔫𝔞, v.12, n6, p.715; "Johannes Steinseifer (1698–1757)" by Ryan Stansifer in 𝔅𝔢𝔶𝔬𝔫𝔡 𝔊𝔢𝔯𝔪𝔞𝔫𝔫𝔞, v.10, n.5, p.583.

Huffman, John, #1. For the estate of John Huffman, on 25 JUN 1741, a Henry Huffman was the administrator and George Oots (Utz) was a bondsman. There was no will. The estate inventory was returned 21 JUL 1741. These are recorded in *Orange W.B. 1*, p.155–6 and 161. The presence of George Utz who was the step-father of the wife of John Huffman, see next entry, suggests the John Huffmans here may have been related.

Huffman, John, #2 (Hofmann). John Huffman was a member of the First Colony of 1714 but he moved to the Robinson River area around 1729. The probable motivation for his move arose when his first wife (Anna Catherina Häger) died and he married Mary Sabina Volck (sometimes given as Folg), the daughter of the wife of George Utz. For the Volck and Utz story see Margaret James Squires, "The Mother of My Wife," in 𝔅𝔢𝔶𝔬𝔫𝔡 𝔊𝔢𝔯𝔪𝔞𝔫𝔫𝔞, v.1, n.1, p.4. with essential parts reproduced here in Part I. The patents and grants of this John were summarized in Part I.

John and Mary had twelve children, all recorded in John Huffman's family Bible and all lived to adulthood and married. The family is treated in *Germanna Record* 3 and in *Germanna Record* 5. A three generation chart is given in 𝔅𝔢𝔶𝔬𝔫𝔡 𝔊𝔢𝔯𝔪𝔞𝔫𝔫𝔞, v.12, n.1, p.667 but the statement that only two children from the first marriage survived is in error. It was proven after that chart was made that the daughter Agnes did live and she became the first wife of Steven Harnsberger. See Wanda Cunningham, "Who Was Agnes Harnsberger?" in 𝔅𝔢𝔶𝔬𝔫𝔡 𝔊𝔢𝔯𝔪𝔞𝔫𝔫𝔞, v.12, n.4, p.695.

Hume (Home). The Humes were of Scottish origins and were cousins of Alexander Spotswood. Francis and George Hume had participated in the failed Jacobite rebellion of 1715 but were captured and sentenced to transportation. Francis became the overseer of the Germans at Fort Germanna but he died in 1718 and is buried along the Rapidan River. George Hume did not arrive in Virginia until 1721 after serving a few years on slave ships. He obtained a license as a surveyor which led to a long career as a major surveyor in Virginia. Descendants of George Hume married into the Crigler, Willheit, and Finks families. For an introduction to the Hume families see, Karl R. Hume's "George (Hume) Home, Surveyor" in 𝔅𝔢𝔶𝔬𝔫𝔡 𝔊𝔢𝔯𝔪𝔞𝔫𝔫𝔞, v.7, n.1

Hupp (Hoop). Philip Hoop died in Culpeper County in 1761 leaving his wife, Elizabeth, and children, George, Baltus, Philip and Elizabeth (see *W.B. A*, pp.264–65). His will refers to "that land and plantation I had of Robert Hutcheson on top of Greens and Moors Mounting and all the grain that is growing on the same." The executors of the will were the wife, Elizabeth, and Henry Aylor (Henry was connected through the Thomases to Philip Hoop). Eberhard and John Hoop were deeded land in 1762 which they sold in 1769. Many members of the family moved to Washington County, Pennsylvania very early in the history of the region including the mother, Elizabeth, who was remarried to Matthias Ault. Besides the children in the will there were Everhard, born 1745, John, and Francis.

Everhart Hupp, George Bumgarner from Culpeper County, Virginia, and Abraham Teagarden went to Ten Mile Creek in 1766. The wife of Everhart was Margaret Thomas, the daughter of Michael Thomas. It is said that she was the first known white woman west of the Monongahela River. They had eleven children. John Hupp, brother of Everhart, was born in 1747. He married Anne Rowe (Row) daughter of Adam. George Hupp married a Delaware Indian and they had four children. Philip was a woodsman, adventurer and soldier. Balser married first Mary_____with seven children and then Barbara Grove with four children. He is buried on his farm along the Shenandoah River.

More history is included in "The Hupp Family" in 𝔅𝔢𝔶𝔬𝔫𝔡 𝔊𝔢𝔯𝔪𝔞𝔫𝔫𝔞, v.5, n.1, p.243–4, and in v.5. n.2, p.251–2 with several references.

Isom. The name Isom was probably a phonetic spelling of Eastham at the German Lutheran Church. Maria Isom was a sponsor at the birth of Maria of Adam Broyles and his wife Maria.

Jacobi (Jacoby). This family has not been studied enough. Some things are known about John Francis Lucas Jacobi who married Johanna Friederika Lotspeich in London in 1764. Several records pertaining to land suggest that the Jacobi family had a presence in Virginia earlier than this. Daniel Jacobus, had a warrant for land in the Northern Neck in 1747 in the Little Fork of the Rappahannock River. In this same year he was a chain carrier for John Strother on a tract in the North Fork of the Rush River. Daniel Jacobi was also a chain carrier for Francis Strother. John Francis Lucas Jacobi assigned his warrant of 1751 to John Oldham. John Francis Lucas Jacobi applied for a grant of land that was escheated from John Daniel Jacoby. The father had intended to leave the land to Francis who would pay his brothers and sisters something but the will was declared invalid because he was an alien. Apparently the family was German as the father was an alien and they were involved with many Germans. See the Lotspeich family section here.

Jesse. John Jesse and his wife Susanna Carpenter were sponsors for children of Peter Cook and his wife Mary Carpenter.

Kabler (Kappler, Cobler). Apparently Frederick Kabler lived at Sulzfeld where Christopher Zimmerman was a godparent when Kabler's son Christoph was baptized in 1713. This son died in 1714. In the so called "Fifth Return Party," (see Part I) Frederick Kabler was the head of a family containing three people in 1717 (apparently himself, his wife Barbara, and an unspecified person) who were petitioning for funds to return to Germany. Thus, he is one of the families who left their home in Germany in 1717 but did not get to Virginia until 1719. The adjacent names to his on the "Return Petition" were George Lang and Christopher Uhl who were also from Sulzfeld. There is no good evidence for a Susanna whom many people say was the wife of Adam Yager.

In Virginia, Kabler settled close to his friend Christopher Zimmerman in the Mt. Pony area where he had a patent for 289 acres next to Conrad Amberger and Zimmerman (*Virginia Patent Book 13*, p. 477, 28 SEP 1728). He was deeded 200 acres by Christopher Zimmerman 7 APR 1729 (Crozier, *Spotsylvania County Records*, p. 106). He was deeded 290 acres by Adam Yager 25 NOV 1736 (*Orange County D.B. 1*, p.407).

His will, dated 6 MAR 1779 and probated 17 JAN 1780 (*Culpeper W.B. B*, p. 349) shows that he had four children: Conrad, Nicholas, Christopher, and a daughter who married a Watts.

> Christopher is thought to be the youngest son who was named for the deceased first son. His wife was Mary. He was granted 136 acres (*Grant Book M*, p. 181) on the south arm of Mt. Pony adjacent to the Adam Yager tract which was sold to Frederick Kabler and given to Conrad Kabler. Christopher and Mary sold part of this land in 1775 to William Joel. Apparently the couple moved away after his father's death in 1780 for he does not appear on the 1782 tithables list. In 1768 he had signed a petition to Gov. Josiah Martin of North Carolina. In 1784 he had a grant of land in Rockingham County, North Carolina. That same year he also had a grant of land in Wentworth County, North Carolina. He does not appear in the 1790 census so it is presumed he was deceased by then. Christopher had a son Frederick as is shown in the will of the grandfather. The children of Christopher were:
>> Lewis (there is only one reference to him),
>>
>> Harvey, buried in Mt. Olivet Cemetery in Nashville, Tennessee,
>>
>> Frederick, born 14 Aug 1758 according to his pension application for service in the Rev. War. He married Martha_____(perhaps Pryor) and moved with his brother Harvey to Davidson County, Tennessee where he died in 1840.
>>
>> Thomas was born in North Carolina in 1765. He married Elizabeth Grogan and they had four children,
>>
>> Nicholas was born in 1769 in North Carolina. He married Prudence_____. This family moved to Bedford County, Virginia. He died there in 1859.
>
> Nicholas, perhaps the second son, was granted 162 acres on 22 NOV 1752 (*Grant Book H*, p.236) on Mt. Pony adjacent to Christopher Kabler, Minor Winn, and Thomas Brown. This land was sold by Nicholas and his wife Nanny to John Brown in 1773. Nicholas died in 1806 and his will, dated 10 JAN 1788, was probated 15 DEC 1806 (*Culpeper W.B. E*, p. 190). It names two sons, Frederick and John Kabler and an unmarried daughter Anna but says there were five children in all. The daughter may have been the Anna Kabler who married John Yager 5 SEP 1809. The son John was apparently a Methodist minister and he officiated at a number of marriages in Culpeper County.
>
> Conrad, probably the eldest son, was married twice as shown by his will. The first wife's name is unknown and the second wife was Joan or Joanna. Conrad died in 1778 before his father did. Conrad's will was probated in Culpeper County 20 JUL 1778. By his first wife he had a son William and a daughter Barbara who married_____Thackett. By his second wife, there were four daughters and a son Frederick who married Ann Threlkeld.

The land transactions which have been given are only a part of the many transfers of land by members of the family. More is known about the German ancestry of Frederick Kabler, see "The Ancestry of the Snyder, Amburger, Kerker, and Kapler Families, "*Before Germanna*, v.8.

Käfer. Michael Käfer was a bachelor who came with his sister, Apollonia, and her husband, John Nicholas Blankenbaker. Later he married Anna Maria Blankenbaker, the widow of John Thomas and the sister of John Nicholas, so that Michael's children were double cousins of Nicholas' children. Michael was sued by Spotswood in 1724 and was granted 400 acres in the Robinson River neighborhood 24 JUN 1726 (*Virginia Patent Book 12*, p. 479). He bought 100 acres of Timothy Johnson for £16 on 15 JUL 1735 (*Orange D.B.* 1, 67ff). His daughter Elizabeth married Adam Garr at least as early as 5 FEB 1740(OS), as on this date Michael deeded 100 acres to Adam Garr (*Orange D.B. 4*, p.384). In JAN 1762 Michael Käfer made deeds of gift of 100 acres apiece to his sons-in-law and daughters, so that his children are known to be:

   Elizabeth who married Adam Garr,

   Dorothy who married John Clore,

   Barbara who married John Weaver,

   Mary who married George Utz, and

   Margaret who married Nicholas Crigler.

These are to be found in *Culpeper D.B. C*, pp.640, 642, 644, and 646; also, *D.B. D*, p.48. The will of Michael Käfer, dated 28 DEC 1762 and probated 17 NOV 1768 (*Culpeper W.B. A*, p.467), names his five daughters and their husbands as above and leaves bequests to "my deceased wife's children," John Thomas, Michael Thomas, Magdalena wife of Michael Smith, and Margaret wife of Henry Aylor (given in the will as Collier but by analysis shown to be Aylor). This shows that he married Anna Maria (Blankenbaker) Thomas, perhaps a 1717 immigrant with her husband and two children, John and Anna Magdalena. Michael Käfer's descendants occur through his five daughters in the Clore, Crigler, Garr, Utz and Weaver families.

A little is known from Germany about the Käfer family and it is given in "The Ancestry of the Clore, Kaifer, and Thomas Families," *Before Germanna*, v. 2. They were from Ansbach in Bavaria. There is one record from Dietenhofen in Mittelfranken which might be the grandparents of Michael Käfer. Conrad Käfer and his wife Margaretha had two children, Margaretha and Magdalena, with these dates 11 NOV 1655 and 26 SEP 1658 (LDS film 0542001). Another sibling might be Wolfgang Käfer, the father of Michael (Wolf Michael). These dates in Dietenhofen suggest that the family might have been emigrants from Austria. The author here believes that the Käfer family was related to the Blankenbakers.

Kahl (uncertain German spelling). Perhaps Wilhelm Kahl was from Eisern as he seems to associate with the Huffman and Railsback families, who were from there. This would mean he was Reformed. When John Sneider wrote his will in 1760, the witnesses were William Cawl, John Knuesbay, and Henry Huffman. On 6 MAR he witnessed a deed along with James Graves, John Thomas, William Catton, Michael Smith, Christopher Moir [Moyer], and Adam Barlow. This deed was a sale of 288 acres by John Wiland and Katherine to Henry Railsback. In October of this year, William Call sold land in Culpeper to Charles Taylor. This was 170 acres of the John Paul Vaught tract. William stated he was moving away. He is found after this in Rowan County, North Carolina, in the presence of many other Germanna names. The will of Wilhelm Kahl was dated 1778 and proved 4 MAY 1784 in Rowan County. One witness was Henry Railsback. A descendant Eva Alford gives the following names as children of Wilhelm Kahl.

   Adam, born 1758,

   John, born 1760,

   Daniel, born 1761,

   Dorothy, born 1765, married Henry Railsback, Jr. 16 FEB 1788, in Rowan County, (she is an ancestor of Eva Alford),

   Henry,

Maria Margaret married Henry Railsback as his second wife,

Eva,

Christiana,

Anne Mary,

Margaret Elizabeth.

More work on this family would be desirable including perhaps finding the origins in Germany.

Kaines (or Kines). John Kains patented 400 acres in the Robinson River Valley in 1736 (*Virginia Patent Book* 17, p.57) on Comical Run, on the branches of Deep Run adjacent to John Huffman, Christian Clayman [Clemons], and Edward Ballenger. He had been living in the community for he was appointed to appraise the estate of William Rush 16 MAR 1735(OS). He proved his importation in May 1741. He died in Culpeper County in 1767 and his will mentioned his grandson John Harriss and Joseph Harriss and his wife. His friends Harmann Spilman and John Stinecyfer, Jr. were appointed executors. It would appear that John Kaines was of the Reformed faith. There was a John Kyner in the 1739 Orange County tithables with three tithables. This may have been Kaines.

Kerker. Andrew Kerker came in 1717 with his wife Margaret and his daughter Anna Barbara and was granted 850 acres in the Robinson River section 28 SEP 1728 (*Virginia Patent Book 13*, p. 389) as Andrew Kirker. While his patent of 850 acres was granted two years after the majority of the 1726 patents, it was in the midst of the 1726 patents. His original stake or land claim must have been made at the same time as the other early settlers. The German Lutheran Church was later built on his patent. He made a proof of importation in which he stated that he came in 1717. He was churchwarden of the Lutheran Church in 1733 and 1734 and was the treasurer of the church. His church account is recorded in *Orange W.B. 1*, p.54ff (see "The Hebron Church Account" in 𝔅𝔢𝔶𝔬𝔫𝔡 𝔊𝔢𝔯𝔪𝔞𝔫𝔫𝔞, v.6, n.4). When Andrew Kerker died in 1738, John Carpenter was appointed his administrator 27 JUL 1738 (*Orange W.B.1*, pp.50–51). John Carpenter's wife, Anna Barbara, was Andrew Kerker's daughter as proven by deeds of gift made by John Carpenter and Barbara his wife on 17 MAR 1762 to their sons, Andrew, William, and Michael, of land which was part of the 1728 patent to Andrew Kerker described as "father of Barbara" (*Culpeper D.B. C*, pp.663, 664 and 666). Thus, all the Carpenters are descended from Andrew Kerker, for John Carpenter's brother William had no children.

Kiester (Küster). Georg and Margaretha Kiester communed 26 OCT 1783 at the Lutheran Church. Several years later, a Johannes Küster communed twice at the church.

Kinslow (Kuntzly, Kensel, Censley, Genessle, Kunzle, Kenselow, etc.). Conrad Kinslow was four years old when he came with his parents to Pennsylvania in 1750. His father was also a Conrad. The father has a traceable trail in Pennsylvania and the Shenandoah Valley including fighting in the French and Indian War. On 16 August 1758, the Augusta County, Virginia Court recognized the death of Conrad, Sr. It named the children as Conrad 12, Savina [Sabina] 8, and Katrina 6. Sabina became the ward of Henry Sellers and Conrad was bound to Jacob Nicklos, a son-in-law of Henry Sellers. Catrine was bound to Robert Shanklin. Jacob Nicklos lived in the Peaked Mountain area where he was a member of the local church. The Rev. George Samuel Klug of the Culpeper County Lutheran Church served the church by visitations. Later the Rev. Schwarbach visited the church also. Conrad was free when he was 21 and he appears to have moved soon after this (about 1767) to Culpeper County on the east side of the Blue Ridge Mountains. There he married Rachel Barlow. There is no date for the marriage but in 1772 Rachel Kuenzle was a sponsor for Abraham, son of George and Anna Magdalena Christler. Anna Magdalena was Rachel's maternal aunt. Rachel Barlow is a Germanna descendant of the Barlow, Smith, Thomas, and Blankenbaker families.

The births of nine children of Conrad and Rachel are recorded in the Baptismal Register of the Lutheran church. Later two more children were born to them, Ezekiel about 1798 in Mercer County and Andrew Carpenter Kinslow about 1800 in Washington County, both counties being in Kentucky. The children were:

Elizabeth, born 2 NOV 1773, married Andrew C. Carpenter 19 DEC 1792 in Culpeper County (eleven children),

Nimrod, born 18 DEC 1775, was the father of six children but the name of their mother is unknown,

Ambrose, born 13 FEB 1778 married first Barbara Coleman in Barren County, Kentucky (eight children), married second 18 JAN 1830 Mahaly Emerson in Barren County, married third Patsy Jones 17 NOV 1842 in Barren County,

Joshua, born 18 OCT 1780 in Culpeper County, married Jane Adams on 25 FEB 1809 in Washington County, Kentucky (eleven children),

Adam, born 2 FEB 1783, married first Charlotte Drake on 22 JAN 1809 in Barren County (five children), married second Lousia Pickett on 30 MAY 1826 in Barren County (nine children),

Nancy Jane, born 22 NOV 1785 Culpeper County, married Joseph Coleman 27 AUG 1807 in Barren County (three children),

Aaron, born 4 JAN 1792 in Culpeper County, married Jane Jones 28 DEC 1814 in Barren County (seven children),

Margaret (Peggy) Kinslow, born 20 DEC 1794 in Culpeper County, married William Adams 30 DEC 1814 in Barren County (seven children),

Ezekiel, born 1798 in Cave City, Barren County, married Elizabeth Anderson,

Andrew, born 1800 Cave City, Barren County, married Sarah Gertrude Emerson (eleven children).

For more information on the Kinslow family, see several articles in Beyond Germanna: "The Wife of Conrad Künzle" in v.12, n.3; a correction appears in v.12, n.4; Jefferey Jewell et al, "The Family of Conrad Kinslow," in v.12, n.5; Mariettta Mansfield, "Conrad Kuntzley," in v.13, n.1. The attempts to equate the names Kinslow and Kincheloe are misguided, see Linda L. Hope, "Kinslow and Kincheloe," in v.13, n.1.

The church records for Oberöwisheim and Neuenbürg in Baden (the origins of the Blankenbaker and Thomas families) have names that could easily have become Kinslow.

Klug. George Samuel Klug was born at Elbing, near Danzig (now Elblag, Poland). He studied at Helmstedt University and was chosen as the assistant pastor by Johann Casper Stoever, Sr. during the European fund raising tour of the German Evangelical Lutheran Church of Orange County, Virginia. He was ordained at Danzig on 30 August 1736. He proceeded to London where he spent some time and perhaps learned the English language. He arrived in Virginia in late 1738 or early 1739. His duties in Virginia were to be the assistant pastor with responsibilities for missionary work with the Indians and teaching in a school connected to the Lutheran church in the Robinson River Valley. Upon the death of Rev. Stoever on his return trip, Rev. Klug became the pastor of the church in Virginia. One of his first duties was to oversee the construction of a new church and the purchase of a farm and slaves to support the church. For a while, Klug also taught school in a building near the church (perhaps the original chapel). The subjects taught were reading, writing, arithmetic, and religion. But the labor of serving other churches at great distances made it impossible for him to continue to teach in the school. Among the German congregations that he served across the Blue Ridge Mountains in the Shenandoah Valley were Naked Creek, (Lower Peaked Mountain), Upper Peaked Mountain, Frieden's, Hawksbill (Mt. Calvary), and the Opequon Cedar Creek settlement. Many of these were Union churches serving both Reformed and Lutheran congregations. Klug admonished the people to beware of the Moravians and they admitted they could make little headway in Virginia because of Klug's work. In 1749, Klug visited the Pennsylvania Ministerium where he met Henry Melchior Muhlenberg who wrote that Klug, "lamented that he was so entirely alone in that vast, extensive country and had no opportunity to be cheered and edified by his clerical brethren since most of his inhabitants are English." The distances to Pennsylvania discouraged Klug and there is no evidence that he was actually invited to the meetings of the Ministerium. He was pastor for twenty-four years but not without some critical observations on his performance. Muhlenberg did not like Klug's position on slavery, his abandonment of the school, and his style of living.

Klug also served his English neighbors in the Robinson River Valley. His services in this capacity were recognized by the Council of Virginia on 16 APR 1752 when they awarded him twenty-five Pounds for "his Services for Many years past to the Neighbouring English inhabitants of Culpeper County .. and for his Good character and on Consideration of this small Allowance and indigent Circumstances."

At the Virginia Council of 2 NOV 1752, the following petition was read:

> To the Revd George Samuel Klug, Michael Thomas, Nicholas Knot, Jacob Burner, Henry Bochman, Abraham Mayer, Stephen Suel, Abraham Brown, Adam Wayland, Adam Broil, Adam Barler, Henry Ailer, Matthew Smith, Nicholas Smith, Michael Russell, John Ralchbach [Railsbach], John Barler, and Paul Ledderer, Leave is granted them to take up and survey Thirty Thousand Acres of Land, lying between Green Briars to the south and Youghyoughganie to the North, bearing the Name of Mannangelie upon a River called Goose-River, beginning at a Run known by the Name of Muddy Run up the River upon a white Walnut Tree marked M.T. provided it does not interfere with any prior Grant, and four Years Time is allowed them, to survey and pay Rights upon Return of the Plans to the Secretary's Office.

Several of these names are Robinson River Valley names. Apparently Michael Thomas (M.T.) had scouted and found the land. Then Klug became the leader in taking the position to the Council. Some of the names are from the Shenandoah Valley where Klug visited on his trips to the churches there. Not long after the petition above was made and granted, war broke out which made the Valley an unsafe place. Then on 28 APR 1762, Klug asked the Council for a renewal of the grant and other items:

> i) About Ten Years ago (viz.) 1752 in November there was granted unto George Samuel Klug (after he had been naturalized) and until his Company in the General Council a Certain Tract of Land containing 30,000 Acres of Land of which the said George Samuel Klug for himself petitioned for 10,000 Acres, and received an Order for it made by the said Honourable Council present the late Governour, which had been surveied in the Time alloted if we had not been prevented be [by] Reason of War. Now as he shall by Mr. Walthoe humbly petition for renewing of the said Order. His Houour is intreated of his Patronage in Obtaining a renewed Order, the Old one having been entered in the Auditor's office at Williamsburgh and in the office of Augusta County.
>
> ii) That it has been extremely hard for George Samuel Klug to pay his Witnesses which appeared on his behalf, when he was spitefully prosecuted by disaffected persons, for by those means his debts contracted in the Time of his Distress, were increased very much. Now since for Peace's sake he hath a mind to give up the urging [paying?] of the full Payment of the Costs and Charges during the lawsuit. He asks leave to beg for an Order from the Honourable General Court or the Honourable Council, to sell a Couple of Negroes out of the Estate recovered by Judgment, that his great damages sustained by the Malice of his Adversaries, who wanted (if they could) to disallow the said estate given for my Maintenance as the gentlemen of the Court of Culpeper County very well know; by this the said George Samuel Klug would be able to satisfy his Creditors and also incouraged to pray incessantly unto the Supreme Governour of the World to pour all possible Blessings upon his Honour our Gallant Governour and upon all the Honourable Persons which sit with him at the Helm of the Goverment of Virginia.

Michael Klug, the son of Rev. Klug, renewed the petition for the grant on 6 NOV 1770 but the Council postponed action.

Shortly after he came to Virginia, Rev. Klug married Susannah Castler. Nine children were born to them:

Michael, born about 1741, m. Elizabeth Fisher. He was in the militia of 1781 in Culpeper Class number 70 and the 1787 personal property tax list living north of Criglersville.

Samuel, born about 1744, became an Anglican pastor after studying at William and Mary College,

Ephraim, born about 1756, married 24 August 1792 Elizabeth Major. He was in the militia of 1781 in Culpeper Class 92 and in the 1787 tax list for Culpeper (living south of today's town of Madison),

Elizabeth, m. Michael Broyles,

Eva, m. Matthias Broyles, youngest brother of Michael Broyles,

Magdalene, m. William Lotspeich,

Daughter, m. Godfrey Yager as his first wife,

Child eight, and

Child nine.

Rev. Klug left no will when he died in 1764. He was buried beneath the chancel of the German Lutheran Church. Susanna was appointed the administrix of the estate (*Culpeper W. B. A*, p.369 where the personal property in the estate was appraised at £361). She was granted the use of the glebe for seven years. Susanna later married Jacob Medley but only after an agreement was signed on 20 OCT 1774 between the two which preserved the prenuptial assets of each for their own purposes. She lived until 1801.

Strangely, there are hardly any mentions in the Lutheran church records of members of the Klug family. Some members of the family turned more to their English neighbors than to their German ones.

An article, by Mary C. Padget et al, "George Samuel Klug," appeared in Beyond Germanna, v. 11, n.1.

Langenbühler. The entry with this name made 16 MAY 1786 in the Lutheran Baptismal Register was a mistake for Blankenbaker (Blankenbühler).

Leatherer / Leathers. Johann Paulus Lederer was born 17 JAN 1709 in Schwaigern (now in Baden-Württemberg). In Germany he married Anna Maria Schlötzer 3 OCT 1730 in Schwaigern. They had a daughter Maria Magdalena Lederer who was born 2 SEP 1731. The circumstances are not clear but he came to America leaving Anna Maria and Maria Magdalena behind. He arrived at Philadelphia from the *Johnson* on 28 SEP 1733. The daughter died 19 OCT 1741 and the wife married John Daniel Schreiber on 19 JUN 1742, with both events in Schwaigern.

Many people in Schwaigern had emigrated to Virginia and this is probably the reason Paul Leatherer came to Culpeper County. He may have lived for a while in the Shenandoah Valley as he was called as a witness in the suit of Jacob Stover vs. George Home [Hume] in 1734. On 20 JUN 1751, Michael and John Clore sold him 100 acres. Presumably Leatherer was married to Margaret Clore who would appear to be several years younger than he was. He died between writing his will in 1780 and the 1785 probation of it. Paul and Margaret were the parents of nine children:

Samuel Leatherer, born 1745, died in Carroll County, Georgia,

Paul Leatherer, born 1 APR 1747, died at Georgetown, Scott County, Kentucky,

Michael Leathers, born before 1755, died 1805/6 in Pendleton District, South Carolina,

John Leathers, born about 1752/5 in Culpeper County, Virginia, died in 1817/8 in Madison County, Virginia,

Nicholas Leatherer, born about 1754, died 1817/8 in Madison County, Virginia,

Joshua Joseph Leathers, born 13 DEC 1759, in Culpeper County, Virginia, died 23 MAY 1825, at Georgetown, Scott County, Kentucky,

Susannah Leatherer served as a sponsor at the baptism of Elizabeth Lederer on 29 OCT 1776. This required that she be confirmed which typically might be at the age of 16 so perhaps she was born before 1760. After a mention in her father's will, there is no further record,

Mary Leatherer, no further information,

Margaret Leatherer was confirmed Easter Sunday 1776 at the German Lutheran Church. In the next two years, she was a sponsor twice at baptisms. After a mention in her father's will, there is no record.

There is more information in "The Ancestry of the Zimmerman, Yowell, Mercklin, Wegman, and Leatherer Families," *Before Germanna*, v.9.

Lehman. The Lehman family has a few mentions in the German Lutheran records and in the Culpeper County, Virginia, civil records in the period around the time of the Revolution. On Christmas Day in 1775, Georg and Michael Lehman were communicants at the Lutheran church without any wives (they may have been present but non-Lutherans). The next September, Georg Lehman signed the church petition of 1776. Georg Lehman, age 21, and Joh. Lehman, age 15, were confirmed at church on 22 May 1785. This same day, one other Lehman, another Georg, is a communicant who is presumably their father, probably the Georg of Christmas Day 1775. George Layman was a landowner in the Robinson River Valley. The family moved to Tennessee after the Revolution. Family links to the longer established residents of the Robinson River Valley were few if any.

The Lehman name is well known in Pennsylvania and the originator of the family in Pennsylvania was probably an Anabaptist from Switzerland. Sources of information on the family include: 1) Beyond Germanna, "The Lehman Family," in v.11, n.2 and in v.11, n.3); *National Genealogical Society Quarterly*, v. VIII, n.3, p.38, October 1919; Rupp, *History of Lancaster County*; Howard Lehman Spessard, *A Brief History of the Lehman Family and Genealogical Register of the Descendants of Peter Lehman of Lancaster County*, Pennsylvania, Hagerstown, MD, 1960.

Leyerele (many variations in spelling). Johann Christoph Leyrle arrived at Philadelphia 30 SEP 1754 on the *Richard and Mary*. Almost immediately he was found in Harpers Ferry and married Christina_____. They moved to Culpeper County where Zachariah (born 2 JUN 1756), Peter (1757), Christopher (1763), and perhaps Barbara, Margaret, and Catherine were born. About 1767, the family moved to Rowan County, North Carolina. Another son, Jacob, was born about the time of the move.

Christopher Lyerly was very active at the Organ Church in North Carolina. His feelings were strongly in favor of Germans as is attested by his will of 12 OCT 1784.

His son, Zacharias, was in the Revolutionary War and his pension application states he was born in Culpeper County in 1755 where he lived about ten years.

In Culpeper County, Christopher Lyrle was appointed administrator of Christian Reapman on 21 APR 1763 (A. M. Prichard, compiler, *Abstracts from the County Court Minute book, 1763–64*, 1930, p.16).

Probably the reason that the family has no mentions in the baptismal records at the Lutheran church is that they had moved away by the time the Baptismal Register was rewritten in 1774. Families who had moved away were omitted. For more information, see "A Trilogy of Family Stories," Beyond Germanna, v.9, n.2.

Lipp. The first members of the family in the Robinson River Valley seem to be Henry and Elizabeth Lipp who attended church in 1776. They had children:

> Caroline (perhaps) who married Benjamin Huffman about 1780. Benjamin was the son of Jacob Huffman and Barbara Sauder (the evidence for Caroline is weak),
>
> Jacob, confirmed at the age of 18 in 1782 married Margaret _____ who was probably not a Zimmerman,
>
> Daniel, confirmed in 1777,
>
> Elizabeth, confirmed in 1782 at the age of 16,
>
> Anna Maria, confirmed in 1777. The report that she married Christopher Zimmerman is to be doubted as he married Mary Tanner,
>
> Friedrich Lipp signed the petition of 1776 so he was confirmed before this date.

When Jacob Lip and his wife Margaret had their daughter Elizabeth and son Thomas baptized, the sponsors included Daniel, his brother, Elizabeth Lip, his sister, and Anna Maria Lip, his sister. When Aaron Wilheit and his wife Maria Yager had their son Benjamin baptized in 1788, one of the sponsors was Maria Lip. This might have been the Anna Maria above but it is a mystery why she was chosen. When Christoph Zimmerman and his wife Maria Tanner had their daughter Lea baptized in 1786, one of the sponsors was Maria Lip who might have been the daughter of Jacob above.

The reason for stating that Jacob Lipp did not marry Margaret Zimmerman is that a simple age analysis shows that Margaret Zimmerman was about ten years older than Jacob. Another Margaret Zimmerman, a niece of the first Margaret, was too young to be the wife of Jacob Lipp. On the contrary, the Margaret Zimmerman who was the daughter of John, was almost certainly the second wife (of three) of Matthias House.

The name Lipp or Lepp is found in the church records for Neuenbürg and Oberöwisheim.

Long / Lang. John George Long by his proof of importation said that he came in 1717 with his wife Rebecca (see below) but this seems to be an error as he was one of the people who petitioned 16 September 1717 for funds to return to Germany from London. At this time the Long party consisted of four persons. It may be that he was thinking of when he first stepped on English soil. He said the ship was the *Mulberry* and this may have been the ship that brought the Second Colony from Rotterdam to London. On 28 SEP 1731 he was granted 300 acres (as Lang) in the first fork of the Robinson River adjacent to Andrew Kerker, J. Huffman and M. Castler (*Virginia Patent Book 14*, p.359). In 1739 he deeded land to Matthias Castler, a neighbor (*Orange D.B. 3*, p.325). He appears among the Orange tithables in 1739 as George Lung with one tithable (see Part I). On 22 JUL 1742 he was excused from the county and parish levies (Orange County O.B. 3, p.169). In 1750 and 1751 he deeded land to Michael Russell and to Martin Hirsch (Deer). The latter deed was for his 300 acre grant (*Culpeper D.B. A*, pp.203 & 304). There are Longs in the Shenandoah Valley who are associated with Germanna descendants and these may be descendants of George Long.

Lotspeich. The origins of this family prior to Virginia are in Frankenthal, a village located a few miles northwest of Ludwigshafen. The name is spelled variously in the records there, e.g., Lotschberg, but it generally settles on the Lotspeich spelling. Three members of the family came to Virginia and it appears that the first person to come, Johanna Friederika Lotspeich, married John Francis Lucas Jacoby in London at the Parish of St. Martins in the Fields on 16 JUL 1764. The Jacobi family had a presence in Virginia before this so the return to Virginia was natural. This family moved to Kentucky. They are assigned twelve children. She died in 1822. Apparently after John Francis Lucas and Johanna Friederika Jacobi came to Virginia, two of her Lotspeich brothers came to Virginia.

One was Johann Wilhelm Lotspeich who married Magdalena Klug in Virginia, the daughter of Rev. George Samuel Klug who died in 1764. Probably this marriage was after the Rev. Klug died. Wilhelm was active in Virginia real estate. His wife's brother-in-law, Matthias Broyles, gave a power of attorney to him from Greene County, Tennessee. Eventually Johann Wilhelm is found in Kentucky where, at Lexington, he died in 1828. Five children, possibly six, are assigned to him.

A second brother, Johann Christopher Lotspeich came through Philadelphia on 19 OCT 1772 on the ship *Catherine*. His signature appears on several documents in Culpeper County, Virginia, not long after his arrival. However, he moved to Greene County, Tennessee, where he married Rebecca Barbara Hartley. He had a North Carolina land grant for 122 acres in 1788. He acquired other land, including a parcel where a neighbor was a Broyles. He wrote his will in 1830. Fourteen children were named in the will and it is believed there was another one. Christopher was a Quaker who would not allow any work, even cooking, on Sunday.

There are elements in the history of the Lotspeich family that are unusual. The uncle of the three immigrants (a brother of their mother) was Ralph (Rudolph) Ladenberger, a wine merchant in London. Though he was married twice in England, he had no children and he left his estate to his siblings and/or nieces and nephews. This created a fair amount of testimony with respect to the American heirs. Articles with much more information by Robert Lotspeich et al, "The Lotspeich Family," appeared in *Beyond Germanna*, v.12, n.1, in v.12, n.2, and in v.12, n.3.

Lutz. Michael Lutz and his wife Susanna and Daniel Lutz and his wife Maria communed at the Lutheran church on 2 APR 1786.

Majors. Franky Majors married George Racer and they were sponsors in 1788 for Elizabeth, the daughter of Christian Racer and his wife Sarah Simms. Also, they sponsored Margaret, the daughter of Jacob Racer and Susanna Snyder in this same year.

Manspile (the German spelling is uncertain). Jacob Manspile was granted 400 acres of land in 1734 on Deep Run adjacent to George Martin, Joseph Bloodworth, and Edward Ballenger (*Virginia Patent Book* 15, p.351). He paid for the land with eight head rights, namely, Jacob Bryell, Rose Paulitz, Susanna Hance, Peter Hance, Margaret Hance, Jacob Manspoil, Catherine Hance, and Adam Hance. The five members of the Hance family are unknown but they were residents of Orange County in 1746 and 1747 (see Hance). On 26 SEP 1739, Manspoil purchased 100 acres from John Sutton for £15 (*Orange D.B. 3*, p.328). In 1739 Jacob Manspeil was the head of a household with one tithable (this in Orange County). He was naturalized 24 FEB 1742(OS) with other Germans from the Robinson River Valley.

He may have had a son John who in 1752, with his wife Ann, deeded land to John Deer in Culpeper County. Apparently Jacob and his wife Mary deeded some of his original land to John Broyle in 1779. In this same year Jacob Manspile made a deed of gift of his property to William Adkins and Margaret his wife of Culpeper County and to James Shearer and Anna his wife of Orange County on the condition that Jacob and his wife Mary be maintained for the rest of their lives (*Culpeper County D.B. K*, p.89). It would seem there were three children, John, Margaret who married William Adkins, and Anna who married James Shearer.

The statement that Jacob had a daughter Elizabeth who married Michael Yager is false for it has been proven that the wife of Michael Yager was Elizabeth Crigler.

In the Lutheran communion lists, Jacob Mansbeil and his wife are found once, on 26 MAY 1776 when they were elderly. He did not sign the Constitution for the Lutheran Community nor did he sign the petition for relief from support of the Anglican church (both of these were in 1776).

Marbes. Johannes Marbes was a communicant on five occasions at the German Lutheran church from 1790 to 1792. A man of this name married Catherine Smith, the daughter of John Michael Smith, Jr. and his wife Anna Magdalena Thomas, but it is uncertain if it is the same person. It is recorded in the Lutheran Baptismal Register that Catherine had a child by someone other than her husband.

Mauck. Matthias Mauck with his wife Barbara appears in deeds in Culpeper County in 1772, 1774, and 1779. George William Glore (Clore) married Elizabeth Mauck 5 JAN 1786 in Culpeper County. Barbara Harnsberger married Daniel Mauk.

Milcher. There are two families on the Spotswood head right list for which the history is minimal. In the Gemmingen departure list, there is a family of Hans Michael MichlEkler, wife Sophia Catharina, daughters Anna Margaretha age 7 and Anna Catharina age 4 plus the wife's sister who is not named. This could be the family shown by Spotswood as Hans Michel Milcher, Sophia Catharina Milcher, and Maria Parvara Milcher. The difference in the spelling of the surname is not significant. In the Gemmingen church books the spelling is extremely varied. The two Gemmingen daughters and the wife's sister must have died and a new child was born. (Alternately, the wife's sister might have been entered erroneously as a Milcher, a not unlikely event.) It is unknown what happened to this family. One thought is that the family decided not to stay in Virginia but slipped away quietly, perhaps to Pennsylvania.

Miller, George. George Miller was a brother of Henry, see following. George with his wife Maria Margaretha came to the Robinson River community with three children who had been baptized elsewhere but they were recorded in the German Lutheran church in Culpeper County. Very little is known about this family.

Miller, Henry. Henry and Susanna Miller moved to Robinson River community from Pennsylvania not long before the Revolutionary War. They already had a number of children but most of them were baptized at the Lutheran church in the Robinson River Valley. Apparently the family was complete by 1772. In the Baptismal Register, there are errors in the history of the family probably as the result of the parents failing to remember the birthdays. Henry Miller signed the church petition of 1776. He purchased land in Culpeper County, some near the Lutheran church and some in the area that fell into Rappahannock County. Henry wrote his will in 1796 and it was settled in 1807. Of his twelve children, nine were still living as was his wife Susanna.

There is some record of Susanna who came to Philadelphia bringing a "birth certificate" which was preserved within the family. The certificate states she was born 21 FEB 1731, the daughter of Michael Sibler, a citizen and master carpenter, and his wife Barbara. The parents were Evangelische Lutherans in legal and honest wedlock. She was born at Auerbach and the birth was recorded at Langensteinbach (both in Baden). The certificate was made 7 APR 1752 which probably means she arrived in 1752. The first child was born in 1756. From the will and the church records, the children are:

> Unknown Miller. Tradition says that Mary was the second child,
> Mary (Mollie), born 17 SEP 1756, married Isaac Haines 15 FEB 1779,
> Sarah, born 7 NOV 1757, no further information,
> Henry, born 4 JAN 1759, married first 14 MAY 1782 Achsah Warner, married second before 1810 Margaret _____, died 7 JAN 1833,
> John, born 5 FEB 1762, married 16 DEC 1789 Nancy Hitt, died 3 AUG 1841,
> Susanna Catherine, born 4 DEC 1763, no further information,
> George (twin), born 6 FEB 1766, christened 17 JAN 1772, no further information,
> Margaret (twin), born 6 FEB 1766, christened 17 JAN 1772, no further information,
> Elizabeth (Betty), born 8 DEC 1767, married 18 APR 1802 Francis Le Campion in Philadelphia,
> Adam, born 17 DEC 1768, married Mary Wilhoit, died 5 JUL 1813 in War of 1812,
> Sophia, born 23 OCT 1771, married 15 OCT 1792 Burgess Rogers, no further information,
> Anna, born 27 JAN 1773, married 15 JUL 1790 Jesse Berry and they moved to Monroe County, Indiana where he died in 1849.

For more information, see Louise Keyser Cockey, "Henry and Susanna Miller," Beyond Germanna, v.1, n.5. Also, see Louise Keyser Cockey et al, *History of the Descendants of Charles Keyser and Henry Miller*.

Miller, Jacob. Jacob Miller had a patent (*Virginia Patent Book 15*, p.110) of 47 acres on the side of Mt. Pony adjacent to John Gordon and Adam Eager [Yager]. This patent was issued 17 AUG 1733. A Jacob Miller petitioned 25 FEB 1741(OS) to be levy free since he was 67 years of age and unable to work (*Orange County O.B. 3*, p.105). He was naturalized 24 FEB 1744(OS) (*Orange O.B. 3*, p.346).

Möller. Heinrich Möller was called to the German Lutheran Church in the Robinson River Valley as a catechist after Johannes Schwarbach resigned. Möller spent a few months at the church and it is probably he who rewrote the Baptismal Register. He was engaged to a lady in Pennsylvania and she did not want to move to Virginia. Möller resigned from the church and returned to Pennsylvania.

Morton. James Morton and his wife Susanna brought Rebecca in 1799 for baptism at the German Lutheran Church. There were no sponsors and the record was written in English. Perhaps, the parents were concerned about the health of the infant and came to Rev. Carpenter for an emergency baptism.

Motz. John Motz came to Virginia in 1717 with his wife, Maria Pelona (Apollonia). Very little history in Germany is known but the marriage record of 28 FEB 1716 for Johannes Motz and Maria Apollonia Maubars is in the Lutheran Church at Bonfeld, Baden (Annette Kunselman Burgert, *Eighteenth Century Emigrants from German-Speaking Lands to North America*). In this marriage record, Johannes Motz was the son of the late Galli Motz, citizen at Ditzingen, Leonberger Ambt [Amt Leonberg]. Maria Apollonia was the daughter of Johann Leonhard Maubars, citizen at Hecklingen in the Markgrafschaft Anspach [Ansbach], near Gunzenhausen. The village of Bonfeld, five miles north of Schwaigern, is on the northern edge of the area from where many Second Colony

Germans came. Ditzingen is about 26 miles south of Bonfeld close to Stuttgart. Hecklingen is unidentified but Gunzenhauser is in Bavaria to the east of Illenschwang from where Andreas Gaar came.

On 24 JUN 1726 John Motz was granted 400 acres jointly with John Harnsberger (*Virginia Patent Book 12*, p. 475) which may mean that Motz and Harnsberger or their wives were kinsmen. John Motz and Cyriacus Fleshman were the two deputies sent by the congregation to London to inquire about a pastor. They arrived in London in the last week of summer 1726 and were still there in December. After this, John Motz completely disappears from the records, and must have died early, for he is not shown among the tithables of Orange in 1739. His property is mentioned in a deed dated 19 AUG 1762 (*Culpeper D.B. D*, p.85) in which John Christopher Nelson and his mother, Elizabeth Nelson, deeded Adam Yager 200 acres which were part of the patent granted to John Motz. Therefore it looks as if he left a daughter Elizabeth whose husband was perhaps a Philip Nelson and whose orphan, Christian Nelson, was placed under the guardianship of Adam Barlow in 1763. Shortly afterwards Christian Nelson was removed from Barlow's supervision (*Culpeper Minute Book 1763–4*, pp.369 and 450). Nothing else is known of the possible descendants of John Motz. Keith omitted John Motz from his account of the 1717 families. See "John Motz" Beyond Germanna, v.15, n.1 for a short note. It is a possibility that earlier elements of the family were transients, perhaps from Austria.

Moyer (**Moyers, Mayer, Myers**). A family of Hans Georg Majer (Maier, Mayer) and his wife Barbara has been found in Gross Sachsenheim, Württemberg by Zimmerman and Cerny as reported in "The Ancestry of the Broyles, Paulitz, Moyer, and Motz Families," *Before Germanna*, v.6. While many elements of the history are correct for the 1717 immigrant family, it is not certain that this is the family. If the authors are correct, George Moyer was 43 years of age when he arrived in Virginia. Though George Moyer does not appear on Spotswood's list of head rights, he was sued by Spotswood in 1724 for more than £24. Circumstantial evidence says that his transportation had been paid by Robert Beverley, a partner of Spotswood. The jury only awarded Spotswood £15 but this was the largest award that Spotswood was allowed in all of the lawsuits against the Germans.

George Moyer was granted 400 acres in the first fork of the Rappahannock 24 JUN 1726 (*Virginia Patent Book 12*, p.478) in the first fork of the Rapidan River on the upper side of a run off Island Run (now called White Oak Run) in the Robinson River Valley. His adjacent neighbors, Michael Käfer, John Harnsberger, and John Motz also had land patents of this same date. On 28 SEP 1728 he patented another tract of 498 acres (*Virginia Patent Book 14*, p.107) in the Great Fork of the Rappahannock River down Deep Run adjacent to George Utz, Peter Weaver, Michael Stoltz, Lawrence Crees' corner, and Matthias Castler (though some of these neighbors were later).

The first Grand Jury in Orange County in 1735 found that George Moyer had on the first Friday of October 1735 insulted and abused Michael Cook and diverse other persons gathered for worship at the German Chapel. He was found guilty and ordered to pay Michael Cook. Perhaps George Moyer had relatives amongst the Robinson River group for George Utz had married Anna Barbara (Majer) Volck in Germany. George Moyer, Sr. and Barbara his wife sued Frederick Baumgardner and Catherine his wife for trespassing on 23 MAR 1743 (*Orange County O.B.4*, p.74).

The eldest son, Christopher, was old enough to be mentioned in law-suits in 1738 (*Orange County O.B.1*, pp.325 and 340) and was head of a family with himself as the one tithable in 1739. George Moyer himself appears in the 1739 tax list with two tithables, indicating another son, born prior to 1723. George Moyer made a deed of gift of 300 acres from his 1728 patent to Christopher Moyer 24 MAR 1740(OS) (*Orange County D.B.4*, p.356). A Michael Moyer witnessed a deed along with George Moyer on 1 AUG 1744 from Christopher Moyer and his wife Catherine to Michael Clore for the 300 acres mentioned above (*D.B.9*, p.197).

George Moyer sold the balance of the 1728 patent to Peter Weaver 9 JAN 1745(OS) (*D.B.10*, p.294–5), but kept the 1726 patent of 400 acres for some years. He increased the tract to 496 acres on 5 JUL 1744 when William Eddings sold him 96 acres of land adjacent to the southeast section of his 1726 patent. This deed was witnessed by George Hume, Silas Hart, and Thomas Dillard (*Orange Co. D.B. 10*, p. 198–90).

On 10 MAR 1753, George, Sr. sold Adam Broyle 100 acres including some waste land. The chain carriers were George Holt and Adam Wilheit. A dispute occurred concerning the amount of waste land. Broyle sued Moyer and won the case for on 6 AUG 1754 George Moyer for 60£ 18s transferred 100 acres plus 275 acres of waste land to Adam Broyle. Witnesses were Robert Coleman and William Brown (*Culpeper D.B. B*, p.171).

On 15 MAR 1753 George, Sr. made a deed of gift of 100 acres to each of his sons, Christopher and George, Jr. (*Culpeper D.B. A*, p.486–7). About twelve years later, Christopher mortgaged his 100 acres to Hugh, Lenox, Wm. Scott Co. for one year (*D.B. D*, p.642 on 16 MAY 1765). Then thirty-nine years later on 16 APR 1792, Christopher and wife Mary Catherine made a deed of gift of the 100 acres to their son-in-law Nathaniel Smith with life estate retained by Christopher and Mary Catharine Moyer. Witnesses to this were Henry Chrisler, George Crisler, and Adam Yager. George, Jr. and his wife Sarah sold their gift of 100 acres to Jacob Broyle on 21 OCT (*D.B. B*, p.507).

George, Sr. sold the 96 acres he bought from William Eddings to George, Jr. in May of 1754 and the next month he gave George, Jr. all of his personal property and sold the remaining 100 acres of his land. Witnesses to both deeds were Benjamin Powell, Conrad Delph, and Matthias Castler (*Culpeper D.B. B*, p.492). The last year in which George Moyer, Sr. appears in the records was 1754 and he probably died soon thereafter.

Records from the German Lutheran Church up to 1795 show the names of the following Moyers, Meyers, or Mayers. Jacob Mayer and wife Margaret were sponsors in 1762 for a child of Henry and Susannah Miller. Christopher Moyers, Sr. appears on the communion rolls 1775 to 1790. His wife Catherine's last church appearance was in 1795. Christopher Mayer, Jr. and wife Susanna appear on the communion rolls from 1775 to 1777. All seven children of Christopher, Jr. and wife Susanna were born in Culpeper County but only the daughter, Amelia, born 19 APR 1777, was baptized in the German Lutheran Church. Christopher Mayer, Jr. served in the Rev. War (North Carolina Army Volunteer, #1, p.74, Folio #4) and received land in what is today Jefferson County, Tennessee. He and his son-in-law Henry Randolph were the earliest settlers in the immediate area of the present day town of White Pine, Tennessee.

> Other children of Christopher Mayer, Sr. found on the communion rolls were:
>
> Adam Mayer (Christmas 1775). Adam served in the Rev. War (North Carolina Army, Vol. #5, p.91, Folio #4) and received land in what is today Greene County, Tennessee.
>
> Anna Barbara married Christopher Berler/Barlow (son of Adam Berler) and they had a son, Ludwig, baptized at church 24 MAR 1776. Two of the sponsors were her brother, Christopher Mayer, Jr. and her sister, Magdalena Moyer. Anna Barbara and Christopher Barlow were in church 1776 to 1778. They migrated to Kentucky with his father Adam Barlow.
>
> Susanna Mayer, confirmed at church Easter Sunday 1776, was on the church rolls until 1790. In 1809, Susanna Mayer and her husband Nathaniel Smith bought land in Washington County, Tennessee not many miles from her brother Adam.
>
> Daughter Magdalena Mayer appears at church in 1776 and 1777.
>
> Daughter Maria Mayer attended church from 1776 through 1783.

(The Margaret Mayer who attended church from 1776 to 1778 was probably not Christopher, Sr.'s daughter but was the wife of Jacob. It has not been determined if or how the Jacob and Margaret Mayer who in 1762 sponsored a child of Henry and Susannah Miller fit into the George Moyer, Sr. family. Also, the relationship, if any, of Philip and Catherine Mayer on the church rolls in 1783 in the George Moyer, Sr. family is unknown.)

The second son, Michael Myers, of George Moyer, Sr. received no land in Virginia which may be because he had moved to North Carolina. Michael married the widow Mary (Gerhard/Garrett) Blankenbaker whose first husband was George Blankenbaker, the eldest son of the 1717 immigrant Matthias Blankenbaker. Michael probably married Mary shortly after 1746 and they soon moved to Rowan County, North Carolina. There they are identified in the will of John Garrett (Gerhard) who names daughters Mary Mires and Catherine Wollox (Walke) in 1757 (*Rowan County, North Carolina W.B A*, p.59). Michael Myers left a will dated 20 OCT 1768, (*Rowan W.B. A*, p.110) in which he names his wife Mary, daughter Elizabeth married to Henry Doland, Jr., daughter Barbara (later married James Alexander McMackin, Sr.), daughter Mary (later married to Nicholas Isenhauer), daughter Hannah (later married to to Michael Holtzhauser) and son Michael. Land was left to Susannah Myers (later married to David Smith) and his wife's son John Blanket Pickler (Blankenbühler initially but later uniformly Pickler). Mary Myers left a will, date 14 JUL 1784 (*Rowan W.B. B*, p.157).

The third son, named after his father, was George Moyer, Jr., who died in Culpeper County, Virginia prior to 16 MAY 1763 for on this date George Moyer (III) and Sarah his mother sold 161 acres of land to James Barbour, Jr. (*Culpeper D.B. D*, p.244). On 21 JUL 1763, George III and his mother sold 35 acres to John Wayland, with Adam and Nicholas Broyles as witnesses (*D.B. D*, p.253). George, Jr. was married prior to 1744 as he and his wife brought suit in that year against Conrad Broyle and his wife for trespassing (*Orange O.B. 4*, pp.74, 149, and 279).

Because George Moyer, Sr. left no will (he had disposed of his property before death), there is no record as to whether there were any daughters.

The assistance of Nancy Moyers Dodge for this family is appreciated.

Nunnamacher (perhaps the name was Nonnenmacher in Germany). Lewis Nunnamacher married Barbara Blankenbaker, daughter of John Blankenbaker and granddaughter of the 1717 Matthias Blankenbaker. They were sponsors for Rosina (her parents were John Peck and his wife Barbara) in 1776. The relationship of John Nunnenmacher who was confirmed in 1777 to Lewis is unknown but perhaps they were of a similar age and brothers.

George Ludwig Noonemacher arrived on 26 OCT 1754 at Philadelphia on the ship *Mary and Sarah* with a known Germanna immigrant, George Raüser (Racer, Razor). It may be that Lewis (Ludwig) and John were sons of George Ludwig. In Kentucky, Barbara Blankenbaker, the daughter of Samuel Blankenbaker and Amy Yager, married George Henry Nonnenmacher on 22 AUG 1797. The Nonnenmach name is found in the communities close to those from where many Second Germanna colonists came, for example, Neuenbürg, whence the Blankenbakers came. Some individuals believe the name Moneymaker in America is derived from Nunnenmacher.

Ohlscheitt. Conrad Ohlscheitt with Catharina Daher had Henry baptized 3 JUL (1782). Apparently, the parents were not married. Sponsors of the boy were Joseph Holtzclaw and his wife Elizabeth and Daniel Daher and his wife Maria Elisabetha.

Ohlschlager. Johannes Eberhard Ohlschlager was deeded land in Culpeper County in 1768.

Paulitz. Philip Paulitz came to Virginia on the *Scott*, bringing his wife Rose (born 1671), and daughters Margaret (born 1705) and Catherine (born 1708) (*Spotsylvania W.B. A*, p.142). His origins have been found in Germany at Ottmarsheim, Württemberg and given in "The Ancestry of the Broyles, Paulitz, Moyer, and Motz Families," *Before Germanna*, v.6. He was sued by Spotswood in 1724. He did not have a land grant, but in 1729 was deeded land in the Robinson River neighborhood by Nicholas Yager, part of which he sold back to Yager 4 DEC 1733 (Crozier, *Spotsylvania County Records*, pp.107 and 128). After this he does not appear in the records, though the land of Philip "Powlet" is referred to in a deed of Adam Yager, son of Nicholas, in 1762. Very probably Paulitz had died before then as his wife would have been 89 years old then. Keith has a short paragraph on him (p. 187).

Peck (Beck?). John Peck and Barbara had a daughter, Rosina, baptized 8 AUG 1776 at the Lutheran church. The sponsors were Ludwig Nunnemacher and his wife Elis. (Blankenbaker). There was a Lorentz Bekh in the Gemmingen departure list but there is no strong reason to identify him with John Peck.

Perler (Barlow). Aaron Perler and his wife Catharina Beemon were the parents of Alpha, Lucia, and Jonas who were baptized from 1802 to 1806 at the Lutheran Church with only the parents serving as sponsors. Aaron Perler was the son of Christopher Barlow.

Perry. The name Perry occurs in the German Lutheran Church records but it is believed to be a mistake for Berry.

Pinnegar (Pinegar, Benninger, Pinnegar, and similar spellings). Peter Benninger of Epfenbach (Kreis Sinsheim) was permitted to emigrate in 1751 with his wife and four children (Don Yoder, editor, *Rhineland Emigrants*, Genealogical Publishing Co., 1985). They arrived at Philadelphia that same year on the *St. Andrew*. Research by Kevin Peniger in the German records shows that Peter Beninger married, on 30 AUG 1729, Anna Christian Ziegler who was born 1 MAY 1705. One of their sons was Peter Pinegar, born 1735, who was married by 1755 in Page County, Virginia to Mary Magdalena_____.

Peter and Magdalena Pinegar sold land in Augusta County, Virginia, 15 AUG 1771 (*D.B. 16*, p.30) to Frederick Wolfaarth. On 12 AUG 1778, Peter Pinnegar purchased 275 acres of John Deer and wife Catherine of Culpeper County, Virginia in the Goard Vine Fork of the Rappahannock River (technically, this would have been outside the Robinson River Valley). This land had been a part of grant made to Francis Brown in 1749. In the Culpeper Classes of 1781, William Pinegar and Matthias Pinnegar are names. The Culpeper Classes also show John Flinchan, John Flinchan, and Robert Flincham who are in the same neighborhood as the Pinegars. Christopher Zigler is also a near neighbor.

In February of 1793, Peter Pinnagor of Stokes County, North Carolina sold 275 acres in Culpeper County, Virginia to William Sampson. The will of Peter Pinnegor, dated 4 SEP 1793, in Stokes County names his wife Mary, son Matthias, son William and three daughters.

> William Pinegar married Elizabeth Zimmerman, the daughter of John Zimmerman, Jr. and a granddaughter of John and Ursula (Blankenbaker) Zimmerman. The marriage seems to have taken place in Culpeper County as William Pinegar and Elizabeth Pinnegar were witnesses to the will of Richard Ship of Culpeper County dated 9 FEB 1781. William and Elizabeth were the parents of William, Jr. and Leonard who are named in the father's will.
>
> Matthias Pinager's wife is unknown. They were the parents of five sons, John, Peter, William, James, and Matthias, all of whom are named in the father's will.
>
> Mary Pinegar married Robet Flincham and they were the parents of John, William, Thomas, Jacob, Robert, Samuel, Catherine, Thenia, and Mary.
>
> Christine married_____Mounce.
>
> Catherine married_____Flinchan.

There was a strong association between the Flinchums, Zimmermans, Ziglars, and Pinegars who all moved to North Carolina where the families intermarried even more.

Preiss. The name Preiss is a German phonetic spelling of Price. A few mentions of the name Price occur at the German Lutheran Church. Whether we are dealing with an English family or a German family is not clear.

Printz. Georg Printz was a communicant on Easter Sunday in 1798.

Prosie. Jacob Prosie was the administrator of Barbara Cooper in 1735.

Raüser (Racer, Rasor, Razor). George Adam Raüser came to America from Germany on the ship *Mary and Sarah* which had sailed from Amsterdam via Portsmouth, England. The ship arrived in Philadelphia on 26 OCT 1754 and carried another potential Germanna immigrant, George Ludwig Nonnenmacher. George Razor married Margaret_____before his arrival in Virginia, perhaps in Sussex County, New Jersey where he lived before moving to Virginia. On 14 MAY 1774, George bought 100 acres in the Robinson River area from Frederick and Sarah Baumgardner. For the next fourteen years the family can be found in the Lutheran church records. About 1794 George Razor, Sr., his sons Peter and Christian, son-in-law George Swindle, several members of the Swindle family and, possibly at the same time, Aaron Clore moved to the Abbeville district of South Carolina. Family tradition says that George, Sr. died during the move and was buried along the way. In South Carolina the family name consistently became Rasor whereas the family name in Virginia became Racer.

Counting George Adam as the first generation, the second generation was:

Jacob, born about 1756 in Sussex County, New Jersey, married first Susanna Snyder 6 FEB 1786 in Culpeper County, Virginia. Second he married Elizabeth Delph 24 JAN 1801 in Madison County, Virginia. He had six and five children, respectively, by his two wives;

Peter, born about 1758 in New Jersey, married Frances Deer in OCT 1786 in Culpeper County, Virginia. He died 4 NOV 1831 in Spencer County, Indiana after a stay in Dearborn County, Indiana where he had moved from Abbeville County, South Carolina.

Christian, born 14 AUG 1760 in New Jersey, married Sarah Sims 29 DEC 1780 in Culpeper County, He died in 1848 in Abbeville County, South Carolina.

Susannah Rasor, born about 1762 in New Jersey, married Andrew Deer about 1779 in Culpeper County. Andrew died in 1798 in Madison County. Susannah moved with her children to Boone County, Kentucky.

Catherine, born about 1764 in New Jersey, married George Swindle, 30 JUL 1786, in Culpeper County, Virginia. (There is confusion about the wife or wives of George Swindle which is perhaps confounded by there being two Georges, an uncle and a nephew of about the same age.)

George, born about 1766 in New Jersey, married first Frances Major on 8 FEB 1789 in Culpeper County, Virginia. Second, he married Mary Brookings 7 NOV 1805 in Madison County, Virginia. He died in 1842 in Madison County. He and his first wife, Franky, had six children.

More information down to the third generation has been given by Gene Dear in "George Razor, the Immigrant" in Beyond Germanna, v.3, n.4, p.154.

Railsback, Henry. Johann Heinrich Rehlsbach in Germany was the younger brother of John Railsback (see following) and Henry came to Virginia in 1750. Though he was christened as just Heinrich, his two brothers who had been christened as Johann Heinrich had died. Heinrich became Johann Heinrich to fulfill the vacant role. Johann Heinrich married Anna Maria Enteneur in Eisern on 13 SEP 1757. Two children of these parents are in the church records at Oberdorf about one mile from Eisern. Since the second child was born in 1761 and the father Henry appears in a March 1762 record in Culpeper Co, Virginia, the travel to America must have taken place in 1761. The children of the marriage are:

Henry, Jr. born 1758 and christened in Obersdorf,

Edward, born 1761 and christened in Obersdorf, died in Rowan County, North Carolina,

Elizabeth, born 1764 in Culpeper County, married Isaac Ellis in North Carolina,

Mary, born 21 APR 1766 in Culpeper County, married John Lowry 24 AUG 1786 in Rowan County,

David, born 12 DEC 1768 probably in North Carolina, married twice and he died in Indiana,

Daniel, born about 1773 in Rowan Co, married first Charity Little and married second Elizabeth Dossee,

Rosa/Rosannah, born 9 FEB 1777 in Surrey County, North Carolina, married Morgan McMahan,

Lydda, born 8 JAN 1780 in Rowan County, North Carolina, married Samuel Austin,

Anna, born 2 MAY 1782 in Rowan County, North Carolina, married apparently Lamb Taylor.

After the death of his first wife, Henry Railsback married Margaret Call (Kahl) of a Culpeper family who lived in the same area as the Huffman, Stonecipher, and Railsback families. Henry and Margaret were the parents of

Sarah, born 27 NOV 1792 in Rowan County, North Carolina, married Oliver Griffen.

The two oldest sons, Henry, Jr. and Edward, died at a young age and it is doubtful that they left any heirs.

Henry Railsback, Sr. wrote his will in Rowan County, North Carolina in 1814. Because both John and Henry Railsback, the immigrants, had sons named Daniel, it should be noted that John's Daniel was born in Virginia and Henry's Daniel was born in North Carolina. The Virginia Daniel married Rosannah Clore/Glore in 1788. They had one son, Edward, who was raised by his grandfather, Adam Glore, after Rosannah died.

Rachel Klug in Virginia married a Railsback as her father Michael Klug gave his permission in 1798 for his daughter Rachel Railsback to marry John Carter. Rachel was the mother of one Railsback son, Thomas Fisher Railsback. Rachel's mother is said to have been Elizabeth Fisher which is the origin of the middle name of Thomas Fisher Railsback.

For a more complete story on Henry Railsback, see Susan Pottenger White et al, "The Railsback Family," in Beyond Germanna, v.12, n.5.

Railsback, John. Hans Georg Rehlsbach was baptized 3 NOV 1697 at Eisern, just southeast of Siegen. The wife of Hans Georg, Maria Catharina Gerhard, was baptized 14 NOV 1706 at Wilnsdorf. The two married in the Chapel at Eisern on 24 OCT 1730. (Hans Georg adopted the name John as his calling name.) Their eldest child, Johannes, born 16 SEP 1731, arrived in this country as Johannes Reesbach on the ship *Nancy* and he took the oath of allegiance at Philadelphia on 31 AUG 1750 (seven consecutive names on the passenger list were Creutz, Brumbach, Gitting, Shneyder, Weissgerber, Reesbach, and Jung). Other families who came from Eisern include Henry Huffman, John Steinseifer, and Henry Railsback. The Huffmans lived in the Robinson River Valley which is undoubtedly the reason that John Railsback settled there also.

John Railsback was a foot soldier of Culpeper County, Virginia in 1756. From 1757 to 1778, he was involved in several land transactions in Culpeper County. His wife was Elizabeth Thomas, the daughter of John Thomas, Jr. and his first wife, Mary. One Railsback record at the Lutheran church occurs when the daughter Catherine is baptized in 1777. In this record he is noted as a Calvanist, i.e., Reformed. The sponsors at the baptism were related to the mother and this helps to identify the wife of John Railsback.

John Railsback left Virginia for Kentucky in 1788 and appeared on tax lists of Mercer County from 1792 to 1795. From Kentucky, he went to Preble County, Ohio where he died intestate in 1810. John and Elizabeth were the parents of eight children:

Mary, born 1761 in Virginia, married Ambrose Huffman,

Susannah, born in Virginia, married Joseph Rouse as his first wife,

Daniel, born Virginia, married first Rosannah Clore 25 MAY 1788, married second Rachel Klug, the daughter of Michael Klug. Daniel died in Virginia in 1799,

Annie, born Virginia, married Christopher Smith 12 SEP 1792, Mercer County, Kentucky,

Leah/Layanne, born about 1775 Virginia, married Reuben Dooley 26 MAY 1795, Mercer County, Kentucky,

Catharine, born 17 FEB 1777 Virginia, christened at the Lutheran Church in the Robinson River Valley, married John Pottenger 19 FEB 1800, Nelson County, Kentucky,

Jacob, born 1780 in Virginia, married Martha Hill 31 DEC 1802, Barren County, Kentucky,

John, Jr. born 5 AUG 1784 Virginia, married Hannah Conger 3 APR 1805, Barren County Kentucky.

A note on the family, "John Railsback", by Susan Pottenger White appears in Beyond Germanna, v.2, n.5, p.101. She was the source of much of the Railsback information, both for John and his brother Henry. The church records of Eisern were obtained by Mr. and Mrs. Guy Railsback in 1983.

Redman. Peter Redman attended communion twice in late 1775 at the German Lutheran Church. Peter and Jacob attended communion at the Easter 1776 service.

Reiner (also Riner, Ryner in America). The Reiner family was from Schwaigern, Württemberg. The first representative of the family to come to Virginia was Mary Barbara Reiner who had married Michael Cook in Germany and came with him as members of the Second Colony. Her brother, Hans Dieterich Reiner, with several adult members of his family, came in 1750 on the ship *Fane*, docking in Philadelphia on October 17. They immediately went to Virginia and became involved in the life of the community. The German records state that six children came with the family but, of these, there is no record of Johannes in Virginia. The youngest son, Eberhardt, who was only 17 at the time, purchased 530 acres of land from Ambrose Powell in 1750. This land was divided between Eberhardt and Christopher (Christian).

> Mary Sarah, born 2 MAY 1724, married George Cook, her first cousin,
>
> Mary Magdalena, born 21 SEP1720, married Nicholas Smith,
>
> John Christian, born 10 APR 1718, (sometimes called Christopher) married Elizabeth Fleshman. They were the parents of John, Daniel, Christian, Mary, Elizabeth, and Sarah. (All of the Germanna people of the Reiner surname descend from John Christian),
>
> Everhardt never married and his will mentions his sister Witham,
>
> Mary Margarethe, born 12 FEB 1723, married_____Witham. Apparently they were the parents of Peter. Mary Margarethe appears in the German Lutheran Communion Lists and this is probably the sister to whom Eberhard referred. Margaret was called a widow 29 AUG 1784.

The history of the Reiners in Schwaigern can be traced back to almost 1600. *Before Germanna*, v. 7, and *The Pennsylvania Genealogical Magazine*, v.XXI, n.3, 1960, p.242, and *Beyond Germanna*, v.3, n.5, p.165 have more information.

Rinehart. Michell Rynehard signed a petition to the Orange County Court to have a road cleared from the part of "Sharando called Mesenuting to Thorntons Mill." In Dunmore County, George Rindhart had a grant in 1761 in which the Germanna names of Moyers or Meyers and Gabbert are mentioned. Matthias Rinehart and Elizabeth his wife appear in deeds in Culpeper County from 1767 to 1776. Jonas Rynehart was a chain carrier for Catharine Fox in 1775 in Dunmore County. George Rinehart was mentioned in a grant to John Fry in 1777. Micall Rindhear was a chain carrier for Andrew Kyzer in 1779 in Shenandoah County. In the same county in 1778, Michael Rindhart had a grant of 218 acres. Matthias Rynehart appears in the 1787 tax lists of Culpeper County in the area from which Rappahannock County was formed. There is a separate entry for Elizabeth Rineheart who seems to have lived in the region of modern Culpeper County. She paid the tithe for Henry Smith and Leven Vinson.

Rise. Benjamin Rise and his wife Hanna brought Franke (born 15 NOV 1777) to the church for baptism on 8 MAR 1778. Michael Schneider and his wife were sponsors.

Rodeheaver. Johannes Rothöfer and wife Maria brought David for baptism on 25AUG 1776 to the German Lutheran Church. Sponsors were Nicolaus Jager, Johannes Jager and wife Maria. John Rodeheifer is in the Culpeper Classes (106) and he is in the Culpeper 1787 tax list in the area of southern Madison County. A deed in 1787 shows his wife's name to be Sarah. John Rodeheaver died in 1790 and his will mentions two daughters, under 18, and three sons, John, Joseph and David (*Culpeper W.B. C*, p.385). In 1791, the widow Sarah married Ephraim Yager, son of Godfrey Yager and grandson of Adam Yager.

Rossel. Maria Rossel was a communicant in 1778 at the German Church. Mary and Elizabeth Rossel were sponsors for the child Elisabetha of Johannes Becker and his wife Elisabetha Clore in 1771. When the natural child of Ephraim Klugge and_____Rossel was baptized in 1776, one of the sponsors was Maria Rossel.

Rookstool (Rückstuhl in America). It is thought that the origins of this family were in Switzerland. Soloman Ruckstuhl, born 1679 at Zurich, married Barbara Buchi, born 1682. Their son Solomon, born 1707 in Switzerland, married Olive(?)_____. Solomon and Olive's eldest son was George, born 1744 in Montgomery County, Pennsylvania. He married Susanna, maiden name unknown. Their children were probably all born in Pennsylvania but the family is to be found in the Robinson River Valley. The following are believed to be children of the family:

> George, Jr. married Cathy House 14 JUL 1798. (He was the father of a natural son William, born 29 JAN 1794. The sponsors were Valentin Bunger and the child's mother, not otherwise specified.) George, Jr. and his wife Cathy are in the church records up to 1808. They moved to Preble County, OH,

Elizabeth (Betsy) was confirmed in 1798,

Sally,

Jacob,

Henry married Ann Bunger,

Susanna,

Catherine married George House (some say this was a second marriage for her but the marriage license gives her name as Rookstool,

John married Eve Cline in Greenbrier County, now West Virginia,

Polly.

Why the family moved to Virginia is not clear but one wonders if the mother was related to people already living there. None of the family appears in the Culpeper Classes of 1781 nor do they appear in the personal property tax list for Culpeper County for the year 1787. The earliest record is for a Susanna Rookstool who appears at the German Lutheran Church in 1788. Two members appear at church up to 1802.

Row / Rowe. This family may be of English origin but their name is mentioned several times in connection with the German families. George Row received a payment from the estate of William Nash in 1759. He was a witness to the will of Richard Burdyne, along with John Clore, Peter Clore, and John James. In this same will, dated 22 JUL 1761, George Row is named as co-executor. Witnesses to the will of Michael Clawr (Clore) were Christopher Crigler, Henry Jones and George Row. Anne Rowe, born in 1747 as the daughter of Adam Rowe, married John Hupp, This Anne Hupp, with her younger brother, Jacob, led the defence of Miller's Blockhouse against an Indian attack in 1782 (in southwest Pennsylvania). Anne later married John May. In the Culpeper personal property tax list of 1787, there are five Rowe men, Benja., Benjamin, George, George, Jr., and William. The name Row/Rowe does not appear in the Culpeper Classes of 1781.

Rouse (perhaps Rausch in Germany but the origins have not been found). John Rouse was granted 610 acres in the First Fork of the Rapidan, adjoining Thomas Wayland, on 28 SEP 1728 (*Virginia Patent Book 14*, p. 110). This is the earliest mention of him in Virginia though it seems he would have been in Virginia several years by then. He is mentioned as John Raussen in 1733 in the Lutheran Church accounts (*Orange W.B. 1*, pp.54–57). In 1739 he had two tithables in his family, indicating a son born by 1723. John Rouse was dead by 7 MAR 1747 when Mary, his widow, petitioned for the transfer of the land of John Rouse to the sons Martin, Matthias, and Adam, saying that John Rouse, a German, had failed to naturalize himself. The petition was granted 8 OCT 1750 when Mary Rouse, widow, and Martin, Matthias and Adam Rouse were granted 318 acres of land near Michael Holt (*Grants Book G*, p.423). Mary Rouse had died by 15 MAR 1764 when Matthias Rausch and wife Elizabeth deeded to Martin Rausch the land granted to Mary Rausch in 1750 by Lord Fairfax. That Adam did not participate in this suggests that he had died by this time.

Martin Rouse and his wife, Frances, deeded land in 1762 and 1772. In 1793 Martin and his wife, Elizabeth, communed at the Lutheran Church. His Madison County will (*Madison W.B. 2*, p.192), dated 11 JUL 1802 and probated 26 JAN 1809, names four children:

Elizabeth who married John Loyd,

John left no known heirs,

Adam who married Tabitha Vawter in 1795 and he died in 1847,

Samuel died in 1817 and left his property to his brothers (*Madison W.B. 3*, p.309).

Matthias Rouse was probably born about 1723 and he was a foot soldier of Culpeper County in 1756. From 1762 to 1788 he was involved in several land transactions. With his wife, Elizabeth, he was a communicant in 1775 at the Lutheran Church. He died in Madison County, Virginia in 1806. His will, dated 8 MAY 1796 and probated 26 JUN 1806 (*Madison W.B. 2*, p.92), mentions his wife Elizabeth, and "all my children." The Lutheran Church records show seven sons.

> Joseph married first Susannah Ralsbach (Railsback) and second Mary Magdalen Tanner. He moved to Indiana,
>
> Samuel married Maria Weaver and died in Boone County, Kentucky,
>
> Michael married first Catherine_____ and second Nancy_____,
>
> Jacob married Anna Weaver and moved to Boone County, Kentucky,
>
> Lewis married Elizabeth Garriott in Virginia and died in Henderson County, Kentucky,
>
> Ephraim married first Maria Huffman and second Barbara Deer and died before 1850,
>
> George married Betsy Zimmerman and died in Ralls County, Missouri,
>
> Mary seems to have been the only daughter and she married Frederick Tanner, son of Christopher Tanner.

An Ibrahim (Abraham) Rausch, age 18, was confirmed in 1782. Whether he was a son of Matthias or of his brother, Martin, is uncertain. In either case, he seems to have died before his father.

John Rouse of Virginia and His Descendants 1717–1980 by Mrs. Robert (Nancy E.) Rouse, privately printed, 1982, should be consulted for much more extensive information.

An Edward Rouse made a proof of importation from England at the Orange County Court (*O.B. 1*, p. 46) on 18 NOV 1735. Very often the Germans were said to be immediately from England because all of the ships had to leave from an English port so this record does not prove he was English or German.

Rungo. Christian Rungo seldom missed a communion service at the Lutheran church from 1790 to 1822. He was always alone.

Schad. Commencing in 1804, Friederich J. Schad and his wife Catherina appear in the Lutheran communion lists. He was the organist at the Lutheran church and school teacher. The last appearance of this couple was in 1806. They had a son Philip. It is not yet proven but it appears that Friedrich Julius Schad was a Brunswicker who deserted the British auxiliaries sometime after 1779. He appears in the Frederick County, Maryland church records in the 1780s and he is in the Maryland 1790 census as Julius Schade.

Schlatter (Slaughter in America). A George Slaughter had a 300 acre patent on 28 JAN 1733(OS) (*Virginia Patent Book 15*, p.144). This land was noted as being adjacent to George Long and Matthew Castler which may indicate that George "Slaughter" was German. George Schlatter and his wife Margaretha attended the German Lutheran Church. Other Schlatter names in the Lutheran church include Elisabeth, John, Maria, and Rosina. John and Elisabetha were confirmed at the church in 1777. A Margaretha Schlatter was confirmed in 1778. Conrad Slaughter is mentioned in deeds but this may have been Conrad Slater. The last mention in the church records is in 1784. The family needs more work.

Schwarbach. Johnannes Schwarbach was the pastor at the German Lutheran Church from about 1764 to 1774. After Rev. Klug's death, there was a gap of about a year before Schwarbach came to Culpeper. He had been born in Europe (8 MAR 1719) before he moved to Pennsylvania where he was a teacher. He moved to the Valley of Virginia where he was a catechist. On his own authority he undertook to be the minister in Culpeper. When challenged on the question of ordination, the elders of the Culpeper church (Adam Gaar, Adam Jeger, Adam Weyland plus Nicholaus Grigler, Michael Schmidt, Michael Jeger, Hinrich Ehler, Johannes Carpenter, Christoph Grigler, Adam Broyl, Adam Koch, Michael Blankenbicher, Johannes Weber, Johannes Feischmann, Philip Schneider) wrote to the Pennsylvania Ministerium (in letters of 20 DEC 1765, 9 FEB 1766, and 17 MAY 1766) requesting his early ordination. Schwarbach attended the meeting of the June 1766 meeting of the Ministerium and he was examined and ordained. At the Lutheran church in Culpeper County in 1768, he wrote, "I am overburdened with work . . . in six months, I have instructed and confirmed young people in seven different congregations at a considerable distance from each other." Deacons Adam Garr and Adam Wayland wrote at the same time that "The efforts of Mr. Schwarbach . . . please us very much." (The deacons complained at the same time that Mr. Schwarbach was not allowed to officiate at their weddings because of the colonial policy which required marriages to be performed by an Anglican minister.) His retirement seems to have been motivated by a desire to escape the heavy physical duties involved with congregations far away. His wife was Margaretha and they were sponsors for the Henry Miller twins in 1772. Margaretha Schwarbach was a sponsor twice for children of Zacharias Broyles and his wife Delia in 1771 and 1774. Later Rev. Schwarbach was the minister at Ben Salem Lutheran Church in Carbon County, Pennsylvania. He died 4 OCT 1800 and is buried in the cemetery at Ben Salem.

Selser. Mary Selser married Samuel Lederer and they had Elizabeth baptized in 1776 at the Lutheran Church. In 1778, they had Mary baptized. Surnames of sponsors include Lederer, Yager, Carpenter, and Cook.

Sheible. George Scheible was born in 1670 at Neuenbürg, Baden, which was the origin of several Germanna families. George Sheible was excused from levies in 1723, probably for a disability, not for age. Spotswood sued him in 1724. He was on Spotswood's importation list as Hans George with his wife, Maria Clara (in his marriage record in Germany, she is given as Maria Eleanora), and three daughters, Anna Martha, Anna Elizabeth and Anna Maria who make the identity complete. George Sheible was granted 78 acres which fell on both sides of the Robinson River 24 JUN 1726 (*Virginia Patent Book 12*, p.481) amid other emigrants from Neuenbürg. He accompanied Johann Caspar Stöver, Sr., the first pastor of the German Lutheran Church, to Pennsylvania in 1733 in order that Stöver might receive ordination (*Orange W.B. 1*, pp.54–57). He appears in the Robinson River community in 1739 with only 1 tithable, see Part I. He probably died soon after this date. Keith has a short paragraph on Sheible (p. 187). The daughter Elizabeth was the wife of Michael Holt for on 15 APR 1737 George Shuble made a deed of gift of his 78 acres to his grandson, George Holt (*Orange D.B. 2*, p.287). Therefore the Holts are descended from George Sheible. Whether the other two Scheible daughters had families is unknown.

The *Oberöwisheim-Neuenbürg Ortssippenbuch* has good information on the family. Some of this was reported in 𝕭𝖊𝖞𝖔𝖓𝖉 𝕲𝖊𝖗𝖒𝖆𝖓𝖓𝖆 in the article "Ortssippenbücher," in v.14, n.5. The Ortssippenbuch tells us that Johann Georg Schaible was born 11 FEB 1670. He was a weaver who married Maria Eleanora Ockert 13 NOV 1692. They had five children:

    Anna Martha, born 14 MAR 1697,

    Anna Elisabeth, born 17 SEP 1700,

    Anna Maria, born 18 MAR 1708, d. 4 APR 1708,

    Anna Maria, born 15 JUN 1709, d. 12 JUL 1710, and

    Anna Maria, born 27 JUL 1711.

Maria Eleanora's parents were Johannes Ockert, citizen in Oberöwisheim in 1676, and Anna Maria _____ born in Kleingartach about 1637. Information is available in "The Ancestry of the Sheible, Peck Milker, Smith, and Holt Families," *Before Germanna*, v. 5 though it is in error on Maria Eleanora's parents.

It is the belief of the author that Hans Scheiblin's family originated in Austria, probably on the Schaiblau farm which is about one-half mile from the Plankenbichl farm which was the origin of the Plankenbühlers/Blankenbakers. George Scheible lived along with the Blankenbakers in Neuenbürg and he had land in the midst of the Neuenbürg emigrants in Virginia. The families are probably related.

The difference between the Neuenbürg records and Spotswood's head right list is probably an error in the head right list for Maria Eleanora Scheibel was a sponsor in London in September of 1717. (Hanß Jürgen Scheibeler was also a sponsor on another occasion.)

Sluchter. Henry Schlucter was the step-son of Cyriacus Fleshman and a half-brother of the Blankenbakers and Fleshmans. His birth (7 MAY 1697) in Neuenbürg, Baden is known and he is recorded on Spotswood's importation list. Cyriacus Fleshman deeded land to Sarah Sluchter in 1737. In 1737, William Carpenter was appointed surveyor of roads in place of Henry Sluchter (*Orange County O.B. 1*, p.200). Whether Sarah was the wife of Henry or a daughter is not clear. The 1739 tithe list contains a Conrad Slater in the midst of the Blankenbaker, Sheible, and Fleshman names. It may be that the Schlucter name has become Slater by then and that Conrad is a son of Henry. In settling an estate in 1741, Conrad Sluchter is said to owe one shilling and three pence (see 𝕭𝖊𝖞𝖔𝖓𝖉

Germanna, v.15, n.5). [B.C. Holtzclaw says that Henry Sluchter deeded land to John Shafer in 1749 but this statement has not been verified.] Except for this last statement, it appears that Henry Sluchter married young with at least a son Conrad. Henry died about 1736 and Cyriacus Fleshman deeded property to Sarah Sluchter who was probably his wife. More clarification of the information is needed.

Smith, Matthew (Schmidt in Germany). Matthew Smith came in 1717 with Regina Catharina, his wife, when they were in their late twenties. They were one of the families from Gemmingen. When the family left in July 1717, there were two children, Matthaus, 3½, and Anna Margaret, 1½. In London, while they waited for the ship, a boy named Johann was born on 29 AUG 1717 and baptized two days later. In his proof of importation, no claim was made for any children so it appears that their three children died during the trip. The surviving children were born in Virginia. The family was not on Spotswood's importation list and this presumably is the reason Matthew Smith was not one of the people whom Spotswood sued. On 24 JUN 1726 he was granted 400 acres of land jointly with Matthias Bellar or Barlow (*Virginia Patent Book 12*, p. 480). Keith (pp. 187–188) confused Matthew Smith with his brother, Michael Smith, who came at the same time.

Matthew Smith is shown with two tithables in Orange County in 1739 and the second tithe was probably a son. Matthias Smith made a deed of gift of 100 acres of land 16 AUG 1750, part of the 1726 patent to Matthias Smith and Matthias Barler, (*Culpeper D.B. A*, p.202) to Nicholas Smith. On 21 JUN 1753 Matthias Smith made a deed of gift of the other 100 acres of the patent to his son, Matthias Smith, Jr. (*D.B. A*, p.507). So far as is known, Nicholas and Matthew Smith, Jr. were the only sons of Matthew Smith, Sr., and the Culpeper Rental of 1764 shows Nicholas Smith and Matthew Smith, each with 100 acres. Matthew Smith, Sr. probably died 1753–64, at least, he does not appear in the records after 1753.

Nicholas Smith married Maria Magdalena Reiner (born 21 SEP 1720 at Schwaigern, Württemberg). They were sponsors for children of George and Mary Sarah (Reiner) Cook in 1751, 1753, 1756, 1758 and 1768. The two wives were sisters. Nicholas and Mary Magdalena appear quite often on the communicant rolls of the German church. Nicholas died in Madison County, Virginia in 1797 and his will, dated 7 APR 1792 and probated 28 SEP 1797, left his property to his sons, John, Nicholas, Michael, and Godfrey (*Madison W.B. 1*, p.146).

Matthew Smith, Jr. married Mary_____. On 19 SEP 1765 Matthias Smith (who must have been Matthew, Jr., as his father had already deeded away his land and was probably dead) deeded the 100 acres on which he lived to Michael Smith and Matthias Smith, Jr. (i.e., Matthew III) with Michael Klug, Adam Cook and others being witnesses (*Culpeper D.B. E*, p.46). It would appear that Michael and Matthew III were children at the time of this deed, for Matthew, Jr. died before 1782, and his widow, Mary Smith, is shown with only one tithable in her family in that year, namely, Michael Smith. Matthew III and another son, Samuel Smith, were under 16. The tithables of 1787 show Mary Smith with all three sons, Michael, Matthias and Samuel Smith in her family; 1788 shows Mary Smith 3 tithables; 1789, "Samuel Smith son to Mary and your brothers 3"; 1790, Samuel Smith son to Mary 2, Michael Smith 1; 1791, Samuel Smith and brothers 3; 1792, the same. It would appear that Mary died about 1790/91. Possibly there were two daughters. A Leah was confirmed in 1789 and married Joshua Wayland in 1790.

The later descendants of the seven grandsons of Matthew Smith, the 1717 immigrant, are somewhat uncertain, and the lines need work.

Smith, Michael. Hans Michael Schmidt was the older brother of Matthew Smith. Both came from Gemmingen and appear on the Gemmingen sexton's list of 1717 emigrants. Michael's family consisted of his wife, Anna Margaretha, his son Hans Michael 5½, his son Christopher ½, and his "in-laws". His wife's father was a Sauter but he had already died. Therefore "in-laws" may mean her mother and her step-father. While the family is on Spotswood's importation list, the names of Christopher and the "in-laws" are missing. Michael was sued by Spotswood in 1724 and on 24 JUN 1726 was granted 400 acres in the Robinson River neighborhood (*Virginia Patent Book 12*, p.478). In 1733 he and Cyriacus Fleshman were collectors of funds for the German Evangelical Lutheran Church and he was a churchwarden there in 1733 and 1740 (*Orange W.B. 1*, pp.54–57). In 1734 he and Michael Holt accompanied the first pastor of the Lutheran Church, Rev. John Caspar Stöver, to Europe to collect funds for German Lutheran Church. Michael Smith returned to this country with Rev. Stöver in the latter part of 1739 and witnessed the latter's will when he died on the voyage back to Philadelphia (*Orange W.B. 1*, pp.83–9). In 1739 he had three tithables in his family which would normally indicate two sons born before 1723. However, if there were two sons, the younger one must have died early, for Michael Smith died in Culpeper County in 1761, and his will, dated 25 FEB 1760 and probated 19 FEB 1761, leaves all his property to "my only son, John Michael Smith, Jr." (*Culpeper W.B. A*, pp.243–4). It is uncertain whether Michael Smith, Sr. had any daughters. Based on the baptismal records at the church, the odds are strongly against this.

Michael Smith, Jr. was born in 1712. His wife was Anna Magdalena Thomas, sister of John Thomas, Jr. and stepdaughter of Michael Käfer (see Thomas and Käfer). In 1742 Michael Smith, Jr. was deeded 600 acres by Christian Clement, part of a grant to Clement on 1 NOV 1734 (*Orange D.B. 7*, pp.6–8. The original deed does not call Michael "Jr.", but the acknowledgment by Clement 26 NOV 1742 specifically named the grantee as "Michael Smith, junr."). After his father's death in 1761, Michael Smith II was thus the owner of 1,000 acres of land, all of which he disposed of by deeds of gift to his three sons and four sons-in-law during the years 1762 to 1772. The 1762 deeds were as follows: 28 JAN 1762, Michael Smith for love and affection to John Berry, Jr. and his wife Susannah, my daughter, 100 acres, signed Michael Smith, Ann Magdalene Smith (*Culpeper D.B. C*, p.678); 15 APR 1762, deeds of gift from Michael Smith of 100 acres to his son-in-law, Adam Barler; of 117 acres to his son Zachariah Smith; and of 117 acres to his son Adam Smith, all the land being from the Christian Clements tract (*Culpeper D.B. D*, pp.3, 5). Michael Smith's wife, Anna Magdalena Thomas, is shown by the above to have been living in 1762. She does not appear in the deeds of gift made in 1771 and 1772, so had probably died in the interval. In accordance with the 1762 deeds, the Culpeper County Rental of 1764 shows Michael Smith with 666 acres, Zachariah Smith "of Michael" 117 acres, and Adam Smith "of Michael" 117 acres. On 31 DEC 1771 Michael Smith made deeds of gift to his son Zacharias; to his son-in-law, George Christler; to his son-in-law, John Marbes; and a joint deed of gift to his sons Adam and John Smith and his son-in-law Adam Barler (*Culpeper D.B. F*, pp.418, 419 and 420). On 16 MAR 1772 he made deeds of gift as follows: 117 acres to his son-in-law George Christler; 146 acres to his son John Smith; 155 acres to his son Adam Smith (*D.B. F*, pp.421, 422 and 423); and on 17 MAY 1772, he made a deed of gift of 161 acres to his son-in-law, John Marbes (*D.B. F*, p.461). These deeds show that Michael Smith II had seven children,

- Susannah, wife of John Berry, Jr.,
- Mary, wife of Adam Barler,
- Zachariah who died in Mercer County, Kentucky about 1816. He married first about 1760, Ann Elizabeth Fishback, daughter of John Frederick Fishback and his wife, Ann Elizabeth Holtzclaw. The Lutheran church records show "Zacharias Schmidt and Anna Schmidt" as sponsors at the christening of a child in 1767, and Ann Elizabeth probably died around 1770, certainly before 1777, when Zachariah Smith and wife, Sarah Ann, deeded away land in Culpeper. Zachariah raised a crop of corn in 1776 in Kentucky County (later Lincoln and finally Mercer County, Kentucky) and took out his land rights 1779–1780. He served in the Revolutionary War in a detachment of Lincoln County militia. See 𝕭𝖊𝖞𝖔𝖓𝖉 𝕲𝖊𝖗𝖒𝖆𝖓𝖓𝖆, v.4, n.2 for more information,
- Adam, married first Unknown and married second Elizabeth_____,
- Anna Magdalene married John George Christler (her children, born 1767–1792, are shown in the *Garr Genealogy*, p.66),
- Catherine, wife of John Marbes (see the Baptismal Records for the Lutheran Church), and
- John married Elizabeth, perhaps a Böhme.

It appears, after John Michael Smith, Jr. had disposed of his land, that he became a minister. In the period around 1782 to 1785, he was minister at the German Lutheran Church in the Robinson River Valley but he was not successful and the elders relieved him of his duties. This question is examined in "Who Was J. Michael Schmidt?' in 𝕭𝖊𝖞𝖔𝖓𝖉 𝕲𝖊𝖗𝖒𝖆𝖓𝖓𝖆, v.15, n.2.

The following deeds show how the heirs disposed of this land: *Culpeper D.B. F*, p.217, 18 DEC 1770, John Berry, Jr. and Susannah his wife to Adam Yager; *D.B. F*, p.553, 21 SEP 1772, Adam Smith and Elizabeth his wife to Henry Field, the land given them by Michael Smith; *D.B. H*, p.234, 11 MAY 1776, John Marbus to Adam Barlour, 17 acres; *D.B. H*, p.499, 15 AUG 1777, John Smith and Elizabeth his wife to Henry Field, Jr. 246 acres; *D.B. H*, p.500, 15 AUG 1777, Zacharias Smith and Sarah Ann his wife to Henry Field, Jr., 359 acres. After 1777 the Culpeper County records show no trace of Zacharias, Adam, and John Smith who had moved to Kentucky.

Smither. Joseph Smither was a communicant in 1782 at the Lutheran church.

Snyder, Henry. Hans Heinrich Schneider was born on 4 DEC 1667 in Botenheim, Württemberg. Details of his German history are available in "The Ancestry of the Snyder, Amburger, Kerker, and Kapler Families," *Before Germanna*, v.8. He married Anna Dorothea Schilling and they had one child, Anna Magdalena Schneider, who married Hans Jacob Öhler in 1712 (see Aylor). While the Snyder family came in 1717, the Aylors did not come at that time. Henry Snyder was sued by Spotswood in 1724 and was granted 78 acres across the Robinson River 24 JUN 1726 (*Virginia Patent Book 12*, p.475) as Schnider. He died in Orange County, Virginia in 1747. His will, written 30 NOV 1742 and probated in Orange County 26 MAR 1747, mentions his wife Dorothea, daughter Anna Magdalena Aler (Aylor) who was a widow, and grandchildren, Elizabeth Tanner and Henry Aler (*Orange W.B. 2*, pp. 106–7). Keith (pp. 188–189) erred in naming a grandson, Henry Snider. There were no Snyder descendants of Henry Snyder but all the Tanners and Aylors are descended from him. Other Snyders were descendants of John or Philip Snyder, who came over later and who seem to have no relationship to Henry Snyder.

Snyder, John. John Snyder does not seem to be related to Henry Snyder, the 1717 colonist. He first appears in Virginia in 1742 when he witnessed the will of Michael Wilhoite, the Germanna pioneer. John Snyder's will of 1760 and probated that same year was witnessed by William Cawl, John Knuesbay, and Henry Huphman (Huffman). This group of people were probably members of the Reformed community and suggests that John Snyder may have been Reformed himself and from the Nassau-Siegen area. The will names three sons, John, Adam and Michael and states there were five daughters but without giving their names. The sons are:

John, born perhaps about 1740–45, married Elizabeth_____,
Adam, born perhaps about 1745–50, married first Nancy Towles, second Mrs. Mildred (Wright) Long,
Michael, born perhaps about 1750–55, married Martha (Patsy) Stigler.

A history of the family by Claude Yowell appears in *Germanna Record* 12. Also, see Stigler here.

Snyder, Philip. Philip Snyder seems to have come to America about 1740 through Philadelphia. He married Margaret, daughter of Michael Cook, 1717 colonist. His family appears several times in the German Lutheran records suggesting that he was not a brother of John Snyder. Philip Snyder died about 1795, leaving four sons and three daughters.

Michael, probably born before 1750 and for that reason none of the children of Philip Snyder appear in the baptismal register. He married Mary Delph,
Mary Margaret, born about 1750, married Michael Delph,
Elizabeth, born about 1755, married George Conrad Delph,
Joseph, born about 1757, married Mary Christopher,
Mary, born 1762, never married,
Susanna, born about 1764, married Jacob Rasor,
Philip, a communicant in 1778, perhaps at an age of 18, would have been born about 1760, never married,
Samuel, confirmed 1789 perhaps at an age of 19 would have been born 1770, married Elizabeth Cook.

The birth years are estimates. Claude Yowell wrote a note on the family of Philip Snyder in *Germanna Record* 12.

Souther (Sauder in German). There are Sauders in the German ancestry of families who are discussed here but whether these are related to the Southers in Virginia is unknown. For example, the mother of John Michael Smith, Sr.'s first wife was a Sauter. In the 1739 Orange County tithes list, there is a Henry Crowder close to Michael Smith. Perhaps this name should be Sauder. (Crowder might be mistake in the writing or in the reading.)

Henry Souther was granted 324 acres in 1748 on German Ridge in present day Madison County The chain carriers were Daniel(?) Crisler and Steven Hansburger. Prior to this he seems to be in the Shenandoah Valley where he was claimed as a head right by Jacob Stover in 1733. In 1735 he was involved in a court action concerning lands of Stover. In the 1787 Culpeper tax list, there are two Southers, Jacob and Michael, who lived west of the present day town of Madison. When David Christler and wife Elizabeth had the child Nancy baptized in 1780, the sponsors included Jacob Sauther and Catharina Sauther. About the same time, on three occasions, Jacob Sauder was a sponsor for children of Henry Wayland and his wife Hanna. The wife of Jacob Sauder was Catherine, the daughter of John Wayland, son of Thomas Wayland, the Germanna pioneer. John Wayland had married Catherine Broyles, daughter of Jacob Broyles.

Spilman. Harman Spilman was the son of the 1714 colonist John Spilman. Harman lived for a while in the Robinson River Valley. He married Catherine, the daughter of the 1714 colonist, John Huffman. See *Germanna Record* 3 and 5.

Stär. Elizabeth Stär was confirmed in 1782 at the Hebron Church at the age of 17.

Stature. Rosina Stature was confirmed in 1782 at the Hebron Church at the age of 17.

Steiner. This is a mistake for Reiner.

Steinseifer (there are several variations in spelling in America). Johannes Steinseifer was born 6 JUL 1698 at Eiserfeld, a neighboring village to Eisern in Germany where the Hofmanns lived. On 3 AUG 1723 Johannes Steinseifer married Elisabeth Schuster (born 1705) of Eisern. (The wife of Henry Huffman was also a Schuster but the relationship between the two women is unknown.) The family lived in Eisern and had nine children baptized in the parish of Rödgen. They and their baptismal dates were:

Johannes Henrich, 1 OCT 1724,

Elisabeth, 24 NOV 1726 (d. 1727),

Johann Heinrich, 18 JUL 1728,

Elisabeth, 17 JAN 1734,

Agnes Catharina, 26 AUG 1716,

Henricus, 2 AUG 1739,

Maria Agnesa, 14 JAN 1742,

Johannes, 2 FEB 1744,

Anna Margaretha, 7 APR 1748.

Some names were favored and two children bore the same name. The family emigrated in 1749 except for the eldest son who came in 1753. John Steinseifer wrote his will 2 APR 1754 but it was not probated for three years. The four sons were called John the Elder, Henerecus, John the Younger, and Henry. The lands of John Steinseifer adjoined Michael Smith, John Kains, Major Roan, Henry Hoffman, and Jacob Manspile.

John Steinsiffer and his wife Jemima Clore brought Veronica, born 1 DEC 1776, for baptism at the Lutheran church. An interesting article on the family by Ryan Stansifer, "Johannes Steinseifer (1698–1757)" appeared in *Beyond Germanna*, v.10, n. 5.

Stigler. Samuel Stigler, born about 1729, moved to the Robinson River area where he purchased land in 1765. Samuel's daughter, Martha (Patsy or Patty), married Michael Snyder (son of John Snyder and Mary). Michael and Martha had eleven children. These children married Yager, Wayland, Fray (two), Aylor, Peyton, Taylor (two), and Thornton descendants plus Rev. Thornton Rucker.

Apparently, Samuel was the son of James Stigler who may have come to Virginia as an infant. This family lived in King George County where there are several records pertaining to them. Several Stigler records are to be found in Fauquier County (see John P. Alcock, *Fauquier Families 1759–1799*, Iberian Publishing Company, Athens, Georgia, 1994). There may be a relationship to the Berry family. Descendants were soon found in Kentucky and Missouri. This information on the Stigler family came from Suzee Oberg.

Stöver. Johann Caspar Stöver was baptized 13 JAN 1685 at Frankenburg, Hesse where his father was Dietrich Stöver and his mother was Magdalena the daughter of Andreas Eberwein, the Lutheran pastor there. Johann Caspar Stöver's first wife was Gertrud_____. There are blank periods in his German history and his marriage and the birth of a daughter have never been found. His namesake son was born in Lüdorf, Solingen Amt, in Duchy of Berg in December of 1707. (Lüdorf is about 14 miles east-southeast of Düsseldorf.) By 1717, Johann Caspar Stöver was living at Annweiler where he was a teacher and organist. He remained here until 1724. Then there is a short blank until he appears in America in 1728.

Johann Caspar Stöver, Sr. and Jr. plus the daughter Elizabeth Catherine arrived at Philadelphia on the *James Goodwill* on 11 SEP 1728. One of the two men was a "theological student" and the other was a "missionary." The son was probably the theological student for the father had been a teacher and organist in Germany. Though he was not ordained, the son commenced clerical duties in Pennsylvania almost immediately (he was just twenty years old).

It is known that the senior Stöver was in North Carolina where there are documents attesting to his presence. There he married Mary Magdalena whose maiden name may have been Pool as that was her mother's name but this may have been a second marriage for the mother. Late in 1732 or early in 1733, the father was going to Pennsylvania from North Carolina and stopped at the Robinson River community. Finding that he had a good education, the congregation offered him the position as pastor if he could be ordained. After inquiries were made, Johann Caspar Stöver and George Scheible of the congregation went to Pennsylvania. There, apparently on the same day 8 APR 1733, the Rev. Johann Christian Schultz ordained both the father and son and held a marriage ceremony for the son. The wife was Maria Catharina Mercklin originally of Lambsheim. She was perhaps a cousin of Dewald Christler who later moved to the Robinson River community. This thesis is developed in "A Possible Connection Between Theobald Christler and Johann Caspar Stöver. Jr.," Beyond Germanna, v.14, n.6.

Services with communion were held in the spring of 1733 in the Robinson River. The congregation had raised the funds to purchase a glebe from William Carpenter and to build a house for the new pastor. They felt they could pay him only 3,000 pounds of tobacco a year as they had to pay tithes to the Anglican church.

The decision was reached to send Rev. Stoever, Michael Smith, and Michael Holt to Europe to raise money. This trip started in September of 1734. The effort was very successful. On the voyage home in 1739, Rev. Stöver died, leaving a will which was witnessed by Michael Smith and two other men.

The daughter of the senior Stöver, Elizabeth Catherine, married Johannes Kuntz at Earl Town, Pennsylvania on 25 JUN 1738.

Mary Magdalena Stöver, his second wife, surely was considerably younger than her husband. (She was the mother of Philip and Elizabeth). After Stöver died on the return trip, she married George Holt, the Virginia-born son of the early immigrant Michael Holt. Since he could hardly have been twenty years old in 1740, it is probable she was a little older than he was. Presumably when Mary Magdalena married John Caspar Stöver, Sr., she must have been very young and perhaps a student of his. She was asked by the Orange Court whether she would take the responsibility for the guardianship of her children, 26 FEB 1741(OS) (*Orange O.B. 3*, p. 106). An account of the estate of John Gaspar Stoever was delivered to the Orange Court on 25 NOV 1742 by Jonathon Gibson and James Porteus (*O.B. 3*, p.290).

Vernon Stiver privately published in 1992 a book of genealogy of the family entitled *Stöver-Stoever-Staver-Stiver*. Many articles pertaining to the life and duties of Johann Caspar Stöver have been published in Beyond Germanna.

Stoltz. John Michael Stoltz was first granted 400 acres in Hanover County on both sides of Owens Creek in 1725 (*Virginia Patent Book 12*, p.246). He was granted 291 acres in the Robinson River area in 1732 (*Virginia Patent Book 14*, p.438) adjacent to George Moyer. (Peter Weaver's 400 acre patent for land in 1736 up Deep Run was adjacent to Frederick Pamgarner, John Michel Stolts, and George Moyer). John Stolts is in the 1739 Orange County tithe list. At an inquiry in 1741, it was found that the property of John Michael Stolts, deceased then, had reverted to the state. William Fowler claimed it and sold it to Michael Utz in 1745. B.C. Holtzclaw says that John Michael Stoltz died in 1741/2 and his son of the same name was appointed his administrator (*Orange W.B.1*, p.194). The son had great difficulties in administering the estate which required lawsuits against several of his neighbors such as Weaver, Utz, Towles, and Bobo to name a few. The estate was appraised by Francis Michaels, John Thomas, Jacob Broyles, and Peter Fleshman. *Before Germanna*, v.10, "The Ancestry of the Yager, Stolts, Crees, and Beyerbach Families," gives information on two different individuals in Germany who might have been this man.

Swindle / Swindell / Schwindel (The origin or even the nationality of this family is not certain). The name Schwindel is found in Germany. Variations of the name are found in parts of Virginia where there were few, if any, Germans. So the national origins of Timothy Swindle are not known. His wife, Rebecca Crees (Crest, Greys), was clearly German as delineated in "The Ancestry of the Yager, Stolts, Crees, and Beyerbach Families," *Before Germanna*, v.10. A number of records at the German Church shed some light on this family. From the church records, it is possible to discern five children which may be taken as the family of Timothy and Rebecca (Cree) Swindel:

Sarah who married Frederick Baumgardner,

Michael who married Elizabeth Utz, the daughter of Michael and Elizabeth Utz. Michael and Elizabeth Swindle moved to South Carolina where they died. More information can be found in B. Dale Swindle's *The Swindle Family—Three Centuries in America*.

John who married Hannah Weaver. Hannah Weaver was the daughter of Peter and Elizabeth Weaver. She was not married when her father wrote his will. Her marriage to John is established by the sponsorships at the church.

George Swindle, a son, is listed twice in the Culpeper County, Virginia marriage records but these pertain to two different individuals, the son here and a nephew. In the first on 30 JAN 1786, George Swindle married Catherine Razor. Later, on 21 JAN 1790, a George Swindle married Hannah Cornelius. Records in Laurens County, South Carolina show that the widow of George (of Timothy) was named Hannah. The marriage to Catherine is thought to be this George's nephew. The nephew, in the tax lists in 1787, was living in 1817 when he received a distribution from the estate of Michael (of Timothy).

Rebecca who married John Fray. Virginia Fray Lewis' *A History & Genealogy of John Fray of Culpeper County, Virginia* states it was a tradition within the Fray family that John Fray's wife was Rebecca Yowell, the daughter of Nicholas Yowell. B.C. Holtzclaw doubted this claim. From the baptismal records at the Lutheran Church, it is almost certain that Rebecca Swindle married John Fray. There is no record of a Rebecca Yowell.

More information on the family and its descendants are given in the article by T.M. and W.H. Sutherland, "The Timothy Swindle Family" in 𝔅𝔢𝔶𝔬𝔫𝔡 𝔊𝔢𝔯𝔪𝔞𝔫𝔫𝔞, v.7, n.4, p.391.

Tanner. The name Tanner is found in Switzerland, Germany, and Austria but the origins of the family have not yet been proven. At the Lutheran Church in the Robinson River Valley, the name of the male head is given as Urban Tanner when he was paid in 1733 for going to Williamsburg on business for the church though he generally used the name Robert Tanner. Urban Tanner is believed to be the first Germanna citizen to leave Germany. In 1709 he and his wife Anna Maria had their daughter, Anna Catharina, baptized. It was recorded in the Catholic church in Westhofen (near Worms) which also served nearby chapels. In this record it is stated he was from Argersheim by which Ergersheim is probably meant as there is no known Argersheim in Germany but there are two Ergersheims, one in Bavaria and one in Alsace. On the June 10th of 1709, Urban Danner with wife and four children is recorded in the 3rd departure list from Rotterdam for London. Urban Tanner, a cooper and brewer aged 33, and his wife, and daughters aged 6, 4, 3, and 1 were in the 3rd arrivals in London. He is recorded as one of the Palatines in Ireland. There he appears as Urban Damur (or Damus) 13 July 1715. The names of his wife and the one daughter agree with Virginia records. His origins may have been in Switzerland where there are many Tanners in the German-speaking parts of it. The attempt in Virginia to suggest that the name was Gerber was a misguided effort, probably introduced by Heinrich Möller who was a candidate minister in 1774/5 and who rewrote the Baptismal Register.

On 8 NOV 1727 Robert Turner, German, testified that he came into this country in 1720 and brought with him his wife Mary and his five children, Christopher, Christiana, Katherine, Maria, and Parva (Barbara) (*Spotsylvania O.B. 1724–30*, p.214). Probably he adopted the name Robert because the name Urban is rare and easily misunderstood. He was granted 216 acres in the Robinson River section adjoining Jacob Crigler 28 SEP 1728 (*Virginia Patent Book 14*, p.96) and on 18 AUG 1735 he received another grant of 200 acres adjoining Henry Snider (*Virginia Patent Book 16*, p.156). Turner in the record is a mistake of the clerk of the court for Tanner as confirmed by the fact that Robert Tanner had a son, Christopher, to whom on 24 AUG 1737 he deeded the 200 acres that had been granted him in 1735 (*Orange D.B. 2*, p.78). On 21 MAR 1738/9 he deeded to Richard Burdyne the 216 acres for £50 granted him in 1728 (*Orange D.B. 3*, p.117). The 1739 tithables (see Part I) of Orange County show a George "Tenner" with one tithable next to Robert "Tenner" who has two tithables (himself and his son Christopher). George Tanner is a mystery as he does not appear in the later records of Orange and Culpeper Counties.

In 1734, Robert Tanner applied and was approved to be levy free because he was sick and incapable of work (*Orange O.B. 1*, p.13).

When Robert Tanner deeded the 200 acres to Christopher, he stated he was giving his real estate and personal property to Christopher in return for Christopher taking care of Mary, Robert's wife (*Orange D.B. 2*, p.83). Robert stated at this time that he designed to depart this country for Germany and the transfer of property was to put his affairs in order. Whether he did visit Germany and where he died are unknowns. On 24 SEP 1742 the action of debt brought by Robert Tanner against Christopher Tanner was dismissed (*Orange O.B.3*, p.244). Just slightly later, his action of trespass, assault, and battery against Christopher Tanner was dismissed (*Orange O.B. 3*, p.263). At the same time, the action of trespass by Robert Tanner against Henry Eller (Aylor) was dismissed (*Orange O.B. 3*, p. 273). It would appear that Robert Tanner did die in Virginia.

On a petition of 1 JUN 1731 of Robert Tanner, he was denied the discharge of public levies by the County Court (*Spotsylvania O.B. 1730–1738*, p.49). Robert Tanner was sued by George H_____(unreadable) for one thousand pounds of tobacco 29 JAN 1731. At the trial, Robert won completely with the plaintiff being assessed attorney's fees for the defendant (*Spotsylvania O.B. 1730–1738*, p.82). In another lawsuit, brought by Alexander Spotswood, Esquire, against Robert Tanner for thirty-two shillings (or four barrels of corn) for rent, Spotswood won a judgment of three barrels of corn (*Spotsylvania O.B. 1730–1738*, p.66). The basis of this lawsuit is not understood and it may not be the Germanna Robert Tanner.

There is no record at present that shows who married his daughters. Katherine is believed to have married Richard Burdyne. There is a weak possibility that Mary was the first wife of John Thomas, Jr. (see 𝔅𝔢𝔶𝔬𝔫𝔡 𝔊𝔢𝔯𝔪𝔞𝔫𝔫𝔞, v.7, n.2, p.376). There is no information on Christina and Barbara.

All the known Tanners of Culpeper and Madison Counties are descended from the son, Christopher. Christopher Tanner was born after the departure from Germany and before Virginia and at least as early as 1716, for he was presumably 21 years old when his father deeded him land in 1737. He married around the year 1740 Elizabeth Aylor, daughter of Hans Jacob Aylor and Anna Magdalene Schneider. Christopher Tanner is shown with 200 acres of land in the Culpeper County Rental of 1764. He and his wife Elizabeth deeded 34 acres to his brother-in-law Henry Aylor 15 JUL 1779 (*Culpeper D.B. I*, p.377). His will, dated 12 MAY 1781 and probated in Madison County 27 JUN 1797 (*Madison W.B. 3*, p.314), names his children:

- Jacob, married Dorothy Zimmerman, daughter of John Zimmermann and granddaughter of the 1717 immigrant, Christopher Zimmermann.
- Frederick married Mary Rouse and most of the births of their fourteen children are given in the church records.
- Christopher married Susannah Huffman.
- John did not marry and he died in Madison County in 1816.

Abraham married Elizabeth Huffman about 1778.

Dorothy married Reginald Burdyne, her first cousin, as his second wife.

Mary Magdalen married Joseph Rouse as his second wife with no issue.

Researchers of the Tanner family should consult Leatrice Tanner Wagner's book *Robert Tanner and His Descendants, A Family History*. This large, well documented tome is a major Germanna book which has an excellent general history besides the family history. A shorter history by B.C. Holtzclaw is given in *Germanna Record* 12.

Teter. Johann George Dieter was born in Schwaigern, Württemberg, the home of many other Germanna settlers. Born in 1699, he married Mary Margaret Luttmann in 1720. Two children were born in Schwaigern, John Michael and Mary Christina. They arrived at Philadelphia 30 SEP 1727 on the *Molly*. A third son John George was christened in Lancaster, Pennsylvania in 1730. This information is from "The Ancestry of the Christler, Baumgartner, Deer, Dieter, and Lotspeich Families," *Before Germanna*, v.11 where more is given. He obtained a patent for 200 acres on the south side of the Robinson River adjacent to Roger Quarles and Michael Cooke, 10 JAN 1735(OS) (*Virginia Patent Book 16*, p.475). George Teter is in the 1739 Orange County tithe list next to Lewis Fisher, George Tanner, Robert Tanner and Henry Snider. He died in Orange County. In 1743/4 his widow, Mary Margaret, was appointed his administratrix. His widow and children moved to Rowan County, North Carolina and then to Pendleton County in today's West Virginia. See the *Henckel Genealogy* by Junkin and *Henckel Genealogical Bulletin* for more information on the descendants of the son John George. More on the family is in Franklin H. Cochran, "George Teter of the Robinson River Settlement in Virginia," in *Beyond Germanna*, v.9, n.5, p.525 which gives some additional references.

Thallert. Christoph and Elizabeth Thallert were communicants 2 APR 1786 at the German Lutheran Church.

Thomas. John Thomas probably came over in 1717 with his wife Anna Maria Blankenbaker, his son John and his daughter Anna Magdalena but proof of this is lacking. Since her family all came at that time, it seems likely that the Thomas family would have come also but they may have been one of the families that was delayed. John, Sr. died early, but his sons, John, Jr., and Michael Thomas were granted 156 acres of land (under the name of Tomer) on 24 JUN 1726 (*Virginia Patent Book 12*, p. 476) along with the other 1717 colonists. Neither boy was of age at this time; Michael may have been only six years old. The mother Anna Maria Thomas married second Michael Käfer, the 1717 colonist, and his will mentions her four children, John Thomas, Michael Thomas, Magdalena wife of Michael Smith, and Margaret wife of Henry Coller (but the latter name was a clerical mistake for Aylor).

John Thomas, Jr., the eldest son, patented 400 acres when he was 16 in the Robinson River section 28 SEP 1728 (*Virginia Patent Book 14*, p. 97). On 27 FEB 1744(OS) he was deeded 570 acres by John Paul Vogt (Vaught) and Mary Catherine his wife (*Orange D.B. 9*, p. 259). John Thomas, Jr., born in Germany, was admitted to citizenship with other German Protestants of the German Lutheran Church community 27 JAN 1742(OS) (*Orange O.B. 3*, p.313).

In February 1742(OS), John Thomas, Jr. and his first wife, Mary, sold to Michael Thomas his half interest in the 156 acres which had been patented jointly by John and Michael in 1726 (*Orange D.B. 7*, p.98). Michael was probably born in this country about 1720. Michael was married twice with twenty-five descendants. The first wife was Catherine_____ and the second wife was Eve Susannah Hart. Many of the children, but not all, have been identified. At the 24 NOV 1743 Orange County Court, Michael requested that Christian Mood be added to his tithables. Michael was a participant in a proposed development in the west, see the section here on the Klug family. Michael continued to live in Culpeper County until 1769. On 20 JAN 1769 he and Eve Susannah Margaret Hart, his wife, deeded the 156 acres to Elliott Bohannon (*Culpeper D.B. E*, p. 734). After this Michael Thomas does not appear in the records as he moved initially to southwestern Pennsylvania and later to Kentucky. Many of the children made this same migration.

The Thomas, Sr. daughter, Anna Magdalena Smith is discussed in the section on Michael Smith. The daughter Anna Margaret married Henry Aylor.

John Thomas, Jr. and his wife Mary gave land to three daughters and their husbands for natural love and affection:

> Susannah, wife of Jacob Holtzclaw (*Culpeper D.B. C*, p. 439, 20 NOV 1760),
>
> Mary, wife of Joseph Holtzclaw (*Culpeper D.B. D, p. 5*, 15 APR 1762),
>
> Mary Barbara, wife of Jacob Blankenbaker (*Culpeper D.B. C*, p. 441, 20 NOV 1760) near Jacob Broyle, Mary Thomas, John Railsback, and Jacob Holtzclaw.

The two Holtzclaws were the youngest sons of Jacob Holtzclaw, the 1714 Germanna colonist. Jacob Blankenbaker was the son of Nicholas Blankenbaker, the 1717 immigrant (see Nicholas Blankenbaker).

John Thomas, Jr. had another daughter and a son,

> Elizabeth,
>
> Michael.

The evidence for them is of a different nature. John Thomas created five parcels of land of about the same size (approximately 100 acres). Three of these were gifts to sons-in-law as indicated above. Two of five parcels went to John Railsback who paid something for them because he got more land in the two parcels. That John Railsback's wife, Elizabeth, was a daughter of John Thomas, Jr. is indicated by a baptism at the Lutheran church. The Railsbacks were the parents of Catherine, christened on 16 MAR 1777 with sponsors Jacob Blankenbaker, Dorothea Tanner, and Mary Zimmerman. This indicates a strong likelihood that Elizabeth was a daughter of John Thomas, Jr.

Members of a Thomas family from North Carolina had a tradition that their ancestor was a Michael Thomas of Culpeper County, Virginia who moved to North Carolina. DNA testing has confirmed that the male descendants of this North Carolina Michael match almost perfectly the DNA of male descendants of Michael Thomas, the brother of John Thomas, Jr.

This sequence of events came about when John Thomas had planned to give each of five children about 100 acres of land. The son Michael of John Thomas, Jr., chose not to take the land or he was a minor. With the fifth parcel available, John Thomas sold two parcels to John Railsback charging something for the land because John Railsback got more land. After disposing of his land, John Thomas, Jr., his wife Sarah, and his son Michael moved to North Carolina.

The appearance of the wife, Sarah, shows that John Thomas, Jr. was married twice. The daughters all seem to have the mother Mary while the mother of Michael is problematic. The maiden names of both Mary and Sarah are unknown though there is a possibility that Mary was a Tanner (see *Beyond Germanna*, v.7, n.2). The speculation that she might have been a Vaught does not seem well founded. John Thomas and Sarah his wife also deeded 100 acres on 10 APR 1762 to Michael Smith (his brother-in-law) out of the tract bought from John Paul "Focht" in 1744 (*Culpeper D.B. C*, p. 702). A John Thomas was sworn in as an Ensign in the military 2 JUL 1742 (*Orange County O. B. 3*, p.169) but this may be another man.

The Culpeper Rental of 1764 shows two John Thomases owning land, one English and the other, German. It has not always been easy to distinguish the two men. John Thomas (the German) and wife Sarah seem to have deeded away the balance of his land from 1769 to 1771: to John Finnell in 1769; to John Hantsberger (Harnsberger) of Augusta County, again to Michael Smith, and to Zachary Smith (Michael's son), all in 1771 (*Culpeper County D.B. F*, pp. 10, 240, 345, and 365). After this there is no record of John Thomas, Jr. and he appears to have moved to North Carolina with his son Michael.

Since some of the descendants of the English John Thomas married Germanna people, it might be well to recap some of the genealogy of the English John Thomas. The English John Thomas is probably identical with the person who was granted 106 acres of land near William Banks 10 SEP 1753 (*Northern Neck Land Grants, Book H*, p. 408), and with his wife, Betty, deeded to Philip Rootes 100 acres of land 24 DEC 1754, the land having been deeded him by Benjamin Rush and originally patented to William Rush (*Culpeper D.B. B*, p.229). He died at an advanced age in Culpeper County in 1785, his will mentioning a number of grandchildren and one great-grandchild. The will, dated 29 April 1782 and probated 21 FEB 1785 (*Culpeper W.B. C*, p.100), mentions his son John, son-in-law William Powell, son Benjamin, daughter-in-law Elizabeth (widow of son Massey, decd.), son-in-law Robert McKey, son-in-law Jeremiah Kirk, great-granddaughter Lucy (daughter of John Thomas son of Massey Thomas), grandson John (son of Massey Thomas), grandson Jesse (son of John Thomas), grandson Reuben, and son William. Of the four sons mentioned in the will, John Thomas died in Madison County, Virginia in 1793. His wife was named Elizabeth, as shown by a deed to William Powell April 16, 1791 (*Culpeper D.B. Q*, p.262). The will, dated Sept. 9, 1793 and probated 24 OCT 1793 (*Madison W.B. 1*, p.12), mentions his children, Jesse, Massey, Elisha, George, William, Betsy, Rhoda wife of Joshua Barler, and Jemima wife of Benjamin Rush. The daughter, Rhoda Thomas, m. Joshua Barler 24 MAY 1789 (Knorr, *Culpeper County Wills*, p.4), Joshua being the eldest son of Adam Barler and grandson of Christopher Barler, the 1717 immigrant (see Barlow). Massey Thomas (apparently son of John II) m. Elizabeth Barbour 20 DEC 1785, and Elisha Thomas m. Leanna Zigler 28 DEC 1788 (Knorr, p. 88). Leanna Zigler was a granddaughter of Leonard Ziegler and his wife, Barbara Zimmerman, daughter of Christopher Zimmerman, the 1717 colonist (see Ziegler). Massey Thomas, son of John Thomas who died in 1785, died in Culpeper County in 1776, his appraisement occurring May 22 of that year (*W.B. B*, p.174). Massey Thomas' wife, too, was named Elizabeth, and he left six children, Reuben, John, William, Massey, Jesse and Susannah Thomas, all of whom were of age 6 MAR 1782, when they turned over to their mother, Elizabeth Thomas, their interest in the estate of their father, Massey Thomas, deceased. (*Culpeper D.B. M*, p. 185). Massey's son, William Thomas, had moved to Sullivan County, North Carolina by 16 FEB 1783, on which date his grandfather, John Thomas, deeded him a negro (*D.B. L*, p.257).

Tivall. Christian Tival is called a son-in-law of Andrew Garr (see Garr). Another member of the family is Henry. Nothing more is known about the family and they represent a problem in the general history. See the section on the Garrs.

Trumbo. George Trumbo and his wife Margaretha had Andreas baptized 17 NOV 1776 at the German Lutheran Church in Culpeper County. Andrew had been born 19 AUG 1776. The sponsors were George Utz, Jr. and his wife. Margaret's father was George Utz (II) and her mother was Mary Käfer.

The following information was supplied by Marge Willhite. "Andrew Trumbore (Andreas Drumbor) emigrated from the Rhenish Palatinate to Pennsylvania between 1724 and 1727. On 27 March 1728 he purchased two hundred five acres of land for fifty-five pounds, seven shillings from John Budd and Humphrey Murrey...After living here twenty-five years, Andrew sold his large plantation to his second son Andrew, Jr. and gave a conveyance date 6 JUN 1754..."

Branches of the Trumbos moved to Virginia in the area which is now Pendleton County, West Virginia. This was in a valley to the west of Shenandoah Valley and separated from it by the Shenandoah Mountains. Fort Seybert was a prominent early feature and its location is still known. Jacob and Mary Trumbo were the parents of seven children: Elizabeth who married Matthias Rheinhart (see Reinhard), Andrew who married Margaret Harness, John who married Mary Custer (Küster), George (the subject of this note), Dorothy, Margaret, and Jacob, Jr. who married Elizabeth Lair and Hannah Hawes Cowger. The family history gives the wife of George as Margaret Rockefeller Oats. The identity with Margaret Utz is clear. (Since the grandmother of Margaret Utz Trumbo was Anna Maria Blankenbaker, the Rockefeller name was probably a misreading of German script.)

There is a book of family history by Conrad Feltner, *The Trumbo Family*, 1974. George Trumbo lived on the west side of the Valley of Virginia and business took him east of the Blue Ridge Mountains on occasions. On one of these trips he appears to have met Margeret Utz, the daughter of George Utz and his wife Mary Käfer. This George Utz was the son of George Utz, the 1717 immigrant. Mary Käfer was the daughter of Michael Käfer and Anna Maria (Blankenbaker) Thomas. Probably, when Andrew was due to be delivered, Margaret came home to her mother and stayed a short while. Before returning to their home, Andrew was baptized. The George Utz who was a sponsor could have been her brother, George, or her cousin, son of Michael Utz.

Urbach / Arbach. Adolph and his wife Anna Maria Urbach had Anna Barbara, born 31 AUG 1776, baptized 22 SEP 1776, at the German Lutheran church with Daniel Doser and his wife as sponsors. Five pages of information on the Arbaugh/Orebaugh/Orebach family is given by Ardys V. Hurt in Larry Shuck's book *Our Families*. Names in the text that could be Germanna names include Snider, Baker, Dozer, Fleshman, Soward, Baumgardner and Miller.

Utz. Ancestors of George Utz are found in the villages of Haundorf, Mosbach, Seiderzell, Bergnerzell, and Kühnhard in Mittelfranken in Bavaria, just east of the line dividing Bavaria and Württemberg. Georg Utz emigrated to Wagenbach, an estate farm just outside Hüffenhardt in Baden. There he married the widow Anna Barbara (Majer) Volck in 1709, see page 44 for a longer discussion. In Virginia, the three surviving children, Michael, Mary Margaret, and George, were born.

Michael Utz married Susanna Crigler the daughter of Jacob Crigler a 1717 colonist and they had six children:

George who married Margaret Weaver,
Michael who married Mary Crigler,
Margaret who married John Broyles,
Adam who married Mary Wayman,
Elisabeth who married Michael Swindle, and
Daniel who married Mary Finks.

Mary Margaret Utz married John Blankenbaker, the son of Matthias Blankenbaker a 1717 colonist. John's will mentions these children:

John who married Elizabeth Weaver (not Elizabeth Utz),
Elizabeth who married Henry Huffman,
Barbara who married Lewis Nonnenmacher, and
Mary Magdelena who married Henry Wayman.

George Utz married Mary Käfer the daughter of Michael Käfer a 1717 colonist. They had eight children:

Margaret who married George Trumbo,
George who married Dinah Carpenter,
Mary who never married,
Ephraim who married Christina Blankenbaker,
Susanna who married Lewis Blankenbaker,
Lewis who married Mary Carpenter,
Elizabeth who married George Wilhoit, and
Michael who had no known heirs.

The existence of this last Michael is inferred from the church documents, as is the existence of his sister Elizabeth and her husband.

Veil. David Veil was a communicant in 1775.

Vinegunt (See Weingard also). William Vinegunt had a 500 acre patent on the north end of the early German settlement (*Virginia Patent Book 14*, p.32, 28 SEP 1728). After this patent, little is known though his name appears in the Orange County Court records for a number of years. In 1735, John Winyard brought suit against Francis Brown. John Vynyard lost a trespass suit 16 MAR 1735(OS). The suit of trespass brought by Isaac Smith against John Vynyard was dismissed 21 SEP 1736.

Vogt / Vaught (many variations of this name occur in the records, as for example, Vaut, Faut, Wacht or Bellfaut). John Paul Vogt was born about 1680 in Frankfurt, Germany. He married Maria Catharina and four children, born in Germany, came with them to Philadelphia in OCT 1733. On 15 JUL 1735 he applied for six head rights in the Orange County Court, naming himself, his wife, and children John Andrew, John Caspar, Catherine Margaret, and Mary Catherine. He had a patent for 640 acres on 10 JAN 1735(OS) adjoining Christopher Clemmon (Clements) which he paid for with the six head rights named above plus £1 15s (*Virginia Patent Book 16*, p.510). Christopher (Christian) Clements, whose land was on Deep Run, married Catherine Vogt which is presumably Mary Catherine as Germans generally used their second name as the "calling" name. By June of 1734, John Vought was a security for the administrator of the estate of Barbara Cooper who lived at some distance from where John Vought had his land. It is unusual for an emigrant to have such a responsible duty so soon after his arrival. One wonders if there was some relationship to the Cooper family. On 17 JUN 1735, Gaspar Stoever and Mary his wife brought suit against John Vought for assault and battery. The Rev. Johann Casper Stoever, Sr. was, at this time, on the fund raising trip to Germany. The suit was later dismissed.

John Paul and his wife sold 170 acres to William Caul (Kahl) on 7 JUL 1744. They also sold 470 acres to John Thomas. The family, along with the Clements, moved to the Massanutten Mountain area in the Shenandoah Valley in 1744. John Paul died at his home in the Shenandoah Valley in 1761. His will, dated 9 OCT 1759, was proved 18 AUG 1761. Besides the sons Andrew and Gaspar, only one daughter, who had married Christian Clements, is mentioned in the will.

John Andrew Vaught moved to southwest Virginia on tributaries of the New River. His wife is known only as Elizabeth and they are believed to be parents of Andrew, George, John, Gaspar, Christian, David, and Henry. During the Revolution these southwestern Vaughts were sympathetic to the Loyalists and not to the Revolution. The sons moved to Kentucky and Tennessee while two remained in Wythe County, Virginia.

Gaspar Faught, son of John Paul and Catherine, married Elizabeth Wilkiss about 1750. At first he lived near North River in the Valley close to his father. In the 1770s he sold his land and moved to Botetourt County, Virginia on the headwaters of the James River. The nine children of Gaspar and Elizabeth (Wilkiss) Faught are: Martin, Paul, Adam who married a Catherine, Sarah, Gaspar (his birth is in the Peaked Mountain Church records), Leonard, Barbara who married John Edwards in 1785, Elizabeth who married Thomas Jackson in 1786, and George who married Mary Persinger in 1789.

A three part article on the family by Helen Spurlin appeared in Beyond Germanna, v.2 in issues 2, 3 and 4. The article was based on the book, *Descendants of Christley Vaught* by Helen Spurlin and Mickey Martin.

Walk. Hans Martin Valk landed at Philadelphia 11 SEP 1728 from the *James Goodwill*. It is interesting that two other passemgers were Johann Caspar Stöver, Sr. and Johann Caspar Stöver, Jr. (The senior Stöver became the first pastor in 1733 of the German Lutheran Church in the Robinson River Valley.) Shortly after this, Michael Clore sold 100 acres to Martin Wallick. Presumably, Martin Walk was married to Catherine Clore by then.

Martin Walk with Tobias Willhide had a patent of 400 acres on branches of Deep Run (*Virginia Patent Book 17*, p.127, 20 JUL 1736) adjacent to William Beverley's Meander Run Mountain Land on the German Road. It is not clear why the two men would have gone into this partnership but Tobias might have married a sister of Martin Walk (there are other possibilities). On 22 SEP 1748, Walk and Willhide divided their joint tract equally. Nineteen days later Martin Walk and wife Catherine sold their 200 acres to Michael Yager. Martin Vallick was naturalized 27 JAN 1742(OS) (*Orange O.B. 3*, p.313). At the same time, Martin Vallick brought a suit of trespass against Michael O'Neal.

He purchased 165 acres on Yadkin River in North Carolina. Thereafter he appears many times in the court and land records in North Carolina. The will of Martin Wallox was proved 8 FEB 1785. He was married twice, possibly three times. The question is hard to answer as all of the wives appear to be named Catherine. The memoirs of his daughter, Catherine, say that her mother, Catherine Clore died about 1745. We know that he married before 1759 Catherine Gerhard, the daughter of John Garrett (see Gerhard here) who was living in Rowan County, North Carolina.

A son Martin (Jr.), in North Carolina, became a Moravian. Martin left a story of his life, in accordance with Moravian custom, which is in the Moravian archives. This has been translated by Elke Hall and published in 𝔅𝔢𝔶𝔬𝔫𝔡 𝔊𝔢𝔯𝔪𝔞𝔫𝔫𝔞, v.9, n.2. In it he states he was born in Culpeper County, Virginia on 2 APR 1737. He lost his mother early on and when his father remarried some time later, he often endured harsh treatment from his stepmother. In his 13th year he moved to North Carolina with his parents and some other families who now belong to the *Gemeine* (congregation). He left his parents' home in his 22nd year. In 1767 married the Elizabeth Fiscus. From this union there were 12 children.

Wayland (Wieland in German). Thomas Wieland was born 27 NOV 1681 in Lehrensteinfeld, Württemberg. He married Maria Barbara, daughter of Abraham Seppach, 18 AUG 1711, at Willsbach, Württemberg. Two children, Hans Jacob and Anna Catharine Clara, were born at Waldbach, Württemberg. More information is available in "The Ancestry of the Wayland, Albrect, and Cook Families," *Before Germanna*, v.12. Also, see *Germanna Record* 11, "Carpenter and Wayland."

Thomas Wayland stated on 4 NOV 1729 that he came to this country with his wife Mary and his children, Jacob and Catherine (*Spotsylvania O.B. 1724–30*, p.356) but no date for entry was given. The family was at St. Mary in the Strand in London in 1717 for Maria Barbara Wieland was a sponsor at a baptism. On 28 SEP 1728 Thomas Wayland was granted 504 acres in the Robinson River neighborhood (*Virginia Patent Book 13*, p.433). Because of the later date, the Wayland family may have been delayed in getting to Virginia. He lost 384 acres of the 504 acres to John Broyles because it overlapped Broyles who had the earlier claim. The remaining 120 acres were sold to Michael Smith for £20 (*Orange D.B. 2*, p.63). In the deed book, Thomas Weyland is called a blacksmith.

In 1739 he is shown with one tithable in Orange County which indicates that his son, Jacob, was dead and that the younger sons, Adam and John, were born after 1723. The Vestry of St. Mark's Parish ordered, on 12 OCT 1741, that the wardens pay 30 shillings to Tho. Wayland's wife out of the money for the use of the poor. Apparently, she had rendered substantial aid to a person or family and was to be reimbursed. He was excused from all county and parish levies on 22 JUL 1742 (*Orange O.B. 3*, p.169). Thomas Wayland last appears in the records 12 JUL 1748, when he sold 120 acres to Adam Garr and perhaps he died soon after this. What became of Thomas Wayland's daughter, Catherine, is uncertain but speculation has made her the wife of a Germanna settler. Adam and John Wayland, who appear in the 1750s at the Lutheran Church, were almost certainly Thomas' surviving sons, born about 1725–30.

Adam Wayland married Elizabeth, daughter of the 1717 immigrant, Balthasar Blankenbaker, and the church records show that they were already married before 1754. Elizabeth (Blankenbaker) Wayland was still living on

16 MAY 1775, when Adam Wayland wrote his will, but the church records show that she died in that year. By 7 APR 1776 Adam was married to his second wife, Mary Finks, the daughter of Mark Finks and his wife Elizabeth. They had a son Adam, born 12 FEB 1777. Adam Wayland's will, dated 16 MAY 1775 and probated 15 OCT 1781, mentions the wife Elizabeth, "all my children" (no names given) and makes his son John Wayland and Godfrey Yager executors (*Culpeper W. B. B*, p.451). The division of Adam Wayland's estate 25 APR 1788 (*W.B. C*, p.285) shows that he had six surviving children by his first marriage and two by the second, the heirs being John Wayland, Godfrey Yager, Joshua Wayland, Anney Wayland, Lewis Wayland, Morton Christopher, Adam Wayland, and Hannah Wayland. The record states that the widow was a second wife and that Adam and Hannah were her children. Of his children,

> Elizabeth Wayland, one of the older children of his first marriage, was married to Morton Christopher by 1766 and their first child was born in 1767.
>
> John Wayland married Rosina Wilhoit, daughter of John Wilhoit and granddaughter of the Germanna pioneer, Michael Willheit; their children are given in the Lutheran Church records.
>
> Mary Wayland, the third child of the first marriage, became the second wife of Godfrey Yager prior to 1775 (he was the youngest son of Adam Yager and grandson of the 1717 colonist, Nicholas Yager).
>
> Joshua Wayland, apparently the fourth child, seems to be the Joshua who married Rachel Utz 18 DEC 1781 (Knorr, *Culpeper County Marriages*, p.95). She was the daughter of George Utz III, granddaughter of George Utz II and great-granddaughter of George Utz, the 1717 colonist.
>
> Anney Wayland, seems to have been unmarried in 1788 and still living but Knorr shows that an Anne Wayland married 22 DEC 1785 Nicholas Yager, son of Nicholas, grandson of Adam, and great-grandson of Nicholas Yager, the 1717 colonist.
>
> Lewis Wayland, son of Adam by his first marriage, was still a minor 15 SEP 1783, when he was put under the guardianship of his brother, John (*Culpeper W.B. C*, p.22). He was probably of age in 1788, when the estate was distributed. Jane Crouch Williams published an article "Lewis Wayland, Sr.," in 𝕭𝖊𝖞𝖔𝖓𝖉 𝕲𝖊𝖗𝖒𝖆𝖓𝖓𝖆, v.7, n.6.

Of the two children of the second marriage,

> Adam (born 1777) married Judah Burke 24 NOV 1803 (Knorr, p. 93) and they had a son, John Burke Wayland, born 24 NOV 1804 (Lutheran Church records).
>
> Hannah Wayland, the youngest child of Adam, was put under the guardianship of Adam Utz about 1785 (*Culpeper W.B. C*, p.137) and she married _____ Jones.

John Wayland, son of Thomas Wayland, the Germanna pioneer, married Catherine Broyles, daughter of Jacob Broyles and granddaughter of John Broyles, the 1717 colonist. John Wayland died in Madison County, Virginia in 1804. His will, dated 2 FEB 1793 and probated 22 MAR 1804 (*Madison W.B. 1*, p.435), mentions the wife Catherine and daughter Margaret McDonald, and "all my children" (no names given), but a list of property that he had given his children shows ten of them as follows:

A daughter, name not given, who married Jacob Souther,

Henry Wayland who with Hannah his wife had children christened at the Lutheran Church 1778 1790,

Elizabeth Wayland who married David Crisler (see *Garr Genealogy*, p. 67),

Mary Wayland married Joshua Yager, son of John, grandson of Adam, and great-grandson of Nicholas Yager, the 1717 colonist,

Anna Magdalena Wayland who married Andrew Carpenter 11 JAN 1791 (Knorr, p. 19), Andrew Carpenter being a son of Andrew Carpenter and grandson of John Carpenter, the 1721 Germanna immigrant (there was another Andrew Carpenter, son of Michael Carpenter and grandson of John, but the Lutheran Church records show that the wife of Michael's Andrew was named Elizabeth),

Cornelius Wayland,

Margaret who married McDonald,

Eleanor Wayland married Matthias Weaver 22 DEC 1791 (Knorr, p. 95), who was son of Matthias Weaver and grandson of Peter Weaver, the1717 immigrant to the Hebron Church neighborhood,

Joshua Wayland, probably the Joshua Wayland who married Alin Ward 16 FEB 1792 (Knorr, p. 95), and

A daughter who was the wife of William Roebuck.

Wayman. Georg Weidmann emigrated from Nassau-Siegen in Germany in 1738 and arrived in Virginia from the ill-fated ship *Oliver*. George Wayman leased 100 acres in the Little Fork from William Beverley which was located on Little Indian Run (*Orange D.B. 3*, p.389). He had two sons, Harman and Henry, who lived among the Robinson River people.

Harman, born 19 AUG 1750, married first Elizabeth Clore, the daughter of Peter Clore and granddaughter of Michael Clore, 1717 colonist. After Elizabeth died Harman married Frances Clore, daughter of John Clore and another granddaughter of Michael Clore. He died 20 JAN 1837 in Boone County, Indiana after he had lived for a while in Kentucky. He is listed in the *DAR Patriot Index*. His immediate descendants are traced in *Germanna Record* 16, "The First Four Generations of the Michael Clore Family."

Henry Wayman was also married twice. In Harman's pension application, it is stated that Henry also served during the Rev. War. His first wife was Magdalena (Finks?), the daughter of Zacharias Blankenbaker's wife by her first husband. Second, he married Magdalena Blankenbaker, the daughter of John and the granddaughter of Matthias Blankenbaker. For information on his two marriages, see "The Two Wives of Henry Wayman," *Beyond Germanna*, v. 15, n.5. *Germanna Record* 5 has more history of the Waymans. The book *Some Martin, Jefferies, and Wayman Families and Connections of Virginia, Maryland, Kentucky and Indiana* has information.

Weaver (Weber in Germany). Joseph and Susanna Weber are to be found in the Gemmingen church books. The baptisms of their children are recorded there and may be found on Latter Day Saints film 1189134. A transcription of these was given in "Gemmingen Baptisms of the Children of Joseph Weaver and his Wife Susanna Klaar" in *Beyond Germanna*, v.15, n.6. One of these children was the person who became known as Peter Weaver in Virginia. He was christened on 8 NOV 1710 as Hans Dieterich Weber. The departure of the family from Germany was recorded by the sexton at Gemmingen. The family at this time was given as Joseph Weber (age 30), Susanna (age 25), Hans Dietrich (age 7), and Sophia (age 4) who would be the future wife of Peter Fleshman. They appear on the importation list of Alexander Spotswood in a family which then contained a fifth member, Wabburie [Walburga] Weber. The name Dieterich became, in the familiar form, Dieter which became Teter and Peter. The father, Joseph, must have died at an early age as the importation list is the only time his name appears in Virginia. The mother, Susanna, who was a sister of Michael Clore, married secondly, Jacob Crigler. After his death, she married Nicholas Yeager. The youngest member of the family, Wabburie, married John Willheit and she appears in the church records as Burga. Peter, Burga, and Sophia Weaver should be called Second Colony members though, due to their very young age, they were almost a generation younger than other members. More information from Germany is given in "The Ancestry of the Weaver, Utz, and Folg Families," *Before Germanna*, v. 4 where it also traces the evolution of the name from Dietrich to Peter.

Peter Weaver purchased land from William Rush on 1 OCT 1734. He proved his importation to Virginia in 1736 without stating when he arrived (*Orange O.B. 1*, p. 72). A land grant for 400 acres on 20 JUL 1736 added to his holdings (*Virginia Patent Book 17*, p.127). The land he acquired from Rush was sold to Henry Frederick Beyerbeck on 1 FEB 1741(OS) (*Orange D.B. 8*, p. 13). He acquired still more land by purchase from George Moyer on 9 JAN 1746. Peter Weaver was appointed guardian of Michael Clore, son of George Clore who was deceased. Michael was a first cousin once removed to Peter. On 17 MAR 1762, Peter Weaver, transferred 200 acres to each of his sons, John, Matthias and Peter. He wrote his will on 27 MAR (1763) and named his wife Elizabeth and the seven children. Of the children:

John married Barbara Käfer, daughter of Michael Käfer,

Anna Barbara married first George Clore and then Andrew Carpenter,

Matthias married Elizabeth, the daughter of Mark Finks,

Peter, Jr. married Mary Huffman, daughter of Henry Huffman, brother of the 1714 colonist, John Huffman,

Elizabeth married Henry Christler, son of Theobald Christler,
Margaret married George Utz, Jr,
Catherine married Lewis Garr,
Hannah married John Swindle.

The German Lutheran Church records are full of Weaver information. *Germanna Record* 13, "Blankenbaker, Weaver, and Wilhoite" is a source of information but it does have some errors.

Wegman. An unknown family from Spotswood's head right list is the family of Hans Jerich, Anna Maria, Maria Margaret, and Maria Gotlieve Wegman. (The other family was the Milchers.) The origins and the eventual fate of this family are unknown. Possibly, Hens Jerich died and the women had no record or perhaps the family left Virginia.

Weingart. Johannes Weingart and his wife, Anna Maria, had Susanna (born 27 JUL 1776) baptized 4 AUG 1776. John Winegard signed the church petition of 1776. In 1728, William Vinegunt had a land patent for 500 acres on the north end of the early German settlement in the Robinson River Valley. "Vinegunt," especially as heard by English-speaking individuals, could be the same name as Weingart but other than the similarity of the name there is no reason to believe they are of the same family. John Vinyard appears several times in the early Orange County records.

Willer. John Willer made a donation to the Lutheran Church in 1734. Individuals who were specifically named were usually not members of the church but had wives who were members.

Willheit (Wilhite, Wilhoit, and similar variations in America). Johann Michael Willheit was christened in Schwaigern, Württemberg on 25 JAN 1671 with his twin, Matthias, who would die two weeks later. Michael married first Anna Dorothea Müller on 29 JAN 1696. She had been married previously to Hans Michael Boger and had a surviving daughter who eventually came to Virginia as the wife of Johann Friedrich Gebert. Michael and Anna Dorothea had no surviving children from four births. At the time of the fifth child, Anna Dorothea died. Michael married second Anna Maria Hengsteler who would be mother of all Michael's surviving children. Five births are recorded in Schwaigern and of these, two were to come to Virginia. These were Tobias, christened 15 JUL 1708, and Johannes, christened 1 JUL 1713. Adam, Matthias, Eva, and Phillip were born in Virginia. Pioneering research in depth was conducted on this family by Mary F. Mickey which was reported in *Wilhite-Wilhoit Connexions*, Marge Willhite, editor. Also Volume 1 of *Before Germanna*, "The Ancestry of the Johann Michael Willheit and Anna Maria Hengsteler," is devoted to the family.

Michael Wilhide was granted 289 acres adjoining George Woods (i.e., Utz) on 28 SEP 1728 (*Virginia Patent Book 14*, p.113). On 6 MAY 1729 he was freed from levies. He did not prove his importation until 15 MAY 1736 as Michael Wilhite (*Orange O.B. 1*, p.72) when he said he came immediately from England. This same day, John and Tobias Wilhite also made their proofs of importation stating, as did their father, that they were imported from England. Michael died in Orange County in 1746, leaving a will which mentions his wife, Mary, sons and a daughter:

Tobias may have married Catherine Walke but the case for this is very weak. The circumstantial evidence is the joint patent of Tobias and Martin Walke. Tobias was naturalized 24 FEB 1743(OS) (*Orange O.B. 3*, p.346).

John married Walburga Weaver, the daughter of Joseph Weaver and Susanna Clore. Burga, as she was known at church, was born enroute to America since she was not on the Gemmingen departure list but she was on Spotswood's head right list as Wabburie Weber. John was naturalized on the same day as his brother Tobias.

Adam married Catherine Broyles.

Matthias married Mary Ballenger first and Hannah_____ second but all of his children are Mary's.

Philip married Rachel_____ and _____,

Eva married Nicholas Holt, Jr.

The exact division of the children between Tobias and Matthias is not certain. Some researchers believe that five of the children (Catherine, Joel, John, Lewis, and Tobias) who are often assigned to Matthias (see *Germanna Record* 13) were children of Tobias. (The will of Tobias names two oldest sons and two youngest sons and adds that, if the youngest sons should die, their inheritance should go to the "next older sons.")

In Schwaigern, Württemberg, it is possible to trace ten generations of Willheits (various spellings) in the church records of baptisms, marriages, and deaths. Johann Michael Willheit was of the fifth generation. Many relatives of Michael came to America. Michael Willheit's first cousin, Johann Friederich Willheit, arrived in Philadelphia on 11 SEP 1731 on the *Pennsylvania Merchant* and he settled in York County, Pennsylvania. His descendants are generally known as Willhide or Wilhide though some use Wilhite. Johann Friederich Baumgarner, a nephew of Johann Michael, arrived in Philadelphia in 1732 on the *Johnson*. He settled in Orange County, Virginia near his uncle. This latter Friederich had a younger brother, Gottfried, who arrived on the *Fane* in 1749 at Philadelphia. Anna Rosina (Willheit) Abendschön, a first cousin of Johann Michael, also arrived on the *Fane* with Friederich. Johann Michael's previously mentioned step-daughter, Susannah Catharina, came in 1731 and settled in the Shenandoah Valley.

Germanna Record Number 13, "Blankenbaker, Weaver, Wilhoite" has information on the early American history.

Williams. Eva Williams communed at the Lutheran Church 7 JUN 1778.

Wolber. Adolph Wolber and Anna Maria, his wife, were communicants 26 MAY 1776.

Wolfenberger. This family lived for a few years in the Robinson River Valley at the time of the Revolution. The vestry of St. Mark's Parish in 1780 refunded one levy to Woolfenbarger who had been overcharged in the previous year. See "Vestry Minutes of St. Mark's Parish," Beyond Germanna, v.7, n.1 where the information is taken from R. E. Davis, *St. Mark's Parish Vestry Book 1730–1785*. The Wolfenberger family had probably been in America for several decades before the appearance of some members in Culpeper County. The immigrant family was Johannes Wolfensberger and his wife Anna Margaretha Entzminger who had seven children, some of whom were born in Alsace though the earlier family origins were in Switzerland. This family arrived at Philadelphia on 29 AUG 1730 on the *Thistle* and settled in Lancaster County, Pennsylvania. One son was Peter and he had a son George Michael who went to Culpeper County, Virginia. Others of the family went to the Shenandoah Valley, and to the area which became West Virginia (later to Ohio). One member went to North Carolina.

Wrede. See Frady.

Yager, John, Sr. (Piney Woods John). The study of the Yager family or families is compounded by the presence of Yagers who do not fit into the family of Nicholas Yager. Piney Woods John came to Culpeper County from the area of Woodstock in the Shenandoah Valley. His father and mother were Adam and Susannah Yager. (Note that Adam, the son of Nicholas in the next section, is said to have married Susanna Kabler.) Adam purchased two lots in the town of Woodstock from Jacob Miller and Barbara his wife in 1762. Adam Yager's son Joseph married Barbara Miller, the daughter of Jacob Miller, Sr. and his wife Barbara. Adam's daughter Rebecca married first Jacob Miller, Jr.

Adam's son John is the one who became known as Piney Woods John and he purchased 221 acres of land in Culpeper County from his sister Rebecca and her husband Jacob Miller, Jr. The tax assessor adopted the practice of calling this newcomer Piney Woods John to distinguish him from the existing John Yagers. Jan Creek wrote an article, "John Yager, Sr. of the Piney Woods," which appeared in Beyond Germanna, v. 15, n.3.

Yager, Nicholas (Jäger in German but Yager, Yeager, Yaeger, Jaeger are variations in America). Nicholas Yager in his proof of importation stated that he came in 1717 with his wife Mary and his two children, Adam and Mary. Nothing more is known of Mary (she did not marry Matthias Blankenbaker). Nicholas was naturalized by Lt. Gov. Spotswood 13 JUL 1722 in one of his last official acts as Governor. Nicholas was sued by Spotswood in 1724. He patented 400 acres of land in the Robinson River area (*Virginia Patent Book 12*, p.483.) It is uncertain when the wife, Mary, of Nicholas died. He married Susanna Clore Weaver Crigler between the time her husband died and the 1739 Orange County tithe list. At the 27 APR 1738 Orange County Court, Nicholas Yeagor was to be "free from working on the road and from mustoring but he still had to pay the levy." A very extensive family history as a typescript was prepared by A. L. Keith. The original is in the Newberry Library in Chicago but a microfilm copy is available from The Church of Jesus Christ of Latter Day Saints.

All of his descendants are through his son Adam who is said to have married Susanna Kabler but there is little evidence, if any, for this. Adam Yager had six children:

    Michael, born 29 JUN 1728, married Elizabeth Crigler (not Elizabeth Manspeil),

    Barbara, born 7 SEP 1730, married first Peter Clore and second Phillip Chelf,

    John, born 15 SEP 1732, married Mary Willheit,

    Nicholas, born 1735, married Susanna Willheit,

    Adam, born 9 MAY 1738, married Juriah Berry,

    Godfrey, born 6 JUN 1747, married first _____ Klug and second Mary Wayland.

Zimmerman and Cerny report in "The Ancestry of the Yager, Stolts, Crees, and Beyerbach Families," *Before Germanna*, v. 10, that Nicolaus Jäger married Anna Maria Sieber in Marienthal in the Palatinate on 11 MAY 1706. Adam was born 30 September 1708 at Falkenstein, a nearby village. Four other children were born there also but only Mary and Adam arrived in America. Though there is some information about Nicholas' German ancestry, it is conflicting. For the best survey of current findings, see Elizabeth Yates Johnson *Following John, Documenting the Identity and Path of John Yager*, Gateway Press, Inc., Baltimore, 2004.

When John Huffman and his wife Maria Sabina baptized their twelve children, one of the sponsors was Nicholas Yager for eleven of the children; for one, the wife of Nicholas Yager was a sponsor. The question of why Nicholas was chosen is unanswered. Difficulties in the genealogical study of the descendants of Nicholas Yager is compounded by the presence in the community of other Yager families. Many of the published papers contain errors as people have been assigned to the wrong family. Also, people of the same name have been confused.

Yowell (Uhl or Uhle in German). Birth records for six children born to Christopher Uhl and Eva Gottsaurin were found in Sulzfeld, Baden, where records of the Zimmerman and Kabler families are also found.. Though Christopher Uhl gave his origins as Württemberg when he was naturalized in 1745, this is not unrealistic. The line dividing Baden and Württemberg is not far from Sulzfeld and it would have been easy for Christopher Uhl to have been born in Württemberg even though his children were born in Baden. The children born in Sulzfeld were Jerg Friedrich (1705), Magdalena (1706), Anna Catharina (1709), Friedrich David (1712), Anna Barbara (1714), and Hans Jacob (1717). The match between the German family and the Virginia family is not perfect. The family was in London in the late summer of 1717 when Christopher Uhl signed a petition asking for money to return to Germany. In this list he is the head of a party of eight. Adjoining names were Kabler and Lang who have been found in Sulzfeld. Apparently Christopher Uhl was delayed in coming to America.

Christopher Atwell was granted 400 acres of land on 28 SEP 1728 (*Virginia Patent Book 14*, p. 103) as adjoining Michael and John Clause (Clore) and on 12 SEP 1733 (as Christopher Awel) received an additional patent of 124 acres adjoining Michael Awell, his own land, and Michael Clause (*Virginia Patent Book 15*, p. 120). Since there is no Michael Awell among the children of Christopher, there may be a mistake for some other name or it is possible that Christopher had a brother Michael who came over to this country. However, nothing further is known of Michael. Christopher Uhl is mentioned in the German Lutheran Church accounts in 1734 (*Orange W.B. 1*, pp.54–57) and on 27 JAN 1742(OS) Christopher Uhl was admitted to citizenship along with other Germans of the Robinson River community (*Orange O.B. 3*, p.313). The name Uhl disappears, to be replaced occasionally as Owell, but finally Yowell is used exclusively.

Virginia records show that Christopher Yowell had four sons, John, David, Christopher and James Yowell. Christopher had a wife named Mary 8 MAR 1742(OS) and his wife was Margaret in 1750. Possibly he was married three times. He died intestate in Culpeper County, Virginia in 1762.

The following are the pertinent records: *Orange D.B. 7*, p.155, 8 MAR 1742(OS), Christopher Owell to John Owell 100 acres, part of 400 acres granted him in 1728 and signed by Christopher Owell and Mary Owell; *Orange D.B. l*, p.136, 9 MAR 1748(OS), Christopher Owell to John Owell 100 acres; Same, p.133, Mar. 17, 1749(OS), Christopher Yowell to Peter Clore 203 acres and signed by Christopher Yowel and Margarethe Yowel; *Culpeper D.B. H*, p.60, 31 DEC 1751, David Yewell granted 53 acres of land in the Great Fork; same, p.250, 1752, Christopher Yowell granted 80 acres adjoining John Thomas; *Culpeper D.B. A*, p.534, 19 JUL 1753, Christopher Yowell to Christopher Yowell, Jr. for 124 acres patented in 1733 and 80 acres patented in 1752; *Culpeper D.B. B*, p.112, 20 JUN 1754, Christopher Yowell and Margaret his wife to Michael Clore 400 acres adjoining James Yowell, Peter Glore, and Nicholas Crigler; the Culpeper County Rental of 1764 shows Christopher Yowell with 511 acres, David Yowell with 162 acres, Christopher Yowell, Jr. with 220 acres, and James Yowell with 230 acres (the son, John, is not shown and may have died), Christopher Yowell died in 1762 with Joseph King as his administrator and an account of his estate in 1763 shows many payments to various people, but mentions the widow's dower, showing that his last wife survived him (*Culpeper W.B. A*, pp.98 and 101).

Separating the children in the later generations is not easy as names are duplicated so many times.

Ziegler (often Ziglar in America). Johann Leonhart Ziegler came through Philadelphia in 1732 and moved on to Virginia where he married Barbara Zimmerman, the daughter of Christopher Zimmerman, the 1717 immigrant. His origins in Germany were at Epfenbach in Kreis Sinsheim, see Don Yoder *Rhineland Emigrants*. He died in 1757 and his will mentions children, Christopher, Leonard, Elizabeth, Ann, and Susannah. Leonard, Jr. married Ann_____ and he died in 1772 leaving all of his possessions to his wife Ann. A pension application (W 4107) adds information. It was made on behalf of Leonard Ziglar (or his widow) who was born 2 JUL 1762. This Leonard was the third and in 1783/4 he married Nancy Zimmerman, the daughter of John the son of John the son of the immigrant Christopher. Leonard III moved in 1789 to Surry County, North Carolina (later Stokes County and then Forsyth County). Leonard III and Nancy were the parents of fourteen children. See Gene Dear, "The Ziegler/Ziglar Family," in 𝔅𝔢𝔶𝔬𝔫𝔡 𝔊𝔢𝔯𝔪𝔞𝔫𝔫𝔞, v.3, n.2.

Zimmerman. The Zimmerman family was in Steffisburg in the Canton of Bern in Switzerland before 1665 when some members moved to Ravensburg in Baden, Germany. Ravensburg is an estate very near to Sulzfeld where a Lutheran church is located. The Sulzfeld Evangelische Church shows the birth of Johann Christoph Zimmerman on 16 MAR 1692 and his baptism the following day. He was the third son of Christian Zimmerman and Eva Dünstler of Langenbruck who was the daughter of Michael Dünster. Eva died when Christoph was six years old. Christoph's father remarried and the new wife was Maria Barbara Edel. A large second family followed. Christoph's brother, Johann Conrad who was two years older, died when Christoph was eight years old.

Johann Christoph, the future Virginia immigrant, at the age of eighteen married (27 JUL 1710) a woman who five or six years older. This was Dorothea Rol or Rottle (the writing is very confusing) who was the daughter of Martin Rol of Horndorff. Their first child Johannes was born 11 APR 1711 and was baptized the next day. Dorothea died at the age of twenty-seven years on 16 JAN 1714. Christoph was a widower at twenty-two years of age with a son Johannes of less than three years of age.

Later Christoph appears in the Sulzfeld parish with a wife Anna Elizabeth of unknown origin and surname. A child Johann Martin was born 15 JUN 1715 and baptized the next day. At two of the baptisms of children of Christopher Zimmerman, sponsors were Ludwig Fischer and Anna Barbara Fischer (one each). In 1717 the Zimmerman family emigrated to Virginia where they arrived with sons John and Andrew. It is presumed that Johann Martin died during the trip and Andrew was born during the journey.

In Virginia, Christopher Zimmerman settled southeast of Mt. Pony and south of Stevensburg (in today's Culpeper County) where he had several parcels of land (24 JUN 1726, 400 acres, *Virginia Patent Book 12*, p.483; 28 SEP 1728, 280 acres, *Book 13*, p.390; 25 AUG 1731, 240 acres, *Book 14*, p.250; 7 JUL 1735, 440 acres, *Book 16*, p.13).

In some records, he is described a cooper and perhaps he felt the need to be closer to the market for casks and barrels. In 1734 he petitioned the Orange County court to be permitted to establish an ordinary at his home. He claimed that he lived in a very public place and he was much oppressed by travelers seeking accommodations. He was a Lieutenant in the Orange County militia in 1735. His will dated 1748 and probated the next year mentions this wife and six children. He had nine children, the first two by Dorothea and the others by Anna Elizabeth. They were:

> John who lived in the Robinson River Valley away from the rest of the family, He is in the 1739 tithables for Orange County. He was naturalized 27 JAN 1742(OS) (Orange O.B.3, p.313),
>
> A still born child in Sulzfeld,
>
> Johann Martin whose fate is uncertain,
>
> Andrew, no record after his arrival in Virginia is noted,
>
> Frederick who married Sarah and had three children Reuben, Frederick, and Christopher,
>
> Barbara who married Leonard Zeigler and had several children. Christopher Zimmerman sold land to Barbara Ziegler,
>
> Christopher who did not marry but is noted with Kabler and Brown connections,
>
> Elizabeth is thought to have married and _____ Conner and _____ Weaver have been suggested,
>
> Katherine who married William Slaughter and is said to have Thomas, William, John, Gabriel, and Smith as children.

John Zimmerman, above, married Ursula Blankenbaker had seven children:

> John who married in turn Katherine _____, Elizabeth Fewell, and Jemima Rivercomb,
>
> Dorothey who married Jacob Tanner,
>
> Elizabeth who married Joseph Holtzclaw as his second wife,
>
> Christopher who married Mary Tanner,
>
> Mary never married,
>
> Margaret probably married Matthias House as his second wife, and
>
> Rosanna married Moses Samuel.

Margaret James Squires published her findings in "The Immigrant Christopher Zimmerman," in **Beyond Germanna**, v.2, n.3. Also, Cerny and Zimmerman published information in "The Ancestry of the Zimmerman, Yowell, Mercklin, Wegman, and Leatherer Families," *Before Germanna*, v. 9. Keith has comments about the Zimmermans. More information about Frederick, the grandson of Christopher Zimmerman (via Frederick) was given by Gene Dear, "Frederick and Judith Zimmerman," **Beyond Germanna**, v.3, n.3. The only child of the immigrant Christopher Zimmerman to appear in the German Lutheran records in the Robinson River Valley is John who married Ursula Blankenbaker. The name always appears there as Zimmerman for members of this family. (Sometimes, the descendants of John Carpenter are called Zimmerman in the church records and one must be on the watch for these.)

Zollicoffer / Zollikoffer / Zollickoffer. Jacob Christoph Zollikoffer, a merchant who was in business probably not too far from Germanna, went to Europe in 1719 and was asked to solicit aid for the 1714 Germanna colonists in securing a pastor and building a church and school. In London, it appears that he turned the original request made by the First Colony into one that appeared to ask for aid for both colonies. Perhaps, he was attempting to broaden the appeal to obtain a response from both German Reformed and Lutherans. Therefore some of the historical aspects of the two colonies were not obtained from the colonists but from his second hand understanding. He was back in Spotsylvania County, Virginia by 3 SEP 1723 and 2 OCT 1723, on which dates he sued William Thompson (*Spotsylvania W. B. A*, p. 46 and 56) and his land is mentioned in 1724 (Crozier *Spotsylvania County Records*, p. 93). Nothing further has been found about him in the Virginia records. He originated in St. Gall, Switzerland and was a son-in-law of Christoph von Graffenried though he divorced his wife.

Part III

Photographs from Germany and Austria

John and Eleanor Blankenbaker visited Germany and Austria for three weeks in May of 2000 and again in May of 2002. They did many things but, whatever they did, they took thousands of photographs. (Another source of the photographs here is Thomas Faircloth who has visited on several occasions.) Some of those photographs are reproduced here in black and white. Though the originals were in color, the conversion to black and white does convey the sense of the scene. Many of these photographs are available in color on a CD, "Germanna Villages, Photographic Essays" which is available from the Germanna Foundation (see germanna.org) or from John Blankenbaker (see germanna.com).

There are two purposes in showing the photographs here. One is to supplement the text. Another is to convey the fun of the trips. To achieve this latter aim, the presentation, at times, will take a personal tone. When the pronoun "we" is used it means Eleanor and John whereas "I" refers to John. The conditions under which we made the trip were that we traveled in a rental car (getting around is easy with a book of detailed maps). Except for our stays in larger cities, which were rare, we made no reservations but searched for a place to stay where we found ourselves that evening. So our travel was informal and casual though we did have a travel agenda which we followed in a general way. Only occasionally did we have fixed appointment times.

The people we met were extremely kind and helpful to us. The average English is better than the average English in the United States though not everyone speaks English. We had a few critical phrases in German memorized. John had a tour of the tower of the Bönnigheim church even though the guide spoke no English and John really does not speak German. People went out of their way to do special things for us.

Many churches are shown. It must be emphasized that, in the three hundred years since our ancestors left, church buildings have changed. Maybe a part will be retained while another part will be rebuilt or enlarged. Sometimes this is obvious in the style which is not early eighteenth century. Sometimes, the multiple styles of a church are a clue that the building was not all built at the same time. The longest lasting part of a church building is the tower.

The homes and villages we see today are not typical of what might have been seen in the eighteenth century. This is shown here by one photograph. One just does not see today what the physical conditions were like in the eighteenth century. Still, to see the house where one's ancestors lived in 1600 is awesome even though the windows have been enlarged and glassed and the roof has been converted from thatch to tiles. The landscape changes little.

This is the church in Bönnigheim where Conrad Amberger lived. It would seem that Conrad might not recognize this building because the style is later than the early eighteenth century.

Gaining entrance to Protestant churches is not easy. To prevent damage, the churches are generally kept locked. On one occasion, when I really wanted to get into a church, I inquired at the pastor's house which was close by. Though he was away, his wife opened the church for us.

The Bönnigheim church was open and people were cleaning it and the organist was practicing. Another man beckoned to me and suggested by sign language that we go up the tower. I followed him and the next photo shows what he wanted me to see.

The mechanism at the left controls the ringing of the bells. For a long time, the churches have been the "official" keeper of the time. Almost every church has a clock with a face on four sides of the tower. In addition to this visual indication of time, some churches ring the bells to indicate the hours and quarter hours. That is the purpose of the mechanism here. My guide was the keeper of the mechanism. He oiled it, cleaned it, and tuned it up. There was a tool box, oil can, and a maintenance manual on the spot. The entire mechanism was housed in a glass enclosure to keep the dirt (and the birds) out.

In times past, nearly all villages were walled to keep out undesirable elements. As a part of the wall, there were watch towers where men lived and stayed on the alert to prevent people from entering the village whom they did not want. Sometimes these towers were used as communication elements to adjacent villages. Castles also had these watch towers.

As a result of expansion of the villages, the walls and towers became a part of the central core of the village while the village grew outside the walls and became a town. Some of the towers have been preserved though their original purpose is no longer valid. Usually the walls have been destroyed as the stones of the wall were used in other building projects.

At the base of this tower in Bönnigheim one can see the arch where the gate or doors would have been installed. The main street of the village would have been the one that led through the gate.

Gemmingen, Schwaigern, Botenheim, Bönnigheim, Cleebronn, and Gross Sachsenheim (and some others) are very close to one another, almost in a line, albeit a crooked one. It is not unusual in the Germanna histories to find people who have associations with more than one of these villages and towns.

This is the church at Botenheim with the village Maypole (Maibaum). The custom of raising a Maypole early in May is popular in Germany. There are some rules which are supposed to govern the erection such as it must be done by manual labor only. This requires many able bodied men to turn out. The work is hard and beer breaks are required.

Botenheim is the home village of Hans Jacob Öhler (aka Jacob Aylor). This is where he was baptized. He married Anna Magdalena Schneider here. Her parents came to Virginia first and the Öhlers came later.

In Cleebronn, a near neighbor to Botenheim, the church shows evidence of modifications. This might be repair work to fix damage. It could also be the result of an enlargement of the church which raised the roof to allow a balcony to be installed inside.

Cleebronn is also an ancestral village of Jacob Aylor as ancestors of his were born here.

Cleebronn, Botenheim, and Bönnigheim lie at the apexes of a triangle about two miles from each other. A few miles to the south of them lies the larger village of Sachsenheim.

Notice that the suffix, "heim," is very popular in the names of villages. It means "home."

Gross Sachsenheim is misnamed for it means "large Sachsenheim." Actually it is smaller than Sachsenheim itself.

This is the church door at Gross Sachsenheim. The church itself is located in an awkward situation for photographing. It is a pity for the architecture is unusual.

Most churches have the entry or door way on the side of the church as here. This is a very beautiful door of blonde wood.

It is thought that George Moyer originated here.

One sees very good designs in Germany. The new exists along side the old and they are harmonious. This Gross Sachsenheim entry way is a good example of modern design installed in an nineteenth century building.

The villages and towns love date stones. They are usually based on the first written record showing that the village existed. Many times these are the ecclesiastic records. Of course, the village surely existed before it was first mentioned.

Falkenstein was a castle. The neighboring village which supported it was also called Falkenstein. The castle was situated on a hillside because the site aided the fortification of the castle. As a result, the hillside village was crowded. The villagers went elsewhere to go to church. In the eighteenth century there were two alternatives, Marienthal and Winnweiler.

The castle is now in ruins.

The archeologists have had fun cleaning up the castle site. Major parts of it are missing but enough remains to show how it may have looked. The overwhelming characteristic is that it was not large but the parts were massive. The seats in the lower left corner here are a modern adaptation.

Another view reinforces the idea that parts of the castle were massive. All of this was on the top of a hillside which made it difficult to storm the castle.

The village of Falkenstein which lies below the castle site is narrow with essentially one street through it. This photograph of a portion of the village was taken from the castle site. In back of the castle, the hill falls away very sharply. Another hill rises on the far side of the village.

Just about in the dead center of the photo is a modern church. In the time of Nicholas Yager, there was no church in Falkenstein.

The Falkenstein area is a popular camping and recreational area today.

This is the church at Marienthal (Valley of Mary). Nicholas Jäger (Yager) married Anna Maria Sieber here in 1706. Marienthal is within walking distance of Falkenstein though Americans today might not want to walk that far.

Probably Nicholas and Mary would not recognize the church were they here today. It looks as if were built in the nineteenth century and perhaps updated again in the twentieth century. The tower though may date from an earlier time. This is a common practice. The fact that there are no clock faces on the tower suggests it may be quite old.

The Yagers also attended the church at Winnweiler which is in the opposite direction from Falkenstein.

Marienthal has its own date stone though apparently the village is not quite as old as Falkenstein. It is hard to tell because no date gives us a clue when the stone was made. In keeping with the name of the village, Mary and the Baby Jesus are depicted.

Typically, we would think of the presence of Mary as indicating a Catholic community and church. During the Reformation when many churches converted to a form of Protestantism, the emblems of the Catholic religion were kept. Some Lutheran churches in Germany look more Catholic than Catholic churches in America.

This house in Marienthal is said to be the home of a Jäger family. Through the years, the building has probably been modified and many details have been changed.

It is my opinion that buildings in Germany never die. They are rebuilt, changed, and updated. Today, it is hard to tell what the original building would have looked like.

The tile roof was once probably wood or straw. Since both of these were fire hazards and wood was sometimes scarce, it was mandated that tiles be used. Undoubtedly, the windows have changed, certainly enlarged. Originally, there may have been no glass in the opening and shutters would close the opening.

The church in Gemmingen is obviously not a eighteenth century building. When one reads the church records for Gemmingen when they were resumed just before the start of the eighteenth century, one is struck by how much smaller the village must have been then. By now is not appropriate to call it a village for it has become a town or a city.

For Germanna people, a more important feature is the records of the church which detail the departure of the Clore family, the Weaver family, the two Smith families, and the Milcker (Mühleckher) family. Also, the sexton, in writing the record, added a bit of general history which helps our understanding of their decision.

Today the town has become large enough to support other churches. These "free" Protestant churches do not receive the tax support that the Lutheran, Reformed, and Catholic churches do.

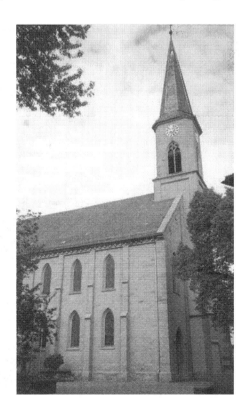

Above is the Gemmingen church baptismal record for Peter Weaver as he became known in Virginia. The copy here has been cleaned up on the computer to remove the extraneous material such as ink spots, bleed through, and what is generally called fly specks.

In the left most column is the date, in this case November 8. The year, shown elsewhere, is 1710. The new style calender is in effect. By the old style calender the day would be October 29. Nothing in this record says whether the date is a christening date or a birth date but, most probably, it is a christening date. The birth date could be the same or any day previous, perhaps the previous day.

The child was named Hannss Dieterich. Following the German custom where the second name is the calling name, Dieterich became Dieter and then Peter in Virginia.

In the third column, the parents are Joseph Weber, day laborer, and his wife Susanna [Klaar/Clore].

In the last column are the sponsors and in this area the writer often writes in a cramped style. The first of these was Martin Zehendbauer who was a citizen and day laborer in Gemmingen.

This tower in Schwaigern is called the witch's tower. In 1713, Anna Maria Heinrich was burned as a witch. It is thought that she was the last person to be burned at the stake in Schwaigern.

Several families left from Schwaigern for Virginia, including the Willheits, Frederick Baumgärtner, the Koch family, members of the Reiner family, Johann Georg Dieter (Teter), and Paul Lederer, not all in 1717.

Schwaigern was the victim of several fires which destroyed major parts of the town.

It is very difficult to get a photograph of the Schwaigern Church because other buildings are built so close to it and the trees at the front door obscure it. However, one can go along the side of the building to get a photograph of the upper tower. This very ornate structure was there in 1717 for an etching of an earlier date shows exactly the same features.

By the clock we would say it was about half past four. Germans would say though it was half to five or they might say it was 16:30. They use the 24 clock much more than we do.

Schwaigern and Gemmingen are only about four miles apart. Anyone who had an ancestor from one of these towns should read Aaron Spencer Fogelman's *Hopeful Journeys*. This book is very informative about the troubled and chaotic life in the early eighteenth century in Schwaigern and Gemmingen.

Schwaigern lies in a region where many grapes are grown. The smaller farmers used a communal wine press, called a Kelter. Shown is the cooperative winery in Schwaigern dating to 1659.

It was not unusual for a sponsor at a baptismal in Gemmingen to live in Schwaigern. This pair of villages contributed more Germanna immigrants than any other close region in Germany.

Lambsheim has a watch tower also but this one does not show a gate. The wall has long since disappeared, at least in the vicinity of the tower.

Lambsheim was the home of Theobald Christele (Crisler). He came as a young boy with his family to Pennsylvania then later he moved down to Virginia. It is probable that a cousin of his married Johann Caspar Stöver, Jr. and that he learned about Virginia at the time of the ordinations of the Stövers when Stöver, Jr. was also married.

Frankenthal is very close to Lambsheim. These two localities plus Falkenstein (and Marienthal and Winnwiler) are in the Palatinate. The Lotspeich family lived in Frankenthal. Three members of the family emigrated to Virginia about the time of the Revolution.

Another member of the family was a wine merchant in London. Apparently Johanna Friederika Lotspeich was visiting him in London where she married John Francis Jacoby who had been living in Virginia. They returned to Virginia. Later two brothers of Johanna Friederika came to Virginia.

This building has an unusual purpose (if we understood our informant correctly). This is a building where urns containing ashes of deceased people may be kept.

The pastor who ordained the Stövers came from the very small village of Schainbach. Accordingly, the church is very small as you may judge by the comparative sizes of the nave and the entry way on the side. If you look for the clock, you will not find it. Instead, there is a sundial on the southern side.

The pastor was Johann Christian Schultz (he came on the same ship as did the Andreas Gaar family) who did not stay in America very long. He realized that help was needed for the struggling congregations here and he returned to Germany to raise funds. However, he yielded to temptations and used the money he obtained for his personal uses

John Broyles and his wife Ursula Ruop with their children came from Ötisheim. The present day church is shown.

Again, the church shows evidence of being built at different times. Halfway up the tower is an old date stone which precedes the presence of the Broyles. At some point there was a remodeling which yielded this building. Also, at the extreme left of the building is the remnant of an arch which is stylistically different from any of the elements we see here.

As is often the case, the church is built on one of the highest elevations in the village.

This is the Wappen for Ötisheim. The dictionary defines a Wappen as a family coat of arms as used in a shield or heraldry. In these more democratic times, the Wappens have become a community symbol, not a personal symbol. By now almost every political jurisdiction has a Wappen. This one was mounted on the Ötisheim Maypole.

Many people seek their "coat of arms." This is a farcical endeavor as they do not exist. Occasionally an individual will be awarded a coat of arms but it belongs to him personally and not to the family.

Our Germanna ancestors were usually poor and many were from the lower half of the social spectrum. They came to America to escape their life in Germany. Those that had a good life in Germany did not come to America.

In Ötisheim the tax collector's office shows a half-timbered construction and overhang that is seen in buildings, especially the older buildings.

A town which has a significant number of half-timbered buildings is Eppingen. Many other towns also have a substantial quantity of half-timbered buildings, some to the extent that they are tourist attractions, not only for foreigners but for the Germans.

In Schönenberg, a suburb of Ötisheim, there is a Waldesian church. In the yard, we can barely see a statue of a man who was an early eighteenth century pastor at this church. A plaque at the base tells why he is being remembered. In essence, it says that he was the "first to plant potatoes" and this was in 1722.

At the time most of our ancestors left Germany, the potato and the tomato were regarded as items to be avoided. A noted German historian once said that in 1700, the three meals of the day were bread, bread, and bread. In 1800, the three meals of the day were potatoes, potatoes, and potatoes.

Before you think your ancestor lived in a stylish place, take a look at this home. It is in Östheim (no relation and not even close to Ötisheim).

This is a old village being preserved to show how people lived. It is a small walled village with watch towers and a large church at the center. There are no "streets." Inside there are footpaths, some with steps. The roof tiles here are modern. Earlier, the roof would have been wood or straw. For windows, there were openings which could be covered over with shutters. Glass was an expensive item.

This is the church in Stetten, less than two miles southwest of Schwaigern. Hans Michael Hold (Holt) was baptized on 30 December 1696 in Stetten.

Jonas Hold, the oldest known ancestor of Michael Holt, was the mayor here about 1640 during the Thirty Year's War. His first wife died in Schwaigern, perhaps because of the war which forced many people to relocate.

The first two children of Thomas Wieland (aka Wayland) and Maria Barbara Seppach were born at Waldbach. The church at Waldbach is too new in design to have been there in this form in 1717. Around the site there are parts of an earlier structure which were not used in this building.

The Wielands are in the London church records of 1717 but it would appear they did not make it to Virginia until 1719.

Waldbach is to the east of the major center of the 1717 emigrants. It is an easy trip east of Heilbronn.

This is a "downtown" view of Neuenbürg, the home of the Blankenbakers, Schlucters, Fleshmans, Thomases, and the Scheibles. The church is Catholic since Neuenbürg was a part of the domain of the Catholic Bishops of Speyer. Neuenbürg is not a well organized village as can be judged by the random orientations of the houses. The village is so small there is hardly any commercial activity in it. Today, the community has expanded but it is largely a bedroom community for larger nearby towns.

145

This is the Catholic church in Neuenbürg and there was no Protestant church in the village. The Protestants walked to Oberöwisheim about two miles away to attend a Lutheran church there.

Elements of this church suggest it may be old. Some details of the building are unusual. There is lots of stained glass which casts a warm multi-colored glow over the interior.

Apparently, the Protestants and Catholics lived in peace. The baptismal records in Oberöwisheim for the Lutherans often show Catholic sponsors.

In the Neuenbürg cemetery, there are a series of Jewish gravestones. Toward the end of World War II, the village was taken over by the Allied occupation forces and converted into a convalescent camp for refugees from the labor camps. Many of these people were very weak and sick and not all of them lived. Berek Steinbok died on his 32nd birthday.

I have had communications with a person who was evicted from the village and with a person from a labor camp who was moved here. Neither of them was happy about their experiences and neither of them lives in Germany today.

This is the tower (right) of the Lutheran church in Oberöwisheim. The residents of Neuenbürg (including the Blankenbakers, the Schlucters, the Fleshmans, Thomases, and the Scheibles) who wanted to attend a Lutheran church, went to church here. Again, it is difficult to date the church though it has existed here for centuries. Parts of the earlier church are preserved. At the left, portions of an earlier altar and perhaps even the remains of a tomb are shown.

When we visited the church in Oberöwisheim, it was lunch time. So we dropped down to the street below and bought some bread, cheese, and orange juice (very popular in Germany) which we ate in the church yard. Since the church sits on a hill above the city, we had this view of roof tops. The random orientation of the buildings made an interesting pattern so we took a picture.

When we bought the items for the lunch, we went to a bakery to get the bread. Bakeries do not sell cheese so we had to go to the room next door where the same sales person sold us the cheese and the drinks.

Unteröwisheim is not too far from Oberöwisheim. Many of the same names are to be found in the church records for these two villages. For example, there was a Nicholas Blankenbaker who died here in 1742. This shows that not all of the Blankenbakers who lived in this area came to America. Some of them stayed. In this particular case, we do not know how Nicholas was related to the others. Oberöwisheim and Unteröwisheim might be called the Upper- and Lower-öwisheims.

In Oberderdingen, about twenty miles from Neuenbürg, Matthias Blankenbühler married Anna Maria Mercklin. Matthias was described as a tailor. Probably in his training he had worked for a master tailor here and became acquainted with Ann Mary. They had one son, George, who was born here. In Virginia this George married Mary Gerhardt and one son, John, was born to them. George died, Mary remarried and moved to North Carolina. The son John was the patriarch of the family which took the name Pickler. So all of the Germanna Picklers go back to this church.

When Matthias married, his relatives from Neuenbürg probably walked to Oberderdingen for the wedding. It was rare that one had a horse (cattle were more common than horses and were used as draft animals). Also, most of Matthias' relatives were weavers and probably did little farming.

The home of the Käfers was in Zaberfeld (earlier they had lived in the Ansbach district of Bavaria). Nicholas Blankenbaker married Apollonia Käfer in Neuenbürg. It appears that she had been living for a while in Neuenbürg since she was a sponsor at a baptism before her marriage.

The wedding of Nicholas and Apollonia was the day before the wedding of Matthias Blankenbaker. So it made a very busy two or three days for the family.

Apollonia had a brother, Michael, who came in 1717. He later became the husband of the widow Anna Maria Blankenbaker Thomas.

I lean to the view that the Käfers had emigrated from Austria to Bavaria, probably about 1655 when several of the Blankenbakers (and probably the Scheibles) were leaving Austria. The chances are good that these families were related.

Another resident of Zaberfeld who at least has a mention in Virginia is Georg Wegmann. Except for his inclusion in Alexander Spotswood's head right list, nothing is known about him in Virginia.

The Lutheran church at Sulzfeld suggests a Catholic church. During the Reformation, when many of the churches converted, some of them kept the characteristics, especially the elaborate altar pieces and the emblems of the preceding Catholic church. Though this building is much newer than the Reformation, they have preserved some of the stylistic characteristics.

Sulzfeld is the home of four Germanna families, those of Christopher Zimmerman, of Christopher Uhl, of George Lang, and of Frederick Kappler. The last three of these, even though they left Sulzfeld in 1717, did not arrive in Virginia until about 1719. George Lang left a confused head right application in Virginia in which he appears to have been thinking of when he stepped onto the soil of England as opposed to the soil of Virginia.

Just to the east of Sulzfeld, is a small hill on which the Ravensburg castle once stood. Parts of it are still inhabited. It is especially noteworthy because of the views from the hill and from the tower there. The scene here is to the southwest and on the right is the village of Sulzfeld. Land use is agricultural including many vineyards as seen in the left foreground.

The view is also from Ravensburg. With a telephoto lens, Sulzfeld has been brought into a closer perspective. It is too large to be called a village. Many farmers live in Sulzfeld and drive out to their fields. Looking slightly to the right of center, at a distance of about nine miles lies the village of Neuenbürg (it cannot be seen here).

The Volck and the Utz families lived on the Wagenbach estate farm. The nearest community with a church is Hüffenhardt. Wagenbach itself is a community of many homes. Most of them are modern, but some are old and some are a mixture like the one here. On the near end is a modern structure. In back of it is an older structure which combined the features of a barn and home. Down below, through the large door, was the barn while the people lived on the upper two floors.

George Utz had lived earlier in Bavaria. There are a series of villages just over the line from Württemberg where the Utz family lived. Here at Haundorf, the oldest known ancestor of George lived. This church is noteable for its wooden tower (which leans slightly). Two other nearby villages were Seiderzell and Kühnhard though they had no churches. Ancestors of George lived there also.

The interior of the church at Mosbach is very colorful, especially in May when confirmations take place. The baptismal font is a unique piece. Many records of the Utz family are to be found in Mosbach for the parish was much larger than the village itself.

Bergnerzell is also prominent in the history of the Utz family. In fact it is still the home of many Utz families. When we visited, I asked a man on the street if there were any Utz families there. He thought it was an odd question and he answered by going into a nearby business and bringing out a telephone book and showing me a page filled with the Utz name.

The villages of Haundorf, Seiderzell, Kühnhard, Mosbach, and Bergnerzell form a circle of about a four mile diameter. The valley in and around them is very pretty.

Just a short drive beyond the villages of the Utz family lies Illenschwang, the village whence Andreas Gaar and Eva Seidelman with five children left for America. The interior of the Lutheran church there is shown. It is typical with a side entry and a balcony on one side and the rear. Organs are very popular and they are usually placed in the rear of the church.

I enlisted the aid of my seventh cousin, Fritz Gaar, his wife Gisela, and their eldest daughter Martina. We are in the Illenschwang Church waiting for the pastor. I wanted to give him, for the church there, a photograph of Hebron Church and a book of history of Hebron. Here we are talking before the pastor joined us.

On Sunday morning, we attended church here and the pastor showed the photograph and the book to the people. He also worked Andreas Gaar into his sermon.

Martina, the young girl here, was our interpreter as her parents and the pastor did not speak English. Martina did a great job. The family lives a couple of miles from Illenschwang and they go a Lutheran church in their own village. Fritz descends from a brother of Andreas Gaar. There are two other children in the family and the family has a five piece band.

On the left is the church in Beyerbach which is rich in history for Eva Seidelmann. Twelve of her ancestors were baptized here, four couples were married, and fourteen were buried in the graveyard.

We can view one of Eva's descendants in the graveyard here. Fortunately, he is upright and above ground.

On the right is the Maypole in Frankenhofen, the village of Andreas Gaar's birth. For sheer pride in their village, the residents rate an A+. Their Maypole was the largest and most elaborately decorated of any we saw.

When Hans Gahr, the earliest identified Gaar, was married in Regensburg in 1570, it was recorded that he was a farmer (cabbage grower) from Kolnpach. Locating this place was not easy for the name is not correct. It was Kolmbach which is a farm and it does not appear on maps we owned though we did have some clues as to its general location. Our friend, Jost Gudelius, in Germany had access to a ordinance map which showed it. So armed with Jost's details we went to Kolmbach which is in the southeast corner of Germany. In fact it is only fifteen miles from Austria and in an area where many Gaars, Gahrs, Gars, and a few Garrs live today. The buildings here are undoubtedly of modern origin though they may incorporate parts of older structures.

I believe that a great-great-grandfather of Andreas Gaar lived at Zenzing which is today a "community" of about five homes plus this chapel. The stucco is yellow and the wood trim is white. It is well kept and a delight to look at. Zenzing is within walking distance of Walderbach. Both of these can be found on a detailed map. Look in a northeast direction about fifteen miles from Regensburg.

Broadly speaking, we have been moving from Baden-Württemberg eastward, first to Waldbach, then to the Utz villages, and on to Illenschwang. Finally, at Kolmbach we are about out of Germany. The next photographs come from Austria, mostly from the area of Gresten which again requires a detailed map to locate it. It is about fifty miles west of Vienna.

Gresten lies in the foothills between the plains to the north where the Danube River flows and the Alps to the south. Around Gresten, the land is hilly enough so that meadow-based agriculture is followed. From one of the hills, we took this photo of Gresten. The Plankenbichl farm lies just in back of us.

The nearest set of buildings are on the Planckenbichl farm outside Gresten, Austria. There is one very large building consisting of three parts. At the left is the old house; in the center is the barn; and on the right end is a new set of apartments. Immediately in back of the large building is another building which is hardly visible. The ground slopes away from this complex on three sides. For a scale, observe the cows on the hillside.

The name Plankenbühler comes from the farm name after the modern word for "hill" (-bühl) is substituted for the old word for "hill" (-bichl). The use of a "c" before the "k" is erratic in Germany and Austria. In back of the photographer about half a mile on another hill is the Pletzenberg farm where a Plankenbühler son lived.

From the Plankenbichl farm, one see the Scheiblau farm at a distance of about a half mile. I am betting that this is where the Germanna Scheible family originated. Scheiblau is now a wood products factory so many buildings have been added around the house.

Probably one of the Scheiblaus left here about 1655 when the Plankenbühlers left. George Scheible is found in Neuenbürg with the Blankenbakers and, then in Virginia, George has land with the Blankenbakers.

In Vienna, there is a short street (Gasse) about four blocks long which has this name. In Austria, the name was spelled with a "P." Some of the family, but not all, who moved to Germany changed to a "B." All of those who came through Germany have omitted the "c" before the "h."

I have been told that the man for whom this street was named was a sub-mayor of Vienna.

"Downtown" Klings in Germany is shown. The buildings (homes) are very large, probably a holdover from the times when barns and homes were combined.

Klings was in East Germany, not far over the border dividing East and West Germany. We were not sure what the conditions would be but they seemed to be the equal of homes in West Germany. Our motivation for visiting here is that this was the home of Cyriacus Fleshman.

The pastoral setting of Klings is shown. Some of the residents farm based on meadows. We saw several cow herds and a flock of sheep. In May when we were here in the full sunshine, the setting was very beautiful with green fields and red-tiled roofs. .

There could hardly be any doubt about Klings being the home of the Fleshmans. This truck was spotted just outside the town.

The stone is in the graveyard. The most common name on the gravestones, and it occurred quite often, was Fleischmann. Of course they spell it with all of the letters. Germans almost never use words if a numeral suffices. They also follow the logical sequence in a date of day, month, and year. The symbol * is widely used to mean "born" amd + or a cross means "died."

Along the Rhine River there many castles, most of which are in at least a partial state of ruin. The claim is made that only one has been preserved intact. That is Marksburg shown here. The fact that it was never destroyed may be due more to politics than to its being a strong fortification. It is now a museum and worth a visit when one tires of looking at churches.

The siting, for defensive purposes was excellent. It was on a steep hill that would make it difficult to approach it. Cannon shots, either offensively or defensively, would be difficult.

The use of space in Marksburg Castle is random. Leaving one area, one encounters another area with what seems like an unrelated function. Here is the kitchen which is an overgrown, walk-in fireplace. From the size of the kettles, probably all of the food for the inhabitants of the castle was cooked here.

One room was the ladies room. It had a better decor with better polished wood and painted walls in a soft floral pattern. Shown here is a piece of furniture which was more the work of a blacksmith than a carpenter.

Traveling along the Rhine River, one cannot help but be amazed at the vineyards which seem to be vertical, not horizontal. We saw one in which cultivators and sprayers were being winched up and down the hillside by a cable from a tractor on an upper road in the yard. We have yet to understand how erosion control is practiced. Also, the soil is very stony.

Perhaps the largest castle along the Rhine was Rheinfels which was huge. It is almost entirely in ruins now though a few rooms have been restored enough to permit a museum to be installed. Within its outer walls, the population could exceed ten thousand people.

These castles were the strongholds of the many principalities that were a part of the Holy Roman Empire before there was a Germany. They controlled the use of the Rhine River and extracted fees from boats on it. It would have been impossible for boats to have challenged this castle.

Even in a state of ruin, one can see the grand scope of the architecture at Rhinefels. It would be hard to imagine the number of servants and laborers it would take to run an establishment of this size. Besides the civil government, there would be the security forces to feed and house.

This is the old house on the Plankenbichl farm outside Gresten, Austria. As late as 1930 the roof was made of thatch. The windows appear to have been enlarged.

These old houses do not afford the best living conditions. In recent times, this house was slated to be torn down but it has been granted a reprieve. In back of it is the barn. And in back of the barn is a new apartment building.

The farms such as Plankenbichl are no longer economically viable and alternative uses are sought. On the Pletzenberg farm, the old farm house is being remodeled into apartments.

In the closing section are a few pictures intended to show what a delight it can be to visit Germany.

A few years ago I became acquainted with Jost Gudelius, a native German, via the Internet. We corresponded at some length. When we made our trips to Germany, he invited us to visit his family.

The Gudelius family has a connection with the Germanna families. The first pastor at Oberfischbach after the end of The Thirty Year's War was an ancestor of these two Gudelius boys. Also, a Gudelius once owned the house in Trupbach that is now owned by Horst Bocking-Schmidt.

Though the Gudelius family lives in southern Germany, almost to the Austria border south of Munich, we have never felt it was out of the way to visit them. The two young men here are Axel (left) and Jost, Jr.. Besides their parents they have another brother and a sister. For more about this sports minded family, see their web site www.gudelius.de.

This is John with his tenth half-cousin, Richard Plankenbühler who lives in Nürnberg (not to be confused with Neuenbürg). Our common ancestor lived on the Plankenbichl farm outside Gresten, Austria in 1600. About 1655 several Plankenbühlers left Austria and all but one settled in Mittelfranken in Bavaria. Matthias Blanckenbühler though went on to Neuenbürg. Today there about fifteen Blankenbühlers and a few Plankenbühlers in Germany.

Richard and his wife Gisela, with the help of Pastor Kuhr of Nürnberg (Nuremberg to English speakers), traced the Plankenbühler family back to Austria. This was not an easy job considering the scarcity of Austrian records. Richard, Gisela, and John have written up this research for English readers.

Richard's English is good. He learned this as a POW in England and in the United States. He has one son, Dr. Roland Plankenbühler, a computer engineer which is what John sometimes says his occupation was.

One of the delights in visiting Germany is the unexpected. There is a lot to surprise one. Once we were touring with Jost Gudelius not far from his home. We had been in the woods for quite a distance when we emerged into a small village. There was a large church which was rather plain on the outside. Inside it took our breath away. It was the finest example of the rococo style that I have witnessed. As I understand this church, it is associated with a convent.

In 2002, Eleanor worked where there was a cafeteria managed by Clemens Meyers who came from Austria. He wanted us to visit the "home village." It was not out of our way so we stopped to take pictures to prove to him that we had visited. It being lunch time, we decided to eat there. Eleanor asked the waiter if he knew Georg Meyer (the brother of Clemens). Yes, Georg was a good friend of his. So the waiter phoned Georg and asked him to come to the restaurant. We talked and finished lunch. Georg and Eleanor struck it off very well. So well that Georg got the biggest laugh out of Eleanor in the fifty years that John has known her. Georg then asked us to come by his home and meet his father and mother. We did do that and we talked for more than two hours. At the end, the mother asked us to take some cookies to Clemens. We did and Eleanor said that Clemens was teary eyed when she gave him the cookies. Within a couple of years we were pleased to have Clemens and his family and Georg with a friend to lunch at our house.

In short, having ancestors in and visiting Germany and Austria can be a lot of fun.

Index

Abendschön
    Anna Rosina(Willheit) Abendschon, 129
Adams
    Jane Adams, 96
    William Adams, 96
Adkins
    Margaret Adkins, 101
    William Adkins, 101
Alcock
    John P. Alcock, 117
Alexander
    E.P. Alexander, 53
Alford
    Eva Alford, 94
Altap
    Elizabeth Altap, 59
Ambargo, see Amberger
Amberger (Ambargo, Ambergey, Amburga, Amburgey, Ambyon), 54
    Anne Amberger, 59
    Barbara Amberger, 59
    Connorat Ambyon, 59
    Conrad Amberger, 13, 22, 28, 59, 60, 68, 93, 134
    Hans Conrad Amberger, 59
    John Ambargo, 59
    John Amberger, Jr., 60
    John Amburger, 59, 60
    John Amburger, Jr., 59
    Margaret Amburger, 59, 60
    Peggy Amburga, 60
    William Amburger, 59
Ambergey, see Amberger
Amburgey, see Amberger
Ambyon, see Amberger
Anderson
    Elizabeth Anderson, 96
Atwell, see Yowell
Ault
    Matthias Ault, 91
Austin
    Samuel Austin, 107
Awel, see Yowell
Aylor (Ailer, Aler, Ehler, Eiler, Öhler), 54
    Abraham Aylor, 60
    Absalom Aylor, 40
    Anna Magdalena Aylor, 60, 88, 115
    Anna Margaret Aylor, 120
    Barbara Aylor, 60, 70
    Benjamin Aylor, 40
    Delilah Aylor, 60
    Elizabeth Aylor, 60, 91, 119
    Frances Aylor, 60
    Georg Catharina Aylor, 60
    Georg Heinrich Aylor, 60
    Henry Ailer, 97
    Hans Jacob Aylor, 60, 115, 119, 135
    Heinrich Aylor, 42
    Heinrich Ehler, 42, 112
    Henrich Aylor, Jr., 39
    Henrich Aylor, Sr., 39
    Henry Alyor, 28, 48, 60, 61, 77, 88, 91, 94, 98, 115, 119, 120
    Henry Aylor, Sr., 80
    Henry Eiler, 61
    Jacob Aylor, 60, 135, 136
    John Jacob Aylor, 60
    Magdalena Aylor, 60, 80
    Margaret Aylor, 60, 61, 94
    Mary Aylor, 60
    Susannah Aylor, 60

Baccon
    Maria Baccon, 61
Bach
    Henry Bach, 61
    Hermann Bach, 61
    John Bach, 61
Backer
    John Backer, 42
Bädl
    Margaretha Bädl, 61
Bahmer, see Beemon
Baker
    John Baker, 64
Ballenger (Bellenger, Balynger)
    Agatha Ballenger, 61
    Andreas Bellenger, 13
    Andrew Ballenger, 61, 72
    Edward Ballenger, 22, 28, 61, 72, 95, 101
    Edward Ballenger, Sr., 61
    Francis Ballenger, 61
    James Ballenger, 61
    John Ballenger, 61
    Margery Ballenger, 61
    Mary Ballenger, 61, 129
    Sarah Balleger, 61
    Sarah Balynger, 61
    Susannah Ballenger, 61
Bangert, see Bunger
Banks
    Betty Banks, 121
    Ralph Banks, 18, 28
    William Banks, 18, 28, 121

Barbour
    Elizabeth Barbour, 122
    James Barbour, Jr., 81, 105
Barger
    Adam Barger, 73
    Casper Barger, 73
    Catharine Barger, 73
    Christa Barger, 73
    Eve Barger, 73
    Jacob Barger, 73
    John Barger, 73
    Philip Barger, 73
    Philip Barger, Jr., 73
Barler, see Barlow
Barlow (Barler, Beller, Berler, Carler, Parlur, Parlow, Perler)
    Aaron Barlow, 62, 65
    Aaron Perler, 105
    Adam Barler, 41, 98, 114, 122
    Adam Barlow, 41, 97, 114, 122
    Adam Berler, 104
    Alpha Perler, 105
    Ambrose Barlow, 62
    Anne Barlow, 62
    Barbara Barlow, 63
    Catherine Barlow, 62, 65
    Catherine Barlow, 84
    Christopher Barler, 75, 84, 122
    Christopher Barlow, 42, 61, 62, 63, 64, 65, 84, 104, 105
    Christopher Barlow, Jr., 63
    Christopher Berler, 104
    Christopher Parlow, 61
    Christopher Parlur, 15
    Cornelius Barlow, 63
    Daniel Barlow, 62, 64
    Elizabeth Barlow, 63
    Enoch Barlow, 62
    Ephraim Barlow, 62
    Jacob Barler, 64
    Jacob Barlow, 62, 63, 70
    Jane Barlow, 63
    Jemima Barlow, 62, 84, 91
    John Barler, 63, 97
    John Barlow, 62, 63
    John Parlor, 63
    Jonas Perler, 105
    Joseph Barlow, 62
    Joshua Barler, 122
    Joshua Barlow, 62
    Leah Barlow, 62
    Lewis Barlow, 63
    Lucia Perler, 105
    Ludwig Berler, 104
    Margaret Barlow, 62
    Mary Barlow, 62, 63
    Matthew Barlow, 28
    Matthias Barler, 113
    Matthias Barlow, 20, 62, 113
    Matthias Beller, 20, 62
    Matthias Carler, 71
    Michael Barlow, 62
    Pauera (Barbara) Barlow, 61
    Pauera Parlur, 15
    Rachel Barlow, 49, 62, 95
    Rhoda Barlow, 62, 122
    Samuel Barlow, 63
    William Henry Barlow, 63
Battan, see Battern
Batteley
    Elizabeth Batteley, 20, 28
Battern (Battan, Batten, Batton)
    Anna Battern, 63, 75
    Elizabeth Battern, 63
    George Battern, 63
    John Battan, 75
    John Battern, 63
Baugh
    Sally T. Baugh, 64
Baumgardner (Baumgarner, Baumgartner, Bumgarner, Pamgarner), 28
    Adam Baumgardner, 64, 65
    Adam Bumgarner, 85
    Catherine Baumgardner, 63, 64, 79, 103
    Dorothy Baumgardner, 63, 64, 84
    Elizabeth Baumgardner, 64
    Eva Baumgardner, 79
    Eve Baumgardner, 63, 64
    Frederick Baumgardner, 24, 32, 63, 64, 65, 79, 103, 106, 118, 140
    Frederick Bumgarner, 32, 80
    Frederick Pamgarner, 63, 117
    George Baumgardner, 64
    George Bumgarner, 91
    Gottfried Baumgardner, 63
    Gottfried Baumgarner, 129
    Hans Jacob Baumgartner, 63
    Jesse Baumgardner, 64, 65
    Joel Baumgardner, 64
    Johann Frederick Baumgardner, 63
    Johann Frederick Baumgartner, 64
    Johann Friederich Baumgarner, 129
    Sarah Baumgardner, 118
Baumgartner, see Baumgardner
Beale
    William, 72
Beatty
    David Beatty, 91

Becker
    Elisabetha Becker, 109
    Elizabeth Becker, 65
    Jesse Becker, 65
    Johannes Becker, 65, 109
    Samuel Becker, 65

Beemon (Bahmer, Boehme, Böhme, Peemon, Perler)
    Harman Bahmer, 64
    Anna Beemon, 65
    Catharina Beemon, 105
    Catharine Beemon, 65
    Catherine Beemon, 62, 65
    Daniel Böhme, 39
    Daniel Beemon, 48, 64, 65, 71
    Daniel Peemon, 42
    Elizabeth Böhme, 61, 114
    Elizabeth Beeman, 64
    Elizabeth Beemon, 65
    Eva Beemon, 65
    Eve Böhme, 75
    John Beemon, 64
    Joshua Beemon, 64
    Margaret Beemon, 64, 65
    Mary Beemon, 64, 65
    Nancy Beemon, 48, 64, 65
    Peggy Beemon, 64
    Rosina Beemon, 65
    Susannah Beemon, 64

Bekh
    Lorentz Bekh, 105

Bell
    John Bell, 69

Bellenger, see Ballenger
Beller, see Barlow
Bender (Painter, Pander)
    Aaron Bender, 65
    Adam Bender, 65
    Adam Painter, 65
    Adam Pander, 41, 65
    Heseckiel Bender, 65
    Johann Adam Bender, 65
    Johann Jorg Bender, 65

Bennett
    Charles M. Bennett, 76

Benz
    Alfred Benz, 60

Berler, see Barlow
Berry (Berrey), 54, 117
    Acrey (Acra) Berry, 66
    Anna Berry, 102
    Anthony Berry, 48, 66
    Elijah Berry, 66
    Elizabeth Berry, 66
    Jemima Berry, 65
    Jeriah Berry, 66
    Jesse Berry, 102
    John Berry, 65
    John Berry, Jr., 66, 114
    John Berry, Sr., 66
    Juriah Berry, 130
    Susannah Berry, 114

Beverley
    Robert Beverley, 3, 4, 11, 14, 103
    William Beverley, 24, 28, 125, 127

Beyerbach, see Beyerback
Beyerback
    Anna Catharina Beyerbach, 66
    Hannah Beyerback, 66
    Heinrich Friedrich Beyerbach, 66
    Henry Frederick Beyerbach, 66, 127

Blackmore
    Richard Blackmore, Sr., 3

Blakenbaker, see Blankenbaker
Blanckenbühler, see Blankenbaker
Blancumbaker, see Blankenbaker
Blankebuchner, see Blankenbaker
Blankenbücher, see Blankenbaker
Blankenbühler, see Blankenbaker
Blankenbaker, (Blakenbaker, Blankenbecker, Blankenbeckler, Blan(c)kenbühler, Blancumbaker, Blankenbeker, Blankenbicher, Blankenbucher, Blankebuchner, Blankenbücher, Blankenbuecher, Blankenbühler, Pickler, Plancit-Pecker, Plankenbühler, Plunkapee)
7, 145, 146, 154, 160
    Aaron Blankenbaker, 48
    Aaron Blankenbücher, 40
    Adam Plankenbühler, 43
    Alcy Blankenbaker, 82
    Anna Barbara Blankenbaker, 82
    Anna Barbara Blankenbühler, 43
    Anne Margaret Blankenbaker, 66
    Anna Maria Blankebuchner, 9
    Anna Maria Blankenbaker, 67, 74, 83, 90, 94, 120, 122
    Anna Maria Blankenbühler, 43, 44, 66
    Apollonia Blankenbaker, 67, 84
    Applona Blankebuchner, 9
    Appollonia Blankenbaker, 67
    Balthasar Blankenbaker, 18, 24, 28, 32, 66, 82, 83, 125
    Balthasar, Blankenbeker, 48
    Balthasar, Blankenbucher, 13, 66
    Barbara Blankenbaker, 75, 105, 123
    Blasius Plankenbühler, 43
    Christina Blankenbaker, 67
    Christina Blankenbaker, 123
    Christoph Blankenbücher, 39
    Christoph Blanckenbühler, 36
    Christopher Blankenbaker, 67, 82

Christoph Plankenbühler, 43
Davis Pickler, 67
Dorothy Blankenbaker, 86
Dorthea Blankenbaker, 67
Eleanor Blankenbaker, 133, 161
Elis Blankenbaker, 105
Elizabeth Blankenbaker, 48, 67, 79, 84, 87, 123, 125
Elizabeth Blankenbecker, 67
Elizabeth Barbara Blankenbaker, 68
Elisabetha Plankenbühler, 43
Els (Alcy) Blankenbaker, 48, 67
George Blankenbaker, 63, 67, 88, 104
George Blankenbühler, 148
Gisela Plankenbühler, 42, 44, 160
Hanna Blankenbaker, 67
Hannes Jerg Blankenbühler, 44
Hannss Plankenbuühler, 43
Hans Balthasar Blankenbühler, 43, 44
Hans Jerg Blankenbaker, 67
Hans Jerich Blankebuchner, 9
Hans Matthias Blankenbühler, 43
Hans Nicholas Blankebuchner, 9
Hans Niclas Blankenbühler, 43
Hans Thomas Blankenbühler, 43
Jacob Blankenbaker, 48, 67, 87, 121
Jacob Blankenbicher, 39
Jacob Blankenbücher, 40
Jesse Pickler, 67
John Nicholas Blankenbaker, 67, 86, 87
John Nicholas Blankenbeckler, 67
Johan Nicolas Blankenbühler, 44
Johann Mattheus Blankenbühler, 44
Johannes Blankenbücher, 39
Johannes Blankenbüchner, Jr., 40
John Blankenbaker, 44, 45, 50, 51, 67, 75, 105, 123, 127, 133, 160
John Blankenbaker, Jr., 67
John Nicholas Blankenbaker, 48, 86, 87, 94
John Nicholas Blankenbeckler, 67
John Pickler, 67
Jonas Blankenbücher, 40
Joseph Pickler, 67
Julius Blankenbaker, 49
Kilian Plankenbühler, 43
Lewis Blankenbaker, 123
Ludwig Blankenbücher, 40
Magdalena Blankenbaker, 127
Magdalena Plankenbühler, 43
Margaret Blankebuchner, 9
Margaret Blankenbaker, 66
Margaretha Blankenbühler, 43
Maria Barbara Blankenbühler, 44
Mary Barbara Blankenbaker, 120
Mary Blankenbaker, 50, 79, 104
Mary Pickler, 67

Mary Barbara Blankenbaker, 67
Mary Magdalena Blankenbaker, 48, 123
Mary Margaret Blankenbaker, 67
Martha Plankenbühler, 43
Mathas Plancit-Pecker, 67
Mathiaas Blanebuchner, 9
Mathias Blankenbaker, 32, 66, 67
Mathias Blankenbucher, 13
Mathias Plankabeaner, 32
Matther Blanckenbücher, 67
Matthew Blankenbaker, 28
Matthew Plunkapee, 18, 67
Matthias Blankenbaker, 18, 24, 48, 66, 67, 82, 83, 123, 127, 130
Matthias Blankenbucher, 67
Matthias Blankenbühler, 43, 148
Matthias Plankenbühler, 43
Micall Blancumbaker, 86
Michael Blankenbaker, 67, 68, 79, 86
Mich'l Blankenbecker, 42
Michael Blankenbicher, 112
Nancy Pickler, 67
Nicholas Blancumbaker, 67
Nicholas Blankenbaker, 24, 28, 32, 66, 67, 83, 84, 90, 121, 147, 148
Nicholas Blankenbucher, 13, 67
Nicholas Plancabeaner, 32
Nicholas Plunkapee, 67
Pale Blankebuchner, 9
Pals Plunkabeaner, 32
Paltas Blancumbaker, 66
Paul Plankenbühler, 43
Paul Plunkapee, 18, 66
Paultus Blankenbaker, 68
Paulus Blancumbaker, 18
Potentiana Plankenbühler, 43
Richard Plankenbühler, 42, 44, 160
Samuel Blankenbaker, 105
Samuel Blankenbücher, 40
Sophia Plankenbühler, 43
Susanna Blankenaker, 123
Thomas Blankenbücher, 40
Tivall(?) Blancumbaker, 86
Ursula Blankenbaker, 67, 106, 132
William P. Blankenbeckler, 54, 67
Zacharias Blancumbaker, 86
Zacharias Blanc…buchler, 41
Zacharias Blankenbaker, Jr., 67
Zacharias Blankenbaker, Sr., 75
Zachariah Blankenbaker, 58
Zacharias Blankenbaker, 48, 49, 67, 82, 127
Zacharias Blankebuchner, 9
Zacharias Blankenbücher, 39
Zacharias Blankenbühler, 44
Zachory Blancumbaker, 86

Blankenbecker, see Blankenbaker
Blankenbeckler, see Blankenbaker
Blankenbeker, see Blankenbaker
Blankenbicher, see Blankenbaker
Blankenbucher, see Blankenbaker
Blankenbuecher, see Blankenbaker
Blanton
    John Blanton, 61
Bloodworth
    J. Bloodworth, 22
    Joseph Bloodworth, 22, 28, 33, 59, 61, 68, 101
Bobo
    Mary Bobo, 90
Bochman
    Henry Bochman, 97
Bocking-Schmidt
    Horst Bocking-Schmidt, 159
Boeringer
    Anna Magdalena Boringer, 60
Boger
    Hans Michael Boger, 128
Bohannon
    Elliott Bohannon, 120
    Margaret Bohannon, 68
Bond
    John Bond, 10
Boughan
    Eve Boughan, 64, 79
    Mordecai Boughan, 64
Braun
    David Braun, 68
Breil, see Broyles
Breuel (Breyhel), see Broyles
Breul, see Broyles
Breyel, see Broyles
Broil, see Broyles
Brooke
    Robert Brooke, 18, 28
Brookings
    Mary Brookings, 107
Browel, see Broyles
Brown
    Abraham Brown, 97
    David M. W. Brown, 10
    Francis Brown, 106, 124
    James Brown, 30
    James E. Brown, 82, 83
    John Brown, 79, 93
    Thomas Brown, 93
    William Brown, 104
Broyles (Breil, Breuel, Breul, Breyel, Briles, Broil, Browel, Bryell, Bryoll, Prial)
    Aaron Breil, 40
    Adam Breil, 46
    Adam Briles, 68
    Adam Broil, 42, 98

Adam Broyles, 68, 92, 103, 104, 105, 112
Catherine Broyles, 68, 78, 82, 116, 126, 128
Christley Browel, 32
Christley Broyles, 32, 69
Conrad Breyel, 68
Conrad Briles, 68
Conrad Broil, 69
Conrad Broyles, 32, 68, 69, 71, 80, 105
Conrad Bryoll, 15
Cortney Browel, 32
Cyrus Broyles, 68
Delia Broyles, 112
Demilia Broyles, 65
Elizabeth Briles, 68
Elizabeth Broyles, 65, 68
Elizabeth Bryoll, 15
Frederick Briles, 68
George Briles, 68
Hans Jacob Broyles, 68
Jacob Broil, 32, 41, 69
Jacob Broyles, 18, 28, 32, 41, 68, 69, 78, 83, 84, 104, 116, 117, 121, 126
Jacob Bryell, 101
Jacob Bryoll, 15
Jerg Martin Broyles, 68
Johannes Breuel (Breyhel), 68
John Broil, 69
John Broyles, 20, 28, 42, 68, 69, 71, 101, 123, 125, 126, 143
John Bryoll, 13, 15
John Prial, 20, 68
Margaret Briles, 68
Margaret Broyles, 123
Margaretha Breyel, 68
Maria Broyles, 92
Maria Elisabetha Broyles, 68
Mary Briles, 68
Mary Broyles, 68
Mary Catherine Broyles, 68, 78, 83
Mattheus Broyles, 68
Matthias Broyles, 68, 97, 100
Michael Broyles, 68, 97
Moses Broyles, 65
Nicholas Breul, 41
Nicholas Broyles, 68, 78, 105
Peter Breil, 39, 42
Peter Broyles, 48, 49, 68
Rachel Briles, 68
Rebecca Briles, 68
Stephen H. Broyles, 68
Steven Broyles, 20
Susanna Briles, 68
Urseley Broyle, 68
Ursley Bryoll, 15
Ursula Broyles, 68
Zacharias Breil, Jr., 40

Zacharias Breil, Sr., 40
Zachariah Broyles, 41
Zacharias Broyles, 68, 112
Ziriakus Breil, 42
Bruce
John Bruce, 20, 28
Brückmann
Anna Maria Brückmann, 89
Hans Jerg Brückmann, 89
Bryell, see Broyles
Bryoll, see Broyles
Buchi
Barbara Buchi, 110
Budd
John Budd, 122
Bumgarner, see Baumgardner
Bunger (Bangert, Bungert)
Ann Bunger, 111
Anna Margaret Bungard, 69
Annette Kunselman Bungert, 102
Barbara Bungard, 69
Catherine Bunger, 69
Elisabeth Bungert, 90
Elizabeth Bungard, 69
Elizabeth Bunger, 69
Eva Bunger, 69
Felta Bunger, 69
Henry Bunger, 69
Jacob Bungard, 40, 69
Jacob Bunger, 69
Jacob Bungert, 91
Johannes Bungard, 40
John Bungard, 69
John Bunger, 90
Magdalena Bungard, 69
Margaret Bunger, 69
Margaret Catherine Bunger, 54
Mary Bunger, 69
Philip Bunger, 69
Vallendin Bangert, 41
Valentin Bungard, 39, 69
Valentin Bunger, 69, 111
Valentin Bungert, 90
Burdyne (Burdine)
Carol Ann Burdine, 50
Catherine (Tanner) Burdyne, 81
John Burdyne, 81
Reginald Burdyne, 50, 120
Richard Burdyne, 28, 33, 50, 66, 67, 81, 109, 119
Burgert
Annette K. Burgert, 102
Burgud, see Harnsberger
Burke
Judah Burke, 126
Burner
Jacob Burner, 97

Butler
John Butler, 22, 28
Byrn
Martha Byrn, 10
Thomas Byrn, 10

Cain
Winton Burell Cain, 54
Calhoun
John Calhoun, 87
Call, see Kahl
Care, see Garr
Carehaut, see Gerhardt
Carler, see Barlow
Caroland
Ellie Caroland, 63
Carpenter (Occasionally members of the Carpenter family were called Zimmerman.) 54
Aaron Carpenter, 70
Abraham Carpenter, 40
Andreas Carpenter, 39, 41
Andreas Carpenter, Jr., 40
Andreas Zimmerman, 36
Andrew Carpenter, 65, 70, 71, 73, 95, 126, 127
Andrew C. Carpenter, 96
Ann Barbara Carpenter, 70
Anna Carpenter, 70
Anna Barbara Carpenter, 69, 81
Anna Magdalena Carpenter, 80, 126
Barbara Carpenter, 60, 65, 70
Cornelius Carpenter, 40, 70
D. R. Carpenter, 16, 18
Dinah Carpenter, 70, 123
Dorothy Carpenter, 70, 75, 80
Elizabeth Carpenter, 15, 69, 70, 71, 96, 126
Ephraim Carpenter, 70
Jeremias Carpenter, 40
Joel Carpenter, 40
Johannes Carpenter, 42, 112
Johannes Carpenter, Jr., 39
Johannes Carpenter, Sr., 39
John Carpenter, 18, 26, 28, 32, 69, 70, 71, 73, 74, 78, 80, 81, 95, 126
John Carpenter, Jr., 70, 74, 75
John Carpenter, Sr., 42, 70, 80
John Zimmermann, 69
Jon Carpenter, 32
Joseph Carpenter, 40, 70
Margaret Carpenter, 70
Margaretha Carpenter, 70
Maria Carpenter, 70
Mary Carpenter, 70, 75, 93, 123
Michael Carpenter, 39, 42, 70, 71, 78, 80, 95, 126
Michael Carpenter, Sr., 39
Michael Zimmerman, 42
Moses Carpenter, 70

Nancy Carpenter, 70
Peggy Carpenter, 70
Rebecca Carpenter, 70
Rev. Carpenter, 102
Salomon Carpenter, 40
Samuel Carpenter, 64, 70
Samuel Carpenter, Sr., 39
Simeon Carpenter, 40, 70
Solomon Carpenter, 70
Susanna(h) Carpenter, 70, 80, 93
W. Carpenter, 26
Wilhelm Carpenter, Sr., 39
Willhelm Carpenter, 41
William Carpenter, 15, 32, 56, 69, 70, 71, 81, 84, 95, 112, 117
William Cimberman, 70

Carr, see Garr

Carter
John Carter, 108

Castler, 7
Anna Magdalena Castler, 71, 80
M. Castler, 100
Matthew Castler, 28, 112
Matthias Castler, 24, 32, 71, 77, 80, 100, 103, 104
Susannah Castler, 71, 97

Catton
William Catton, 94

Caul, see Kahl

Cave
Robert Cave, 20, 28

Cawl, see Kahl

Cerny
Johni Cerny, 5, 51, 89

Chelf (Chelf, Jelf, Scheff, Schelf, Schnepff, Zelf), 8
Anna Chelf, 72
Barbara Yager Clore Chelf, 71, 72
Catherine Chelf, 72
Elias Chelf, 72
Hans Schnepff, 72
Isaac Chelf, 72
Johannes Scheff, 71
Nancy Chelf, 48, 64, 71
Philip Chelf, 48, 64, 71, 72, 74
Philip Jelf, 39, 42
Phillip Chelf, 130

Chively, see Scheible

Chrisler, see Christler

Christele, see Christler

Christler (Chrisler, Crisler, Christele, Christler)
Abraham Christler, 40, 95
Adam Christler, 39, 78
Anna Magdalena Christler, 95, 114
Catherine Crisler, 72, 78
Daniel Crisler, 116
David Christler, 78, 116
David Crisler, 126
Debold Christler, 86
Debold (Theobald) Christler, 77, 86
Dewald Christler, 117
Deobold Christler, 78, 86
Deval Christler, 78
Dorothy Christler, 78
Elizabeth Christler, 116, 126
Georg Christler, 39, 42
George Christler, 95, 114
George Crisler, 114
Henrich Christler, 39, 41
Henry Chrisler, 104
Henry Christler, 78, 127
John George Christler, 78, 114
Henry Crisler, 88
Leonard Christler, 78
Leonard Crisler, 72
Lewis Crisler, 72
Margaret Christler, 78
Mary Christler, 70, 78
Michael Christler, 78
Nancy Christler, 116
Rosina Crisler, 86, 88
Theobald Christele, 142
Theobald Christler, 70, 78, 127
Theobald Crisler, 86

Christopher
Ann Christopher, 72
John Christopher, 72
Mary Christopher, 115
Morton Christopher, 72, 126
Nicholas Christopher, 65, 72
William Christopher, 72

Clar, see Clore

Clause, see Clore

Clawr, see Clore

Clawse, see Clore

Clayman, see Clements

Clemans, see Clements

Clement, see Clements

Clements (Clayman, Clemans, Clement, Clemmon)
Catherine Clements, 72
Christian Clayman, 95
Christian Clements, 22, 33, 72, 73, 114
Christopher (Christian) Clements, 124
Christopher Clemmon 124
Elizabeth Clements, 73
Eve Clements, 73
Gaspar Clements, 72, 73
John Clements, 72, 73
Mary Catherine Clements, 73

Cline
Eve Cline, 111

Clore (Clar, Clause, Clawr, Clawse, Glore, Klaar, Klar), 139
    Aaron Clore, 106
    Adam Clore, 42, 78
    Adam Glore, 107
    Agnes Margaret Cloar, 9
    Agnes Margaretha Clore, 73
    Andrea Claus Cloar, 9
    Andreas Clore, 73
    Ann Elizabeth Clore, 73
    Anna Maria Parva Cloar, 9
    Barbara Clore, 70, 73
    Barbara Yager Clore, 71
    Catherine Clore, 74, 125
    Elisabeth(a) Clore, 64, 65, 109, 127
    Frances Clore, 127
    George Clore, 70, 73, 89, 127
    George William Glore, 101
    Hans Jerich Cloar, 9
    Hans Michael Clore, 9
    Hans Michael Klaar, 73
    Jemima Clore, 116
    Johann Georg Clore, 73
    John Clawse, 18
    John Clore, 18, 28, 42, 73, 74, 78, 86, 94, 98, 109, 127, 130
    John Clore, Jr., 42
    Katherine Clore, 74
    Margaret Clore, 72, 73, 74, 78, 98
    Maria Barbara Clore, 73
    Michael Clause, 130
    Michael Clawr, 109
    Michael Clawse, 18
    Michael Clore, 13, 18, 28, 33, 42, 54, 73, 77, 98, 103, 125, 127, 130, 131
    Michael Klaar, 45
    Peter Clar, 42
    Peter Clore, 61, 71, 72, 73, 74, 78, 109, 127, 130, 131
    Peter Klor, 39
    Rosannah Clore, 107, 108
    Susanna Clore, 49, 50, 77, 127, 128
    Susanna Klaar, 45, 46, 127, 140
    Veronica Clore, 116
Cob(b)ler, see Kabler
Cochran
    Franklin H. Cochran, 120
Cock
    Secretary Cock, 3
Cockey
    Louise Keyser Cockey, 102
Cofer (see also Käfer)
    George Cofer, 74
    Jacob Cofer, 74
    Joel Cofer, 74
    Thomas Cofer, 74

Coleman
    Barbara Coleman, 96
    Joseph Coleman, 96
    Robert Coleman, 28, 104
    Robert Coleman, Sr., 22
    Samuel Coleman, 59
Coller
    Henry Coller, 120
    Margaret Coller, 48
Conger
    Hannah Conger, 108
Connor
    Margaret Connor, 61
Coock, see Cook
Cook (Koch)
    Aaron Cook, 75
    Adam Cook, 62, 63, 74, 75, 84, 113
    Adam Cook, Jr., 75
    Adam Koch, 39, 41, 112
    Ambrose Cook, 75
    Ambrosius Koch, 40
    Ann Cook, 75, 76
    Ann (Rhoda Ann) Cook, 63
    Ann Yowell Cook, 55
    Anna Maria Cook, 75
    Aron Koch, 40
    Barbara Cook, 63, 74, 75, 84
    Barbara Koch, 7
    Cornelius Cook, 75
    Daniel Cook, 75
    Daniel Koch, 40
    Dina Cook, 75
    Dorothy Cook, 70, 74, 75, 80
    Elizabeth Cook, 75, 76, 115
    Ephraim Cook, 76
    Ephraim Koch, 40
    Eva Cook, 75
    Frederick Cook, 75
    Georg Koch, 39
    George Cook, 74, 75, 91, 109, 113
    George Koch, 41
    Jemima Cook, 75, 76
    Johann Michel Koch, 7
    Johannes Koch, 40
    John Cook, 75
    Leanna Cook, 75
    Lewis Cook, 75
    Ludwig Koch, 40
    Magdalena Cook, 75
    Margaret Cook, 74, 75, 80, 115
    Maria Dorothea Cook, 74
    Maria Dorothea Koch, 7
    Maria Sarah Cook, 75, 113
    Mary Barbara Cook, 75
    Mary Cook, 9, 15, 70, 74, 75, 93
    Mary Sarah Cook, 75, 116

Michael Cook, 13, 18, 28, 32, 42, 69, 70, 71, 74, 75, 77, 103, 108, 115
Michael Cooke, 120
Michael Koch, 39
Michel Cook, 9
Michell Cook, 15
Michial Coock, 12
Moses Cook, 75
Peter Cook, 75, 93
Peter Koch, 40
Rosanna Cook, 75
Sarah Cook, 75
Solomon Koch, 40
Susan Cook, 75
Susanna Cook, 75

Cooper
Barbara Cooper, 76, 106, 124
Joseph Cooper, 76
Susie House Cooper, 54, 90

Copeland
Nicholas Copeland, 28

Cornelius
Hannah Cornelius, 118

Cornwell
Larry P. Cornwell, 73

Cotton
Joseph Cotton, 59

Cowger
Hanna Hawes Cowger, 122

Crane
James Crane, 73

Crecelius (Cretselious, Krekel)
Anna Magdalena Crecelius, 76
Anna Margarethe Crecelius, 76
Anna Ursula Crecelius, 76
Catharina Barbara Crecelius, 76
Christian Crecelius, 76
Dietrich Theodore Krekel, 76
Dorothea Crecelius, 76
Elizabeth Crecelius, 76
(Maria) Elisabetha Crecelius, 76
Elizabeth Cretselious, 76
Jacob A. Crecelius, 76
Johann Crecelius, 76
Johann Cristophal Crecelius, 76
Johannes Crecelius, 76
Maria Barbara Crecelius, 76
Maria Elisabetha Crecelius, 76
Otto Rudolph Crecelius, 76
Peter Crecelius, 76
Rudolph Crecelius, 42
Rudolph Crecilius, 80
Rudolph Isaac Crecelius, 76
Ruldolph Crecelius, 42, 76
Rudolph Cretselious, 76
Samuel Crecelius, 76

Creeglar, see Crigler

Creek
Jan Creek, 129

Crees (Crest, Grays, Greys, Greyss)
Henriabout Louise Greyss, 76
Lancelot Crest, 77
Lau Crees, 32
Laurentius Greyss, 76
Laus Crest, 24, 77
Lawrence Crees, 28, 32, 103
Lawrence Grays, 77
Lorenz Crees, 24
Maria Euphrosina Gress, 76
Peter Cree, 76, 86
Rebecca Crees (Crest, Greys), 118
Rebecca Greyss, 76

Cretselious, see Crecelius

Crible
George Frederick Crible, 76

Crigler (Creegler, Griegler, Grickler, Grigler, Krug(l)er)
Ann Crigler, 70
Anna Crigler, 72, 77
Aaron Crigler, 77, 78
Abraham Crigler, 77
Abraham Grickler, 40
Abraham Grigler, 40
Adam Grickler, 42
Ann Crigler, 69
Anna Crigler, 72, 77
Aron Grickler, 39
Arthur D. Crigler, 78
Catherine Crigler, 77, 81
Caty Crigler, 77
Christoph Crigler, 42
Christoph Grickler, 39
Christopher Creeglar, 78
Christopher Crigler, 46, 74, 77, 81, 82, 109
Christoph Grigler, 112
Elizabeth Crigler, 46, 49, 71, 77, 78, 88, 101, 130
Jacob Crigler, 12, 13, 18, 28, 31, 40, 46, 49, 68, 77, 78, 82, 119, 127
Jacob Krugler, 18, 74, 77, 123
James Crigler, 77
Joel Crigler, 40
John Crigler, 77
Josua Crigler, 40
Lewis Crigler, 77
Lewis Crigler, Jr., 40
Ludwig Grickler, 40
Margaret Crigler, 49, 77
Mary Crigler, 77, 123
Nicholas Creeglar, 78
Nicholas Crigler, 46, 49, 77, 78, 94, 131
Niclos Griegler, 39
Nicolaus Crigler, 40

Nicolaus Grickler, 36
Nicolaus Grigler, 112
Reuben Crigler, 77
Ruben Grickler, 39
Susannah Creagler, 77
Susanna Crigler, 31, 45, 46, 49, 77, 78, 123, 130
Susannah Crigler, 77, 78
William Crigler, 77

Crowder
Henry Crowder, 32, 33, 115

Crozier
W. A. Crozier, 53

Cunningham
Wanda Cunningham, 88, 92

Custer, see Küster

Daher, see also Ohlscheitt
Catharina Daher, 105
Daniel Daher, 105
Maria Elisabetha Daher, 105

Damur or **Damus**, see Tanner

Daughtary
Edward Daughtary, 20
John Daughtary, 20

Davis
Jane Davis, 67
Margaret G. Davis, 53
Margaret Grim Davis, 41
R. E. Davis, 129

DeBolt
Mary Ann DeBolt, 78

Dearet, see Deer

Deer (Dear, Hirsch, Hirsh)
Abner Deer, 79
An. Maria Deer, 79
Andreas Hirsch, 39
Andrew Deer, 79, 107
Barb Hirsch, 79
Barbara Deer, 79, 110
Catharina Deer, 76
Catharina Hirsch, 80
Catherine Deer, 79, 106
Elizabeth Deer, 79
Ephraim Deer, 79
Frances Deer, 79, 107
Gene Dear, 132
Jemima Deer, 79
Jeremiah Deer, 79
Johannes Hirsch, 39, 79
John Dear, 79
John Dear, Sr., 42
John Deer, 79, 101, 106
John Deer, 64
Jonas Deer, 79
Larkin Deer, 79
Lewis Deer, 79
Lucy Deer, 79
Maria Dear, 79
Martin Deer, 79
Martin Deer, Jr., 79
Martin Hirsch, 79, 100
Martin Hirsch, Jr., 40
Martin Hirsch, Sr., 39
Martin Hirsh, 42
Mary Deer, 79
Mildred Deer, 79
Moses Deer, 79
Reuben Deer, 79
Sarah Deer, 79
Simeon Deer, 79
Susanna Deer, 79
Thomas Deer, 79
Veronica Deer, 79

Delph (Delp)
Adam Delph, 60, 71, 80
Ann Delph, 80
Anna Magdalena Delph, 71, 80
Conrad Delph, 39, 41, 71, 80, 104
Daniel Delp, 42
Daniel Delph, 80
David Delph, 80
Elizabeth Delph, 115
George Conrad Delph, 62, 80, 115
Henry Delph, 80
John Delph, 62
Magdalena Delph, 60
Margaret Delph, 62
Mary Delp, 80
Mary Delph, 80, 115
Mary Margaret Delpp, 115
Matthias Delph, 80
Michael Delp, 39
Michael Delph, 71, 80, 115
Nancy Delph, 80
Rebecca Delph, 80
Samuel Delph, 71, 80
Susannah Delph, 80

Dicken (Dikons)
Benjamin Dicken, 81
Charles Dicken, 81
Christopher Dicken, 81, 86
Daniel Dicken, 81
Elizabeth Dicken, 81
Ephraim Dicken, 81
Isaac Dicken, 81
John Dicken, 81
Joseph Dicken, 81
Lot Dicken, 81
Rhode Dikons, 81
Richard Dicken, 81
Sarah Dicken, 81
Susannah Dicken, 81
William Dicken, 81
Winifred Dicken, 81

Dickinson
    Lynnea Dickinson, 66
Diederle
    Maria Elisabetha Diederle, 76
Diefenbacher
    Karl Diefenbacher, 44
Diehl (Deal, Deel, Deale, Diel)
    Alexander Deale, 80
    Christina Diel, 80
    Daniel Deel, 80
    Daniel Diehl, 76, 80
    Elias Deal, 80
    Elisabetha Diehl, 76
    Elizabeth Diehl, 80
    John Deal, 80
    Johann Diel, 80
    Marg Diehl, 76, 80
    Margaret Diehl, 76
    Peter Diel, 80
    Rosanna Deale, 80
Diemer
    Darryl J. Diemer, 49, 54, 84
Dieter, see Teter
Dikons, see Dickens
Dillard
    Thomas Dillard, 103
Dodge
    Nancy Dodge, 87
    Nancy Moyers Dodge, 48, 51, 105
Doland
    Henry Doland, Jr., 104
Dooley
    Reuben, 108
Doser (Dosser, Dozer, Dozier)
    Daniel Doser, 81, 123
    Daniel Dosser, 42
    Friedrich Dosser, 81
    Henrick Dosser, 81
    Leonard Dozier, 81
Dossee
    Elizabeth Dossee, 107
Dougharty
    Edward Dougharty, 28
    John Dougharty, 28
Downs
    Henry Downs, 18
Drake
    Charlotte Drake, 96
Drysdale
    Lt. Gov. Drysdale, 83
Dünstler
    Eva Dünstler, 131
    Michael Dünstler, 131
Duff
    William Duff, 28

Eberhart
    Anna Maria Eberhart, 81
    Elizabeth Eberhart, 81
Eberwein
    Andreas Eberwein, 117
    Magdalena Eberwein, 117
Eddings
    John Eddings, 20, 28
    William Eddings, 20, 28, 89, 103
Edel
    Maria Barbara Edel, 131
Edwards
    Barbara Edwards, 124
    John Edwards, 124
Ehler, see Aylor
Eiler, see Aylor
Eisenberg
    William Edward Eisenberg, 53
Ellis
    Isaac Ellis, 107
Emerson
    Mahaly Emerson, 96
    Sarah Gertrude Emerson, 96
England
    John England, 28
Enteneur
    Anna Maria Enteneur, 107
Entzminger
    Anna Margaretha Entzminger, 129
Evans
    Rachel Evans, 28

Fähr
    Adam Fähr, 81
    Caspar Fähr, 81
    Catharina Fähr, 81
Faircloth
    Thomas Faircloth, 133
Fairfax
    Lord Fairfax, 26, 110
Fargarson
    Thomas Fargarson, 33
Feischmann, see Fleshman
Feiser
    Melchior Feiser, 8
Feller
    P. S. Feller, 53
Feltner
    Conrad Feltner, 122
Fewell
    Elizabeth Fewell, 132
Field
    Henry Field, 114
    Henry Field, Jr., 114
Fincks, see Finks

Finder
    Michael Finder, 81
Fink, see Finks
Finks (Fincks, Fink), 63, 66
    Alcy Finks, 67, 82
    Andrew Finks, 82
    Anna Finks, 82
    Catherine Finks, 46, 77, 81, 82
    Christina Finks, 67, 82
    Elizabeth Finks, 49, 81, 82, 126, 127
    Eve Finks, 82
    Hannah Finks, 82
    James Finks, 82
    Johannes Fincks, 39
    John Fink, 41
    John Finks, 82
    Magdalena Finks, 127
    Marck Fincks, 39
    Marck Fink, 41
    Mark Finks, 32, 67, 77, 81, 82, 89, 126, 127
    Mark Finks, Jr., 82, 83
    Mark Finks, Sr., 48
    Mary Finks, 123
    Mary Finks, 67, 81, 82, 89, 126
    Mary Magdalena Finks, 82
    Sarah Finks, 82
Finnell
    John Finnell, 121
Fischer, see Fisher
Fiscus
    Elizabeth Fiscus, 125
Fishback
    Ann Elizabeth Fishback, 114
    John Frederick Fishback, 114
Fisher (Fischer)
    Adam Fisher, 81, 83
    Anna Barbara Fischer, 66, 82, 131
    Barnett Fisher, 83
    Bernhard Fischer, 41
    Elizabeth Fisher, 50, 83, 97, 108
    Elizabeth Garr Fisher, 81
    Eve Fisher, 82, 83
    Lewis Fisher, 32, 33, 66, 82, 83, 87, 120
    Lodowick Fisher, 32, 82
    Ludwick Ffisher, 82
    Ludwick Fisher, 32
    Ludwig Fischer, 33, 82, 131
    Ludwig Fisher, 82, 83
    Mary Magdalena Fischer, 83
    Mary Margaret Fisher, 50, 83
    Nicholas Fisher, 50
    Stephen Fisher, 42, 83
Fite
    Barbara Fite, 83
    Theobold Fite, 83
Flefhman, see Fleshman

Fleit (Floyd?)
    Agnes Fleit, 91
    Robert Fleit, 83, 91
Fleshman (Feischmann, Flefhman, Fleischmann, Flishman, Floschman), 54
    Anna Barbara Fleshman, 46, 83
    Anna Parva Floschman, 9
    Barbara Fleshman, 63, 74, 75, 84
    Catherine Fleshman, 62, 66, 84
    Cyracus Fleshman, 13, 61-62
    Cyriacus Fleischmann, 64, 68
    Cyriacus Fleishman, 18
    Cyriacus Fleshman, 7, 9, 10, 12, 18, 24, 28, 30, 32, 46, 62, 66, 75, 83, 84, 103, 112, 113, 155
    Cyriax Fleischmann, 30
    Dorothy Fleshman, 64, 79
    Elijah Fleischmann, 40
    Elizabeth Fleshman, 84, 109
    Ephriam Fleischmann, 40
    Fleischmann, Robert, 42
    Hannah Fleshman, 84
    Hans Peter Fleischmann, 43
    Jacob Floschman, 9
    Jemima Fleshman, 76
    Johannes Feischmann, 112
    John Fleischmann, 42
    John Fleshman, 63, 67, 75, 84
    John Peter Floschman, 9
    Joshua Fleshman, 86
    Margaret Fleshman, 84
    Maria Catharina Fleischmann, 43
    Maria Catharina Floschman, 9
    Mary Catherine Fleshman, 68, 83, 84
    Mary Fleshman, 75, 80
    Michael Fleischmann, 39, 41
    Peter Fleshman, 18, 28, 32, 46, 49, 62, 63, 64, 66, 74, 75, 83, 84, 117, 127
    Peter Fleshman, Jr., 49, 84
    Peter Fleshman, Sr., 84
    Robert Fleshman, 63, 64, 84
    Sericus Fleshman, 18
    Sophia Fleshman, 84, 127
    Susanna Fleshman, 75
    Winifred Fleshman, 84
    Zacharias Flefhman, 32
    Zacharias Fleischmann, 40
    Zacharias Flishman, 12
    Zachary Fleshman, 84
Flincham (Flinchan, Flinchman)
    Catherine Flincham, 106
    Jacob Flincham, 106
    John Flincham, 106
    John Flinchan, 106
    Mary Flincham, 106
    Robert Flincham, 106
    Robert Flinchan, 106

Samuel Flincham, 106
Thenia Flincham, 106
Thomas Flincham, 106
William Flincham, 106
Flohr
George Daniel Flohr, 84
Floschman, see Fleshman
Floyd
John Floyd, 91
Susanna Floyd, 90
Focht, see Vogt
Förckel (Forchel)
Hans George Forchel, 8
Johann Georg Förckel, 7
Maria Barbara Förckel, 7
Susanna Förckel, 7
Fogelman
Aaron Spencer Fogelman, 53, 141
Fowler
William Fowler, 117
Fox
Catharine Fox, 109
Frady (Vorete, Vrede, Wrede)
Barbara Wrede, 85
Carl Simon Wrede, 84
Carl Vorete, 85
Carl, Vrede, 39, 85
Carl Wrede, 85
Charles Frady, 85
Elizabeth Frady, 85
Ephraim Frady, 85
George W. Frady, 85
Henry Frady, 85
Rev. Jacob Franck, 85
John Frady, 85
Lewis Frady, 85
Minnie (Winnie) Frady, 85
Polly Frady, 85
Sarah Frady, 85
Thomas H. Frady, 85
William Frady, 85
Franck
Barbara Franck, 85
Jacob Franck, 56, 85
Franklin
Frances L. Franklin, 50
Fray, (Freh, Frey, Fry)
Aaron Fray, 85, 86
Elizabeth Fray, 85, 86
Elizabeth Ann Fray, 85
Ephraim Dutton Fray, 85
Ephraim Fray, 85
Ephraim Freh, 40
Hester Ann Fray, 85
John Fray, 49, 54, 85, 118
John Fry, 109

Johannes Freh, 39, 42
Joseph Martha Fray, 85
Joseph Michael Fray, 85
Lucy Fray, 86
Margaret Fray, 85, 86
Martha Fray, 85
Mary Fray, 85, 86
Moses Fray, 85, 86
Nancy Fray, 85
Rebecca Fray, 85, 118
Rosanna Fray, 85
Sarah Fray, 85
Susannah Fray, 86
Tabitha Fray, 85
Freh, see Fray
Frost
Cathi Clore Frost, 54, 74
Fry
John Fry, 109
Full, see Vogt

Gabbard (Gabbert, Gybert)
Anna Mary Gabbard, 86
Anne Mary Gabbard, 81
Catrina Gybert, 86
Elizabeth Gybert, 86
Frederick Gybert, 86
Matthias Gybert, 86
Michael Gabbard, 86
Sabina Gybert, 86
Gabbert, see Gabbard
Gahr, see Garr
Garhert
Barbara Garhert, 88
Garr (Care, Carr, Gaar, Gahr, Gar), 7
Adam Care, 86
Adam Carr, 32
Adam Gaar, 32, 36, 39, 41, 81, 112
Adam Garr, 87, 94, 125
Andrew Care, 18, 86
And. Garr, 86
Andreas Gaar, 39, 42, 54, 86, 103, 143, 152, 153, 154
Andrew Garr, 18, 28, 68, 78, 86, 87, 122
Benjamin Gaar, 39, 42
Catherine Garr, 127
Dorothy Garr, 86
Elisabeth Garr, 83, 86
Elizabeth Barbara Gaar, 86
Elizabeth Barbara Garr, 68
Eva Gaar, 86
Eve Care, 86
Fritz Gaar, 152
Gisela Garr, 152
Hans Gahr, 153
Jemima Garr, 75

Johannes Gaar, 39, 41
John Adam Gaar, 86
John Adam Garr, 81
John Calhoun Garr, 54
John Gar, 54
John Garr, 91
John Wesley Garr, 54, 87
Lawr. Garr, 86
Lawrence Gaar, 86
Lawrence Garr, 70, 76, 77, 78, 86, 87
Leanna Garr, 75
Lewis Garr, 127
Lorentz Gaar, 40
Margaret Garr, 91
Martina Garr, 152
Mary Barbara Gaar, 86
Mary Barbara Garr, 87
Mary Magdalena Garr, 83
Michael Gaar, 42
Peter Garr, 86
Rosanna Care, 86
Rosina Gaar, 86
Rosina Garr, 78, 81
Simeon Gaar, 40

Garriott (Garratt, Garrett, Garrot)
 Ambrose Garriott, 79, 87
Barbara Garriott, 69, 87
Catherine Garriott, 87
Daniel Garriott, 87
Edward Garrett, 87
Elijah Garriott, 87
Elizabeth Garriott, 87, 110
Elizabeth Blankenbaker Garriott, 79
Jacob Garriott, 79, 87
James Garriott, 87
John Garratt, 87
John Garrett, 87, 125
John Garriott, 87
John Garrot, 87
John S. Garriott, 87
Jonathan Garriott, 87
Judith Garriott, 87
Levina Garriott, 87, 88
Loving Garriott, 87
Lucinda Garriott, 87
Mary Garriott, 69, 87
Moses Garriott, 87
Phoebe Garriott, 87
Reuben Garriott, 87
Rhoda Garriott, 87
Sarah Garriott, 87
Simeon Garriott, 87
Tom Garret, 87
Thomas Garret, 87
Thomas Garriott, 69, 80, 87
Thomas Garrott, 87
William Garriott, 87

Gebert
Johann Friedrich Gebert, 128
Gemelich
Christofle Gemelich, 8
Gensle, see Kinslow
Gerber, see Tanner
Gerhard (Carehaut, Garrett)
Catherine Carehaut, 87
Catherine Gerhard, 88, 125
Cathrin Gerhard, 63
Daniel Carehaut, 87
Daniel Gerhard, 88
Elizabeth Carehaut, 87
Elizabeth Gerhard, 88
Maria Catharina Gerhard, 108
John Carehaut, 87
John Gerhard, 63, 87, 104
Mary Carehaut, 87
Mary Gerhard, 67, 88, 104, 148
Gerlach
Anna Ursula, 76
Gibbs
John Gibbs, 87
Gibson
Jonathon Gibson, 118
Gillison
James Gillison, 59
Gitting, 108
Glatfelter
Charles H. Glatfelter, 53
Glore, see Clore
Gordon
John Gordon, 102
Gottsaurin
Eva Gottsaurin, 130
Graffenried, (Graffenriede, von Graffenried)
Barron Graffenriede, 2
Christoph von Graffenried, 132
Graves
James Graves, 94
Mary Graves, 63
Nancy Graves, 88
Gray
Gertrude E. Gray, 26
Grays, see Crees
Grayson
Elizabeth Grayson, 75
Green
R. T. Green, 53
Grickler, see Crigler
Griegler, see Crigler
Griffen
Oliver Griffen, 107
Griffith
Dorothy Amburgey, 54, 60
Grigler, see Crigler

Grissam
    John Grissam, 76
Grogan
    Elizabeth Grogan, 93
Gudelius
    Axel Gudelius, 159
    Jost Gudelius, 153, 159, 160
    Jost Gudelius, Jr., 159
Gunnell
    Nicholas Gunnell, 22, 28
Gut (Good)
    Catherina Good, 68
    Casper Good, 88
    Daniel Gut, 88
    Elizabeth Gut, 88
    Hans Caspar Good, 88
    Harriet Good, 88
    Jonas Good, 88
    Joseph Good, 87, 88
    Ludwig Gut, 88
    Sarah Good, 88
    Susanna Good, 88

Hadok
    Isaac Hadok, 33
Häger
    Anna Catherine Häger, 88, 92
    Catherina Häger, 92
    Henrich Häger, 47
Haines
    Isaac Haines, 102
    Mary Haines, 102
Hall
    Elke Hall, 5, 34, 45, 125
Hamilton
    Lynn Berry Hamilton, 54, 66
    C. H. Hamilton, Jr., 54
Hamons
    Elizabeth Hamons, 60
Hance
    Adam Hance, 88, 101
    Catharine Hance, 88, 101
    Margaret Hance, 88, 101
    Peter Hance, 88, 101
    Susanna Hance, 88, 101
Handrexson, see Hendricks
Hansbarger, see Harnsberger
Hansborgow, see Harnsberger
Harbinson
    Anne Harbison, 62
    Moses Harbinson, 62
Harness
    Margaret Harness, 122

Harnsberger (Burgud, Hansbarger, Hansberger, Hansborgow, Harrensparger, Heerensparger)
    Adam Harnsberger, 88
    Agnes Harrensparger, 88
    Anna Barbara Harnsberger, 88
    Anna Magdalena Harnsberger, 60
    Anna Parva Heerensperger, 88
    Anna Purve Burgud, 15
    Barbara Harnsberger, 88, 101
    Barbara Harrensparger, 88
    Conrad Harnsberger, 88
    Elizabeth Harnsberger, 88
    Elizabeth Harrensparger, 88
    Hans Heerensperger, 88
    Hans Herren Burgud, 15, 88
    Henry Harnsberger, 88
    John Hansborgow, 32
    John Harnsberger, 20, 28, 32, 60, 88, 103, 121
    John Harrensparger, 88
    Margaret Harnsberger, 88, 91
    Margaret Harrensparger, 88
    Robert Harnsberger, 88
    Stephen Burgud, 15
    Stephen Harnsberger, 88, 92
    Stephen Harrensparger, 88
    Stephen Heerensperger, 88
    Steven Hansbarger, 78
    Steven Hansburger, 116
    Steven Harnsberger, 92
Harrensparger, see Harnsberger
Harrison
    Nathl. Harrison, 2
Harriss
    John Harriss, 95
    Joseph Harriss, 95
Hartley
    Rebecca Barbara Hartley, 100
Hausmann
    Anna Margaret Hausmann, 61
Hawkins
    Ann Hawkins, 60
    John Hawkins, 59, 60
Headlam
    Cecil Headlam, 3
Heer
    George Heer, 8
    Hans George Heer, 8
    Hans Heer, 8
Heerensperger, see Harnsberger
Heinrich
    Anna Maria Heinrich, 140
Helm
    Wesley Kenerly Helm, 73

Hendricks (Handrexson)
    Jacob Handrexson, 42
    Jacob Hendricks, 89
Hengsteler
    Anna Maria Hengsteler, 46, 50, 68, 89, 128
Hennings
    Samuel Hennings, 28
Henrich
    Johann Henrich, 91
Herr
    Hans Herr, 4
Hill
    Martha Hill, 108
Hirsch, see Deer
Hirsh, see Deer
Hite
    Isaac Hite, 72
Hitt
    Nancy Hitt, 102
Hix
    John Hix, 72
Hodge
    James D. Hodge, 85
    Louise F. Hodge, 85
Hoffman, see Huffman
Holdway (Holloway?)
    Tim Holdway, 60
Holl
    Lore Holl, 60
    Magdalena Holl, 60
Holloway
    Major Holloway, 12
Holsklau, see Holtzclaw
Holt (Hold)
    Anna Hold, 89
    Anna Maria Hold, 89
    Barbara Hold, 89
    Christopher Holt, 89, 90
    Elizabeth Holt, 81, 89, 90
    Eva Holt, 89
    George Holt, 89, 103, 111, 118
    Hans Michael Hold, 89, 145
    Jacob Holt, 90
    Jean Holt, 89
    John Holt, 90
    John Michael Holt, 24
    Jonas Hold, 89, 145
    Margaret Holt, 89
    Martin Hold, 89
    Mary Magdalena Holt, 89
    Michael Holt, 13, 20, 28, 30, 31, 32, 48, 81, 89, 110, 111, 113, 117, 118, 145
    Michael Holt, Jr., 89
    Nicholas Holt, 89
    Nicholas Holt, Jr., 129
    Peter Holt, 89
    Rachel Holt, 89

Holtzclaw (Holsklau)
    Ann Elizabeth Holtzclaw, 114
    B. C. Holtzclaw, 54, 55, 65, 69, 80, 90, 113, 117, 118, 120
    Elizabeth Holtzclaw, 90, 105
    Henrich Holsklau, 40
    Jacob Holsklau, 40
    Jacob Holtzclaw, 54, 90, 91, 121
    Jemima Holtzclaw, 61
    John Holtzclaw, 90
    Joseph Holtzclaw, 42, 90, 91, 105, 121, 132
    Mary Holtzclaw, 90, 121
    Susanna Holtzclaw, 61, 90, 121
Holtzhauser
    Michael Holtzhauser, 104
Home, see Hume
Hope
    Linda L. Hope, 96
House (Haus, Hauss)
    Aaron Hauss, 40, 90
    Aaron House, 49
    Adam House, 90
    Catherine Elizabeth House, 90
    Catherine House, 90, 111
    Catherine (Katy) House, 91
    Cathy House, 111
    Elisabeth House, 90
    Eva House, 69, 90
    Gary Lee House, 54
    George House, 90, 111
    Hannah House, 90
    Jacob Hauss, 40
    Jacob House, 90, 91
    John House, 90, 91
    Josua Hauss, 40
    Margaret House, 49, 69, 90, 91
    Maria Margaret House, 90
    Mary Magdalena House, 91
    Mary Margaret House, 49
    Matheis Hauss, 41
    Mathuis Haus, 40
    Mathuis Hauss, 39
    Mathuis Hauss, Jr., 40
    Matthias House, 49, 90, 100, 132
    Matthias House, Jr., 90
    Michael Hauss, 40
    Michael House, 90
    Moses House, 49, 90, 91
    Salome House, 90, 91
    Sara House, 49, 90
    Susanna House, 90
Huddle
    William P. Huddle, 40, 41, 53
Huffman (Hofman, Hoffman, Huphman)
    Agnes Hoffman, 88
    Agnes Huffman, 91, 92
    Ambrose Huffman, 91, 108

Andrew Huffman, 75
Anna Catharina Huffman, 91
Anna Catherine Huffman, 91
Anna Maria Hoffman, 74, 75
Anne Mary Huffman, 91
Annie Huffman, 85
Barbara Huffman, 99
Benjamin Huffman, 99
Catherine Hoffman, 80
Catherine Huffman, 92, 116
Daniel Hoffman, 54
Daniel Huffman, 69
Dietrich Hoffman, 62
Dietrich Hofman, 83
Elisabeth Catherina Huffman, 91
Elisabetha Huffman, 91, 123
Elisha Hoffmans, 86
Elizabeth Huffman, 49, 91, 120
Frederick Hoffman, 86
George Huffman, 69
Henry Hoffman, 74, 116, 123
Henry Huffman, 61, 84, 85, 88, 91, 92, 94, 108, 116, 127
Henry Huphman, 115
J. Huffman, 100
Jacob Huffman, 49, 99
Jemima Hoffman, 62
Jemima Huffman, 91
Johannes Hoffman, 54
John Hoffman, 26, 27, 28, 32, 45, 66, 88
John Huffman, 18, 24, 49, 61, 69, 70, 72, 75, 88, 91, 92, 95, 116, 127, 130
John Huffman, Jr., 69
John Huffman, Sr., 69
Jonas Hoffman, 80
Lewis Huffman, 91
Magdalena Huffman, 69, 75
Margaret Huffman, 88, 91
Maria Huffman, 110
Maria Elisabetha Huffman, 91
Mary Elizabeth Huffman, 91
Mary Hoffman, 45, 85, 86
Mary Huffman, 49, 91, 127
Mary Sabina Hoffman, 49, 66, 130
Michael Hoffman, 80
Nicholas Hoffman, 80
Sarah Huffman, 75
Susannah Huffman, 119
Teter Huffman, 91
Hume (Home)
Francis Hume, 92
George Home, 98
George Hume, 10, 62, 92, 103
Karl R. Hume, 92
Huphman, see Huffman

Hupp (Hoop)
Anne Hupp, 109
Balser Hupp, 92
Baltus Hoop, 92
Eberhard Hoop, 92
Elizabeth Hoop, 92
Everhard Hoop, 92
Everhart Hupp, 92
Francis Hoop, 92
George Hoop, 92
Jacob Hupp, 109
John Hoop, 92
John Hupp, 109
Philip Hoop, 61, 92
Hurt (Hart), 89
Anna Hurt, 66
Anna Maria Hart, 89
Ardys V. Hurt, 64, 123
Elizabeth Hart, 89
Eve Susanna Margaret Hart, 89
Eve Susanna Margaret Hurt, 66
Eve Susannah Margaret Hart, 66, 120
James Hurt, 66
Mary Hurt, 66
Moses Hart, 89
Sarah Hurt, 66
Silas Hart, 103
Valentin Hart, 89
Valentine Hart, 85
Hutcheson, Hutchinson
Robert Hutcheson, 91
Robert Hutchinson, 28

Isenhauer
Nicholas Isenhauer, 104
Isom (Eastham?)
Maria Isom, 92

Jäger, see Yager
Jackson
Elizabeth Jackson, 124
Thomas Jackson, 124
Jacobi (Jacobus, Jacoby)
Daniel Jacobi, 92
Daniel Jacobus, 92
John Daniel Jacoby, 92
John Francis Jacoby, 142
John Francis Lucas Jacobi, 92
John Francis Lucas Jacoby, 100
Jacobus, see Jacobi
Jaeger, see Yager
James
John James, 109
Jeger, see Yager

Jesse
    Johann Jesse, 40
    John Jesse, 93
    Susannah Jesse, 70, 93
Jewell
    Jefferey Jewell, 96
Joel
    William Joel, 93
John
    Ellen John, 50
Johnson
    Elizabeth Yates Johnson, 55, 130
    Timothy Johnson, 94
Johnston
    Thomas Johnston, 59
Jones
    Catherine Jones, 66
    Hanna Jones, 126
    Henry Jones, 86, 109
    Henry Z Jones, 71
    Henry Z Jones, Jr., 8
    Hugh Jones, Rev., 10
    Jane Jones, 96
    Patsy Jones, 96
    Thomas Jones, 72
Joyner
    Peggy Shomo Joyner, 27, 31, 52, 86

Kabler (Cob(b)ler, Kap(p)ler,)
    Anna Kabler, 93
    Barbara Cobler, 15
    Barbara Kabler, 93
    Christoph Kabler, 93
    Christopher Kabler, 93
    Conrad Kabler, 93
    Fredereick Kabler, 33
    Frederick Cob(b)ler, 15, 33, 76, 89
    Frederick Kabler, 93, 94
    Frederick Kappler, 149
    Fredric Kapler, 8
    Harvey Kabler, 93
    Joan (Joanna) Kabler, 93
    Lewis Kabler, 93
    Martha Kabler, 93
    Mary Kabler, 93
    Nicholas Kabler, 61, 93
    Prudence Kabler, 93
    Susanna Kabler, 93, 130
    Thomas Kabler, 93
    William Kabler, 93
Käfer (Kaffer, Kaifer, Kefer, Keiffer) (see also Cofer)
    7, 148
    Anna Magdalena Käfer, 94
    Anna Maria Käfer, 77
    Apollonia Käfer, 44, 67, 94, 148
    Barbara Käfer, 94, 127
    Conrad Käfer, 94
    Dorothy Käfer, 74, 78, 94
    Elizabeth Käfer, 81, 86, 94
    John Käfer, 94
    Magdelena Käfer, 94
    Margaret Käfer, 46, 48, 77, 78, 94
    Margaretha Käfer, 94
    Mary Käfer, 50, 94, 122, 123
    Michael Käfer, 2, 13, 20, 28, 32, 45, 48, 74, 77, 78, 86, 94, 103, 114, 120, 122, 123, 127, 148
    Michael Keiffer, 32
    Wolf Michael Kefer, 9
    Wolfgang Käfer, 94
Kaffer, see Käfer
Kahl (Call, Caul, Cawl)
    Adam Kahl, 94
    Anne Mary Kahl, 95
    Christiana Kahl, 95
    Daniel Kahl, 94
    Dorothy Kahl, 94
    Eva Kahl, 95
    Henry Kahl, 94
    John Kahl, 94
    Margaret Call, 107
    Margaret Elizabeth Kahl, 95
    Maria Margaret Kahl, 95
    Wilhelm Kahl, 94
    William Call, 94
    William Caul, 124
    William Cawl, 94, 115
Kaifer see Käfer
Kaines (Kains, Kynes, Kyner)
    John Kains, 22, 28, 95, 116
    John Kynes, 33
    John Kyner, 95
Kapler, see Kabler
Kappeler, see Kabler
Kappler (Keppler)
Kavanaugh
    Philemon Kavanaugh, 81
Kefer, see Käfer
Keiffer, see Käfer
Keister, see Küster
Keith
    A. L. Keith, 69, 130
    Leslie Keith, 53
Kelly
    William Kelly, 76
Kemper
    Willis Kemper, 14, 48
Kennerl(e)y
    Thomas Kennerley, 28, 59
Kenszle, see Kinslow
Kercheval
    S. Kercheval, 53, 65

Kerker (Kirker), 26
    Andrew Kerker, 15, 20, 24, 26, 69, 73, 95, 100
    Andrew Kirker, 20, 26, 70, 95
    Anna Barbara Kerker, 69, 78, 95
    Barbara Kerker, 15, 74
    Margaret Kerker, 95
    Margeritta Kerker, 15
    Michael Kerker, 95
    William Kerker, 95
Kethley
    T. W. Kethley, Jr., 53
Kiester, see Küster
Kilby (Kilbee, Kilvy)
    Agatha Kilbee, 61
    John Kilvy, 28, 59
King
    James King, 20, 28
    Joseph King, 76, 131
    Robert King, 76
Kinslow (Censley, Genessle, Gensle, Kensel, Kenselow, Kenszle, Kuenzle, Kuntzly, Kunzle)
    Aaron Kinslow, 96
    Adam Kinslow, 96
    Ambrose Kinslow, 96
    Andrew Carpenter Kinslow, 95
    Andrew Kinslow, 96
    Catrine Kinslow, 95
    Conrad Gensle, 39
    Conrad Kenszle, 42
    Conrad Kinslow, 95, 96
    Conrad Kinslow, Sr., 95
    Conrad Kuenzle, 49, 62
    Conrad Kuntzley, 96
    Elizabeth Kinslow, 96
    Ezekiel Kinslow, 95, 96
    Joshua Kinslow, 96
    Katrina Kinslow, 95
    Margaret (Peggy) Kinslow, 96
    Nancy Jane Kinslow, 96
    Nimrod Kinslow, 96
    Rachel Kuenzle, 62, 95
    Savina (Sabina) Kinslow, 95
Kirk
    Jeremiah Kirk, 122
Kirker, see Kerker
Klar, see Clore
Klug
    Elizabeth Klug, 97
    Ephraim Klug, 71, 80, 97
    Ephraim Klugge, 109
    Eva Klug, 97
    Georg Samuel Klug, 56
    George Samuel Klug, 31, 48, 95, 96, 97, 98, 100, 112
    Magdalena Klug, 100
    Magdalene Klug, 97
    Michael Klug, 77, 83, 97, 108, 113
    Rachel Klug, 108
    Samuel Klug, 71, 91, 97
    Susanna Klug, 71, 97, 98
    Susannah Klug, 71
Knittle
    W. A. Knittle, 53
Knot
    Nicholas Knot, 97
Knuesbay
    John Knuesbay, 94, 115
Koch, see Cook
Krauter (Sauter?)
    Henry Krauter, 32
Krekel, see Crecelius
Kruger, see Crigler
Kuenzle, see Kinslow
Kuhr
    Georg Kuhr, 42
Kuntz
    Elizabeth Catherine Kuntz, 117
    Johannes Kuntz, 117
Küster (Kiester), 54
    Georg Kiester, 95
    Johannes Küster, 95
    Margaretha Kiester, 95
    Mary Küster, 122
Kyner, **Kynes** see Kaines
Kyzer
    Andrew Kyzer, 109

Ladenberger
    Ralph (Rudolph) Ladenberger, 100
Lair
    Elizabeth Lair, 122
Lang, see Long
Langenbühler, 98
Le Campion
    Elizabeth Le Campion, 102
    Francis Le Campion, 102
Leathers, see Leatherer
Leatherer (Leather(s), Lederer)
    Anna Maria Lederer, 98
    Elizabeth Lederer, 98, 112
    Johann Paulus Lederer, 98
    John Leathers, 98
    Joshua Joseph Leathers, 98
    Margaret Leatherer, 73, 74, 98
    Maria Magdalena Lederer, 98
    Mary Leatherer, 98
    Mary Lederer, 112
    Michael Leathers, 98
    Michale Leather, 41
    Nicholas Leatherer, 98
    Nicolas Lederer, 39

Paul Leatherer, 73, 98
Paul Ledderer, 97
Paul Lederer, 74, 140
Paulus Leatherer, 41
Samuel Leatherer, 98
Samuel Lederer, 112
Susannah Leatherer, 98
Lederer, see Leatherer
Lehman
Georg Lehman, 42, 98, 99
Georg Lehman, Jr., 98. 99
Joh. Lehman, 99
Michael Lehman, 98
Lentz
Rev. H. Lentz, 53
Lewis
Florence Virginia Fray Lewis, 54, 86
Sarah Aylor Lewis, 54
Virginia Fray Lewis, 68, 118
Leyerele (Leyrle, Lyerly, Lyrle)
Barbara Leyrle, 99
Catherine Leyrle, 99
Christina Leyrle, 99
Christopher Leyrle, 99
Christopher Lyrle, 99
Jacob Leyrle, 99
Johann Christoph Leyrle, 99
Margaret Leyrle, 99
Peter Leyrle, 99
Zachariah Leyrle, 99
Zacharias Leyerle, 99
Lillard
Thomas Lillard, 76
Liner (Lyner)
Henry Liner, 72
Henry Lyner, 73
Lingel
Elizabeth Lingel, 88
Jacob Lingel, 88
Lipp (Lip)
Anna Maria Lipp, 99
Caroline Lipp, 99
Daniel Lipp, 99
Elizabeth Lipp, 99
Friedrich Lipp, 42, 99
Henrich Lipp, 39
Henry Lipp, 99
Jacob Lip, 88
Jacob Lipp, 40, 49, 99, 100
Margaret Lip, 88
Margaret Lipp, 49, 99
Maria Lip, 99
Thomas Lipp, 99
Little
Barbara Vines Little, 87
Charity Little, 107

Lockhart
Jean C. Lockhart, 89
Long (Lang, Lung)
George Lang, 15, 20, 24, 32, 93, 149
George Long, 16, 20, 24, 28, 32, 70, 71, 79, 111
George Lung, 32, 100
Hans George Long, 8
John George Long, 100
Mildred (Wright) Long, 115
Rebecca Lang, 15
Rebecca Long, 100
Lotspeich, 7
Christopher Lotspeich, 100
Johann Christopher Lotspeich, 100
Johann Wilhelm Lotspeich, 100
Johanna Friederika Lotspeich, 92, 100, 142
Magdalena Lotspeich, 100
Rebecca Barbara Lotspeich, 100
Robert Lotspeich, 100
William Lotspeich, 97
Love
Florene Love, 52
Lowry
John Lowry, 107
Loyd
John Loyd, 110
Lucas
Elizabeth Lucas, 59
Francis Lucas, 59
Lung, see Long
Luttmann
Mary Margaret Luttman, 120
Lutz
Daniel Lutz, 100
Maria Lutz, 100
Michael Lutz, 100
Susanna Lutz, 100
Lyner, see Liner
Lynn
William Lynn, 28, 70
Lyrle, see Leyerele

Maier, see Moyer
Majer, see Moyer
Mayer, see Moyer
Majors
Elizabeth Majors, 97
Frances Major, 107
Franky Majors, 100
Malden
John Malden, 18, 28
Richard Malden, 18, 20, 28
Mansfield
Marietta Mansfield, 96

Manspile
    Ann Manspile, 101
    Anna Manspile, 101
    Elizabeth Manspeil, 130
    Jacob Manspeil, 88
    Jacob Manspile, 22, 28, 33, 96, 101, 116
    Jacob Manspoil, 101
    John Manspile, 101
    Margaret Manspile, 101
    Mary Manspile, 101

Marbes (Marbus)
    Catherine Marbes, 101
    Johannes Marbes, 101
    John Marbes, 114
    John Marbus, 114

Marshal
    Jane Marshal, 63

Martin
    Donald J. Martin, 60
    E.P. Martin, 10
    George Martin, 22, 28, 101
    James E. Martin, 10
    Josiah Martin, 93
    Mickey Martin, 55, 124

Maubars
    Johann Leonhard Maubars, 102
    Maria Apollonia Maubars, 102

Mauck
    Barbara Mauck, 101
    Daniel Mauk, 88, 101
    Elizabeth Mauck, 101
    Matthias Mauck, 101

Maulden
    Richard Maulden, 24

Maxwell
    James Maxwell, 28

McDonald
    Margaret McDonald, 126

McKenzie
    John McKenzie, 28

McKey
    Robert McKey, 122

McMackin
    James Alexander McMackin, Sr., 104

McMahan
    Morgan McMahan, 107

McNeil
    Patrick McNeil, 88

Medley
    Jacob Medley, 98

Mercklin
    Anna Maria Mercklin, 48, 67, 148
    Maria Catharina Mercklin, 117

Merdten
    Johann Jost Merdten, 47

Michaels
    Francis Michaels, 117

MichlEkler (Milcher)
    Anna Catharina MichEkler, 101
    Anna Margaretha MichlEkler, 101
    Hans Michael MichlEkler, 101
    Hans Michel Milcher, 9, 101
    Maria Parvara Milcher, 9, 101
    Sophia Catharina MichlEkler, 101
    Sophia Catharina Milcher, 9, 101

Mickell
    John Mickell, 31, 82

Mickey
    Mary F. Mickey, 64, 128

Mielke
    Andreas Mielke, 5, 7, 31, 45, 46, 51, 83

Millbanks
    John Millbanks, 62, 63
    Mary Millbanks, 66, 63

Miller
    Achsah Miller, 102
    Adam Miller, 102
    Anna Miller, 102
    Barbara Miller, 129
    Elizabeth (Betty) Miller, 102
    George Miller, 101, 102
    Henry Miller, 42, 101, 102, 104, 112
    Jacob Miller, 76, 102, 129
    Jacob Miller, Jr., 129
    Jacob Miller, Sr., 129
    John Miller, 102
    Margaret Miller, 102
    Maria Margaretha Miller, 101
    Mary (Mollie) Miller, 102
    Melvin L. Miller, 54
    Nancy Miller, 102
    Rebecca Miller, 129
    Sarah Miller, 102
    Sophia Miller, 102
    Susanna Catherine Miller, 102
    Susanna Miller, 101, 102
    Susannah Miller, 104

Mires, see Moyer

Mitchell
    Margaret Mitchell, 90
    Mark Mitchell, 90

Möller
    Henrich Möller, 56, 102, 119

Moir, see Moyer

Mood
    Christian Mood, 120

Morgan
    Charles Morgan, 76

Morton
    James Morton, 102
    Rebecca Morton, 102
    Susanna Morton, 102

Mossbarger
    Catherine Mossbarger, 69
    Samuel Mossbarger, 69
Motz (Mutz, Mutts) 16, 18
    Elizabeth Motz, 103
    Galli Motz, 102
    Johann Mutz, 30
    Johannes Motz, 102
    John Motz, 12, 15, 20, 28, 30, 70, 83, 88, 102, 103
    John Mutts, 70
    Maria Pelona Motz, 15, 102
Moyer (Maier, Moyers, Mayer, Mires, Moir, Myers)
    Abraham Mayer, 97
    Adam Mayer, 41, 104
    Amelia Mayer, 104
    Anna Barbara Maier, 44, 66
    Anna Barbara Mayer, 46, 104
    Barbara Majer, 103
    Barbara Mayer, 63
    Barbara Moyer, 103
    Barbara Myers, 104
    Catherine Mayer, 104
    Catherine Moer, 104
    Catherine Moyer, 103, 104
    Christoph Maier, Jr., 42
    Christoph Mayer, 42
    Christopher Mayer, Jr., 104
    Christopher Moir, 94
    Christopher Moyer, 103, 104
    Christopher Moyers, Sr., 104
    Clemens Meyer, 161
    Elizabeth Myers, 104
    Geo. Moyers, 32
    Georg Meyer, 161
    George Meyer, 20
    George Moyer, 13, 14, 20, 24, 26, 28, 66, 103, 104, 105, 117, 127, 136
    George Moyer, Jr., 80, 104, 105
    George Moyer, Sr., 103, 104, 105
    George Moyers, 32
    Hannah Myers, 104
    Hans George Majer, 103
    Jacob Mayer, 104
    Magdalena Mayer/Moyer, 104
    Margaret Mayer, 104
    Maria Mayer, 104
    Mary Catharine Moyer, 104
    Mary Myers/Mires, 63, 104
    Michael Mires, 67
    Michael Moyer, 103
    Michael Myers, 63, 104
    Philip Mayer, 104
    Sarah Moyer, 80, 104, 105
    Susanna Mayer, 104
    Susannah Myers, 104

Müller
    Anna Dorothea, 128
Muhlenberg
    Henry Melchior Muhlenberg, 56, 96
Murray
    Frances Murray, 60
    James Murray, 60
    Susannah Murray 60
Murrey
    Humphrey Murrey, 122

Nägelin (Hägelin)
    Anna Barbara Hagelin, 89
Nash
    William Nash, 109
Neff (Naf, Naef)
    Anna Neff, 88
Nelson
    Christian Nelson, 103
    Elizabeth Nelson, 103
    John Christopher Nelson, 103
    Linda Nelson, 63
    Philip Nelson, 103
Newman
    Delilah Newman, 60
    Muscoe Newman, 60
Nicholson
    Robert Nicholson, 90
Nicklos
    Jacob Nicklos, 95
Nugent
    Nell Marion Nugent, 52
Nonnenmacher, Nunenmacher, Noonemacher
    Barbara Nonnenmacher, 123
    George Henry Nonnenmacher, 105
    George Ludwig Nonnenmacher, 106
    George Ludwig Noonemacher, 105
    John Nunnenmacher, 105
    Lewis (Ludwig) Noonemacher, 105
    Lewis Nunnamacher, 105, 123
    Ludwig Nunenmacher, 42
    Ludwig Nunnemacher, 39, 105

Oats (Utz)
    Margaret Rockefeller Oats, 122
Oberg
    Suzee Oberg, 117
Ockert
    Anna Maria Ockert, 112
    Johannes Ockert, 112
    Maria Eleanora Ockert, 111, 112
Ohlscheitt
    Conrad Ohlscheit, 105
    Henry Ohlscheitt, 105

Ohlschlager
    Johannes Eberhard Ohlschlager, 105
Oldham
    John Oldham, 92
O'Neal (O'Neil)
    Agnes Margaret O'Neal, 73
    Margaret O'Neal, 73
    Margaret (Peggy) O'Neil, 89
    Michael O'Neal, 73, 125
    Michael O'Neall, 33
    William O'Neal, 73
Orkney
    Lord Orkney, 11
Otes, see Utz
Ouds, see Utz
Ouell, see Yowell
Owell, see Yowell

Padget
    Mary C. Padget, 98
Painter, see Bender
Pamgarner, see Baumgardner
Pander, see Bender
Parlur, see Barlow
Pater
    Conrad Pater, 32
Paulitz, 68, 103
    Catherine Paulitz, 105
    Katherin Paulitz, 15
    Margaret Paulitz, 15, 105
    Philip Paulitz, 105
    Phillip Paulitz, 13, 15
    Rose Paulitz, 15, 101, 105
Peck
    Barbara Peck, 105
    John Peck, 105
    Rosina Peck, 105
Pecker, see Blankenbaker
Peemon, see Beemon
Penn
    William Penn, 40, 41
Perler, see Barlow
Perry, 105
Persinger
    Mary Persinger, 124
Philips (Phillips)
    David Philips, 20, 28
    Thomas Phillips, 18, 28
    William Phillips, 72
Pickett
    James Pickett, 31, 82
    Lousia Pickett, 96
Pickler, 148
    John Blanket Pickler, 104
Pierse
    William Pierse, 82

Pinnegar (Pinegar, Benninger, Pinnegar)
    Anna Christina Beninger, 106
    Catherine Pinegar, 106
    Christine Pinegar, 106
    Elizabeth Pinnegar, 106
    James Pinager, 106
    John Pinager, 106
    Kevin Peniger, 106
    Leonard Pinegar, 106
    Magdalena Pinegar, 106
    Mary Magdalena Pinegar, 106
    Mary Pinegar, 106
    Mary Pinnagor, 106
    Matthias Pinager, 106
    Matthias Pinnegar, 106
    Peter Beninger, 106
    Peter Benninger, 106
    Peter Pinegar, 79, 106
    Peter Pinnagor, 106
    Peter Pinnegar, 106
    Peter Pinnegor, 106
    William Pinager, 106
    William Pinegar, 106
    William Pinegar, Jr., 106
Plancabeaner, **Plankabeaner**, see Blankenbaker
Plankenbühler, see Blankenbaker
Plunkabeaner, see Blankenbaker
Plunkapee, see Blankenbaker
Pool
    Mary Magdalena Pool, 117
Porteus
    James Porteus, 118
Pottenger
    John Pottenger, 108
Powell
    Ambrose Powell, 109
    Ann Powell, 80
    Benjamin Powell, 104
    Elias Powell, 61
    William Powell, 122
Preiss (Price), 106
Prial, see Broyles
Printz
    Georg Printz, 106
Proctor
    Catherine Proctor, 71
Prosie
    Jacob Prosie, 76, 106
Pulliam
    Sarah Pulliam, 81

Quarles
    Roger Quarles, 120

Raüser (Racer, Rasor, Razor, Reiser)
    Catherine Rasor, 107, 118
    Christian Racer, 100
    Christian Rasor, 100, 106, 107
    Daniel Reiser, 40
    Elizabether Racer, 100, 107
    Frances Racer, 79
    Georg Reiser, 39, 42
    George Adam Raüser, 106, 107
    George Racer, 100
    George Rasor, 100, 105, 106, 107
    George Razor, Sr., 106
    Jacob Rasor, 107, 110, 115
    Margaret Razor, 100, 106
    Peter Racer, 79
    Peter Rasor, 79, 106, 107
    Susanna Racer, 79
    Susannah Rasor, 107, 115

Railsback (Ralsbach, Reesbach, Rehlsbach)
    Anna Maria Railsback, 107
    Anna Railsback, 107
    Annie Railsback, 108
    Catharine Railsback, 108, 121
    Catherine Railsback, 121
    Daniel Railsback, 107, 108
    David Railsback, 107
    Edward Railsback, 107
    Elizabeth Railsback, 107
    Guy Railsback, 108
    Hans George Rehlsback, 108
    Henry Railsback, 94, 95, 107, 108
    Henry Railsback, Jr., 94, 107
    Henry Railsback, Sr., 107
    Henry Ralsback, 91
    Jacob Railsback, 108
    Johann Heinrich Rehlsback, 107
    Johannes Railsback, 108
    Johannes Reesbach, 108
    Johannes Rehlsback, 108
    John Railsback, 49, 97, 107, 108, 121
    Leah (Layanne) Railsback, 108
    Lydda Railsback, 107
    Margaret Railsback, 107
    Maria Catharina Rehlsback, 108
    Mary Railsback, 91, 107, 108
    Rachel Railsback, 108
    Rosa (Rosannah) Railsback, 107
    Sarah Railsback, 107
    Susannah Railsback, 108, 110
    Thomas Fisher Railsback, 108

Randolph
    Henry Randolph, 104

Rausch, see Rouse

Raussen, see Rouse

Reapman
    Christian Reapman, 99

Redman
    Jacob Redman, 108
    Peter Redman, 108

Reesbach, see Railsback

Rehlsbach, see Railsback

Reiss
    Kilian Reiss, 8

Reichert
    Agnes Reichert, 60
    Barbara Reichert, 60
    Hans Reichert, 60
    Ulrich Reichert, 60

Reiner (Riner, Ryner), 140
    Abirhart (Eberhard) Riner, 41
    Barbara Reiner, 74
    Barnet Reiner, 86
    Christian Reiner, 42, 84, 109
    Christopher Reiner, 84, 109
    Christopher (Christian) Reiner, 62
    Christopher Ryner, 75
    Daniel Reiner, 109
    Eberhard Reiner, 39
    Eberhardt Reiner, 108, 109
    Elizabeth Reiner, 48, 67, 84, 109
    Hans Dieterich Reiner, 108
    Johannes Reiner, 108
    John Christian Reiner, 109
    John Dieter Reiner, 74
    John Reiner, 109
    Julian Reiner, 86
    Maria Magdalena Reiner, 113
    Maria Sarah Reiner, 75, 109
    Mary Barbara Reiner, 108
    Mary Magdalena Reiner, 109
    Mary Margarethe Reiner, 109
    Mary Reiner, 109
    Mary Sarah Reiner, 74, 75, 109
    Sarah Reiner, 109

Reiser, see Raüser

Render
    Joseph Render, 81

Rice
    William Rice, 20

Richter
    Hans Jacob Richter, 47

Rider
    Catherine, 79

Rinehart (Reinhart, Rynehard)
    Elizabeth Rinehart, 109
    George Rindhart, 86, 109
    George Rinehart, 109
    Jonas Rynehart, 109
    Matthias Rheinhart, 122
    Matthias Rinehart, 109
    Matthias Rindhart, 109
    Matthias Rynehart, 109

Michael Rindhart, 109
Michael Rindhear, 109
Michell Rynehard, 109
Riner, see Reiner
Rise
Benjamin Rise, 109
Franke Rise, 109
Hanna Rise, 109
Rivercomb
Jemima Rivercomb, 132
Roan
Major Roan, 116
Roberts
John Roberts, 88
Rodeheaver, (Rothöfer)
David Rothöfer, 109
David Rodeheaver, 109
Johannes Rothöfer, 109
John Rodeheifer, 109
John Rodeheaver, 109
Joseph Rodeheaver, 109
Maria Rothöfer, 109
Sarah Rodeheifer, 109
Roeber
A. G. Roeber, 53
Roebuck
William Roebuck, 127
Rogers
Burgess Rogers, 102
Sophia Rogers, 102
Rösser
Klaus Rösser, 44
Rohleder
Anna Catharina Rohleder, 59
Maria Magdalena Rohleder, 59
Rohrbach
Lewis Bunker Rohrbach, 8, 71
Rol
Dorotha Rol, 131
Martin Rol, 131
Rookstool (Rückstuhl)
Ann Rookstool, 111
Catherine Rookstool, 111
Cathy Rookstool, 111
Elizabeth (Betsy) Rookstool, 111
Eve Rookstool, 111
George Rookstool, 91, 110
George Rookstool, Jr., 111
Henry Rookstool, 111
Jacob Rookstool, 111
John Rookstool, 111
Olive Rookstool, 110
Polly Rookstool, 111
Sally Rookstool, 111
Soloman Rookstool, 110
Susanna Rookstool, 111
William Rookstool, 111
Rootes
Philip Rootes, 121
Rose
William Rose, 28
Rossel
Elizabeth Rossel, 109
Maria Rossel, 109
Mary Rossel, 109
Rothgeb
Catharina Rothgeb, 88
Rousch, see Rouse
Rouse (Rausch, Raussen, Rousch)
Adam Rouse, 110
Ann Rouse, 110
Barbara Rouse, 79, 110
Betsy Rouse, 110
Catherine Rouse, 110
Edward Rouse, 110
Elijah Rousch, 40
Elizabeth Rausch, 110
Elizabeth Rouse, 110
Ephraim Rausch, 40
Ephraim Rouse, 49, 79, 110
Frances Rouse, 110
Georg Rausch, 40
George Rouse, 110
Ibrahim (Abraham) Rausch, 110
Jacob Rausch, 40
Jacob Rouse, 110
Johannes Rausch, 40
John Raussen, 110
John Rouse, 20, 28, 32, 54, 110
John Rowse, 32
Joseph Rausch, 42
Joseph Rouse, 108, 110, 120
Lewis Rouse, 87, 111
Ludwig Rausch 40
Mardin Rausch, 41
Maria Rouse, 110
Martin Rausch, 110
Martin Rouse, 110
Martin Roush, 39
Mary Rausch, 110
Mary Rouse, 110, 119
Matheus Rausch, 39
Matthias Rausch, 110
Matthias Rouse, 26, 70, 110
Michael Rouse, 110
Nancy E. Rouse, 54, 110
Nicholas Rausch, 40
Robert Rouse, 110
Samuel Rausch, 41
Samuel Rouse, 110
Susanna Rouse, 110
Roush, see Rouse

Rowe (Row)
    Adam Rowe, 91, 109
    Anne Rowe, 91, 109
    Benjamin Rowe, 109
    George Rowe, 109
    George Rowe, Jr., 109
    Jacob Row, 109
    William Rowe, 109
Rowse, see Rouse
Rucker
    John Rucker, 20, 28, 89
    Margaret Rucker, 49, 84
    Peter Rucker, 89
    Thornton Rucker, 116
Rungo
    Christian Rungo, 111
Ruop
    Hans Jacob Ruop, 68
    Ursula Ruop, 68, 143
Rush
    Benjamin Rush, 18, 28, 121, 122
    Jemima Rush, 122
    William Rush, 18, 28, 95, 121, 127
Russell
    Michael Russell, 79, 97, 100
    William Russell, 82
Ryner, see Reiner

Sampson
    William Sampson, 106
Samuel
    Moses Samuel, 132
Sauder (Sauter), 5
    Barbara Sauder, 99
Schad, Schade
    Catherina Schad, 111
    Friederich J. Schad, 111
    Friedrich Julius Schad, 40, 111
    Georg Philip Schad, 40
    Julius Schade, 111
    Philip Schad, 111
Schaible, see Sheible
Scheff, see Chelf
Scheible, see Sheible
Scheitle
    Ursula Scheitle, 88
Schilling
    Anna Dorothea Schilling, 60, 115
Schleicher
    Mary Margaret, 74
Schlötzer
    Anna Maria Schlötzer, 98
Schlatter (Slaughter), 5
    Conrad Slaughter, 112
    Elisabeth Schlatter, 112
    Elisabetha Schlatter, 112
    George Schlatter, 39, 112
    George Slaughter, 112
    John Schlatter, 112
    Margaretha Schlatter, 112
    Maria Schlatter, 112
    Rosina Schlatter, 112
Schlucter, see Sluchter
Schneider, see Snyder
Schnell
    Susanna Christina Schnell, 71
Schnepff, see Chelf
Schnidow, see Snyder
Schön
    Anna Barbara Schön, 43, 46, 64, 66
    Maria Barbara Schön, 43
    Quirin Schön, 4343
Schott
    Georg Sigmund Schott, 76
    Maria Euphrosina Schott, 76
Schreiber
    John Daniel Schreiber, 98
Schreiner-Yantis
    Netti Schreiner-Yantis, 52
Schultz
    Johann Christian Schultz, 30, 117, 143
Schuricht
    H.Schuricht, 53
Schuster
    Elisabeth Catherina Schuster, 91
    Elisabeth Schuster, 116
    Elizabeth Catherine Schuster, 74
Schwarbach
    Johannes Schwarbach, 56, 102, 112
    Margaretha Schwarbach, 112
    Rev. Schwarbach, 95
Scott
    Captain Scott, 8, 9, 15, 48
    W.W. Scott, 53
Seidelmann
    Eva Seidelmann, 86, 152, 153
Selig
    Robert Selig, 84
Sellers
    Henry Sellers, 95
    Susannah Sellers, 86
Selser
    Mary Selser, 112
Seppach
    Abraham Seppach, 125
    Maria Barbara Seppach, 125
Seraphim
    Hannah Seraphim, 90
Shafer
    John Shafer, 113
Shanklin
    Robert Shanklin, 95

Shearer
    Anna Shearer, 101
    James Shearer, 101
    Mary Shearer, 60
Sheible (Chively, Schaible, Scheible, Shively)
    145, 146, 155
    Anna Elizabetha Chively, 9
    Anna Elisabeth Schaible, 111
    Anna Elizabeth Sheible, 111
    Anna Maria Chively, 9
    Anna Maria Schaible, 111
    Anna Martha Chively, 9
    Anna Martha Schaible, 111
    Elizabeth Scheible, 89, 111
    George Sheible, 13, 24, 28, 30, 32, 44, 89, 111,
        112, 117, 155
    George Shively, 26, 32
    George Shuble, 111
    Hans George Scheible, 111
    Hans Jerich Chively, 9
    Hans Scheiblin, 112
    Hanss Jürgen Scheibeler, 112
    Johann Georg Schaible, 111
    Maria Clora Chively, 9
    Maria Clara Scheible, 111
    Maria Eleanora Scheible, 111, 112
Ship
    Richard Ship, 106
Shirley
    Elizabeth Shirley, 87
    James Shirley, 87
    Nancy Ann Shirley, 87
Shively, see Sheible
Shotwell
    John Shotwell, 28
Shuble
    George Shuble, 111
Shuck
    Larry G. Shuck, 54, 84
    Larry Shuck, 64, 81, 123
Sibler
    Barbara Sibler, 102
    Michael Sibler, 102
    Susanna Sibler, 102
Sieber
    Anna Maria Sieber, 130, 138
Simms, **Sims**
    Sarah Simms, 100
    Sarah Sims, 107
Sipes
    Ina Ritchie Sipes, 69
Slater
    Conrad Slater, 112
    George Slater, 24
Slaughter
    Gabriel Slaughter, 132
    George Slaughter, 20, 28
    John Slaughter, 132
    Smith Slaughter, 132
    Thomas Slaughter, 132
    William Slaughter, 132
Sluchter, **Schlucter**, 145, 146
    Anna Barbara Schlucter, 43
    Conrad Schlucter, 112
    Conrad Sluchter, 112
    Hendrich Schlucter, 9
    Henerich Schlucter, 43
    Henry Schlucter, 33, 66, 67, 83, 112, 113
    Johann Jacob Schlucter, 43
    Sarah Schlucter, 83, 112, 113
Smith (Schmidt)
    Adam Smith, 114
    Ann Smith, 62
    Anna Creda Smiedt, 9
    Anna Magdalena Smith, 62, 65, 78, 101, 114,
        120
    Anna Margaret Smith, 113
    Anna Margaretha Smith, 113
    Anna Schmidt, 114
    Catherine Smith, 101, 114
    Christopher Smith, 108, 113
    David Smith, 104
    Elizabeth Smith, 114
    Godfrey Smith, 113
    Hans Michael Schmidt, 113
    Hans Michael Smiedt, 9
    Hans Michael Smith, 113
    Henry Smith, 109
    Isaac Smith, 124
    Isaac Smith, Sr., 49, 84
    J. Michael Schmidt, 56
    Johann Michael Smith, 115
    Johann Schmidt, 7, 39
    Johann Smith, 113
    Johannes Schmid, 42
    Johannes Schmidt, 39
    John Michael Smith, Jr., 61, 66, 101, 114
    John Smith, 41, 113, 114
    Katherina Smith, 15
    Leah Smith, 113
    Magdalena Smith, 94
    Maria Magdalena Smith, 113
    Mary Smith, 62, 113, 114
    Matthaus Smith, 113
    Matthew Smith, 15, 28, 32, 62, 64, 97, 113
    Matthew Smith, Jr., 113
    Matthew Smith, Sr., 113
    Matthias Schmidt, 7
    Matthias Smith, 20, 62, 113
    Matthias Smith, Jr., 113
    Michael Schmidt, 39, 112
    Michael Schmidt, Jr., 40
    Michael Schmidt, Sr., 40
    Michael Schmitt, 41

Michael Smith, 13, 20, 28, 30, 32, 70, 86, 89, 94, 113–117, 120, 121, 125
Michael Smith, Jr., 62, 72, 78
Michael Smith, Sr., 114
Nathaniel Smith, 104
Nicholas Smith, 109, 113
Nicholas Smith, Jr., 42
Nicolas Smith, 41, 97
Nicolaus Schmidt, Jr., 39
Nicolaus Schmidt, Sr., 39
Regina Catharina Schmidt, 7
Regina Catharina Smith, 113
Richard Smith, 54
Samuel Schmidt, 40
Samuel Smith, 113
Sarah Ann Smith, 114
Susanna Smith, 66
Susannah Smith, 114
Winifred Smith, 49, 84
Zachariah Smith, 114
Zacharias Smith, 42
Zachary Smith, 121

Smither
Joseph Smither, 115

Snyder (Schneider, Snider), 55
Adam Snyder, 115
Anna Dorothea Schneider, 115
Anna Magdalena Schneider, 60, 115, 119, 135
Dorathy Snyder, 9
Dorothea Synder, 115
Dorothy Snyder, 15
Elizabeth Snyder, 80, 115
Hans Heinrich Schneider, 115
Hendrick Snyder, 13
Henrich Schneider, 7
Henry Schneider, 18
Henry Snider, 18, 28, 32, 60, 119, 120
Henry Snyder, 9, 15, 88, 115
John Sneider, 94
John Snider, 27, 28
John Snyder, 55, 115, 116
Joseph Schneider, 40
Joseph Snyder, 115
Lucy Snider, 86
Margaret Snyder, 74, 75, 80, 115
Martha Snyder, 116
Mary Margaret Snyder, 115
Mary Snyder, 115, 116
Michael Schneider, 39, 42, 109
Michael Snyder, 80, 115, 116
Nancy Snider, 85
Philip Schneider, 39, 112
Philip Snider, 75
Philip Snyder, 41, 55, 74, 80, 115
Samuel Snyder, 76, 115
Schnidow, 16
Susanna Snyder, 100, 107, 115

Southall
Edward Southall, 18, 28

Souther (Sauder, Sauther)
Catherina Sauther, 116
Catharina Souther, 116
Henry Souther, 78, 116
Jacob Sauder, 116
Jacob Sauther, 116
Jacob Souther, 116, 126
Michael Souther, 116

Southwell
Edward Southwell, 72

Spade
Anna Maria Spade, 89
John Spade, 89

Spencer
Edward Spencer, 72

Spessard
Howard Lehman Spessard, 99

Spilman
Catharine Spilman, 116
Harman Spilman, 79, 95, 116
John Spilman, 116

Spotswood
Alexander, 1, 2-4, 9-14, 30, 44, 45, 47, 59, 61, 67, 68, 72-74, 77, 83, 89, 91, 94, 103, 105, 111, 113, 119, 127, 130, 148

Spurlin
Helen Spurlin, 55, 124
Squires, Margaret James, 44, 45, 82, 92, 132

Squires
Margaret James Squires, 44, 45, 82, 92, 132

Stär
Elizabeth Stär, 116

Stallboerger
Petra Stallboerger, 31

Stanbery
Nancy Stanbery, 50

Stansifer, see Steinseifer

Stature
Rosina Stature, 116

Stearns
Joy Q. Stearns, 10

Steinbok
Berek Steinbok, 146

Steiner
116

Steinseifer (Stansifer, Stinecyfer)
Agnes Catharina Steinseifer, 116
Anna Margaretha Steinseifer, 116
Elisabeth Steinseifer, 116
Henerecus Steinseifer, 116
Henricus Steinseifer, 116
Henry Steinseifer, 116
Jemima Steinseifer, 116
Johann Heinrich Steinseifer, 116
Johannes Henrich Steinseifer, 116

Johannes Steinseifer, 92, 116
John Steinseifer, 108, 116
John the Elder Steinseifer, 116
John the Younger Steinseifer, 116
John Stinecyfer, Jr., 95
Maria Agnesa Steinseifer, 116
Ryan Stansifer, 91, 116

Stigler
James Stigler, 117
Martha (Patsy, Patty) Stigler, 115, 116
Samuel Stigler, 116, 117

Stinecyfer, see Steinseifer
Stiver, Vernon, 55, 118

Stiver
Vernon Stiver, 55, 118

Stöver, **Stoever**, 31, 55
Dietrich Stöver, 117
Elizabeth Stöver, 118
Elizabeth Catherine Stöver, 117
Gaspar Stöver, 124
Gurtrud Stöver, 117
Johann Caspar Stöver, Jr., 78, 117, 124, 125, 142
Johann Caspar Stöver, Sr., 30, 48, 56, 83, 96, 111, 113, 117, 118, 124, 125
John Caspar Stöver, Sr., 89, 117
Magdalena Stöver, 117
Mary Magdalena Stöver, 117, 118, 124
Mary Stöver, 124
Philip Stöver, 117
Rev. Stoever, 96

Stoltz (Stolts)
John Michael Stoltz, 24, 28, 32, 103, 117
John Stolts, 117

Stone
Ludwig Stone, 72

Stover
Jacob Stover, 72, 98, 116
Mary Magdalena Stover, 89

Streit
Christian Streit, 56

Strother
Anthony Strother, 28
Francis Strother, 92
John Strother, 92

Stuart
Anne Stuart, 59

Suel
Stephen Suel, 97

Sutherland
Hetty Jean Swindall Sutherland, 55
T. M. Sutherland, 55, 118
W. H. Sutherland, 55, 118

Sutton
John Sutton, 79, 101

Swindle (Swindell, Schwindel), 55
B. Dale Swindle, 55, 118
Catherine Swindle, 118
Elizabeth Swindle, 118, 123
George Swindle, 106, 107, 118
Hannah Swindle, 118, 127
John Swindle, 42, 50, 118, 127
Michael Swindle, 42, 118, 123
Rebecca Swindel, 77, 85
Rebecca Swindle, 49, 118
Sarah Swindell, 64, 118
Sarah Swindle, 118
Timothy Swindell, 76
Timothy Swindle, 118

Taliaferro
Elizabeth Taliaferro, 20, 28
Francis Taliaferro, 72
John Taliaferro, 72
Mary Taliaferro, 20, 28
Robert Taliaferro, 20

Tannenberg
David Tannenberg, 56

Tanner (Damur, Damus, Gerber, Tenner, Turner), 55
Aaron Tanner, 40
Abraham Gerber Tanner, 40
Abraham Tanner, 49, 120
Anna Catharina Tanner, 118
Anna Maria Tanner, 118
Anne Mary Tanner, 90
Barbara Tanner, 49, 119
Catherine Tanner, 50
Christiana Turner, 15, 119
Christina Tanner, 119
Christoph Gerber, 39
Christopher Gerber, 42
Christopher Tanner, 60, 61, 75, 110, 119
Christopher Tanner, Sr., 49
Christopher Turner, 15, 119
Dorothea Tanner, 50, 121
Dorothy Tanner, 119, 120
Elizabeth Tanner, 60, 88, 114, 120
Ephraim Tanner, 40
Frederick Tanner, 41, 110, 119
Friedrich Tanner, 39
George Tanner, 32, 33, 119, 120
George Tenner, 32, 119
Jacob Tanner, 40, 119, 132
Johannes Tanner, 39
John Tanner, 88, 119
John Thomas Tanner, Jr., 119
Jurt Tanner, 42
Katherine Tanner, 119
Katherine Turner, 119
Margaret Tanner, 75
Maria Tanner, 99
Maria Turner, 119
Mary Magdalen Tanner, 110, 120
Mary Tanner, 64, 68, 99, 119, 132

Mary Turner, 15, 119
Michael Tanner, 40
Mildred Tanner, 91
Moses Tanner, 40
Parva Turner, 15, 119
Robert Tanner, 18, 28, 32, 33, 118, 119, 120
Robert Tenner, 32, 119
Robert Turner, 15, 119
Sarah Tanner, 88
Simeon Tanner, 40
Susanna Tanner, 91
Urban Tanner, 118
William Tanner, 40

Tarbett
Andrew Tarbett, 1, 4, 8, 9, 13, 48

Taylor, 116
Charles Taylor, 94
Elizabeth Taylor, 63
Lamb Taylor, 107
Thomas Taylor, 18, 28

Teagarden
Abraham, 91

Tenner, see Tanner

Teter, Dieter
Johann Georg Dieter, 140
Johann George Dieter, 120
John George Dieter, 120
John Michael Dieter, 120
Mary Christina Dieter, 120
Mary Margaret Dieter, 120
George Teter, 32, 120

Thallert
Christoph Thallert, 120
Elizabeth Thallert, 120

Thomas, 145, 146
Albrecht Thomas, 44
Ann Margaret Thomas, 80
Anna Magdalena Thomas, 44, 62, 66, 78, 94, 101, 114, 120
Anna Margaret Thomas, 120
Anna Maria Thomas, 74, 77, 89, 90, 94, 120, 122, 148
Benjamin Thomas, 122
Betsy Thomas, 122
Betty Thomas, 121
Catherine Thomas, 120
Elisabeth Thomas, 66
Elisha Thomas, 122
Elizabeth Thomas, 48, 49, 108, 121, 122
Eve Susanna Hart, 120
George Thomas, 122
Hans Wendel Thomas, 44
Henry Thomas, 61
Jemima Thomas, 122
Jesse Thomas, 122
Johann Thomas, 44

John Thomas, 24, 28, 33, 49, 94, 117, 120, 122, 124
John Thomas, Jr., 50, 67, 90, 108, 114, 119–121
John Thomas, Sr., 50, 60, 89, 90, 120
Lucy Thomas, 122
Magdalena Thomas, 120
Margaret Thomas, 48, 60, 61, 91, 120
Mary Barbara Thomas, 67, 121
Mary Thomas, 90, 108, 120, 121
Massey Thomas, 122
Michael Thomas, 24, 28, 33, 50, 61, 66, 78, 86, 89, 91, 94, 97, 98, 120, 121
Reuben Thomas, 122
Rhoda Thomas, 62, 122
Sarah Thomas, 121
Susannah Thomas, 90, 121, 122
Ursula Thomas, 44
William Thomas, 122

Thompson
William Thompson, 132

Thornton
Francis Thorton, 28

Threlkeld
Ann Threlkeld, 93
John Threlkeld, John, 61
Nancy Threlkeld, 61

Tivall
Christian Tivall, 86, 87, 122
Henry Tivall, 86, 122

Tomer (Thomas), 24
Tower (Thomas), 16

Towles
John Towles, 28, 59
Margery Tolls, 61
Nancy Towles, 115
Stokely Towles, 61

Trotter
John Trotter, 78

Trout
Catherine Trout, 72
David Trout, 72
George Trout, 72, 73

Trumbo
Andreas Trumbo, 122
Andrew Trumbo, 122
Andrew Trumbo, Jr., 122
Dorothy Trumbo, 122
Elizabeth Trumbo, 122
George Trumbo, 122, 123
Jacob Trumbo, 122
Jacob Trumbo, Jr., 122
John Trumbo, 122
Margaret Trumbo, 122
Margaret Utz Trumbo, 122, 123
Margaretha Trumbo, 122
Mary Trumbo, 122

Turner, see Tanner

Uhl, see Yowell
Urbach
    Adolph Urbach, 123
    Anna Barbara Urbach, 81, 123
    Anna Maria Urbach, 123
    Rudolph Urbach, 41
Utz (Otes, Oots, Ouds, Woods), 150, 152
    see Oats also
    Absalom Utz, 76
    Adam Utz, 39, 42, 123, 126
    Ann Utz, 76
    Anna Barbara Utz, 123
    Anna Maria Utz, 123
    Barbara Utz, 45, 66, 67
    Christina Utz, 123
    Daniel Utz, 40, 123
    Daniel Utz, Jr., 40
    Dinah Utz, 123
    Elizabeth Utz, 48, 50, 118, 123
    Ephraim Utz, 40, 123
    Ferdinand Utz, 9, 44
    Georg Utz, 42
    Georg Utz, Jr., 39, 42
    Georg Utz, Sr., 39
    George Oots, 92
    George Ouds 12
    George Utz, 12, 13, 24, 26, 28, 32, 44, 45, 49, 50, 61, 66, 67, 70, 71, 77, 81, 83, 91, 94, 103, 122, 126, 128, 150
    George Utz, Jr., 122, 127
    George Utz II, 122, 126
    George Utz III, 126
    Hans Jerich Otes, 9
    Joel Utz, 40
    Johann Georg Utz, 44
    Johannes Utz, 44, 45
    Lewis Utz, 40, 123
    Ludwig Utz, 40
    Margaret Utz, 48, 122, 123, 127
    Mary Margaret Utz, 45, 67, 123
    Mary Utz, 61, 123
    Michael Michael, Jr., 39, 41
    Michael Utz, 41, 42, 45, 46, 49, 50, 77, 117, 118, 122, 123
    Michael Utz, Sr., 39
    Rachel Utz, 126
    Susanna Utz, 77, 123

Valk, see Walk
Vallick, see Walk
Vandyke
    Garriott Vandyke, 87
    Peter Vandyke, 87
Vaught, see Vogt

Vawter
    Tabitha Vawter, 110
Veal
    Jimmy L. Veal, 89
Veil
    David Veil, 124
Vinegunt, See also Weingard
    William Vinegunt, 18, 28, 124, 127
Vinson
    Leven Vinson, 109
Vinyard, see Weingard
Vogt (Bellfaut, Faut, Focht, Full, Vaught, Vaut, Wacht)
    Adam Faught, 124
    Andrew Vaught, 124
    Barbara Faught, 124
    Catherine Faught, 124
    Catherine Margaret Vogt, 72, 124
    Christian Vaught, 124
    Christley Vaught, 55
    David Vaught, 124
    Elizabeth Faught, 124
    Elizabeth Vaught, 124
    Gaspar Faught, 124
    Gaspar Vaught, 124
    George Faught, 124
    George Vaught, 124
    Henry Vaught, 124
    J. Vogt, 53
    John Andrew Vaught, 124
    John Andrew Vought, 124
    John Caspar Vogt, 124
    John Paul Focht, 121
    John Full, 33
    John Paul Vaught, 28, 55, 59, 94
    John Paul Vogt, 22, 33, 72, 120, 124
    John Paul Vought, 22
    John Vaught, 124
    John Vought, 76, 124
    Leonard Faught, 124
    Martin Faught, 124
    Maria Catharina Vogt, 120, 124
    Mary Faught, 124
    Paul Faught, 124
    Sarah Faught, 124
Volck, (Folg, Volk), 8, 150
    Anna Barbara Volk, 44, 103, 123
    Anna Maria Volck, 44
    Elisabeth Volck, 45, 46
    Elizabeth Volck, 78
    Hans Martin Volck, 8
    Hans Michael Volck, 44
    Johann Michael Volck, 44, 66
    Louisa Elisabetha Volck, 44
    Maria Rosina Volck, 44, 45
    Maria Sabina Charlotta Barbara Volck, 44

Maria Sabina Volck, 45, 66
Mary Sabina Volck, 92
Sabina Volck, 9
von Graffenried, see Graffenried
Vorete, see Frady
Vrede, see Frady
Vynyard, see Weingard

Wagner
Leatrice Tanner Wagner, 120
Walk (Valk, Vallick, Walke, Wallick, Wollos, Wollox)
Catherine Walk, 125
Catherine Walke, 73, 128
Cathrin Wollox, 63, 104
Elizabeth Walk, 125
Hans Martin Valk, 125
Martin Walk, 24, 28, 73, 74, 125
Martin Walk, Jr., 125
Martin Walke, 128
Martin Vallick, 125
Martin Wallick, 73, 125
Martin Wallox, 125
Martin Wollox, 63
Walker
Benj. Walker, 18
Benjamin Walker, 28
Isabell Walker, 88
John Walker, 88
Theodore Walker, 86
Wall
Zacharias Wall, 60
Wallick, see Walk
Wallox, see Walk
Wally
Patricia Blankenbeker Wally, 54
Ward
Alin Ward, 127
Warner
Achsah Warner, 102
Waugh
Alexander Waugh, 72
Waydelich
Barbara Waydelich, 89
Wayland (Wieland), 55
Adam Wayland, 41, 62, 66, 72, 81, 82, 97, 112, 125, 126
Adam Weyland, 36, 39, 112
Anna Catharine Clara Wieland, 125
Anna Magdalena Wayland, 126
Anney Wayland, 126
Catherine Wayland, 116, 125, 126
Cornelius Wayland, 126
Eleanor Wayland, 127
Elizabeth Wayland, 66, 72, 78, 125, 126
Hannah Wayland, 116, 126
Hans Jacob Wieland, 125
Henrich Wayland, 39
Henry Wayland, 82, 116, 126
J. W. Wayland, 53
Jacob Wayland, 15, 125
John Burke Wayland, 126
John Wayland, 78, 82, 105, 116, 125, 126
John Wayland, Jr., 41
John Wiland, 94
Joshua Wayland, 113, 126, 127
Judah Wayland, 126
Katherine Wayland, 15
Katherine Wiland, 94
Leah Wayland, 113
Lewis Wayland, 126
Ludwig Wayland, 40
Margaret Wayland, 126
Maria Barbara Wieland, 7, 125
Mary Wayland, 15, 81, 82, 126, 130
Rachel Wayland, 126
Rosina Wayland, 126
Thomas Wayland, 15, 20, 28, 32, 72, 110, 116, 125
Thomas Weyland, 20, 125
Thomas Wieland, 125, 145
Wayman, (Weidmann)
Elizabeth Wayman, 127
Frances Wayman, 127
George Wayman, 127
George Weidmann, 127
Harman Wayman, 127
Henry Wayman, 48, 82, 123, 127
Magdalene Wayman, 127
Mary Wayman, 123
Mary Magdalena Wayman, 123, 127
Weaver (Weber, Wever), 139
Anna Barbara Weaver, 127
Anna Weaver, 110
Barbara Weaver, 70, 73, 127
Catharine Weaver, 72
Catherine Weaver, 127
Edward A. Weaver, Jr., 55
Elisabeth Weaver, 50
Elizabeth Weaver, 48, 67, 78, 118, 123, 127
Hannah Weaver, 50, 67, 118, 127
Hans Dieterich Weber, 45, 46
Hans Dietrich Weber, 127
Hans Fredich Wever, 9, 45
Hans Georg Weber, 45
Hans Martin Weber, 45
Johann Georg Weber, 45
Johannes Weber, 36, 39, 41, 112
John Weaver, 94, 127
Joseph Weaver, 46, 49, 50, 77, 128
Joseph Weber, 73, 127, 140
Joseph Wever, 9, 45

Margaret Weaver, 123, 127
Maria Sophia Weaver, 49
Maria Sophia Weber, 45, 46
Maria Weaver, 110
Mary Sophia Weaver, 84
Maria Sophia Wever, 9, 45
Matheus Weber, 42
Mathias Weaver, 127
Mathuis Weber, 39
Matthias Weaver, 81, 82, 127
Moses Weber, 40
Peter Weaver, 24, 26, 28, 32, 45, 46, 50, 55, 59, 66, 70, 73, 78, 82, 91, 103, 117, 118, 127, 140
Peter Weaver, Jr., 91, 127
Peter Weber, 39, 42
Peter Wever, 46
Phillip Joseph Weber, 45
Sophia Weaver, 46, 74
Sophia Weber, 127
Susanna Clore Weaver, 49, 77
Susanna Weber, 46, 73, 127
Susanna Wever, 9, 45
Susannah Clore Weaver, 77
Wabburie (Walburga) Weber, 127
Wabburie (Walburga) Wever, 9, 45
Walburga Weaver, 50, 128
Walburga Wever, 46

Webster
Thomas Webster, 87

Wegman
Anna Maria Wegman, 9
Hans Jerich Wegman, 9, 127
Maria Gotlieve Wegman, 9, 127
Maria Margaret Wegman, 9, 127

Weidmann, see **Wayman**
Weiland, see **Wayland**
Weingart (Vinyard, Weingard, Winyard)
Anna Maria Wiengart, 128
John Vinyard, 124
John Vynyard, 124
John Winegard, 41, 124, 128
John Winyard, 124
Johannes Weingart, 128
Susanna Weingart, 128

Wever, see **Weaver**
White
Susan Pottenger White, 108
Tebald White, 83

Wieland, see **Wayland**
Thomas Wieland, 145

Wiland, see **Wayland**
Wilkerson
Mary Wilkerson, 75

Wilkiss
Elizabeth Wilkiss, 124

Willer
John Willer, 127

Willheit (Wilhite, Wilhoit, et al)
Aaron Wilheit, 99
Adam Wilheit, 103
Adam Wilhite, 68, 69
Adam Wilhoit, 78
Adam Willheit, 70, 128
Anna Dorothea Willheit, 128
Anna Maria Willheit, 68, 89, 128
Benjamin, Wilheit, 99
Burga Willheit, 128
Catherine Wilhoit, 75
Catherine Willheit, 63, 128, 129
Elizabeth Wilhite, 68
Elizabeth Wilhoit, 83, 123
Eva Wilhoit, 89
Eva Willheit, 128, 129
Eve Wilhoit, 83
Gabriel Wilhoit, 61
Georg Wilheit, 39
George Wilheit, 42
George Wilhite, 68
George Wilhoit, 123
George Willheit, 50
Hannah Willheit, 129
Jemima Wilhoit, 75
Joel Willheit, 129
Johann Friederich Willheit, 129
Johann Michael Willheit, 50, 63, 68, 86, 128, 129
Johannes Willheit, 128
John Connie Wilhite, Jr., 55
John Michael Willheit, 86
John Wilhide, 33
John Wilhite, 68, 128
John Wilhoit, 42, 126
John Willheit, 33, 46, 50, 127, 128, 129
Lewis Willheit, 129
Margaret Wilhoit, 91
Marge Willhite, 122, 128
Mary Margaret Wilhoit, 83
Mary Wilhite, 68, 128, 129, 130
Mary Wilhoit, 102
Mary Willheit, 70, 99, 130
Matthias Willheit, 128, 129
Michael Wilhide, 26, 128
Michael Wilhite, 68–70, 128
Michael Wilhoit, 61, 78
Michael Wilhoite, 84, 115
Michael Willheit, 24, 28, 32, 46, 50, 61, 69, 70, 89, 126
Mitchell Wilhite, 32
Nicholas Wilhoit, 83
Nicholas Willheit, 50
Nicholaus Wilheit, 42

Philip Willheit, 129
Phillip Willheit, 128
Rachel Willheit, 129
Rosanna Wilhoit, 75
Rosina Wilhoit, 126
Susanna Willheit, 130
Tobias Wilhite, 32, 128
Tobias Wilhoit, 61
Tobias Willheit, 24, 28, 32, 128, 129
Tobias Willhide, 125
William Wilhoite, 87

Williams
Eva Williams, 129
Jane Crouch Williams, 126

Winegard, see Weingart

Winn
Minor Winn, 93

Winyard, see Weingart

Witham
Mary Margarethe Witham, 109
Peter Witham, 109

Wolber
Adolph Wolber, 129
Anna Maria Wolber, 129

Wolfaarth
Frederick, 106

Wolfenberger
Anna Margaretha Wolfenberger, 129
George Michael Wolfenberger, 129
Johannes Wolfenberger, 129
Peter Wolfenberger, 129

Wollos, see Walk
Wollox, see Walk
Wrede, See Frady

Wust
Klaus Wust, 4, 53, 61

Yager (Eager, Jäger, Jaeger, Yager, Yeager)
Adam Eager, 102
Adam Jäger, Sr.), 39
Adam Jeger, 112
Adam Yager, 20, 28, 32, 49, 66, 72, 74, 93, 102, 103, 104, 105, 109, 114, 126, 129, 130
Adam Yager, Jr., 66
Adam Yeager, 15, 70
Adam Yeager, Sr., 42
Amy Yager, 105
Anna Maria Jäger, 130
Barbara Jäger, 78
Barbara Yager, 71, 74, 78, 130
Benjamin Jäger, 40
Elizabeth Jäger, 78
Elizabeth Yager, 71, 77, 88, 130
Ephraim Yager, 109
Eva Jäger, 78
Eva Yager, 81

Godfrey Yager, 98, 109, 126, 130
Hanna Jäger, 78
Jemima Jäger, 78
John Jäger, 78
John Yager, 55, 126, 130
John Yeager, Jr., 42
Johannes Jäger, 39, 41
Johannes Jäger, Jr., 39
Johannes Jager, 36, 76, 109
Joseph Yager, 129
Josua Jäger, 40
Joshua Yager, 126
Maria Jager, 76, 109
Mary Yager, 75, 99, 130
Mary Yeager, 15
Michael Jäger, 39, 78
Michael Jeger, 112
Michael Yager, 46, 49, 71, 77, 88, 101, 125, 130
Michael Yeager, 41
Nicholas Jäger, 138
Nicholas Jager, 109
Nicholas Jeager, 13
Nicholas Yager, 28, 31, 32, 46, 74, 78, 105, 126, 129, 130
Nicholas Yeager, 15, 127, 130
Nichs Yager, 32
Niclaus Jaeger, 41
Nicolaus Jäger, 130
Nicolaus Jager, 109
Piney Woods John Yager, 129
Rachel Jäger, 78
Rebecca Yager, 129
Samuel Jäger, 78
Susanna Jäger, 78
Susannah Yager, 78, 129

Yelton
Sandra Yelton, 7

Yewell, see Yowell

Yoder
Don Yoder, 131

Young
Richard Young, 76

Yowell (Atwell, Awel, Ouell, Owell, Uhl, Uhle, Yewell)
Anna Barbara Uhl, 130
Anna Catharina Uhl, 130
Christofle Uhl, 8
Christopher Atwell, 18, 130
Christopher Awel, 18, 130
Christopher Ouell, 33
Christopher Owell, 131
Christopher Yowell, Jr., 131
Christopher Uhl, 93, 130, 149
Christopher Yowel, 18, 28, 33, 89, 131
C.L. Yowell, 68
Claude L. Yowell, 54, 55, 74, 115

Claude Lindsay Yowell, 53
David Ouell, 33
David Yewell, 131
David Yowell, 33, 131
Eva Uhl, 130
Friedrich David Uhl, 130
Hans Jacob Uhl, 130
James Yowell, 87, 131
Jerg Friedrich Uhl, 130
John Owell, 131
John Yowell, 131
Magdalena Uhl, 130
Margarethe Yowel, 131
Mary Owell, 131
Michael Awel, 130
Nancy Ann Yowell, 87
Nicolas Yowell, 118
Rebecca Yowell, 49, 118

Zehendbauer
Martin Zehendbauer, 140
Ziegler (Ziglar)
Ann Ziegler, 131
Anna Christina Zieglar, 106
Barbara Ziegler, 131, 132
Christopher Ziegler, 131
Christopher Zigler, 106
Elizabeth Ziegler, 131
Johann Leonhart Ziegler, 131
Leanna Zigler, 122
Leonard Zeigler, 131, 132
Leonard Ziegler, 122
Leonard Ziegler III, 131
Nancy Ziegler, 131
Susannah Ziegler, 131
Zimberman, see Zimmerman
Zimmerman
Andrew Zimmerman, 15, 131, 132
Anna Elisabeth Zimmerman, 82
Anna Elizabeth Zimmerman, 131, 132
Anne Mary Zimmerman, 90
Barbara Zimmerman, 122, 131, 132

Betsy Zimmerman, 110
Christian Zimmerman, 131
Christoph Zimmerman, 39, 42, 82
Christopher Zimmerman, 8, 15, 33, 59, 61, 64, 67, 68, 71, 76, 81, 90, 93, 99, 119, 122, 131, 132, 149
Dorothea Zimmerman, 82, 131, 132
Dorothey Zimmerman, 132
Dorothy Zimmerman, 119
Elisabeth Zimmerman, 91
Elizabeth Zimmerman, 15, 90, 106, 132
Eva Zimmerman, 131
Frederick Zimmerman, 61, 132
Friederich Zimmerman, 40
Gary Zimmerman, 5, 51, 89
Jemima Zimmerman, 132
John Zimberman, 18
Johann Christoph Zimmerman, 131
Johann Conrad Zimmerman, 131
Johann Martin Zimmerman, 82, 131, 132
Johannes Zimmerman, 39, 41, 42, 82, 131
John Zimmerman, 15, 18, 28, 33, 62, 67, 90, 100, 106, 119, 131, 132
John Zimmerman, Jr., 83, 106
John Zimmermann, 69
Josua Zimmermann, 40
Katherine Zimmerman, 132
Lea Zimmerman, 99
Margaret Zimmerman, 49, 64, 99, 100, 132
Maria Barbara Zimmerman, 131
Mary Zimmerman, 64, 68, 121, 132
Michael Zimmerman, 42
Nancy Zimmerman, 131
Reuben Zimmerman, 132
Rosanna Zimmerman, 132
Sarah Zimmerman, 132
Susanna Zimmerman, 90
Ursula (Blankenbaker) Zimmerman, 67, 106
Zollicoffer
Jacob Christoph Zollikoffer, 46, 47, 132
Zubrod
Margarethe Zubrod,

Made in the USA
San Bernardino, CA
14 August 2019